THE MAKING OF MICHIGAN, 1820–1860

GREAT LAKES BOOKS

A PIONEER ANTHOLOGY

THE MAKING OF MICHIGAN

1820–1860

EDITED BY JUSTIN L. KESTENBAUM

WAYNE STATE UNIVERSITY PRESS DETROIT

ISBN-13: 978-0-8143-1919-2 ISBN-10: 0-8143-1919-X

Library of Congress Cataloging-in-Publication Data

The Making of Michigan, 1820–1860 : a pioneer anthology / edited by
Justin L. Kestenbaum.
p. cm. — (Great Lakes books)
ISBN 0-8143-1918-1 (alk. paper). — ISBN 0-8143-1919-X (pbk. : alk. paper)
1. Michigan—History—Sources. 2. Frontier and pioneer life—Michigan—Sources. I. Kestenbaum, Justin L. II. Series.
F566.M35 1990
977.4'03—dc19 89-5457
CIP

CONTENTS

ACKNOWLEDGMENTS

The editor is grateful to many persons who helped make this book possible. Dr. Robert Mandel, director of Wayne State University Press, supported the project from its inception. Laurel Brandt of Wayne State University Press managed the manuscript; Philip Mason of the Great Lakes Books Advisory Board provided encouragement and support. Richard Hathaway and Richard E. Lucas of the Library of Michigan shared their expertise on Michigan legislative documents and other arcane matters. Geneva Wiskemann, formerly of the State Archives, made important suggestions.

The editor found a high level of professionalism in Michigan's historical libraries and archives. Francis Blouin and his staff at the Michigan Historical Collections were of invaluable assistance. The staff of the Burton Historical Collection of the Detroit Public Library eased access to many treasures in their holdings. LeRoy Barnett of the Michigan State Archives generously (and genially) shared his incomparable knowledge of many obscure aspects of Michigan's history. Fred Honhart and Dorothy Frye of the Michigan State University Archives and Historical Collections went out of their way to assist. The editor found a warm welcome and many valuable materials at the Cass County Public Library in Cassopolis, Michigan.

The editor is especially grateful to his wife, Jan Parisian, who provided not only encouragment but also assisted in many of the tasks of preparing the manuscript. The book would be much the poorer without her help.

All these persons helped strengthen the manuscript. For its faults the editor alone is responsible.

INTRODUCTION

Michigan was settled late in the history of the Great Lakes frontier. For early westward-moving pioneers it was difficult of access, heavily forested, and of uncertain reputation. The traveler William Darby reported in 1819 that "Detroit . . . is separated by an expanse of water, and by an uncultivated waste, from the other part of the United States, and remains, together with the little community in its environs, an isolated moral mass, having . . . but a slight tie of interest" to the rest of the nation.[1] Ohio, Illinois, and Indiana had already become states during the first great migration into the trans-Appalachian west, years before the advent of steam navigation and the opening of the Erie Canal in 1825 brought a flood of settlers into Michigan.

Many factors explain Michigan's tardy settlement.[2] The pioneer who wanted to sell cash crops preferred to settle along the Ohio River and its tributaries or the National Road, where produce could easily be shipped to market, a fact that delayed settlement not only in Michigan but other regions bordering on the Great Lakes. And pioneers knew little about Michigan until the War of 1812, which brought the area to national attention, but even then the reputation of the land was poor. Edward Tiffin, the Surveyor-General of the United States, reported in 1817 that the land of Michigan was "with a very few exceptions, a poor barren, sandy land on which scarcely any vegetation grows except very small scrubby oaks." If the rest of the land were as bad, Tiffin continued, "there would not be more than one acre in a hundred, if there would be one out of a thousand, that would . . . admit of cultivation."[3]

Lewis Cass, who had been Governor of Michigan Territory since 1813, knew the quality of land in Michigan at first hand and urged the federal government to survey the area, build roads, and open the land to settlement. In 1820, as a means of bringing wider attention to Michigan and to attract settlers, Cass led a three-month, 5,000-mile exploring mission around the rim of Michigan Territory—which then included Wisconsin—in order to discover natural resources, determine the mood of the Indians, and promote settlement. The federal government, at Cass's insistence, began surveying the land but growth remained slow.

The advent of steam navigation on the Great Lakes and the opening of the Erie Canal changed everything. The canal boat and lake steamer were faster, cheaper, and vastly more comfortable than an emigrant's wagon or stagecoach. The first canal boat, the *Detroit,* arrived at Buffalo on October 26, 1825; three days later the Hiram arrived with fifty settlers "bound for Michigan."[4] The great emigration from western New York into Michigan had begun. The Erie Canal and steamboats plying Lake Erie created a virtual highway between New York State and Detroit, the point of entry into Michigan. In a single generation a flood of pioneers—most of them from western New York with roots in New England—fanned out all over southern lower Michigan.[5]

By 1835 population sufficed for statehood, and on the eve of the Civil War exceeded 750,000. So rapidly did the area grow that in one single year—1836—land sales in Michigan equalled one fifth of the total of land sales in the history of the United States.

The Michigan settlers of this era—from the 1820s to the outbreak of the Civil War—considered themselves the true "pioneers" of the state. They believed that the rapid transformation of Michigan's forested wilderness into fertile fields, prosperous communities, and a progressive, forward-looking state was one of the great "success" stories of American history. They were also aware of their own place in that history and determined to keep its record alive for posterity. A rich documentary record has, therefore, survived. *The Making of Michigan, 1820–1860: A Pioneer Anthology* celebrates the historic role of Michigan's pioneers with a sampling of original documents in which participants and observers tell their stories in their own words.

The Making of Michigan focuses on the pioneer period, the era from 1820 to about 1860. The collection is not a comprehensive narrative history and cannot include all aspects of Michigan life in this period. After extensive research in all the major libraries and repositories in the state, I have selected documents that illuminate four themes—the physical setting, the "Great Migration" of settlers into the state, the creation of institutions, and the wave of religious and reform enthusiasm.

Sojourners, missionaries, and scientists ranged all over Michigan during this era, from the lower peninsula to Mackinac Island and the Keewenaw Peninsula copper country. Alexis de Tocqueville, Harriet Martineau, Henry R. Schoolcraft, Charles Fenno Hoffman, and the Rev. John H. Pitizel have left arresting descriptions not only of natural phenomena but of whatever human society they encountered—Indians, persons of mixed breed, settlers, the garrison culture of Mackinac Island, and life in the copper country. The settlers who arrived during the great land rush of the 1830s and 1840s wrote diaries and memoirs of the adventure of building homes, schools, and creating institutions in a frontier setting. Edward W. Barber's account of the attempt to create a New England village in the wilds of Eaton County—perhaps the finest pioneer memoir in the *Michigan Pioneer and Historical Collections*—makes engrossing reading; Engbertus van der Veen's evocation of life in Holland, Michigan, eloquently describes one of the remarkable episodes of the American westward movement. Settlers poured in, no doubt with John Farmer's *Gazeteer* and map in hand, staked out land, and "entered" the site of their future homes at various government land offices; they often were preceded by land speculators, at least one of whom—the Baltimore banker John M. Gordon—was ambivalent about his speculations. His diary is an essential source for an understanding of the "Michigan Fever" or land rush of the 1830s.

Once settled in, Michigan's pioneers set about creating schools; A. D. P. Van Buren's account of teaching in a log cabin school bears witness to the high value placed on education, as well as the rigor of the curriculum. Since education was so vital a concern, and since

Michigan's educational system was a model for other states, the collection includes John D. Pierce's account of the founding of the state educational system. Educational systems were still "new" in this era; the 1841 report of the Superintendent of Public Instruction, based on a tour of the state, conveys a sense of the challenge of creating such a system in a rapidly growing pioneer society. Two of Michigan's major universities trace their origins to this era; Henry Frieze, Professor of Latin at the University of Michigan, discusses the impact of President Henry Philip Tappan on the university as well as the ambience of Ann Arbor and campus life in the 1850s. Charles Jay Monroe, a member of the first class at Michigan Agricultural College, describes the scene of desolation which greeted the first students to enroll in the institution. A lively issue at the University of Michigan was whether to admit women, a matter at the discretion of the university's governing board; the collection includes a legislative committee's strong support of such admission.

William W. Upton's portrayal of the legislative decision to place the state capital in Lansing and A. D. P. Van Buren's lively portrayal of Democratic-Whig rivalry in the immediate post-statehood period convey a sense of the political process. The state was also strongly affected by the mid-nineteenth century reform wave; Michigan created a state prison, insane asylum, and reform school for young offenders. The official reports of these institutions make interesting reading and illuminate the social ideas of the period.

The Mormons—a new sect that originated in the religious excitement of western New York State—had adherents in Michigan; the anthology includes an account of the arrest, trial in federal court, and acquittal of "King" James Strang, one of the more interesting Michigan figures of the period. The antislavery movement energized Blacks and their white supporters; the principal issue for Blacks in pioneer Michigan was the right to vote and other ordinary civil rights; the collection includes the minutes of a convention of Black citizens, which demanded such rights—as well as the legislative report, which found reasons to deny them. The Underground Railroad was active in Michigan; few first-hand accounts have survived. There were, however, several successful rescues of suspected fugitives from the hands of slave-catchers or bounty hunters. The abolitionist Levi Coffin, who played a role in one such rescue in Cass County, described the incident in his memoirs. The anthology concludes with the inaugural message of Kinsley S. Bingham, Michigan's first Republican governor, in 1855. Bingham congratulated the state on its splendid material progress and the excellence of its institutions, although he did see room for improvement. Bingham also discussed at some length the specter on the horizon—slavery, especially the issue of territorial slavery—and made clear the moral grounds for keeping slavery out of the public domain.

The Making of Michigan salutes the pioneers of the formative era—those who came from the mid-1820s to the outbreak of the Civil War. These settlers "defined" Michigan by creating many of its progressive institutions. The stamp they placed on Michigan continues even now.

Notes

[1] William Darby, *A Tour from the City of New York, to Detroit* (New York, 1819), p. 188.

[2] For an excellent analysis of the reasons for Michigan's tardy settlement, see Madison Kuhn, "Tiffin, Morse, and the Reluctant Pioneer," *Michigan History* 50 (June 1966): 111–38.

[3] *American State Papers: Public Lands*, vol. III (Washington, DC, 1834), pp. 164–65.

[4] Ronald Shaw, "Michigan Influences upon the Formative Years of the Erie Canal," *Michigan History* 37 (March 1953): 1–19.

[5] See the following on the migration into Michigan from New York and New England: W. Wilmond Parker, "The Migration from Vermont to Northern New York," *New York History* 15 (October 1934): 398–406; Arthur Pound, "Michigan, New York's Daughter State," *New York History* 23 (July 1942): 283–301.

PART I.

THE PHYSICAL SETTING

A FORTNIGHT IN THE WILDERNESS

Alexis de Tocqueville

In summer of 1831 Alexis de Tocqueville, a young Frenchman and member of the minor nobility, visited Michigan Territory in the course of a nine-month fact-finding mission on behalf of the French government, which was interested in American ideas about penology and social reform. One important result of his visit to the United States was his book, *The American Democracy* (1834), an essential source for understanding the United States in the 1830s. Tocqueville, who was twenty-five years old when he sojourned into Michigan, was interested in testing an idea about the evolution of society from simple to more complex forms. His Michigan essay, *Quinze Jours au Désert* (A Fortnight in the Wilderness), was first published in Paris in 1860, after Tocqueville's untimely death.

He expected to find a peasant or primitive society in frontier Michigan—a society a century or at least decades behind that of the settled parts of the country back east. He found nothing of the kind, but rather a "modern society." The New England Yankees who migrated into Michigan, as Tocqueville saw them, were dour and humorless, and willing to undergo the privation of a life in the wilds in order to afford their children a better start in life. They were of a practical bent of mind; they had, as Tocqueville correctly discerned, come from a "reasoning and intelligent society." For the New England Yankee, "the log cabin is only a temporary shelter . . . when the fields that surround him are in full production . . . a more spacious dwelling will replace the log house and make a home for those numerous children who will also go out and make themselves a home in the wilds." But Tocqueville was also interested in nature—the Michigan forest—as much as he was drawn to the observation of society. Little escaped his notice—he observed Indians, persons of mixed breed, Yankee settlers, and other frontier types. It seems remarkable that no one would have believed that Tocqueville and his traveling companion were interested only in sightseeing; this was almost never done.

The chapter appearing here is an extract from *Quinze Jours au Désert*, in George Wilson Pierson, *Tocqueville and Beaumont in America* (New York: Oxford University Press, 1938), pp. 231–82. By permission of George Wilson Pierson.

At ten o'clock in the morning of the 19th July [1831] we boarded the steamboat Ohio going towards Detroit. A strong breeze was blowing from the northwest and gave the waters of Lake Erie the very look of the waves of a stormy ocean. To the right stretched a limitless horizon. To the left we hugged the southern shores of the lake so close that we often came within earshot of it. These shores were perfectly level and different from those of all the lakes I have ever chanced to visit in Europe. Neither were they any more like the shores of the sea. Immense forests shaded them and formed round the lake as it were a thick belt that was seldom broken. From time to time, however, the country suddenly changes its look. Just around a wood one sees the elegant spire of a clock tower, houses striking in their whiteness and cleanness, and shops. Two paces further on, the primeval and apparently impenetrable forest reclaims its dominion and again reflects its foliage on the waters of the lake.

Those who have passed through the United States will find in this picture a striking emblem of American society. Everything there is abrupt and unexpected; everywhere, extreme civilization borders and in one sense confronts nature left to run riot. That is something that one cannot conceive in France. As for me, in my travelers' illusions—and what class of men has not its own—I was imagining something quite different. I had noticed in Europe that the more or less withdrawn position in which a province or town is placed, its wealth or its poverty, its smallness or its extent, exercised an immense influence on the ideas, the morals, the whole civilization of its inhabitants, and often caused a difference of several centuries between the various parts of the same area.

I had supposed that it was like that, but to an even greater extent, in the New World, and that a country peopled as is America in an incomplete and partial fashion ought to show all conditions of existence and provide a picture of society in all its ages. America, according to me, was then the only country where one could follow step by step all the transformation which social conditions have brought about for man and where it was possible to discover something like a vast chain descending ring by ring from the opulent patrician of the town right down to the savage in the wilds. It was there, in a word, that I counted on finding the whole of humanity framed within a few degrees of longitude.

Nothing is true of this picture. Of all the countries in the world America is the least adapted to provide the sight that I went to seek. In America, even more than in Europe, there is one society only. It may be rich or poor, humble or brilliant, trading or agricultural, but it is made up everywhere of the same elements; it has been leveled out by an egalitarian civilization. The man you left behind on the streets of New York, you will find him again in the midst of almost impenetrable solitude: same dress, same spirit, same language, same habits and the same pleasures. Nothing rustic, nothing naive, nothing that smells of the wilds, nothing even that resembles our villages. The reason for this peculiar state of affairs is easy to understand. The parts of the territories which have been longest and most completely peopled have reached a high degree of civilization. Education has been lavishly and profusely bestowed. The spirit of equality has stamped a peculiarly uniform pattern on the habits of private life. Now, note this well, it is precisely these same men who yearly go to inhabit the wilds. In Europe each man lives and dies on the ground where he was born. . . . Those who dwell in isolated places [i.e., Americans] arrived there yesterday, bringing with them the morals, the ideas, and the needs of civilization. If night overtaking you does not force you to take shelter under a tree, you have a good chance of reaching a village where you will find everything down to French fashions and poor copies of boulevards. The merchant of Buffalo or of Detroit is as well stocked as the one of New York; the factories of Lyon work for the one as for the other. When you leave the main roads you force your way down barely trodden paths. Finally, you see a field cleared, a cabin made from half-shaped tree trunks admitting the light through one narrow window only. You think you have at last reached the home of an American peasant. Mistake. You make your way into this cabin which seems the asylum of all wretchedness but the owner of this place is dressed in the same clothes as yours and he speaks the language of the towns. On his rough table are books and newspapers; he himself is anxious to take you on one side to know exactly what is happening in old Europe and asks you to tell him what has most struck you in his country. He will scribble on paper a plan of campaign for the Belgians, and will solemnly tell you what still needs to be done to make France prosperous. One might think one was meeting a rich landowner who had come to spend just a few nights in a hunting lodge. And in fact the log cabin is only a temporary shelter for the American, a concession circumstances have forced on him for the moment. When the fields that surround him are in full production, and the new owner has time to concern himself with the amenities of life, a more spacious dwelling and one better adapted to his needs will replace the log house and make a home for those numerous children who will also go out and make themselves a home in the wilds.

But to come back to our journey. We sailed slowly along the whole day in sight of the shores of Pennsylvania, and later of Ohio. We stopped for a moment at Presqu'Ile, now called Erie. It is there that the Pittsburgh canal will end. By means of this undertaking the whole execution of which is, they say, easy and now assured, the Mississippi will be connected to the river of the north, and the wealth of Europe will flow freely along the five hundred leagues of land that lie between the Gulf of Mexico and the Atlantic Ocean.

In the evening, the weather having turned favorable, we moved quickly toward Detroit across the middle of the lake. On the following morning we were in sight of the little island called *Middle Sister,* near to which Commodore Perry won a celebrated naval victory over the English.

Soon afterward the level coast of Canada seemed to be moving quickly toward us, and we saw the Detroit River opening in front of us and the houses of Fort Malden in the distance. This place, founded by the French, still bears many traces of its origin. The houses are placed and shaped like those of our peasants. The Catholic bell tower with a rooster on the top rises in the middle of the hamlet. One might think of a village near Caen or Evreux. A strange sight turned our attention away from these sentimental reminders of France; on the bank to our right [i.e., on the Canadian side] was a Scotch soldier mounting guard in full uniform. It was the uniform made so famous by the battle of Waterloo. Feather in cap, jacket, all complete; his clothes and arms glinted in the sunlight. To our left, as if on purpose to point the contrast, stark naked Indians, their bodies streaked with dyes, rings in their noses, came up at the same moment from the opposite bank. They were in a bark canoe with a coverlet for a sail. Letting their frail boat run with wind and current, they shot like an arrow towards our ship and in an instant had turned round it. Then they went off quietly to fish near the English soldier who, still glinting and unmoving, seemed put there as the symbol of the high civilization of Europe in arms.

We reached Detroit at three o'clock. Detroit is a little town of two or three thousand souls, founded by the Jesuits in the middle of the forest in 1710, and still having a great number of French families.

By this time we had crossed the whole State of New York, and gone a hundred leagues over Lake Erie; by now we were touching the limits of civilization, but we had no idea whatsoever whither to wend our way next. To get information was not as easy as one might have thought. To break through almost impenetrable forests, to cross deep rivers, to brave pestilential marshes, to sleep out in the damp woods, those are exertions that the American readily contemplates if it is a question of earning a guinea; for that is the point. But that one should do such things from curiosity is more than his mind can take in. Besides, living in the wilds, he only appreciates the works of man. He will gladly send you off to see a road, a bridge, or a fine village. But that one should appreciate great trees and the beauties of solicitude, that possibility completely passes him by.

So nothing is harder than to find anyone able to understand what you want. You want to see forests, our hosts said smiling, go straight ahead and you will find what you want. They are there all right around the new roads and well-trod paths. As for Indians, you will see only too many in our public places and in the streets; there is no need to go very far for that. Those here are at least beginning to get civilized and have a less savage look. We were not slow to realize that we should not get the truth out of them by frontal attack and that it was necessary to maneuver.

So we went to call on the official appointed by the United States to see to the sale of the still uninhabited land that covers the district of Michigan. We [i.e., Tocqueville and his traveling companion Beaumont] represented ourselves to him as people who, without any decided intention of settling in the country, might yet have distant interest in knowing what land cost and how it was situated. Major Biddle, that was his name, this time understood wonderfully well what we wanted to do, and entered at once into a mass of details to which we paid avid attention. "This part here," he said to us, pointing out a map of the St. Joseph River which, after a bend, flows into Lake Michigan, "seems to me best suited for your scheme. The soil is good there; there are already some fine villages established there; and the road leading thither is so well maintained that public conveyances traverse it daily." "Good," we said to ourselves. "Now we know where not to go, at least unless we want to visit the wilderness in a mail van." We thanked Major Biddle for his advice, and asked him with an air of casualness and a pretended scorn, what part of the district had so far least attracted the attention of immigrants. "In this direction," he told us without attaching more importance to our question, "towards the northwest. As far as Pontiac and in the neighborhood of that village some fairly good settlements have been established. But you must not think of settling further on; the ground is covered by an almost impenetrable forest which stretches almost endlessly to the northwest, where one finds only wild beasts and Indians. The United States are always considering opening up a road, but so far it has barely been begun and stops at Pontiac. I say again, that is a part you should not think about." We thanked Major Biddle for his good advice, and left determined to take it in a contrary sense. We could not maintain ourselves for joy at having at last discovered a place to which the torrent of European civilization had not yet come.

On the next day, the 23rd of July, we hastened to hire two horses. As we contemplated keeping them for ten days or so, we wanted to leave a sum of money with their owner, but he refused to take it, saying that we could pay on our return. He showed no alarm. Michigan is surrounded on all sides by lakes and wilds; he led us into a sort of corral of which he held the door. When we had bought a compass as well as provisions, we set out on our way, rifle on shoulder, as thoughtless of the future as a pair of schoolboys leaving college to spend their holidays at their father's house.

If we had wanted only to see forests, our hosts in Detroit would have been right in telling us that we need not go very far, for, a mile out of town, the road goes into the forest and never comes out of it. The land it passes over is completely flat and often marshy. From time to time along the road one comes to new clearings. As all these settlements are exactly like one another, whether they are in the depths of Michigan or just close to New York, I will try to describe them here once and for all.

The bells which the pioneer is careful to hang round his beasts' necks so as to find them again in the dense forest, give warning in the far distance that one is getting close to a clearing. Soon one hears the echoes of the axe that is cutting down the forest trees, and as one gets closer, signs of destruction make man's presence ever more evident. Severed branches cover the road, and trunks half scorched by fire or cut by the axe, yet stand still erect in your path. As you go on your way, you come to a wood where all the trees seem to have been struck by sudden death. In full summer their withered branches seem the image of winter. Looking at them, you see that a deep circle has been cut in their bark, which, by preventing the circulation of the sap, has brought them to a speedy death. That in fact is usually the planter's first beginning. As he cannot, in the first year, cut all the trees that adorn his property, he sows corn under their branches and, by striking them to death, prevents them from shading his crop. After this field which is an unfinished sketch, a first step of civilization in the wilds, one suddenly sees the owner's cabin. It is generally placed in the middle of some land more carefully cultivated than the rest, but where man is yet sustaining an unequal struggle against nature. There the trees have been cut but not yet grubbed up; their trunks still cover and block the land they used to shade. Round this withered debris, wheat, shoots of oak, plants of all kinds, and weeds of all sorts are scattered pell-mell and grow up together in the untamed and still half-wild ground. It is in the middle of this vigorous and variegated growth of vegetation that the planter's dwelling or, as it is called in this country, his log house, rises. Just like the field around it, this rustic dwelling shows every sign of new and hurried work. It is seldom more than thirty feet long. It is twenty feet wide and fifteen high. Both its walls and its roof are made of unsquared tree trunks between which moss and earth have been rammed to keep the cold and rain from the inside of the house. The closer the traveler gets, the more animated the scene becomes. As they hear his footsteps, the children, playing in the surrounding debris, get up in a hurry and run for shelter to their father's house, as if they were frightened at the sight of a man, while two great half-wild dogs with ears pricked and long muzzles, come out of the cabin growling and covering their young masters' retreat.

It is then that the pioneer himself appears at the door of his dwelling; he takes a good look at the new arrival; signs to his dogs to go back under cover and hastens to give them the example himself without a sign of curiosity and anxiety.

When he gets to the threshold of the log house, the European cannot help casting an astonished glance round the sight before him.

Such a cabin generally has but one window, at which perhaps a muslin curtain is hanging; for in these parts where necessities are not seldom lacking, superfluities often abound. A resinous fire crackles on the hearth of beaten earth, and, better than the daylight, lights up the insides of the place. Over this rustic fire one sees trophies of war or hunt: a long rifle, a deerskin, some eagle feathers. To the right of the chimney a map of the United States is often stretched, and the draft that blows through the gaps in the wall keeps raising and fluttering it. By it on a single shelf of ill-squared planks are a few tattered books; there one finds a Bible with its cloth and boards already worn out by the piety of two generations, a prayer book and, sometimes, a poem of Milton or a tragedy by Shakespeare. Along the wall are some rough seats, made by the hands of the owner himself; some trunks instead of cupboards, some agricultural implements and samples of the harvest. In the middle of the room is a rickety table whose legs, still sprouting foliage, seem to have grown by themselves on the ground they cover. It is there that the family assembles every day to take their meals. One also sees an English china teapot, some spoons usually of wood, some cracked cups and newspapers.

The looks of the master of this dwelling is no less remarkable than the place that gives him shelter. The angular muscles and long thin arms and legs make you recognize at first glance the native of New England. This man was not born in the solitude where he dwells; his constitution alone proclaims that. His first years were spent in the bosom of an intellectual and reasoning society. It's his own desire that has thrown him into the labors of the wilderness for which he does not seem made. But if his physical forces seem beneath his enterprise, in his face, lined by the cares of life, reigns an air of practical intelligence, of cold and persevering energy, which strikes one at once. His step is slow and very regular, his words measured and his face austere. Habit, and pride even more, have imparted to his face that stoic rigidity which his actions belie. The pioneer, it is true, scorns what often most violently moves the heart of man; his goods and his life will never be staked on the throw of the dice or the destinies of a woman; but to become well-to-do he has braved exile, the loneliness and the numberless miseries of the savage life, he has slept on the bare ground, he has exposed himself to the forest fevers and the tomahawk of the Indian. He made this effort one day, he has been renewing it for years, he will continue it for twenty years more perhaps without becoming discouraged or complaining. Is a man, capable of such sacrifices, a cold and insensible being? Ought not one on the contrary to recognize in him one of those mental passions, so burning, so tenacious, so implacable?

Intent on the goal of making his fortune, the emigrant has finally created for himself an altogether individual existence. Family sentiments have come to use themselves in a vast egoism, and it is doubtful if in his wife and children he sees anything less than a detached portion of himself. Deprived of habitual contact with his fellows, he has learned to take a delight in solitude. When you present yourself on the sill of his isolated dwelling, the pioneer comes forward to meet you, he holds out his hand according to custom, but his face expresses neither benevolence nor joy. He only speaks to ask questions of you. It's an intellectual and not an emotional need he is satisfying, and as soon as he has drawn from you the news he wished to learn he falls silent again. One would suppose one's self in the presence of a man who in the evening has retired to his dwelling, tired of the demands and the noise of the world. There is no cordiality in your reception. Interrogate him yourself [and] he will give you the information you need with intelligence; he will even see to your necessities, watch over your safety as long as you are under his roof; but there reigns in all his actions so much constraint, pride; you perceive in them such a profound indifference even for the results of your efforts that you feel your gratitude freezing. Yet the pioneer is hospitable in his way, but his hospitality has nothing which touches you because in exercising it he seems to submit himself to a painful necessity of the wilderness; he sees it a duty which his position imposes on him, not a pleasure. This unknown man is the representative of a race to which belongs the future of the new world: a restless, reasoning, adventurous race which does coldly what only the ardor of passion can explain; a race cold and passionate, which traffics in everything, not excepting morality and religion; a nation of conquerors who submit themselves to the savage life without ever allowing themselves to be seduced by it, who in civilization and enlightenment love only what is necessary to well-being, and who shut themselves in the American solitudes with an axe and some newspapers.

A people which, like all great peoples, has but one thought, and which is advancing toward the acquisition of riches, sole goal of its efforts, with a perseverance and a scorn for life that one might call heroic, if that name fitted other than virtuous beings. It's this nomad people which the rivers and lakes do not stop, before which forests fall and the prairies are covered with shade, and which, after having reached the Pacific Ocean, will reverse its steps to trouble and destroy the societies which it will have formed behind it.

In speaking of the pioneer one cannot forget the companion of his miseries and dangers. Look across the hearth at the young woman who, while seeing to the preparation of the meal, rocks her youngest son in her arms. Like the emigrant, this woman is in her prime; like him, she can recall the ease of her first years. Her clothes even yet proclaim a taste for adornment ill extinguished. But time has weighed heavily on her: in her prematurely pale face and her shrunken limbs it is easy to see that existence has been a heavy burden for her. In fact, this frail creature has already found herself exposed to unbelievable miseries. Scarce entered upon life, she had to tear herself away from the mother's tenderness and from those sweet fraternal ties that a young girl never abandons without shedding tears, even when she is going to share the rich dwelling of a new husband. The wife of the pioneer has torn herself from that innocent cradle of her youth. It's against the solitude of the forests that she has exchanged the charms of society and the joys of her home. It's on the bare ground of the wilderness that her nuptial couch was placed. To devote herself to austere duties, embrace an existence for which she was not made, such was the occupation of the finest years of her life, such have been for her the delights of marriage. Want, suffering, and loneliness have affected her constitution but not bowed her courage. Mid the profound sadness painted on her delicate features, you easily remark a religious resignation and I know not what natural and tranquil firmness confronting all the miseries of life without fearing or scorning them.

Around this woman crowd half-naked children, shining with health, careless of the morrow, veritable sons of the wilderness. From time to time their mother throws on them a look of melancholy and joy. To see their strength and her weakness one would say that she has exhausted herself giving them life and that she does not regret what they have cost her.

The house inhabited by these emigrants has no interior partitions or attic. In the single apartment [room] which it contains the entire family comes in the evening to seek refuge: this dwelling forms of itself a small world. It's the ark of civilization lost in an ocean of leaves. It's a sort of oasis in the desert. A hundred feet beyond the eternal forest stretches about it its shade and the eternal forest begins again.

It was only in the evening after sundown that we reached Pontiac. Twenty very neat and pretty houses, forming so many well-furnished shops, a transparent stream, a clearing about a quarter of a league square, and the eternal forest about: there is the faithful tableau of Pontiac which, in twenty years perhaps, will be a city. The sight of this place recalled to me what Mr. [Albert] Gallatin had said in New York a month before: "There are no villages in America, at least in the sense you give this word." Here the houses of the farmers are scattered through their fields. One assembles in a place only to establish a market for the use of the surrounding population. You see in these so-called villages only men of law, printers, and merchants.

We had ourselves taken to the finest inn of Pontiac (for there are two), and we were introduced, as usual, into what is called the barroom; it's a room where you are given to drink and where the simplest as well as the richest traders of the place come to smoke, drink, and talk politics together, on the footing of the most perfect exterior equality. The master of the shop, or the landlord, was—I shall not call him a huge peasant, for there are no peasants in America—but at least a very large man whose face wore that expression of candor and simplicity which distinguishes the Normandy horse traders. He was a man who, for fear of intimidating you, never looked you in the face while talking to you but waited, to consider you at his ease, until you were busy talking elsewhere; moreover, a deep politician and according to American custom a pitiless questioner. This estimable citizen, with the rest of the company, regarded us at first with astonishment. Our traveling clothes and our guns hardly proclaimed us as businessmen, and to travel to sight-see was something absolutely unusual. In order to cut explanations short, we declared at once that we had come to buy land. No sooner had the word been pronounced than we perceived that in seeking to avoid one evil we had thrown ourselves into another much more redoubtable.

It is true that they stopped treating us like extraordinary beings but each one wanted to bargain with us. To disembarrass ourselves of them and their farms we told our host that before deciding anything we wanted to get from them the price of lands and the method of cultivating them. He immediately led us into another room, spread with appropriate deliberation a map of Michigan on the oak table in the middle of the room and, putting the candle between us three, waited in impassive silence for what we had to communicate to him. The reader, without having the intention of establishing himself in one of the American solitudes, may yet be curious to know how so many thousands of Europeans and Americans who come there each year in search of a refuge go about it. I shall therefore here transcribe the information furnished us by our Pontiac host. Often since we have been in a position to verify its perfect exactness.

"It is not here as in France," said our host after having calmly listened to our questions and snuffed the candle. "With you, labor is cheap and land is dear. Here the cost of land is nothing and the labor of men is beyond price; which I say to you so you may realize that to establish oneself in America one needs capital just as in Europe, even though it is differently employed. For my part, I should not advise any one to seek his fortune in our wilderness unless he has at his disposition from one hundred fifty to two hundred dollars. In Michigan the acre never costs more than ten shillings when the land is still uncultivated. That's about the price of a day's work. A laborer can therefore earn in one day enough to buy an acre of land. But the purchase made, the difficulties begin. Here is how they generally go about surmounting them."

"The pioneer betakes himself to the place he has just acquired with some cattle, a salted pig, two barrels of meal and some tea. If a cabin is to be found near there he goes and receives temporary hospitality. If not, he sets up a tent in the midst of the wood which is to become his field. His first care is to fell the nearest trees with which in haste he builds the rude hut whose construction you have perhaps been able to examine. With us, the keeping of cattle hardly costs anything. The emigrant lets them run in the forest after having an iron bell tied about their necks. It is very rare for these animals, thus abandoned to themselves, to leave the vicinity of their home."

"The greatest expense is the clearing. If the pioneer arrives in the wilderness with a family in a state of aid to him in his first labors his task is easy enough. But it is rarely thus. In general the emigrant is young and, if has children already, they are very young. Then he must all alone provide for the first needs of his family, or hire the services of his neighbors. It costs from three to four dollars to have an acre cleared. The ground prepared, the new proprietor puts an acre into potatoes, the rest into wheat and corn. Corn is the providence of these wildernesses; it grows in the water of our swamps and under the forest foliage better than in the rays of the sun. It's the corn which saves the family of the emigrant from inevitable destruction when poverty, sickness, or carelessness has prevented its making a large enough clearing the first year. There is nothing harder than the first years after the clearing. Later come ease and then wealth."

Thus spoke our host. For our part, we listened to these simple details with almost as much interest as if we had wished to profit from them ourselves, and when he was silent we said to him: "The soil of all the woods left to themselves is generally marshy and unhealthy; does the emigrant, who exposes himself to the miseries of solitude, have nothing to fear for his life?" "All clearing is a dangerous enterprise," resumed the American, "and it is almost without example that the pioneer and his family escape the woods fever [malaria] during the first year. Often, when you travel in the fall, you find all the inhabitants of a cabin down with fever, from the emigrant to his youngest son." "And what becomes of these unfortunates when Providence strikes them in this way? "They resign themselves and wait for a better future." "But have they some assistance to hope for from their fellows?" "Hardly any." "Can they at least procure the services of a doctor?" "The nearest doctor often lives sixty miles from their house. They do like the Indians; they die or get well, as it pleases God."

We resumed: "Does the voice of religion sometimes reach them?" "Very rarely. It has not yet been possible to do anything to assure the public observation of a cult of the woods. Almost every summer, it is true, some Methodist preachers come to make a tour of the new settlements. The noise of their arrival spreads with unbelievable rapidity from cabin to cabin: it's the great news of the day. At the date set, the emigrant, his wife and children set out by scarcely cleared forest trails toward the indicated meeting place. They come from fifty miles around. It's not in a church that they gather, but in the open air, under the forest foliage. A pulpit of badly squared logs, great trees felled for seats, such are the ornaments of this rustic temple. The pioneers and their families camp in the surrounding woods. It's there that, during three days and three nights, the crowd gives itself over to almost uninterrupted religious exercises. You must see with what ardor these men surrender themselves to prayer, with what attention they listen to the solemn voice of the preacher. It's in the wilderness that people show themselves almost starved for religion." "One last question: it is generally believed by us that the wildernesses of America are peopled by the aid of European immigration; whence comes it then that since we have been traversing your forests we have not happened to encounter a single European?"

A smile of superiority and of satisfied pride painted itself on the features of our host on hearing this question.

"It's only Americans," answered he with emphasis, "who can have the courage to submit themselves to such miseries and who know how to buy prosperity at such a price. The European immigrant stops in the great cities along the coast or in neighboring districts. There he becomes an artisan, farm hand, or servant. He lives an easier life than in Europe and, satisfied to leave his children the same inheritance, he is content. It's to the Americans that the land belongs, it's to him that it is given to take possession of the solitudes of the new world, to make them yield to man and to create for himself an immense future."

After having pronounced these immense words, our host stopped. He allowed an immense column of smoke to escape from his mouth and appeared ready to listen to what we had to tell him about our projects.

We thanked him first of all for his valuable advice and his wise counsels, by which we assured him we should profit some day, and we added: "Before settling in your district, my dear host, we intend to go to Saginaw and we want to consult you on this point."

"At this word 'Saginaw,' a singular revolution took place in the expression of the American. It was as if he were being violently withdrawn from the real world to be thrust into the realm of the imagination. His eyes dilated, and the most profound astonishment painted itself on his features.

"You want to go to Saginaw!" cried he, "to Saginaw Bay! Two reasonable men, two well educated foreigners want to go to Saginaw Bay! The thing is hardly credible!" "And why not?" answered we. "But do you realize," retorted our host, "what you are undertaking? Do you know that Saginaw is the last inhabited place till the Pacific Ocean; that from here to Saginaw hardly anything but wilderness and pathless solitudes are to be found? Have you thought that the woods are full of Indians and mosquitoes; that you will have to sleep at least one night in the dampness of their shade? Have you thought of the fever? Would you know how to get yourself out of difficulties in the wilderness, and find your way in the labyrinth of our forests?"

After his tirade, he paused, the better to judge the impression he had made. We replied: "All that may be very true, but we shall leave tomorrow morning for Saginaw Bay."

Our host reflected for an instant, lifted his head, and said slowly in a measured and positive tone: "Only a great interest can induce two foreigners to such an enterprise. You have doubtless imagined, quite wrongly, that it was advantageous to settle in places the furthest removed from all competition?"

We did not answer. He went on: "Perhaps too you are charged by the Canadian fur company to establish relations with the frontier Indians."

Same silence.

Our host was at the end of his conjectures, and he fell silent; but he continued to reflect deeply on the strangeness of our design.

"Have you never been to Saginaw?" we said. "I," he answered, "I unhappily have been there five or six times, but I had an interest in going, and it is impossible to discover that you have any." "But don't forget, my worthy host, that we do not ask you if one should go to Saginaw, but only what are the means to get there with ease."

Thus brought back to the question, our American recovered all his self-possession and all the clearness of his ideas. He explained to us in few words and with admirable practical sense how we should set about to cross the wilderness. He entered into the smallest details and foresaw the most fortuitous circumstances. At the end of his prescriptions he paused anew to see if we would not finally reach the mystery of our trip, and perceiving that neither of us had anything more to say, he took the candle, led us to a room and, having shaken hands very democratically, went to finish the evening in the common room.

The next day we got up with the light and prepared to start. Our host was himself soon afoot; the night had not enabled him to discover what made us stick to a conduct so extraordinary in his eyes. However, as we appeared absolutely resolved to act contrary to his advice, he did not dare return to the charge, but he turned constantly about us. From time to time he muttered: "I can with difficulty understand what can induce two foreigners to go to Saginaw, . . . " and he repeated this phrase several times until finally I said to him, putting my foot in the stirrup: "There are many reasons which carry us there, my dear host!"

He brought up short on hearing those words and, looking me in the face for the first time, he seemed to prepare himself to hear the revelation of the great mystery. But I, calmly forking my horse, made a friendly gesture and went off at full trot.

When after fifty yards I turned my head, I saw him still planted like a hay stack before his door. Shortly he went in, shaking his head. . . .

It has been suggested to us that we apply to a Mr. Williams who, having long traded with the Chippewa Indians and having a son established at Saginaw, might furnish us with useful information.

After having made some miles in the woods and we were beginning to fear that we had already missed our man's house, we encountered an old man busy working a small garden; as we approached him, it was Mr. Williams himself.

He received us with great benevolence and gave us a letter for his son. We asked him if we did not have anything to fear from the Indian tribes whose territory we were going to cross. Mr. Williams rejected this idea with a sort of indignation: "No, no," said he, "you can proceed without fear. For my part, I should sleep more calmly among the Indians than among the whites."

I note this as the first favorable impression about the Indians that I have received since my arrival in America. In the thickly settled regions they are spoken of only with a mixture of fear and scorn, and I believe that there, in fact, they deserve these two sentiments. It has already been possible to see what I thought of them myself when I encountered the first of them at Buffalo. As one advances in this diary and follows me among the Europeans of the frontier and the Indian tribes themselves, one will conceive an idea at the same time more honorable and more just of the first inhabitants of America.

After having left Mr. Williams, we pursued our way in the woods. From time to time a small lake (this district is full of them) appears like a sheet of silver under the forest foliage. It is difficult to imagine the charm which surrounds these pretty places where man has not fixed his dwelling and where still reign a profound peace and an uninterrupted silence.

In the Alps I have visited some fearful solitudes, where nature refused to yield to cultivation but where it deploys, even to the point of horror, a grandeur that transports and impassions the soul. Here the solitude is no less profound, but it does not give rise to the same impressions. The only feelings one experiences in journeying through these flowered wildernesses where, as in Milton's *Paradise,* all is prepared to receive man, are a tranquil admiration, a vague distaste for civilized life, a sweet and melancholy emotion, a sort of wild instinct which makes one reflect with sadness that soon this delightful solitude will be completely altered. In fact, the white race is already advancing through the surrounding woods, and in a few years the European will have cut the trees reflected in the limpid waters of the lake and forced the animals peopling its banks to retire to new wildernesses.

Always progressing, we come into a region of different appearance. The soil was no longer even, but cut by hills and valleys. Several of these hills were most savage in appearance.

It was on one of these trails that, having suddenly turned around to contemplate the imposing spectacle we were leaving behind us, to our great surprise we saw near the crupper of our horses an Indian who seemed to be following us step by step.

He was a man about thirty years of age, tall and admirably proportioned as most of them are. His black gleaming hair fell to his shoulders except for two tresses attached on the top of his forehead. His face was daubed with black and red. He was covered by a kind of blue blouse. He wore some red *mittas;* these are a kind of trouser which only go to the upper thigh, and his feet were garnished with moccasins. By his side hung a knife. In his right hand he held a long carbine, and in his left two birds which he had just killed.

The first sight of this Indian made a rather disagreeable impression on us. The place was ill chosen to resist an attack. On our right a forest of pines rose to an immense height in the air; on our left stretched a deep ravine at the bottom of which tumbled a rocky stream which the thick foliage hid from our view and toward which we were blindly descending! To put our hands on our guns, turn about, and face the Indian was the work of an instant. He himself stopped; we stood for half a minute in silence.

His face presented all the characteristic traits which distinguish the Indian race from all the others. In his perfectly black eyes burned the wild fire which still animates the glance of the half breed and is only lost with the second or third generation of white blood. His nose was arched in the middle, lightly flattened at the point; his cheekbones, very high; and his mouth, deeply cut, revealed two rows of teeth, sparkling white, which gave sufficient proof that the savage, more cleanly than his American neighbor, did not spend his days chewing tobacco leaves.

I have said that the moment we turned about, putting our hands to our arms, the Indian had stopped. He underwent the rapid examination we made of his person with absolute impassiveness, with a glance direct and motionless. As he saw that we on our side had no hostile feelings, he began to smile: probably he saw that he had alarmed us.

That is the first time I was able to observe how completely the expression of gaiety changes the face of these savage men. I have had a hundred occasions since to make the same remark. A serious Indian and a smiling Indian are absolutely two different men. There reigns in the immobility of the first a savage majesty which gives you an involuntary feeling of terror. Does this same man smile, his face takes on an expression of naivete and benevolence that gives it a real charm.

When we saw our man's face relax, we addressed him in English; he let us speak at our ease, then signed that he did not understand. We offered him a little brandy which he accepted without hesitation and without thanks. Speaking always by signs, we asked for the birds he was carrying, and he gave them to us in exchange for a small piece of money. Having thus introduced ourselves, we saluted him and went off at full trot.

At the end of an hour's rapid march, having again glanced behind, I was confounded again to see the Indian again behind the cropper of my horse. He was running with the agility of a wild animal, without pronouncing a single word or seeming to lengthen his stride. We stopped, he stopped; we went on, he followed. We went on at full speed; our horses, raised in this wilderness, cleared all the obstacles with ease; the Indian doubled his pace; I saw him now on the right and now on the left of my horse, jumping over the bushes and falling noiselessly to earth. One would have said one of those wolves of northern Europe which follow riders in the hope they will fall from their horses and be the more easily devoured.

The sight of this set face which, now losing itself in the forest obscurity, now reappearing in the daylight, seemed to float at our side, ended by making us uncomfortable. Not being able to conceive what induced this man to follow us at so precipitate a pace, and perhaps he had long been doing so when we discovered him the first time, it occurred to us that he was leading us into an ambush.

We were occupied with these thoughts when we perceived before us in the woods the end of another carbine; soon we were alongside the bearer. We took him at first for an Indian. He wore a kind of short coat which, folded closely about the waist, revealed an erect and well-proportioned figure. His neck was bare, and his feet covered with moccasins. When we came near him and he raised his head, we at once recognized a European and we stopped. He came to us, shook hands with cordiality, and we began to converse.

"Do you live in the wilderness?" said we to him. "Yes," answered he. "There's my house."

"Alone? Alone? What do you do here?" "I go through these woods and kill from right to left the game to be found on my path, but there are few good shots to be had now." "And this kind of life pleases you?" "More than any other." "But are you not afraid of the Indians?" "Afraid of the Indians! I would rather live in their midst than among the whites. No, no, I am not afraid of the Indians; they are worth more than we, if we had not brutalized them by our liquors, poor creatures!"

We then showed our new acquaintance the man who was so obstinately following us and who had stopped a few feet away and was standing as motionless as a mark. "That's a Chippewa," said he, "or, as the French call them, a *sauteur*. I bet he is returning from Canada, where he has received the annual presents of the English. His family cannot be far from here."

Having spoken thus, the American signed to the Indian to approach and began to speak to him in his tongue with extreme facility. It was remarkable to see the pleasure with which these two men of birth and customs so different found in exchanging their ideas. The conversation evidently turned on the relative merits of their arms. The white, after having examined the gun of the savage very attentively: "That's a fine carbine," said he; "the English have doubtless given it to him to use against us, and he will not fail to do so in the first war. It's thus that the Indians draw on their heads all the misfortunes which overwhelm them, but they don't know any better, poor people!" "Do the Indians," said I, "use these long and heavy guns with skill?" "There are no shots like the Indians," retorted our new friend with the accent of the most profound admiration. "Examine these small birds which he has sold you, sir: They are pierced with one ball, and I am very sure that he shot only twice to get them. Oh!" said he, "there is nothing happier than an Indian in the regions whence we have not yet made the game flee; but the large animals scent us at more than three hundred miles and in withdrawing they make before us a sort of desert where the poor Indians can no longer live, if they do not cultivate the earth." As we resumed our journey: "When you come by again," our new friend called, "knock on my door. It is a pleasure to meet white faces in these parts."

I have related in this conversation, which in itself contains nothing remarkable, to make known a type of man we have since often met on the edges of settlement. They are Europeans who, in spite of the habits of their youth, have ended by finding in the freedom of the wilderness an inexpressible charm. Clinging to the American solitudes by taste and passion, to Europe through their religion, their principles and their ideas, they mingle love of the savage life with the pride of civilization and prefer the Indians to their compatriots, without however acknowledging them as equals.

We resumed our way, then, and, advancing always with the same rapidity, at the end of a half hour we reached the house of a pioneer. Before the door of this cabin an Indian family had taken up temporary residence. An old woman, two young girls, [and] several children were grouped about a fire which exposed the still palpitating parts of an entire deer. A few feet away an Indian, altogether naked, was warming himself in the rays of the sun, while a small child rolled in the dust near him. It was there that our silent companion stopped; he left us without taking leave and went to sit gravely among his compatriots. What had induced this man to follow our horses thus for two leagues? That's something we were never able to divine.

After having lunched at this place we remounted and pursued our way through a tall but rather thin grove. The woods had once been burned, as could be seen from the ashy remains of some trees fallen in the earth. The soil today is covered by ferns, which stretch about as far as one can see under the forest foliage. Some leagues further on my horse lost its shoe, which caused us a lively uneasiness. Near there, fortunately, we met a farmer who succeeded in replacing it. But for this happy encounter, I doubt whether we would have been able to go any further, for we were at the extreme limit of the clearings. This same man, who thus put us in a position to pursue our way, invited us to hasten, the day beginning to fall and two long leagues still separating us from the Flint River, where we wished to sleep.

Soon, in fact, a deep obscurity began to envelop us. It was necessary to walk. The night was serene, but glacial. There reigned in the depth of these forests a silence so profound and a calm so complete one would have said that all the forces of nature were as if paralyzed. One heard only the uncomfortable buzzing of mosquitoes and the footfall of our horses. From time to time one sighted in the distance an Indian fire before which an austere and still profile sketched itself in the smoke.

At the end of an hour we arrived at a place where the road forked, two paths opened on the spot. Which of the two to take? It was a delicate choice. One of the two ended at a stream whose depth we did not know, the other at a clearing. The moon, which was then rising, showed ahead of us a valley filled with a thousand debris; further on we saw houses.

It was so important not to lose ourselves in such a place at such an hour that we resolved to inform ourselves before going further. My companion stayed behind to hold the horses, and I, throwing my gun on my shoulder, descended into the valley. Soon I perceived that I was entering a very recent clearing. Immense trees, with their branches not yet lopped off, covered the ground. By jumping from one to another I came near the houses fairly rapidly. But the same stream we had already encountered separated me from them. Happily its course in this place was obstructed by some great oaks which the pioneer's axe had doubtlessly felled there. I succeeded in working my way along these trees and finally arrived on the other bank.

I approached the two houses with caution, fearing that they might be Indian wigwams. They were not yet finished. I found the doors open and no voice replied to mine. I returned to the bank of the stream, where for some minutes I couldn't keep from admiring the supreme horror of the place. This valley where I found myself seemed to form an immense amphitheater, surrounded by the foliage of the woods on all sides, as by black drapery, and in whose center the rays of the moon, breaking, came to create a thousand fantastic beings which played with each other silently in the forest debris. Beyond that, no sound whatever, no noise of life from this solitude.

At length I thought of my companion, and I shouted to him to tell him the result of my search and to get him to cross the stream to come and find me. My voice echoed a long time in the surrounding solitudes, but I got no response. I shouted again and still listened. The same deathly silence reigned in the forest. Uneasiness seized me, and I ran along the stream to find the trail which I knew crossed it lower down.

Arrived there, I heard in the distance the footfall of horses and soon after I saw Beaumont himself appear. Astonished by my long absence, he had decided to advance toward the stream. He had already begun to descend the slope when I had called. My voice had not then been able to reach him. He told me that on his side he had made every effort to make himself heard and, like me, had been frightened at not receiving a response. But for the ford, which served us as a meeting place, we would perhaps have hunted each other a large part of the night.

We set forth again, promising each other faithfully not to separate any more, and three quarters of an hour from there we caught sight of a clearing, two or three cabins and, what pleased us even more, a light. The river, which stretched like a violet thread at the end of the valley, convinced us that we had arrived at Flint River. Soon, in fact, the baying of dogs made the woods ring and we found ourselves before a log house, separated from it by a single barrier. As we were preparing to cross it, the moon showed us on the other side a great black bear which, upright on its hind feet and drawing its chain in, showed as clearly as it could its intention to give us a friendly accolade.

"What a devilish country it is," said I, "where they have bears for watchdogs." "We'll have to call," said my companion; "if we tried to cross the fence we should have difficulty making the porter understand." We shouted, then, at the top of our lungs so well that a man finally put his head out the window. After having examined us in the moonlight, "Enter, gentlemen," said he. "Trink, go lie down! To your kennel I say! These are not thieves!"

The bear retreated, waddling, and we entered. We were half dead with fatigue. We ask our host if we can have hay for our horses. "Surely," he answered; and he set to work to scythe the nearest field with all the calm of Americans and as he might have done at midday.

Meanwhile, we unsaddled our mounts and tied them, for want of a stable, to the fence we had just crossed.

Having thus cared for our travel companions, we began to think of our own lodgings. There was only one bed in the house; the toss having given it to Beaumont, I pulled my mantle about me and, stretching out on the floor, slept as profoundly as becomes a man who has just done fifteen leagues on horseback.

The next day, 25 July, our first care was to inquire for a guide. A wilderness of fifteen leagues separates Flint River from Saginaw, and the road there is only a narrow path, scarce recognizable to the eye. Our host approved of our plan, and soon after he brought us two Indians in whom he assured us we could place every confidence. One was a child of thirteen to fourteen years, the other a young man of eighteen. The body of the latter, without yet having acquired the vigorous shape of maturity, gave already, however, the idea of agility united to strength. He was of medium height, his figure straight and slim, his limbs flexible and well proportioned. Long tresses fell from his bare head. Moreover, he had carefully painted on his face lines of black and red in the most symmetrical way; a ring passed through the membrane of his nose, a necklace and earrings completed his apparel. His accoutrements of war were no less remarkable. On the one side the battle-axe, the celebrated tomahawk; on the other a long sharp knife, with whose aid the savages lift the scalps of the vanquished. From his neck was suspended a bull's horn which served him as a powderbox, and in his right hand he held a rifle. As with most of the Indians, his glance was fierce and his smile kindly. Beside him, as if to complete the tableau, walked a dog with straight ears, narrow muzzle, much more like a fox than any other animal, and whose fierce air was in perfect harmony with the countenance of his conductor.

After having examined our new companion with an attention of which he did not seem in an instant aware, we asked him what he wanted as the price of the service he was going to render us. The Indian answered a few words in his own tongue and the American, hastening to speak, told us that what the savage asked would be valued at two dollars.

"As these poor Indians," our host added charitably, "do not know the value of money, you will give me the dollars and I shall willingly undertake to furnish him with the equivalent."

I was curious to see what the worthy man called the equivalent of two dollars, and I followed him very softly to the place where the bargain was consummated. I saw him deliver our guide a pair of moccasins and a pocket handkerchief, objects whose total value certainly did not reach half that sum. The Indian withdrew very much pleased and I slipped away saying like La Fontaine: "Ah! If the lions knew how to paint!"

All was ready; we mounted and, fording the stream (Flint River) which forms the extreme boundary between civilization and solitude, we entered once and for all into solitude.

Our two guides walked or rather jumped before us like wildcats across the obstacles in the path. Did a fallen tree, a stream, a marsh present itself, they pointed to the best way, crossed themselves, and did not even look back to see us get out of our difficulties. Used to counting only on himself, the Indian has difficulty conceiving that another has need of help. He knows how to render a service at need, but no one has yet taught him the art of making it appreciated through little courtesies and attentions. This manner of conduct would have elicited some observations on our part, but it was impossible to make our companions understand a single word. And then we felt ourselves completely in their power. There, in fact, the ladder was upside down. Plunged into a deep obscurity, reduced to his own resources, the civilized man was marching like a blind man, incapable not only of guiding himself in the labyrinth he was traversing but of even finding there the means to sustain life. It's in the same difficulties that the savage triumphed. For him the forest had no veil; he was as if at home; he marched there with his head in the air, guided by an instinct more certain than the mariner's compass. At the summit of the tallest trees, under the thickest foliage, his eyes discovered the prey near which the European passes and repasses a hundred times in vain.

From time to time our Indians stopped. They put their hands to their lips to invite us to silence and signed to us to dismount. Guided by them, we managed to reach a place whence the game could be seen. It was a singular spectacle to see the scornful smile with which they guided us near the object which they themselves had seen long ago.

As we advanced, however, the last traces of man disappeared. Soon everything ceased to proclaim the presence of the savage, and we had before us the spectacle we had so long run after: the interior of a virgin forest. In a thin grove through which objects can be seen at quite a distance, rose in a single bound a high clump composed almost entirely of pines and oaks. Obliged to grow on very circumscribed soil and almost entirely deprived of the sun's rays, each of these trees rises by the shortest way to seek the air and the light. As straight as the mast of a vessel, it shoots up beyond the surrounding forest,and it is only in the upper regions that it tranquilly spreads its branches and envelops itself in the shade. Others soon follow it into that elevated sphere and all, interlacing their branches, form as it were an immense dais, above the earth which bears them. Beneath this still humid vault the aspect changes and the scene takes on a new character.

A majestic order reigns above your head. Near the earth, on the contrary, everything offers the image of confusion and chaos: trunks incapable of longer supporting their branches have broken at half their height and present to the eye only a torn and pointed top. Others, long shaken by the wind, have been precipitated to earth in one piece. Torn from the soil, their roots from so many natural ramparts behind which hundreds of men could easily find cover. Immense trees, retained by the surrounding branches, hang suspended in the air, and fall into dust without touching the earth.

With us [i.e., the French] there is no region so little peopled, where a forest is so abandoned to itself that the trees, after having calmly lived out their life, finally fall of decrepitude. It's man who fells them in the prime of their age and who clears the forest of their debris. In the American solitude, on the contrary, all-powerful nature is the only agent of ruin as it is the only power of reproduction. As in the forests within the domain of man, death strikes here without ceasing, but no one takes away the debris it has made; each day adds to their number. They fall, they accumulate, one on the other; there is not the time to reduce them quick enough to dust and prepare new places. There are to be found, lying side by side, several generations of dead. Some, in the last stages of dissolution, present to the eye only a long streak of red dust on the ground; others, already half consumed by time, still preserve their shape. Finally, there are some, fallen yesterday, which stretch their long branches on the ground and at each instant arrest the steps of the traveler by unforeseen obstacles. . . .

When at midday the sun darts its rays at the forest, one often hears in its depths as it were a long sigh, a plaintive cry prolonged into the distance. It's the last effort of the expiring wind; everything about you then enters into a silence so profound, a stillness so complete, that the soul feels penetrated by a sort of religious terror; the traveler stops, then he gazes about. Pressed against each other, their branches intertwined, the forest trees seem to form only a single whole, an immense and indestructible edifice, under whose vaults reigns an eternal darkness. In whatever direction one looks, one sees only a field of violence and destruction, trees broken, trunks torn; everything proclaims that the elements here make perpetual war, but the struggle is suspended, the movement is suddenly arrested. At the order of a great power the half-broken branches have remained hung from trunks which no longer seem able to support them; trees already uprooted have not had the time to reach the ground and have remained suspended in the air.

He listens, he holds his breath fearfully the better to catch the slightest sound of existence which may strike his ear. No sound, no murmur reaches him. It has more than once happened to us in Europe to find ourselves lost in the woods; but always some sounds of life come there to strike the ear. It was the distant ringing of the nearest village bell, the footfalls of a traveler, the axe of the woodchopper, the sound of a shot, the barking of a dog, or only that confused rumor which rises from a civilized country.

Here not only man is missing, but even the voices of animals are not heard. The smallest of them have left these regions to go nearer human habitation, the larger to go further away; those who remain keep hidden under shelter from the rays of the sun. Thus everything is still, everything in the woods is silent under the foliage; one would say that the Creator has for the moment turned his face away and that the forces of nature are paralyzed. . . . In this ocean of foliage who can indicate the road? In vain do you climb on the summit of the highest trees; others higher still surround you. Uselessly do you climb the hills, everywhere the forest seems to go along with you, and this same forest stretches before you even to the arctic pole and the Pacific Ocean.

But it is time to return to the route to Saginaw. We had already proceeded for five hours in complete ignorance of the place when our Indians stopped and the older, whose name was Sagan-Cuisco, made a line in the sand. He pointed to one end of it crying: *Michi-Couteouinque* (the Indian name for the Flint River) and to the other extremity pronouncing the name of "*Saginaw*," and, making a point in the middle of the line, he indicated that we had reached the half-way point and that we should rest a few minutes.

The sun was already high on the horizon, and we would have accepted with pleasure the invitation made us, if we had some water at hand; but not seeing any in the neighborhood we signed to the

Indian that we wished to eat and drink at the same time. He understood us at once and set off with the same speed as before. An hour later he stopped and again showed us thirty yards off in the woods a place where he made a sign that there was water.

Without awaiting our reply, and without helping us to unsaddle our horses, he went there himself; we hastened to follow him. The wind had recently blown away a tall tree at this place; in the hole formerly occupied by its roots, a little rain water was to be found. This was the fountain to which our guide conducted us, without seeming to think that one might hesitate to use such a drink.

We opened our sack. Another misfortune! The heat had absolutely spoiled our provisions, and we saw ourselves reduced for all dinner to a very small piece of bread, all we had been able to find at Flint River. Add to that a cloud of mosquitoes drawn by the nearness of water, and you will have the idea of a picnic dinner in a virgin forest. While we ate, our Indians sat, arms crossed, on the fallen tree of which I have spoken. When they saw we had finished, they made sign that they too were hungry. We showed them our empty sack; they shook their heads without saying anything. The Indian does not know what regular meal hours are; he gorges himself with food when he can, and then fasts until he again finds something to satisfy his appetite; the wolves do the same in like circumstance.

Soon we thought of remounting, but we perceived with great fright that our mounts had disappeared. Bitten by the mosquitoes and pricked by hunger, they had gone from the path where we had left them, and it was only with difficulty that we were able to place ourselves on their trail. The path we were following immediately became more and more difficult to recognize. At each instant our horses had to force a passage through thick clumps or jump over the trunks of the immense trees barring the path. At the end of two hours of extremely hard traveling we finally arrived on the bank of a shallow but extremely inaccessible stream. We forded it and on the top of the opposite bank we saw a field of corn and two cabins quite like log houses. On approaching we discovered that we were in a small Indian settlement: the pretended log houses were really wigwams. Further, the most profound solitude reigned there as in the surrounding forest.

Before the first of these abandoned dwellings Sagan-Cuisco stopped. He carefully examined all the objects round about, then putting down his gun and approaching us, he first traced a line in the sand indicating in the same way that we had yet only covered two thirds of the journey, then getting up he showed us the sun and signed to us that it was fast sinking toward its setting. He then looked at the wigwam and closed his eyes. This language was most intelligible: he wished to have us spend the night at this place. I admit that this news greatly surprised and hardly pleased us. We hadn't eaten since morning and were only moderately anxious to sleep without supping. The somber and savage majesty of the scenes which we had witnessed since morning, the complete isolation in which we found ourselves, the fierce countenances of our guides with whom it was impossible to enter into understanding, none of these was of a nature to beget trust in us.

There was in the conduct of the Indians something singular which did not reassure us at all. The route which we had followed for two hours seemed still less frequented that the one we had been on before. No one had ever told us that we were to pass an Indian village; and every one had assured us, on the other hand, that we could go in a single day from Flint River to Saginaw. . . .

We insisted on going ahead. The Indian indicated that we should be surprised by the darkness in the woods. To force our guides to continue their route would have been a dangerous attempt. We decided to tempt their cupidity. But the Indian is the most philosophic of men. He has few needs, and correspondingly few desires. Civilization has no hold on him. He is ignorant of and despises its comforts.

I had however noticed that Sagan-Cuisco has paid particular attention to a small osier bottle hanging at my side. A bottle that doesn't break! That was a thing whose utility had appealed to his senses and excited his real imagination. My gun and my bottle were the only parts of my European accoutrements which had seemed to excite his envy. I made a sign to him that I should give him my bottle if he conducted us at once to Saginaw. The Indian thereupon appeared violently torn. He looked again at the sun, then the earth. Finally, deciding, he seized his carbine, twice putting his hand on his mouth, he uttered the cry: "ouh! ouh!" and threw himself before us into the brush.

We followed him at full trot and, forcing our way through, we had soon lost the Indian dwellings to view. Our guides ran thus before us with greater speed than they had before made. However the night gained on us and the last rays of the sun had disappeared when Sagan-Cuisco was seized with a violent nosebleed. Habituated though this young man appeared to be, with his brother, to bodily exercise, it was evident that fatigue and want of food were beginning to exhaust his strength. We ourselves began to fear that they would renounce the attempt and want to make us sleep at the foot of a tree. We therefore decided to have them alternately ride the horses. The Indians accepted our offer without astonishment or humility. It was a strange sight to see those half-naked men gravely established on English saddles and carrying our gamebags and our guns slung on bandoleers, while we walked painfully afoot ahead of them.

Night finally came. A glacial humidity began to spread under the foliage. The obscurity then gave to the forest an aspect new and terrible. One saw about one only confused piled-up masses, without order or symmetry, forms bizarre and disproportioned, incoherent scenes, fantastic images which seemed borrowed from the sick imagination of a man in fever. The gigantic and the ridiculous were as close together there as in the literature of our age. Never had our steps awakened more echoes, never had the silence of the forest seemed more formidable. One would have said that the buzzing of mosquitoes was the only breathing of this sleeping world. As we advanced the shadows became deeper; only from time to time a firefly traversing the woods traced as it were a luminous thread in its depths. We realized only too late the justness of the Indian's advice, but it was no longer a question of going back.

We therefore continued on as rapidly as our strength and the night allowed. At the end of an hour we came out of the woods and found ourselves in a vast prairie. Our guides then stopped, and three times uttered a savage cry which echoed like the discordant notes of a tom-tom. An answer came from the distance. Five minutes after we were on the bank of a river whose far bank the darkness made it impossible to see. The Indians halted at this place. They wound their blankets about them to avoid the bites of the mosquitoes and, hiding in the grass, they soon formed but a scarcely perceptible ball of wool in which it would have been impossible to recognize the form of man. We ourselves dismounted and waited patiently for what was to follow. At the end of a few minutes a gentle sound was heard and something approached the bank.

It was an Indian canoe, about ten feet long and, as usual, formed of a single tree. The man who crouched in the bottom of this frail contraption wore the costume and had the appearance of an Indian. He spoke to our guides who, at his orders, hastened to take the saddles off our horses and place them in the pirogue. As I myself was getting in, the seeming Indian came towards me, put two fingers on my shoulder and said to me in a Norman accent that made me tremble: "Don't go too fast; people sometimes drown themselves here."

Had my horses spoken to me I don't think I should have been more surprised.

I stared at the speaker whose face, struck by the first rays of the moon, was gleaming like a ball of copper: "Who are you? French seems to be your tongue," said I, "and you have the appearance of an Indian?" He replied that he was a *bois brulé*, that is to say the son of a Canadian and an Indian woman. I shall frequently have occasion to speak of this singular race of half-breeds which covers all the frontiers of Canada and a part of those of the United States. For the moment I thought only of the pleasure of speaking my native tongue.

Following the counsels of our compatriot the savage, I seated myself in the bottom of the canoe and held myself as steadily as possible; my horse, which I held only by the bridle, entered the river and began to swim, while the Canadian propelled the craft with his paddle, all the while singing softly, to an old French air, the following couplet, the first lines of which alone I caught:

Entre Paris et Saint Denis
Il était une fille, etc.

We arrived thus without accident at the other bank; the canoe returned at once to get my companion. I shall remember all my life the moment when he for the second time approached the bank. The moon, which was full, was then rising over the prairie which we had just crossed; half of its disk only appeared on the horizon; one would have said a mysterious gate through which the light of another sphere was escaping to us. The rays coming from it were reflected in the water and shimmered to where I was. On the very path where trembled this pale light advanced the Indian pirogue. One saw no oars, heard no noise of paddles. It glided swiftly and without effort, long, narrow, and black, like a Mississippi alligator making toward the bank to seize its prey. Crouched in the point of the canoe, Sagan-Cuisco, head on his knees, showed only the gleaming tresses of his hair; at the other extremity the Canadian paddled in silence, while behind him Beaumont's horse made the water of the Saginaw break away under the impulse of his powerful breast. There was in the ensemble of this tableau a savage grandeur which then made and has since left a profound impression on our minds.

Disembarked, we hastened to betake ourselves to a house which the moon had discovered a hundred paces from us and where the Canadian assured us we could find lodging. We did in fact succeed in establishing ourselves comfortably and we should probably have repaired our strength if we had been able to get rid of the myriads of mosquitoes with which the house was filled, but that's what we were never able to accomplish. The creature they call *mosticos* [sic] in English and *maringouin* in French Canadian is a small insect in every respect like the *cousin* of France, from which it differs only in size. It is generally larger, and its sting is so strong and deep that only linen goods can guarantee against it. These small flies are the scourge of the American solitudes. Their presence alone would suffice to make a long sojourn there insupportable. For my part, I declare that I have never experienced a torment like to what they made me suffer during the whole course of this voyage and particularly during our stay in Saginaw. During the day they prevented us from sketching, from writing, from keeping still a single instant; at night they circled us by thousands, each part of the body that we left uncovered instantly served as a rendezvous. Awakened by the pain caused by their bite, we covered our heads with our sheets; their sting went right through. Hunted, pursued by them thus, we arose and went to breathe the air outside until the excess of fatigue finally procured us a painful and interrupted sleep.

We went out very early, and the first spectacle which struck us, on leaving the house, was the sight of our Indians who, rolled in their blankets near the door, slept beside their dogs. We then saw for the first time in broad daylight the village of Saginaw which we had come so far to seek. A small cultivated plain, bordered on the south by a fine tranquil river, on the east, west, and north by the forest, composes at present the whole territory of the city that is coming into being. Near us rose a house whose structure proclaimed the well-to-do character of the proprietor. It was the one where we had just spent the night. A dwelling of the same kind was to be seen at the other end of the clearing. In the interval, and along the edge of the woods, two or three log houses were half lost in the foliage.

On the opposite bank stretched the prairie like the boundless ocean on a calm day. A column of smoke then escaped from it and rose peacefully toward the sky. By following it to earth one finally discovered two or three wigwams whose comic form and pointed peak melted into the prairie vegetation. An overturned cart, some oxen going back of themselves to the plowing, some half-tamed horses completed the tableau.

Wherever one looked the eye sought in vain the steeple of a gothic tower, the wooden cross marking the way or the moss-covered doorstep of the presbytery. These venerable remains of the antique Christian civilization have not been carried to the wilderness. Nothing there as yet recalls the idea of a past and of the future. One doesn't even encounter the asylums sacred to those who are no more. Death has not had time to reclaim its domain nor to mark out its fields. Here man seems to enter life furtively. Several generations do not gather round his cradle to express hopes often fallacious, and give themselves over to premature rejoicings which the future will belie. His name is not inscribed in the registers of the city; religion does not come to mingle its touching sensibilities to the solicitudes of the family. The prayers of a wife, some drops of water sprinkled on the child's head by the father's hand, noiselessly open to him the gates of heaven.

The village of Saginaw is the last point inhabited by the Europeans toward the northwest of the vast peninsula of Michigan. It can be considered an advance post, a sort of refuge that the whites have come to place among the Indian nations.

The revolutions of Europe, the tumultuous clamors rising ceaselessly from the regulated universe, reach here only at long intervals, like the echo of a sound whose nature and origin the ear can no longer distinguish.

Now it will be an Indian who, passing through, will relate with the poetry of the wilderness some of the sad realities of life in society; a newspaper forgotten in the haversack of a hunter, or simply the vague rumor that spreads by unknown ways and rarely fails to warn men that something extraordinary is happening under the sun.

Once a year a vessel, mounting the Saginaw River, comes to tie this detached link to the great European chain which already envelops the world with its coils. It brings to the new establishment the divers products of industry, and in return takes away the fruits of the soil. Thirty persons, men, women, old men, and children, at the time of our passage formed the whole of this little society, scarce formed, germ confided to the wilderness that the wilderness is to make fruitful. Chance, interest, or passions had gathered these thirty persons in this narrow space. Between them were no ties; they differed profoundly from each other. One noted among them Canadians, Americans, Indians, and half breeds. . . .

The men who inhabit this little cultivated plain belong to two races which for more than a century have existed on the American soil and obeyed the same laws. Yet they have nothing in common between them. They are still Englishmen and Frenchmen, such as they show themselves on the banks of the Seine and the Thames. Enter this cabin of boughs, you will meet a man whose cordial welcome, joyful face and half-opened mouth will at once proclaim a taste for social pleasures and a carefree attitude toward life. At first you will perhaps take him for an Indian. Subjected to the savage life, he has voluntarily adopted its clothes, usages, and almost its morals; he wears moccasins, a mink cap, and wool cape. He is a tireless hunter; lies in his blind, lives on wild honey and bison meat. Yet this man has none the less remained a Frenchman, gay, enterprising, glorious, proud of his origins, passionately fond of military glory, more vain than calculating, man of instinct, preferring fame to money and obeying his impulse rather than his reason.

To come to the wilderness, he seems to have broken all the ties which attach him to life. One sees no wife and children with him. This state is contrary to his customs, but he submits himself as easily to it as to everything. There is in the nature of the French something malleable and yet inflexible. Delivered to his natural bent he would normally feel home loving. None more than he prefers to rejoice himself by the sight of his paternal tower. But he has been torn, in spite of himself, from his tranquil rounds; his imagination has been struck by new pictures; he has been transported under another sky; this same man has suddenly felt possessed by an insatiable need for violent emotions, for vicissitudes and dangers. The most civilized European has become the adorer of savage life. He will prefer his savannahs to the city streets, hunting to agriculture. He will play with existence, and live without care for the future.

A few yards from this man lives another European who, subjected to the same difficulties, has stiffened himself against them. This one is [a] cold, tenacious, pitiless arguer. He binds himself to the soil and wrests from the savage life all that he can take from it. He struggles ceaselessly against it, despoils it daily of some of its attributes. Piece by piece he transports into the wilderness his laws, his habits, his customs and, if he can, even the niceties of advanced civilization. The emigrant of the United States esteems only the results of victory: he holds that glory is a vain noise, and that man came into the world only to acquire ease and the comforts of life. [He is] brave, but brave by calculation; brave because he has discovered that there are several things harder to bear than death; adventure surrounded by his family, who yet cares little for intellectual pleasures and the charms of social life.

Placed on the other side of the stream, amid the reeds of the

Saginaw, the Indian throws from time to time a stoic glance at the dwellings of his European brothers. Don't go and believe that he admires their works or envies their lot. In the nearly three hundred years that the American savage has struggled against the civilization which thrusts and envelops him, he has not yet learned to know and esteem his enemy. The generations succeed each other in vain with the two races. Like two parallel rivers they have for three hundred years been flowing toward a common abyss. A narrow space separates them, but they do not mingle their floods.

It is not however that the native of the new world lacks natural aptitude; his nature seems obstinately to reject our ideas and our arts. Lying on his blanket, in the smoke of his hut, the Indian regards with scorn the comfortable dwelling of the European. As for him, he takes a proud pleasure in his misery, and his heart swells and lifts at the evidences of his barbarian independence. He smiles bitterly on seeing us torment our lives to acquire useless riches. What we call industry he calls shameful servitude. He compares the laborer to the ox painfully plowing his furrow. What we call the comforts of life he calls children's toys and women's playthings. He envies us only our weapons. When a man can shelter his head at night under a tent of foliage, when he can light a fire to drive off the mosquitoes in summer and protect himself from cold in winter, when his dogs are good and the country full of game, what more could he ask of the Eternal Being?

On the other bank of the Saginaw, near the clearing of the Europeans and, so to speak, on the confines of the old and new worlds, rises a rustic cabin, more comfortable than the wigwam of the savage, more rude than the house of the civilized man: It's the dwelling of the half breed. When we for the first time presented ourselves at the door of this half-civilized hut, we were surprised to hear in the interior a soft voice singing to an Indian air the canticles of penitence. We stopped for a moment to listen. The modulation of the air was slow and profoundly sad; one easily recognized the plaintive melody which characterizes all the songs of man in the wilderness.

We entered. The master was absent. Seated in the center of the apartment, her legs crossed on a mat, a young woman was making some moccasins. With her foot she was rocking a child whose copper skin and features proclaimed its double origin. This woman was dressed like one of our peasants, except that her feet were bare and her hair fell freely on her shoulders. Seeing us, she fell silent with a sort of respectful fear. We asked her if she was French. "No," she answered, smiling. She lowered her eyes and added: "I am only a savage."

Child of the two races, brought up in the use of two languages, nourished in diverse beliefs and cradled in contrary prejudices, the half-breed forms a composite as inexplicable to others as to himself. The images of the world, when they come to reflect themselves in his crude brain, appear to him only a tangled chaos from which his spirit could not extricate itself. Proud of his European origin, he despises the wilderness, and yet he loves the savage freedom which reigns there; he admires civilization and is unable to submit himself completely to its empire. His tastes are in contradiction with his ideas. Not knowing how to guide himself by the doubtful light which illumines him, his soul struggles painfully in the web of universal doubt: he adopts contrary usages, he prays at two altars, he believes in the Redeemer of the world and the amulets of the charlatan, and he reaches the end of his career without having been able to untangle the obscure problem of his existence. . . .

More tolerant in his rude faith, the Indian limits himself to excluding his European brother from the happy hunting grounds he reserves for himself. Faithful to the confused traditions handed down by his fathers, he consoles himself easily for the evils of life, and dies tranquil, dreaming of the always green forests that the axe of the pioneer will never disturb, where the deer and beaver will come to be shot during the numberless days of eternity.

After dinner we went to see one of the richest proprietors of the village, Mr. Williams. We found him in his shop, busy selling Indians a number of objects of small value, such as knives, glass necklaces, earrings, etc. It was pitiful to see how these unhappy people were being treated by their European brothers. Furthermore, all whom we saw rendered striking justice to the savages. They were good, inoffensive, a thousand times less inclined to theft than the white. It was a pity only that they were beginning to learn the price of things. . . .

On returning from Mr. Williams, it occurred to us to ascend the Saginaw a certain distance to shoot the wild duck which people its banks. As we were busy with this hunt, a pirogue detached itself from the river reeds and some Indians came over to examine my gun, which they had seen from far off. I have always noticed that this weapon, which is not extraordinary in any way, procured me among the savages an altogether special attention. A gun which can kill two men in a second and fires in the rain was, according to them, a marvel above all value, a masterpiece without price. Those who approached us exhibited, according to custom, a great admiration. They asked whence came my gun. Our young guide replied that it had been made on the other side of the great water, among the fathers of the Canadians, which, you might believe, did not render it less precious in their sight. They observed that, as the sight was not placed in the middle of each barrel, one could not be as certain of each shot—a remark to which I admit I did not know well enough what to reply.

Evening having fallen, we re-embarked in the canoe and, trusting to the experience we had acquired in the morning, we set out alone to ascend a tributary of the Saginaw that we had only glimpsed. The sky was without a cloud, the atmosphere pure and still. The river rolled its waters through an immense forest, but so slowly that, to get a just conception of the forests of the new world, one should follow some of the rivers which flow in their shade. The rivers are, as it were, the great roads by which Providence has been careful, since the beginning of the world, to pierce the wilderness to render it accessible to man. When you clear a passage through the woods the view is most often very restricted, even the path where you walk is a human work. The streams, on the contrary, are roads which retain no trail, and their banks freely reveal all that a vegetation vigorous and abandoned to itself can offer in the way of great or curious spectacles.

A solitude flowery, delightful, balmy, a magnificent dwelling, a living palace, built for man but into which the master had not yet entered. The canoe slid without effort or noise. There reigned about us a universal quietness and serenity. We ourselves soon felt as it were softened by such a spectacle. Our words began to come more and more rarely. Soon we expressed our thoughts only in a whisper, finally we fell silent; and, lifting our paddles in unison, the two of us sank into a tranquil reverie full of inexpressible charm. . . . A shot which suddenly rang out in the woods drew us from our reverie. The noise seemed at first to roll with fracas on the two banks of the river; then it retreated growling until it was entirely lost in the surrounding forest. One would have said a long and formidable wary cry uttered by civilization in its march. . . . In a few years these impenetrable forests will have fallen, the noise of civilization and of industry will break the silence of Saginaw. Docks will imprison its banks; its waters which today flow unknown through a nameless wilderness will be thrust back in their flow by the prows of vessels. Fifty leagues separate this solitude from the great European establishments, and we are perhaps the last travelers to whom it has been given to contemplate it in its primitive splendor. So great is the impulse which draws the white race toward the utter conquest of the new world.

It is this idea of destruction, this conception of near and inevitable change which gives in our opinion so original a character and so touching a beauty to the solitudes of America. One sees them with melancholy pleasure. One hastens in a way to admire them. The idea of this natural and wild grandeur which is to end mingles with the superb images to which the march of civilization gives rise. One feels proud to be a man, and at the same time one experiences I know not what bitter regret at the power God has given us over nature. The soul is agitated by these ideas, these contrary sentiments. But all the impressions it receives are great and leave a deep mark.

We wished to leave Saginaw the next day, 27 July, but, one of our horses having a saddle sore, we decided to stay one day longer. For want of other pastime we went hunting in the prairies which border Saginaw just below the clearings.

The prairies are not as marshy as one would believe. They are plains more or less large where the wood doesn't come, though the soil is excellent; the vegetation is thick and three or four feet high. We found but little game, and returned early. The heat was stifling, as at the approach of a storm, and the mosquitoes even more bothersome than usual. We walked surrounded by a cloud of these insects, against whom one had to make perpetual war. Disaster for him who was obliged to stop! He'd delivered himself then defenseless to a pitiless enemy. I recall having been forced to load my gun on the run, it was so difficult to stay still a moment.

As we were crossing the prairie on our return, we noticed that the Canadian who was acting as our guide was following a small path and looking at the ground with the greatest care before making a step. "Why are you being so careful," I asked him. "Are you afraid of getting wet?" "No," he answered, "but I have made it a habit when crossing the prairies always to look where I step so as not to step on a rattlesnake." "What the devil," said I, jumping into the path, "are there rattlesnakes here? "Oh! certainly," replied my Norman American with his imperturbable *sang-froid; "y en a tout plein* [they are most certainly here]."

I reproached him for not having warned us sooner; he maintained, that, as we had on good shoes and rattlesnakes never bit over the ankle, he had not thought that we ran great danger. I asked him if the bite of the rattlesnake was mortal; he replied that one always died of it in less than twenty-four hours if one did not have recourse to the Indians. These knew a remedy which, given in time, saves the victim. . . . The night which followed this burning day was one of the most painful of my life. The mosquitoes had become so bothersome that, even though overwhelmed with fatigue, it was impossible to shut my eyes. Toward midnight the storm which had long been threatening finally broke. Unable longer to hope for sleep, I got up and opened the door of our cabin at least to breathe the freshness of the night. It was not yet raining, the air appeared calm, but the forest was already tossing, and there came from it deep moans and long clamors. From time to time a flash of lightning illuminated the sky. The quiet course of the Saginaw, the small clearing on its banks, the roofs of the five or six cabins, and the belt of enveloping foliage appeared then for an instant like a sublime evocation of the future. Then everything was lost in the most profound obscurity, and the formidable voice of the wilderness made itself heard again.

I was watching this great spectacle, moved, when I heard a sigh at my side, and by the lightning, I saw an Indian leaning like me against the wall of our dwelling. The storm had doubtless interrupted his sleep, for he cast a fixed and troubled glance on his surroundings. . . . His agitated lips seemed to be murmuring some prayers, and all his liniments seemed graven with suspicious terror.

At five in the morning we thought to leave. All the Indians of the neighborhood of Saginaw were absent. They had gone to receive the presents annually given them by the English, and the Europeans were busy with the labors of the harvest. We therefore had to make up our minds to go back through the forest without a guide. The enterprise was not so difficult as one might suppose. In general there is but one path in these vast solitudes, and it's only a matter of not losing the trail to reach the end of the journey.

At five in the morning, then, we recrossed the Saginaw. We received the farewells and the last counsels of our hosts and, having turned our horses' heads, found ourselves alone in the forest. It was not, I confess, without seriousness that we began to penetrate these humid depths. This same forest about us then stretched behind us all the way to the pole and the Pacific Ocean. A single inhabited point separated us from the limitless wilderness, and we had just left it. But these thoughts only led us to hasten our horses along; and at the end of three hours we came near an abandoned wigwam on the solitary banks of the river Cass. A grassy point jutting into the river in the shade of some tall trees served as our table, and we sat down to lunch, having in perspective the river whose waters, limpid as crystal, coiled through the woods.

On leaving the wigwam of Cass River, we encountered several paths. We had been told which one to take. But it is easy to forget some details, or to be misunderstood in such explanations. . . . We did not fail to find it that day. They had spoken of two roads; there were three. It is true that two of these three joined further on in one, as we later learned; but we did not know that then, and our embarrassment was great.

After having well examined, well disputed, we did as do almost all great men, we took a chance. We saw nothing wiser than to abandon our horses, dropping the bridle on their necks, the solution of the difficulty. We forded the stream as best we could and pushed ahead rapidly toward the southwest. More than once the trail seemed about to disappear among the clumps. On other places the road seemed so little frequented that we found it hard to believe that it led elsewhere than to some abandoned wigwam. Our compass, it is true, showed us that we were always going in the right direction; however, we were not completely reassured until the discovery of the place where we had dined three days before.

A gigantic pine, whose wind-torn trunk we had admired, made us recognize it. We continued on our way with no less rapidity, for the sun was beginning to fall. Soon we reached the thinned space that usually precedes the clearings. As night was about to surprise us, we caught sight of Flint River; a half hour afterwards we found ourselves at our host's door. This time the bear received us like old friends and only sat up on his hind legs to celebrate his joy at our happy return.

During the entire day, we did not meet a single solitary human being; on their side the animals had disappeared. They had doubtless withdrawn under the foliage to flee the heat of the day. Only from time to time we discovered, at the bare summit of some dead tree, a hawk which, motionless on one leg and calmly sleeping in the sun's rays, seemed sculptured in the very wood he had made his perch.

It was in the midst of this profound solitude that we suddenly thought of the Revolution of 1830, whose first anniversary (29 July 1831) we had just reached. I cannot say with what impetuosity the memories of the twenty-ninth of July took possession of my spirit. The cries and smoke of combat, the sound of cannon, the rolling of musketry, the still more horrible tolling of the tocsin, this entire day with its inflamed atmosphere suddenly seemed to rise out of the past and place a living tableau before me. This was only a sudden illumination. When, raising my head, I glanced around, the apparition had already disappeared. But never had the silence of the forest seemed colder, its shades more deep, or its solitude so complete.

THE DELIGHTS OF MACKINAC

Harriet Martineau

Harriet Martineau was a famous British writer and reformer who visited the United States from 1834 to 1836. In the course of her visit she toured various parts of the country. In the summer of 1836 she was with a party of sightseers in Chicago who planned to travel overland to Detroit over the Chicago road, when news arrived that heavy rains had made that road impassable. Martineau and several others in the party decided to return to Detroit the long way—up Lake Michigan to Mackinac Island and then down Lake Huron to Detroit. Martineau, who had heard of "the delights of Mackinaw," determined to savor them for herself.

Martineau's fascinating description of the voyage sheds light not only on the conditions of lake travel by sailing vessel in the 1830s but also on the manners and morals of the Americans she encountered, including the garrison culture on Mackinac Island. Her descriptions of the scenery en route—

especially that of Mackinac Island—have a secure place in the American travel literature of this period. The following is an excerpt from Harriet Martineau, *Society in America*, vol. 2 (London: Saunders & Otley, 1837), pp. 1–28.

While we were at Detroit, we were most strongly urged to return thither by the Lakes, instead of by either of the Michigan roads. From place to place, in my previous travelling, I had been told of the charms of the Lakes, and especially of the Island of Mackinaw. Every officer's lady who has been in garrison there, is eloquent upon the delights of Mackinaw. As our whole party, however, could not make so wide a circuit, we had intended to indulge ourselves with a further variation in our travels than to take the upper road back to Detroit; having left it by the lower. On Sunday, June 27th [1836], news arrived at Chicago that this upper road had been rendered impassable by the rains. A sailing vessel, the only one on the Lakes, and now on her first trip, was to leave Chicago for Detroit and Buffalo, the next day. The case was clear: the party must divide. Those who were obliged to hasten home must return by the road we came: the rest must proceed by water. On Charley's account the change of plan was desirable; as the heats were beginning to be so oppressive as to render travelling in open wagons unsafe for a child. It was painful to break up our party at the extreme point of our journey; but it was clearly right. So Mr. and Mrs. L. took their chance by land; and the rest of us went on board the Milwaukee, at two o'clock on the afternoon of the 28th.

Mrs. F. and I were the only ladies on board; and there was no stewardess. The steward was obliging, and the ladies' cabin was clean and capacious; and we took possession of it with a feeling of comfort. Our pleasant impressions, however, were not of long duration. The vessel was crowded with persons who had come to the land sales at Chicago, and were taking their passage back to Milwaukee; a settlement on the western shore of the lake, about eighty miles from Chicago. Till we should reach Milwaukee, we could have the ladies' cabin only during a part of the day. I say a part of the day because some of the gentry did not leave our cabin till near nine in the morning; and others chose to come down and go to bed, as early as seven in the evening, without troubling themselves to give us five minutes' notice, or to wait till we could put up our needles, or wipe our pens. This ship was the only place in America where I saw a prevalence of bad manners. It was the place of all others to select for the study of such; and no reasonable person would look for anything better among land-speculators and settlers in regions so new as to be almost without women. None of us had ever before seen, in America, a disregard of women. The swearing was incessant; and the spitting such as to amaze my American companions as much as myself.

Supper was announced presently after we had sailed; and when we came to the table, it was full, and no one offered to stir, to make room for us. The captain, who was very careful of our comfort, arranged that we should be better served henceforth; and no difficulty afterward occurred. At dinner, the next day, we had a specimen of how such personages as we had on board are managed on an emergency. The captain gave notice, from the head of the table, that he did not choose our party to be intruded on in the cabin; and that any one who did not behave with civility at table should be turned out. He spoke with decision and good-humour; and the effect was remarkable. Everything on the table was handed to us; and no more of the gentry came down to smoke, or throw themselves on the cushions to sleep, while we sat at work.

Our fare was what might be expected on Lake Michigan. Salt beef and pork, and sea-biscuit; tea without milk, bread, and potatoes. Charley throve upon potatoes and bread; and we all had the best results of food,—health and strength.

A little schooner which left Chicago at the same time as ourselves and reached Milwaukee first was a pretty object. On the 29th, we were only twenty-five miles from the settlement; but the wind was so unfavourable that it was doubtful whether we should reach it that day. Some of the passengers amused themselves by gaming, down in the hold, others by parodying a methodist sermon, and singing a mock hymn. We did not get rid of them till noon on the 30th, when we had the pleasure of seeing our ship disgorge twenty-five into one boat and two into another. The atmosphere was so transparent as to make the whole scene appear as if viewed through an opera-glass; the still, green waters, the dark boats with their busy oars, the moving passengers, and the struggles of one to recover his hat, which had fallen overboard. We were yet five miles from Milwaukee; but we could see the bright, wooded coast, with a few white dots of houses.

While Dr. F. went on shore, to see what was to be seen, we had the cabin cleaned out, and took, once more, complete possession of it for both day and night. As soon as this was done, seven young women came down the companion-way, seated themselves round the cabin, and began to question us. They were the total female population of Milwaukee; which settlement now contains four hundred souls. We were glad to see these ladies; for it was natural enough that the seven women should wish to behold two more, when such a chance offered. A gentleman of the place, who came on board this afternoon, told me that a printing-press had arrived a few hours before; and that a newspaper would speedily appear. He was kind enough to forward the first number to me a few weeks afterwards; and I was amused to see how pathetic an appeal to the ladies of more thickly-settled districts it contained; imploring them to cast a favourable eye on Milwaukee, and its hundreds of bachelors. Milwaukee had been settled since the proceeding November. It has good stores; (to judge by the nature and quantity of goods sent ashore from our ship;) it had a printing-press and newspaper, before the settlers had had time to get wives. I heard these new settlements sometimes called "patriarchal:" but what would the patriarchs have said to such an order of affairs?

Dr. F. returned from the town, with apple-pies, cheese, and ale, wherewith to vary our ship diet. With him arrived such a number of towns-people that the steward wanted to turn us out of our cabin once more: but we were sturdy, appealed to the captain, and were confirmed in possession. From this time, began the delights of our voyage. The moon, with her long train of glory, was magnificent to-night; the vast body of waters on which she shone being as calm as if the winds were dead.

The navigation of these lakes is, at present, a mystery. They have not yet been properly surveyed. Our captain had gone to and fro on Lake Huron, but had never before been on Lake Michigan; and this was rather an anxious voyage to home. We had got aground on the sand-bar before Milwaukee harbour; and on the 1st of July, all hands were busy in unshipping the cargo, to lighten the vessel, instead of carrying her up to the town. An elegant little schooner was riding at anchor near us; and we were well amused in admiring her, and in watching the bustle on deck, till some New-England youths, and our Milwaukee acquaintance, brought us, from the shore, two newspapers, some pebbles, flowers, and a pitcher of fine strawberries.

As soon as we were off the bar, the vessel hove round, and we cast anchor in deeper water. Charley was called to see the sailors work the windlass, and to have ride thereon. The sailors were very kind to the boy. They dressed up their dog for him in sheep-skins and a man's hat; a sight to make older people than Charley laugh. They took him down into the forecastle to show him prints that were pasted up there. They asked him to drink rum and water with them: to which Charley answered that he should be happy to drink water with them, but would rather not have any rum. While we were watching the red sunset over the leaden waters, betokening a change of weather, the steamer "New York" came plowing the bay, three weeks after her time; such is the uncertainty in the navigation of these stormy lakes. She got aground on the sand-bank, as we had done; and boats were going from her to the shore and back, as long as we could see.

The next day there was rain and some wind. The captain and steward went off to make final purchases: but the fresh meat which had been bespoken for us had been bought up by somebody else; and no milk was to be had; only two cows being visible in all the place. Ale was the only luxury we could obtain. When the captain returned, he brought with him a stout gentleman, one of the proprietors of the vessel, who must have a berth in our cabin as far as Mackinaw; those elsewhere being too small for him. Under the circumstances, we had no right to complain; so we helped the steward to partition off the portion of the cabin with a counterpane, fastened with four forks. This gentleman, Mr. D., was engaged in the fur trade at Mackinaw, and had a farm there, to which he kindly invited us.

On Sunday, the 3rd, there was much speculation as to whether we should be at Mackinaw in time to witness the celebration of the great day. All desired it; but I was afraid of missing the Manitou Isles in the dark. There was much fog; the wind was nearly fair; the question was whether it would last. Towards evening, the fog thickened, and the wind freshened. The mate would not believe we were in the middle of the lake, as every one else supposed. He said the fog was too warm not to come from near land. Charley caught something of the spirit of uncertainty, and came to me in high joyous excitement, to drag me to the side of the ship, that I might see how fast we cut through the waves, and how steadily we leaned over the water, till Charley almost thought he could touch it. He burst out about the "kind of a feeling" that it was "not to see a bit of land," and not to know where we were; and to think "if we should upset!" and that we never did upset:—it was "a good and a bad feeling at once;" and he should never be able to tell people at home what it was like. The boy had no fear: he was roused, as the brave man loves to be. Just as the dim light of the sunset was fading from the fog, it opened, and disclosed to us, just at hand, the high, sandy shore of Michigan. It was well that this happened before dark. The captain hastened up to the mast-head, and reported that we were off Cape Sable, forty miles from the Manitou Isles.

Three bats and several butterflies were seen today, clinging to the mainsail,—blown over from the shore. The sailors set their dog at a bat, of which it was evidently afraid. A lock of pretty pigeons flew round and over the ship, of which six were shot. Four fell into the water; and the other two were reserved for the mate's breakfast; he being an invalid.

We were up before five, on the morning of the 4th of July, to see the Manitou Isles, which were then just coming in sight. They are the Sacred Isles of the Indians to whom they belong. Manitou is the name of their Great Spirit, and of everything sacred. It is said that they believe these islands to be the resort of the spirits of the departed. They are two: sandy and precipitous at the south end; and clothed with wood, from the crest of the cliffs to the north extremity, which slopes down gradually to the water. It was a cool, sunny morning, and these dark islands lay still, and apparently deserted, on the bright green waters. Far behind, to the south, were two glittering white sails on the horizon. They remained in sight all day, and lessened the feeling of loneliness which the navigators of these vast lakes cannot but have, while careering among the solemn islands and shores. On our right lay the shore, high and sandy, with the dark eminence called the Sleeping Bear conspicuous on the ridge. No land speculators have set foot here yet. A few Indian dwellings, with evergreen woods and sandy cliffs, are all. Just here, Mr. D. pointed out to us a schooner of his which was wrecked, in a snowstorm, the preceding November. She looked pretty and forlorn, lying on her side in that desolate place, seeming a mere plaything thrown in among the cliffs. "Ah;" said her owner, with a sigh, "she was a lovely creature, and as stiff as a church." Two lives were lost. Two young Germans, stout lads, could not comprehend the orders given them to put on all their clothing and keep themselves warm. They only half-dressed themselves: "the cold took them," and they died. The rest tried to make fire by friction of wood; but got only smoke. Someone found traces of a dog in the snow. These were followed for three miles, and ended at an Indian lodge, where the sailors were warmed and kindly treated.

During the bright morning of this day we passed the Fox and Beaver Islands. The captain was in fine spirits, though there was no longer any prospect of reaching Mackinaw in time for the festivities of the day. This island is chiefly known as a principal station of the great north-western fur trade. Others know it as the seat of an Indian mission. Others, again, as a frontier garrison. It is known to me as the wildest and tenderest little piece of beauty that I have yet seen on God's earth. It is a small island, nine miles in circumference, being in the strait between the Lakes Michigan and Huron, and between the coasts of Michigan and Wisconsin.

Towards evening the Wisconsin coast came into view, the strait suddenly narrowed, and we were about to bid farewell to the great Lake whose total length we had traversed, after sweeping round its southern extremity. The ugly light-ship, which looked heavy enough, came into view about six o'clock; the first token of our approach to Mackinaw. The office of the light-ship is to tow vessels in the dark through the strait. We were too early for this; but perhaps it performed that office for the two schooners whose white specks of sails had been on our southern horizon all day. Next we saw a white speck before us; it was the barracks of Mackinaw, stretching along the side of its green hills, and clearly visible before the town came into view.

The island looked enchanting as we approached, as I think it always must, though we had the advantage of seeing it first steeped in the most golden sunshine that ever hallowed lake or shore. The colours were up on all the little vessels in the harbour. The national flag streamed from the garrison. The soldiers thronged the walls of the barracks; half-breed boys were paddling about in their little canoes, in the transparent waters; the half-French, half-Indian population of the place were all abroad in their best. An Indian lodge was on the shore, and a picturesque dark group stood beside it. The sows were coming down the steep green slopes to the milking. Nothing could be more bright and joyous.

The houses of the old French village are shabby-looking, dusky, and roofed with bark. There are some neat yellow houses, with red shutters, which have a foreign air, with their porches and flights of steps. The better houses stand on the first of the three terraces which are distinctly marked. Behind them are swelling green kannols; before them gardens sloping down to the narrow slip of white beach, so that the grass seems to grow almost into the clear rippling waves. The gardens were rich with mountain ash, roses, stocks, currant bushes, springing corn, and a great variety of kitchen vegetables. There were two small piers with little barks alongside, and piles of wood for the steam-boats. Some way to the right stood the quadrangle of missionary buildings, and the white mission church. Still further to the right was a shrubby precipice down to the lake; and beyond, the blue waters. While we were gazing at all this, a pretty schooner sailed into the harbour after us, in fine style, sweeping round our bows so suddenly as nearly to swamp a little fleet of canoes, each with its pair of half-breed boys.

We had been alarmed by a declaration from the captain that he should stay only three hours at the island. He seemed to have no intention of taking us ashore this evening. The dreadful idea occurred to us that we might be carried away from this paradise without having set foot in it. We looked at each other in dismay. Mr. D. stood our friend. He had some furs on board which were to be landed. He said this should not be done till the morning; and he would take care that his people did it with the utmost possible slowness. He thought he could gain us an additional hour in this way. Meanwhile, thunder-clouds were coming up rapidly from the west, and the sun was near its setting. After much consultation, and an assurance having been obtained from the captain that we might command the boats at any hour in the morning, we decided that Dr. F. and Charley should go ashore, and deliver our letters, and accept any arrangements that might be offered for our seeing the best of the scenery in the morning.

Scarcely any one was left in the ship but Mrs. F. and myself. We sat on deck, and gazed as if this were to be the last use we were ever to have of our eyes. There was growling thunder now, and the church bell, and Charley's clear voice from afar: the waters were so still. The Indians lighted a fire before their lodge; and we saw their shining red forms as they bent over the blaze. We watched Dr. F. and Charley mounting to the garrison; we saw them descend again with the commanding officer, and go to the house of the Indian agent. Then we traced them along the shore, and into the Indian lodge; then to the church; then the parting with the commandant on the shore, and lastly, the passage of the dark boat to our ship's side. They brought news that the commandant and his family would be on the watch for us before five in the morning, and be our guides to as much of the island as the captain would allow us time to see.

Some pretty purchases of Indian manufactures were brought on board this evening; light matting of various colours, and small baskets of birch bark, embroidered with porcupine-quills, and filled with maple sugar.

The next morning all was bright. At five o'clock we descended the ship's side, and from the boat could see the commandant and his dog hastening down from the garrison to the landing-place. We returned with him up the hill, through the barrack-yard; and were joined by three members of his family on the velvet green slope behind the garrison. No words can give an idea of the charms of this morning walk. We wound about in a vast shrubbery, with ripe strawberries under foot, wild flowers all around, and scattered knolls and opening vistas tempting curiosity in every direction. "Now run up," said the commandant, as we arrived at the foot of one of these knolls. I did so, and was almost struck backwards by what I saw. Below me was the Natural Bridge of Mackinaw, of which I had heard frequent mention. It is a limestone arch, about one hundred and fifty feet high in the centre, with a span of fifty feet; one pillar resting on a rocky projection in the lake, the other on the hill. We viewed it from above, so that the horizon line of the lake fell behind the bridge, and the blue expanse of waters filled the entire arch. Birch and ash grew around the bases of the pillars, and shrubbery tufted the sides, and dangled from the bridge. The soft rich hues in which the whole was dressed seemed borrowed from the autumn sky.

But even this scene was nothing to the one we saw from the fort, on the crown of the island; old Fort Holmes, called Fort George when in the possession of the British. I can compare it to nothing but to what Noah might have seen, the first bright morning after the deluge. Such a cluster of little paradises rising out of such a congregation of waters, I can hardly fancy to have been seen elsewhere. The capacity of the human eye seems here suddenly enlarged, as if it could see to the verge of the watery creation. Blue, level waters appear to expand for thousands of miles in every direction; wholly unlike any aspect of the sea. Cloud shadows, and specks of white vessels, at rare intervals, alone diversify it. Bowery islands rise out of it; bowery promontories stretch down into it; while at one's feet lies the melting beauty which one almost fears will vanish in its softness before one's eyes; the beauty of the shadowy dells and sunny mounds, with browsing cattle, and springing fruit and flowers. Thus, and no otherwise, would I fain think did the world emerge from the flood. I was never before so unwilling to have objects named. The essential unity of the scene seemed to be marred by any distinction of its parts. But this feeling, to me new, did not alter the state of the case; that it was Lake Huron that we saw stretching to the eastward; Lake Michigan opening to the west; the island of Bois Blanc, green to the brink in front; and Round Island and others interspersed. I stood now at the confluence of those great northern lakes, the very names of which awed my childhood; calling up, as they did, images of the fearful red man of the deep pine-forest, and the music of the moaning winds, imprisoned beneath the ice of winter. How different from the scene, as actually beheld, dressed in verdure, flowers, and the sunshine of a summer's morning!

It was breakfast-time when we descended to the barracks; and we despatched a messenger to the captain to know whether we might breakfast with the commandant. We sat in the piazza, and overlooked the village, the harbour, the straits, and the white beach, where there were now four Indian lodges. The island is so healthy that, according to the commandant, people who want to die must go somewhere else. I saw only three tombstones in the cemetery. The commandant has lost but one man since he has been stationed at Mackinaw; and that was by drowning. I asked about the climate; the answer was, "We have nine months winter, and three months cold weather."

It would have been a pity to have missed the breakfast at the garrison, which afforded a strong contrast with any we had seen for a week. We concealed, as well as we could, our glee at the appearance of the rich cream, the new bread and butter, fresh lake trout, and pile of snowwhite eggs.

There is reason to think that mission is the least satisfactory part of the establishment on this island. A great latitude of imagination or representation is usually admitted on the subject of missions to the heathen. The reporters of this one appear to be peculiarly imaginative. I fear that the common process has here been gone through of attempting to take from the savage the venerable and the true which he possessed, and to force upon him something else which is to him neither venerable or true.

The Indians have been proved, by the success of the French among them, to be capable of civilisation. Near Little Traverse in the north-west part of Michigan, within easy reach of Mackinaw, there is an Indian village, full of orderly and industrious inhabitants, employed chiefly in agriculture. The English and Americans have never succeeded with the aborigines so well as the French; and it may be doubted whether the clergy have been a much greater blessing to them than the traders.

It was with great regret that we parted with the commandant and his large young family and stepped into the boat to return to the ship. The captain looked a little grave upon the delay which all his passengers had helped to achieve. We sailed about nine. We were in great delight at having seen Mackinaw, at having the possession of its singular imagery for life: but this delight was at presently dashed with the sorrow of leaving it. I could not have believed how deeply it is possible to regret a place, after so brief an acquaintance with it. We watched the island as we rapidly receded, trying to catch the aspect of it which had given it its name—the Great Turtle. Its flag first vanished: then its green terraces and slopes, its white barracks, and dark promontories faded, till the whole disappeared behind a headland and lighthouse of the Michigan shore.

Lake Huron was squally, as usual. Little remarkable while we traversed it. We enjoyed the lake trout. We occasionally saw the faint outline of the Manitouline islands and Canada. We saw a sunset which looked very much like the general conflagration having begun: the whole western sky and water being as if of red flame and molten lead. This was succeeded by paler fires. A yellow planet sank into the heaving waters to the south; and the northern lights opened like a silver wheat-sheaf, and spread themselves half over the sky. It is luxury to sail on Lake Huron and watch the northern lights.

On the 7th we were only twenty miles from the river St. Clair: but the wind was "right ahead," and we did not reach the mouth of the river till the evening of the 8th. The approach and entrance kept us all in a state of high excitement, from the captain down to Charley. On the afternoon of the 8th, Fort Gratiot and the narrow mouth of the St. Clair became visible. Our scope for tacking grew narrower every turn. The captain did not come to dinner; he kept the lead going incessantly. Two vessels were trying with us for the mouth of the river. The American schooner got in first from being the smallest. The British vessel and ours contested the point stoutly for long while, sweeping ground and crossing each other, much as if they were dancing a minuet. A squall came, and broke one of our chains, and our rival beat us. In the midst of the struggle, we could not but observe that the sky was black as night to windward; and that the captain cast momentary glances thither, as if calculating how soon he must make all tight for the storm. The British vessel was seen to have come to an anchor. Our sails were all taken in, our anchor dropped, and a grim silence prevailed. The waters were flat as ice about the ship. The next moment, the sky-organ began to blow in our rigging. Fort Gratiot was blotted out; then the woods; then the other ship; then came the orderly march of the rain over the myrtle-green waters; then the storm seized us. We could scarcely see each others' faces, except for the lightning; the ship groaned, and dragged her anchor, so that a second was dropped.

In twenty minutes, the sun gilded the fort, the woods, and the green, prairie-like Canada shore. On the verge of this prairie, under the shelter of the forest, an immense herd of wild horses were seen scampering, and whisking their long tails. A cloud of pigeons, in countless thousands, shadowing alternately the forests, the lake, and the prairie; and an extensive encampment of wild Indians was revealed on the Michigan shore. It was a dark curtain lifted up on a scene of wild and singular beauty.

Then we went to the anxious work of tacking again. We seemed to be running aground on either shore, as we approached each. Our motions were watched by several gazers. On the Canada side, there were men on the sands, and in a canoe, with a sail which looked twice as big as the bark. The keepers of the Gratiot light-house looked out from the lantern. A party of squaws, in the Indian encampment, seated on the sands, stopped their work of cleaning fish, to see how we got through the rapids. A majestic personage, his arms folded in his blanket, stood on an eminence in the midst of the camp; and behind him, on the brow of the hill, were groups of unclothed boys and men, looking demon-like, as even in that scene to remind me of the great staircase in the ballet of Faust. Our ship twisted round and round in the eddies, as helplessly as a log, and stuck, at last, with her stern within a stone's throw of the Indians. Nothing more could be done that night. We dropped anchor, and hoped the sailors would have good repose after two days of tacking to achieve a progress of twenty miles. Two or three of them went ashore to try to get milk. While they were gone, a party of settlers stood on the high bank, to gaze at us; and we were sorry to see them, even down to the little children, whisking bows without ceasing. This was a threat of mosquitoes which was not to be mistaken. When the sailors returned, they said we were sure to have a good watch kept, for the mosquitoes would let no one sleep. We tried to shut up our cabin from them; but they were already there; and I, for one, was answerable for many murders before I closed my eyes. In the twilight, I observed something stirring on the high bank; and on looking closely, saw a party of Indians, stepping along in single file, under the shadow of the wood. Their simplest acts are characteristic; and, in their wild state, I never saw them without thinking of ghosts or demons.

In the morning, I found we were floating down the current, stern foremost, frequently swinging round in the eddies, so as to couch the one short or the other. There seemed to be no intermission of settlers' houses; all at regular distances along the bank. The reason of this appearance is a good old French arrangement, by which the land is divided into long, narrow strips, that each lot may have a water frontage. We were evidently returning to a well-settled country. The more comfortable houses on the Canada side were surrounded by spacious and thriving fields: the poorer by dreary enclosures of swamp. We say a good garden, with a white paling. Cows were being milked. Cow-bells, and the merry voices of singing children, were heard from under the clumps; and piles of wood for the steam-boats, and large stocks of shingles for roofing, were laid up on either hand.

The Gratiot steamer puffed away under the Michigan bank. Canoes shot across in a streak of light; and a schooner came down the clear river, as if on the wing behind the sky and the water. I watched two horsemen on the shore, for many miles, tracing the bay pony and the white horse through the woody screen, and over the brooks, and along the rickety bridges. I could see that they were constantly chatting, and that they stopped to exchange salutations with everyone they met or overtook. These, to be sure, were few enough. I was quite sorry when the twilight drew on, and hid them from me. I saw a little boy on a log, with a paddle, pushing himself off from a bank of wild roses, and making his way in the sunshine up the river. It looked very pretty, and very unsafe; but I daresay he knew best. The captain and mate were both ill to-day. The boat was sent ashore for what could be had. The men made haste, and rode bravely; but we were carried down four miles before we could "heave to," for them to overtake us. They brought brandy for the captain; and for us, butter just out of the churn. The mosquitoes again drove us from the deck soon after dark.

The next morning, the 10th, the deck was in great confusion. The captain was worse: the mate was too ill to command; and the second mate seemed to be more efficient in swearing, and getting the men to swear, than at anything else. After breakfast, there was a search made after a pilferer, who had abstracted certain small articles from our cabin; among them was Charley's maple-sugar basket, which had been seen in the wheel-house, with a tea-spoon in it. This seemed to point out one of the juniors in the forecastle as the offender; the steward, however, offered to clear himself by taking an oath, "on a bible as big as the ship," that he knew nothing of the matter. As we did not happen to have such a bible on board, we could not avail ourselves of his offer. A comb and toothbrush, which had been missing, were found, restored to their proper places: but Charley's pretty basket was seen no more.

It was a comfortless day. We seemed within easy reach of Detroit; but the little wind we had was dead ahead; the sun was hot; the mosquitoes abounded; the captain was downcast, and the passengers cross. There was some amusement, however. Dr. F. went ashore, and brought us milk, of which we each had a draught before it turned sour. He saw on shore a sight which is but too common. An hotel-keeper let an Indian get drunk; and then made a quarrel between him and another, for selfish purposes. The whites seem to have neither honour nor mercy towards the red men.

A canoe full of Indians,—two men and four children,—came

alongside this afternoon, to offer to traffic. They had no clothing but a coarse shirt each. The smallest child had enormous ear-ornaments of blue and white beads. They were closely packed in their canoe, which rocked with every motion. They sold two large baskets for a quarter dollar and two loaves of bread. Their faces were intelligent, and far from solemn. The children looked merry, as children should. I saw others fishing afar off till long after dark. A dusky figure stood in a splendid attitude, in the bow of a canoe, and now paddled with one end of his long lance, now struck at a fish with the other. He speared his prey directly through the middle; and succeeded but seldom. At dark, a pine torch was held over the water; and by its blaze, I could still see something of his operations.

The groaning of our ship's timbers told us, before we rose, that we were in rapid motion. The wind was fair; and we were likely to reach Detroit, forty miles, to dinner. Lake St. Clair, with its placid waters and low shores, presented nothing to look at. The captain was very ill, and unable to leave his berth. No one on board knew the channel of the Detroit river but himself; and, from the time we entered it, the lead was kept going. When we were within four miles of Detroit, hungry, hot, tired of the disordered ship, and thinking of friends, breezes, and a good dinner at the city, we went aground—grinding, grinding, till the ship trembled in every timber. The water was so shallow that one might have touched the gravel of either side with a walking stick. There was no hope of our being got off speedily. The cook applied himself to chopping wood, in order to light a fire, in order to bake some bread, in order to give us something to eat; for not a scrap of meat, or an ounce of biscuit, was left on board.

It occurred to me that our party might reach the city either by paying high for one of the ship's boats, or by getting the mate to hail one of the other schooners that were in the river. The boats could not be spared. The mate hoisted a signal for a schooner, and one came alongside, very fully laden with shingles. Fifteen of us, passengers, with our luggage, were piled on the top of the cargo, and sailed gently up to the city. The captain was too ill, and the mate too full of vexation, to bid us farewell; and thus we left our poor ship. We were glad, however, to pass her in the river the next day, and to find that she had been got off the shoal before night.

As we drew near, Charley, in all good faith, hung out his little handkerchief to show the people of Detroit that we had come back. They did not seem to know us, however. "What!" cried some men on a raft, to the master of our schooner, "have you been robbing a steamboat?" "No," replied the master, gravely; "it is a boat that has gone to the bottom of the lakes." We expected that some stupendous alarm would arouse out of this, when we reached New York, a fortnight after, we found that our friends there had been made uneasy by the news that a steam-boat had sunk on the Lakes, and that eight hundred passengers were drowned. Catastrophes grow as fast as other things in America.

Though our friends did not happen to see Charley's pocket handkerchief from the river, they were soon about us, congratulating us on having made the circuit of the Lakes. It was indeed matter of congratulations.

I have now given sketches of some of the most remarkable parts of the country, hoping that a pretty distinct idea might thus be afforded of their primary resources, and of the modes of life in their inhabitants. I have said nothing of the towns, in this connexion; town-life in America having nothing very peculiar about it, viewed in the way of general survey.

THE ROMANTIC WILDERNESS

Charles Fenno Hoffman

Charles Fenno Hoffman, a New York magazine editor and popular writer, traveled through Michigan in an 1833 sojourn to the Mississippi Valley. His visit occurred just before the peak of the land rush into Michigan during the 1830s; he passed through Dexter, Marshall, and other points before crossing the state line into Indiana. Hoffman was one of those romantic travel writers for whom, in the words of Roderick Nash, "the appreciation of wilderness became a literary genre."[1]

Hoffman was a copious observer of natural phenomena and one of the most admired "travel" writers of his time. In this excerpt from *A Winter in the West* (vol. I, New York: Harper & Brothers, 1835, pp. 166–223), he describes the difficulties of traversing the region on horseback in winter, the Irish Hills,

[1] Roderick Nash, *Wilderness and the American Mind* (New Haven: Yale University Press, 1967), p. 60.

the spectacle of a prairie fire, an encounter with a band of Indians, lengthy talks with setters, the "beautiful Kekalamazoo River," frontier hospitality, oak openings, and the quality of the soil. "You may have already gathered," he concludes, "that neither the grand, the picturesque—hardly even the romantic—are to be numbered among its characteristics. 'The beautiful' comprehends them all."

Letter XIV

Dexter, Washtenaw Co., M. T., Dec. 15th.

I have been waiting here since I last wrote in order to join an exploring party of three or four individuals, to go up into Shiawassee county, to examine lands. A heavy snow-storm has set in to-day, however, and as it will put an end to the expedition, I shall probably start by myself for the Kalamazoo country tomorrow. The journey to Grand River, which I proposed to myself, I shall, from the time it would consume, be compelled now to abandon entirely. I do not regret the time I have spent here, for I am not far from the centre of the territory; and while I have my head-quarters at a good inn, in a well-settled place, I can, in a ride of a few miles, plunge at once into the wilderness. It is a pretty dangerous matter, however, for a stranger to go without a guide reconnoitering through a country where every hill, lake, and wood looks so much like its brother that the ordinary landmarks are of no assistance to the eye. The scenery of Michigan will be far more attractive when cultivation shall have given variety to a landscape which, however beautiful at present, is somewhat monotonous. After visiting nearly a dozen of the transparent ponds of every size which stud the surface of the country, and finding but two or three whose firm banks of some fifteen or twenty feet elevation assumed a picturesque appearance, from the irregular manner in which they pushed their beautifully wooded promontories far into the lakes they bounded, I started, the other day, to visit a sheet of water somewhat elevated, about twelve miles off. My way, after going a mile or two from the village, led through oak openings of rolling land, called " the Short Hills," which I can best assimilate to a collection of enormous graves—the tombs of households, if you choose—thrown confusedly together upon a perfectly level surface; where a patch of wild meadow-land, a cranberry marsh, or a bog that looked like the desolated bed of a lake, and frequently, indeed, the shallow lake itself, filled up the intervals. The huge oaks that crowned the summits of these formal mounds were the only objects that relieved the dreariness of the landscape; even they, I thought, while riding alone beneath their branches, that sighed to the December wind, were not the most enlivening objects in the world. I rode thus for miles without seeing a living thing except a raven, which, as that description of bird is only found in those parts of the Union where wolves still infest the country, I at once took it for granted was hovering near one of the savage beasts to which he so faithfully plays the jackal. Wheeling my horse suddenly from the trail towards a thicket of dwarf oaks, where I expected to find the carrion deer that attracts these worthies, he shied from the bush, and I was thrown upon the spot. After extricating the foot, by which I was dragged a yard or two, from the stirrup, I sprang up but little hurt, and moved as quickly as possible to catch my horse, who, having paused for an instant in a clump of trees near by, turned his head round, like a pointer taken aback with the scent after he has passed a bush, and stood calmly gazing at me. At the first step towards the rascal, however, he moved nearly a rod sideways, and then, ducking his head towards the ground, and throwing his heels high in the air, my ungrateful courser, accompanying these motions with every additional mark of disrespect he could summon to his aid, left his master alone in the wilderness. He disappeared behind a hill in a moment. I could not help ejaculating, with the Kentuckian whose house and family had been burned up by the savages, while he was cleaning his rifle at a brook hard by—"This is very ridiculous." No time was to be lost, however. It was late in the day, and I was far from any house; while the occasional flakes of snow which began to fall from the black lowering sky, threatened a storm which might cover in a moment the only path that could guide me homeward. I sat down at once among the long dry grass, and stripping off my leggings, and disembarrassing my heels of the now useless spurs, stowed all away in my coat-pockets. The coat itself I rolled up in a bundle around my left arm, and taking my gun, to which I applied a fresh cap, in my right, I strode off in as good a humour as one could summon under such provoking circumstances. I could not help thinking, indeed, how much worse matters might have been had I been thus deserted in one of the broad prairies, thirty miles, perhaps, from any house. As for the loss of my horse, I felt so indignant against the inconsiderate brute, that, I confess, it did not much trouble me. Thus did I trudge on, growing momentarily in better humour with myself. The scene around was dreary at present; but having had all the wild flowers that grow in Michigan described to me, I exercised my imagination by conceiving the more attractive appearance it must wear in summer. I thought how the brown woods must look when the lofty oaks around were clothed in their deep-green foliage. I thought of the various vines and flowers which then fill the broad openings between their stems—of the clumps of cluster-roses that here grow wild and cover whole acres—of the crimson daisy and fragrant balm pink, the deep-hued lichnidia, and gorgeous golden rod, which, with jonquils and amaranth, the purple fox-glove and saffron-coloured silk-weed, paint the surface of the soil. I could fancy the glossy leaves of the nightshade with its white blossoms and poisonous berries, the creeping ivy, and red columbine, clustering at the base of the hills. The snow-white lily of the valley, the lilac-tinted adder's tongue, and straw-coloured arrow-head, shooting through the long grass between, while the purple fleur-de-lis bloomed along the wet marshes, where the splendid cardinal-flower tossed its scarlet blossoms in the breeze.

I must have practised horticulture in this way for some time when, on rising a slight eminence in my path, I saw my amiable roan standing quietly looking in the direction whence I was coming, apparently waiting for me. I was completely mollified. I forgave him the little freak, and advanced with a light heart to lay my hand upon the bridle. He moved a little, and so did I. He moved a little more, and I stood still. I spoke to him, but he continued moving. I coaxed him,in a tone that would have melted the heart of one of the marble horses of St. Mark's; he was moved by it—only farther from me. I whistled to him—(I had taught him a day or two before to come to my whistle, when he had obeyed me like a dog)—he stopped, and I advanced once more to lay my hand on the saddle, and the scoundrel broke into a trot just as I was about touching him. I brought my piece to my shoulder, and could hardly forbear drawing the trigger upon him as I stood.

The ground now rolled like the waves of a frozen sea, and my nefarious brute, who soon began to stalk leisurely along about a hundred yards ahead of me, would, to carry out the figure, be just topping the combing while I was in the trough, and vice versa—like two children balancing on a plank. It was perfectly insufferable, mile after mile, to see that eternal saddle bobbing up and down a hundred yards ahead of me. Sometimes, indeed, the vexatious wearer would step aside among a cluster of oaks, to nip the tender grass which still lingered around their roots; and then, as he would arch his neck, and, seeming to admire the Indian blanket and flame-coloured surcingle which, after the gay taste of the West, I had buckled, combining use with ornament, to the back of the ungrateful brute, dash off with a snort into a patch of prairie-land, I could not but admire the eye of fire and gracefully-gathering limbs of the spirited creature. I wished, however, that he was anybody's horse but mine, disporting himself at that rate. At last, at a turning of the path he disappeared behind a hill, and ceasing longer to tantalize, left me comparatively comfortable. I reached the first"clearing" about twenty minutes afterward, and looking along the highway which here commenced, my horse was nowhere to be seen. Tired alike with walking and vexation, and parched with thirst (I had neither eaten nor drunk since breakfast, and it was now nightfall), I advanced to the only shantee near, and knocked at the door. There was no answer, and I shook it violently. A rush-bottomed chair rattled, and a cat, the solitary occupant, sprang out through a broken window. I soon found my way, however, to the dilapidated trunk of a large sycamore-tree near, which formed the top of a well, and drawing up a moss-covered bucket, I placed my lips to the rusty iron-bound brim and took a draught, to which the most delicious of Lynch's chateau were but vile vin-du-pays in comparison. I can remember but one drink in my life before to compare with it, and that was from a similar goblet, after other lips than mine had hallowed the brim. A few moments after a lad rode into the yard with the object of my pursuit, whose bridle had been broken to pieces in the effort of several men to catch him a mile or two off. I was mounted in a moment, and regained my lodgings in an hour; when I found that the adventure of the day had not impaired my relish for a supper of fresh pike and white-fish, just smoking on the table.

The range of hills which traverse the peninsula longitudinally near here, though never, I believe, more than 150 feet high, are said by some to constitute the most elevated part of Michigan. As they abound in game, and consist altogether of oak openings, you can conceive of nothing more animating than to gallop over them on horseback. I was out again among them yesterday; and having a pocket-compass and a map of the country with me, I ventured to leave the trails that wind among the hollows, and scamper over the hills as my fancy led me. A large flock of grouse rose almost from beneath my horse's feet as I topped the first slight eminence, and then,just as the animal was recovering from the flurry into which the rushing sound of their wings threw him, a tall broad-antlered buck, the largest I ever saw, sprang from a small covert, and bounded through the wide forest glades. Away too I went—the feeling was irresistible—I could see the fellow leaping as if he had wings, over the rolling land, and the clear bracing atmosphere had given spirits to my horse, that sent us ahead like one and the same animal. In spite of the deer's prodigious jumps, which were as high as they were long, I had gained decidedly on the chase, when, coming to the brow of a steep hill, he dashed down the side, and was far away over another before my less agile horse could descend the first. I saw two more deer, besides several flocks of grouse, during my morning's ride. Singularly enough, this was the only time that I had moved a mile without a gun since I left New-York; and it was the only opportunity I have had to use one to advantage. If Der Freyschutz were in this region, I should certainly let the wild huntsman make his own terms with me for better luck.

To-day, for the first time, I saw the meadows on fire. They are of vast extent, running far into the woods like the friths of a lake; and as the wild grass, which they supply in the greatest profusion, furnishes the new settler with all the hay he uses for his stock, they are burnt over thus annually to make it tender. These fires, travelling far over the country, seize upon the large prairies, and consuming every tree in the woods, except the hardiest, cause the often-mentioned oak openings so characteristic of Michigan scenery. It is a beautiful sight to see the fire shooting in every direction over these broad expanses of land, which are kindled at a variety of points. The flame at one moment curls along the ground, and seems to lick up its fuel from below, while at the next it tumbles over like the breakers of the sea upon the dried grass, and sweeps it in a wave of fire from the ground. I found myself repeatedly surrounded by the fire, while riding hither and thither, watching its progress; but was only on two occasions exposed to any inconvenience—once when my horse was bogged to the saddle-girths, so that I had to dismount in a morass, covered with high weeds, to which the flame was approaching, and again when I found myself in a small patch of woodland, which crackled and roared like Tophet itself.

As I rode to and fro here, trying to find a point where, if necessary, I might encounter the flame to the least disadvantage, if unable to avoid it altogether, the ridiculous position in which I had placed myself reminded me not a little of that which Andrew Fairservice occupied on the rock, when he trotted hither and thither on his narrow platform, to avoid the bullets of Rob Roy's caterans. A finer subject for reflection, however, presented itself near the spot. A small brook crossed the meadow, and I bethought myself of placing it between me and the fire, which was closing undesirably near around me; but my horse, when I rode him rapidly to the brink, and endeavoured to jump him, recoiled. I wheeled round, and tried it again; but his recent experience in the treacherous marsh made him fear the sedgy margin, and nothing could prevail upon the cautious animal to approach it. At the last attempt, he recoiled so suddenly with a terrified snort, that I was nearly thrown over his head: and looking for the new cause of anxiety where the stream wound around, so as almost to double itself in front of me I saw, on the little peninsula of the burning meadow thus formed, an Indian standing with folded arms amid the wreathing smoke, and surveying my motions with an aspect of perfect calmness. He was a middle-aged man, rather tall, and in the full costume of his tribe. The hair on his forehead, which was seamed with several ghastly scars, was nearly white; but three long plaited locks of raven black fell down behind, from the crimson handkerchief which bound his brows. He wore a white woollen frock, edged with black, with scarlet leggings and moccasins, while armlets of silver, and a belt containing his tomahawk and scalping-knife, completed his equipments. All these, however, were observed afterward, when I had given up the attempt to cross the brook, and spurring through the flame where it was lowest, had placed myself by the side of the old warrior. But for the present I remained fixed in my seat, gazing on the noble apparition with as much delight as if my own call had evoked it from the ground. I had seen a dozen Indians, of all sizes and sexes, in the course of the day, not one of whom had awakened the slightest interest; but there was that about the port and bearing of this grim-looking savage which, with the somewhat theatrical attitude he assumed, and the circumstances under which I first beheld him, carried me away completely. He smiled when I approached him, and saluted me with great kindness of manner; though, as neither of us understood the language of the other, there could be but little interchange of ideas between us. The few Indian expressions of which I am master were soon expended, and he seemed not to have a word of English to give me in exchange. He made me understand, however, that the frightful wounds which disfigure his noble front were received while fighting on the side of the British against the Americans at Sandusky.

Grass Lake, Jackson Co., M. T., Dec. 16.

The storm of yesterday still prevailed when I left my excellent quarters at the growing little hamlet of Dexter, to find my way towards the country watered by the beautiful Kekalamazoo. I had been furnished by mine host with a map of the route for the first eight or ten miles; and it would have amused you to see me occasionally stopping in a furious snow-storm to balance my pocket-compass on the hasty chart thus supplied. I found my way, however, with very little difficulty, through a thick wood, where the heavy coat of snow that robed the trees gave a most fantastic appearance to the forest, and about noon I struck the Washtenaw trail to the west. The travelling, however, was any thing but agreeable. The snow, being soft, would "ball," as it is called, beneath my horse's feet, and what with the stumbling and slipping on this account, I have been unable after a day's travel to make more than twenty miles. There was barely light enough left for me to distinguish my way, when I arrived at a comfortable log-house belonging to an intelligent and hospitable farmer, a recent emigrant from the western part of the sate [sic] of New-York. The owner of the dwelling was absent; and it was not till after a parley of some minutes, between two very pretty women, whom I could distinguish through the window by the light of a tempting-looking fire within, that I gained admittance to pass the night. Once there, however, nothing could exceed the kindness of the family to make the few hours of my sojourn pass agreeable.

Spring-Arbour, Dec. 17.

It snowed when I rose at dawn this morning; but my hospitable entertainer of last night insisted, after an early breakfast, upon accompanying me several miles on my journey; and when he finally parted with me, would not hear of receiving any thing in compensation.

The snow still continues, and the road becoming worse and worse, I have made even less progress to-day. But there is something so wild and picturesque in the country through which I am passing, that even such travelling has its pleasures. I have counted more than a dozen lakes on my route; and though some of them are only dreary-looking pools, covering a few acres, in the midst of an extensive moss-marsh, yet the short sudden hills which surround others, with the beautiful groves of white oak on their banks, and the natural meadows that open upon their mimic friths, make a most romantic appearance. I came unexpectedly upon a travelling band of Ottawas this morning, in one of the most abrupt of these passes. They were returning home amply furnished with presents from the recent treaty held on the Wabash; and their fluttering blankets, gleaming weapons, and gaudy equipments generally, would have made them a fine subject for a painter, as a furious squall of snow swept along the side hill they were descending. We exchanged the customary salutation, "Boju" (probably from the French bonjour), and passed on.

There are several Indian graves immediately before the door of the shantee where I am stopping for the night, which I am told are regularly visited and weeded by the surviving relatives of those here buried. My host has had the good taste to put a fence around them, to keep his cattle from the spot—a piece of attention with which the Indians appeared to be much gratified at their last visit; and I may here observe that the settlers of Michigan, generally, appear to treat this ill-fated race with a degree of kindness and consideration that might well be imitated in other sections of our frontier. This morning I crossed the far-flowing Washtenong, or Grand River, near the new village of Jacksonburg; and the sight of its clear smooth waters inspired a new regret, that I must abandon my original intention of following them down to the last trading-post.

Forks of the Kekalamazoo (Calhoun), Dec. 18.

This never-ending storm still continues, and the trails, where not incessantly travelled, being now completely covered and effaced, I lost my way this morning, and wandered several miles from the track. After traversing a broad marsh, however, where my horse seemed loath enough to venture, I struck a burr-oak opening, and found my way by the blazed trees back to the main trail. A man who is used to it, I am told, can get along very well in this way; but you can imagine, that where one has frequently to cross openings of some two or three hundred yards in width, and then hunt up these primitive guide-posts, which only occur at long intervals, and have their slice of bark taken out at either side, it is not quite so easy to find his way here especially with the snow blowing full in his face, as if walking through the rectangular streets of Philadelphia. It took me three hours to gain six miles in this way, my horse slipping and floundering at almost every step. But, lost as I was, I could not help pausing frequently when I struck the first burr-oak opening I had ever seen, to admire its novel beauty. It looked more like a pear-orchard than any thing else to which I can assimilate it—the trees being somewhat of the shape and size of full-grown pear trees, and standing at regular intervals apart from each other on the firm level soil, as if planted by some gardener. Here, too, I first saw deer in herds; and half-frozen and weary as I was, the sight of those spirited-looking creatures sweeping in troops through these interminable groves, where my eye could follow them for miles over the smooth snowy plain, actually warmed and invigorated me, and I could hardly refrain from putting the rowels into my tired horse, and launching after the noble game.

What a country this is. Into land like this, which is comparatively undervalued by those seeking to settle on the prairie, a man can run his plough without felling a tree; and, planting a hundred acres, where he would clear but ten in the unsettled districts of New-York, raise his twenty-five bushels of wheat to an acre in the very first season. "How is the soil here, sir?" said I to a farmer whose broad fields, though but a year under cultivation, looked as if they had been tilled for ten. "A pretty good gravelly loam of eighteen inches; but I think some of moving off to Kalamazoo, where they have it four feet deep, and so fat that it will grease your fingers." Railroads and canals will make one broad garden of Michigan; and even now there is something singularly pleasing to light upon spots in the wildest districts which, were it not for the rude shantees which indicate their recent settlement,—often of but a few months back,—might be mistaken for the cultivated farms of an old country. The absence of stumps in the land under cultivation, and the open groves adjacent, give a smiling openness to the landscape which, with the myriads of wild flowers that brighten the woods in their season, must make the aspect of the country perfectly delightful. I hardly know, though, how some of your city elegants, the votaries of Delmonico, or the fair visitants at Gardiner's, would meet the inconveniences of travelling here. As for eating, indeed, they might manage with the aid of cranberry sauce to rough it on venison and wild honey, backed by the finest potatoes and best wheat bread in the world; but I think that, when it comes to sleeping, they would be somewhat posed between a bed in the bush and one shared with the hospitable inmates of a cabin, whose dormitory for the whole family is often, as well as their kitchen and parlour, comprised in a single room. Were it not an infraction of the laws of hospitality, I could draw some queer pictures of scenes I have witnessed in this way.

I have now passed the central region where the Eastern and Western rivers of Michigan have their rise; and while I follow down the pebbly waters of the beautiful Kekalamazoo to their western outlet, and from thence pass to the mouth of the St. Joseph's, you must not expect the same regularity in my correspondence that I have hitherto attempted to preserve.

Letter XV

Marshall,Calhoun Co., M. T., Dec.

I confess that it was with some pleasure that—after dividing my time for several days, as described in my last, between roads rendered almost impassable by continual snows and log-cabins, where the recent settler, however hospitable, had but spare accommodation to offer to the passing traveller—on rising an elevation on the northern bank of the Kekalamazoo, I saw a large frame-building, which was evidently an inn, rearing its comfortable-looking chimneys above a group of log-huts on the plain beneath. My horse, who had doubtless repented of former escapadoes in the companionable intercourse which had now for some time subsisted between us, seemed to sympathize in the feeling; and pricking up his ears, as he snuffed the grain in a flour-mill directly beneath us, we descended the slippery height, and were soon tolerably well-housed in the new inn of Marshall. The house was, indeed, not as yet plaistered inside; and the different bed-rooms, though lathed, seemed divided from each other by lines rather imaginary than real; but the bar-room wore already the insignia of a long-established inn in an old community; and apprized me at once, by the placarded sheriffs' notices and advertisements for stolen horses, grain to be sold, and labourers wanted, which indicate the growth of business in country life, that society was in a pretty mature state—at least six months old—in the county town of Marshall. I was, therefore, not at all surprised to find among these notices a call for "a railroad meeting" in the evening, especially as nearly eighteen months had elapsed since the first white man erected his cabin in this section of the country.

The meeting, which might be termed a crowded one, was conducted with more animation than unanimity. There were several intelligent men present, however; and I listened with interest to their exposition of the resources of this section of Michigan, which, as a wheat growing country, may be justly compared to the celebrated Genessee valley of New-York, while the soil, as I have heard it well observed by a resident, "unlike the heavily-timbered land of the Eastern States, instead of wearing out one generation in subduing it for the purposes of the husbandman, invites the plough at once." Nor, if a railroad should be constructed from Detroit to the mouth of the St. Joseph's passing through the counties of Wayne, Washtenaw, Jackson, Calhoun, Kalamazoo, Van Buren, and Berrien, do I think it would be too bold to assert that the amount to be transported by the time the work was completed would be equal to one million of barrels, which is a less estimate by two hundred thousand than I have seen given by an intelligent writer on this subject in a Detroit paper. The route thus designated, I am persuaded, is the right one for a railroad; though, should a different mode of communication be determined upon, it would be difficult to decide whether it were most expedient to construct a canal from the falls of Grand River to Detroit, or from the navigable waters of the St. Joseph's to Monroe. I do not hesitate to add, that before two years have expired, all of these routes will be under contract. The abundant resources of Michigan are developing so rapidly, that they will shortly require all these outlets; and in a country where you may drive a barouche-and-four for hundreds of miles in any direction through the woods, the expense of constructing more artificial ways will be comparatively trivial.

Did I not know how ignorant generally the people of the east are of the resources and condition of this country, it would surprise me that some New-York capitalists have not embarked in some of these works. A tempting speculation might be realized by laying out a railroad on one of these routes above described; having first purchased the land in its vicinity at government prices, to be disposed of afterward when its value should be enhanced by the completion of different sections of the work. The ingenious writer, above alluded to, has already suggested this mode of covering the expense of such an undertaking. You can have no idea of the feeling existing on the subject of internal communications throughout Michigan; and it would amuse you not a little to witness the heart-burnings and jealousies on the subject which pervade a country but just beginning to be peopled. The rapidity with which people establish themselves and collect the indications of agricultural wealth around them, before they have even the ordinary comforts of life, will, in a great measure, account for their looking thus ahead and quarrelling about the game before it is hunted down. The farmer, who has more grain in the sheaf stacked in the field than he can accommodate in his barn, is naturally more eager to find the means of sending a share of it to market.

I was quite diverted at the turn matters took at the meeting which suggested these remarks, when a discussion in relation to the various routes to be recommended to government in case they should consent to make a railroad through the Peninsula, became unpleasantly warm. "This pother reminds me, Mr. Chairman," said an old pioneer, "of two trappers who, in planning a spearing expedition for the next day, quarrelled about the manner in which a turtle, which they proposed taking, should be cooked for their supper, after the day's sport was over. An old Indian happily settled the difficulty, by proposing that they should first catch the turtle! Now, sir, as this railroad,—"the case is not at all parallel"—interrupted a still more ancient speaker, "for Nature has already caught the turtle for us. She meant the railroad to pass right along here, and nowhere else."

The councils of the meeting were not on the whole so harmonious as I could have wished from the courtesies offered me after its termination by the adherents of the two parties of Guelphs and Ghibbelines, which distract the unhappy city of Marshall; but it was surprising to a stranger, upon looking round at the hovels of mud and logs which as yet occupy its site, to find so many persons of intelligence and refinement thus collected within their precincts. The population of Michigan generally,—as I believe I have before observed,—is much superior in character to the ordinary settlers of a new country. The ease with which a man can here support a family as a farmer, induces a great many persons of all professions, in other states, to abandon their former pursuits and become tillers of the soil. The alteration of life, I should judge by the contentment I everywhere witness, is almost always for the better.

I have met with several dispeptics who have been completely cured of that horrible disease by their change of life. With such, health is a sensation—a positive delight; and in duly estimating the blessing, they of course were ever ready to praise the conditions upon which they enjoy it. Others again, bred up in a city, find in the indulgence of that love of rural life which, when it is a natural taste, is inextinguishable, an ample compensation for breaking up established habits and associations. The majority again are men of slender means; and while the necessity of attending practically to the subsistence of their families keeps them employed, the want of pecuniary resources prevents their embarking in the thousand idle schemes which tend so often to the chagrin and the ruin of "gentlemen farmers." But the main cause of Michigan being settled by such respectable people remains yet to be mentioned. It is, that no one can take up an acre of land without first paying cash for it, at one of the three land-offices of the territory. The whole surface of the Peninsula has either been, or is now being, surveyed into townships of six miles square. These again are subdivided into sections of a mile square; which sections are again cut up into lots of forty acres; which is the smallest quantity of land that can be taken up from the government. The price is invariably $1.25 an acre. When you consider, therefore, that every emigrant who means to locate (this is a sound American word, and as indispensable in the vocabulary of a western man as are an axe and a rifle among his household furniture), must, however poor, have some earnings in advance to purchase the spot upon which he is to live, and to bring his family to such a remote distance, it will be easy to conceive that the industrious and the enterprising must constitute the largest portion of such a population of freeholders. The prosperity of a whole community, composed of such aggregate masses, may be safely predicted; and though one sometimes meets with those whom the first process of accumulating renders discontented, and induces to speak ill of the country, yet in general I may say, that the pride of a Michiganian, in the beautiful land of his adoption, is as strong as the home-feeling upon which the citizens of some of the older States pique themselves. As for the sickness which always prevails more or less among the new settlers, to one who is aware of their imprudences the wonder is that the majority of them escape with their lives. Think but of people setting themselves down on a soil of twenty inches in depth, and in the month of June, when the weeds and wild flowers o'ertop the head of the tallest man, turning over the rank soil immediately around their dwellings, and allowing the accumulation of vegetable decomposition to be acted upon by a vertical sun, and steam up for months under their very nostrils; and yet this, I am told, is continually practised by settlers who come in late in the season, and are anxious still to have a crop the first year. Here, as in the case or those settlers who, for the sake of the wild hay, locate themselves near the great marshes, imprudence alone is manifested; but the charge of culpability will justly attach to some other cases, when nuisances, not before existing, are created by the owners of property. I allude to the practice, expressly prohibited by the laws of Michigan, of flooding land while constructing mill-ponds, without removing the green timber growing upon the spot. So pernicious is this to the health of the neighbourhood, that it affects very sensibly the value of property near the new pond; and yet, in their eagerness to have mills erected, and aid the market of their overflowing granaries, the new inhabitants overlook entirely the gross violation of their laws, and the melancholy consequences which ensue to their families. Another cause of sickness is drinking the water of springs or rivers which rise in marshes, and are of course impregnated with their baleful properties, instead of digging wells where water is not liable to such exception. As for general healthfulness of situation, I believe it is agreed that the banks of the small lakes which so abound in the peninsula are—when these transparent bodies of water are surrounded by a sand-beach, which is the case with about a third of them—among the healthiest. They are fed generally by deep springs, and in many instances are supposed to have a subterranean outlet; while so beautifully transparent are their waters, that the canoe suspended on their bosom seems to float in mid-air. These lakes abound with fish; and in some of them, of only a few acres in extent, fish have been taken of forty pounds weight. They generally lie imbosomed in the oak openings, and with their regular and almost formal banks crowned with open groves, these silver pools might be readily taken for artificial trout-ponds in a cultivated park. I need hardly add, that it is necessary to diverge, as I have, from the route generally travelled, to see these scenic gems, so numerous, lonely, and beautiful. Not one in a hundred has a settler on its banks; and I confess I take a singular pleasure in surveying these beauties, as yet unmarred by the improving axe of the woodman, and unprofaned by the cockney eyes of city tourists; nor would I change my emotions, while ranging alone over the broad meadows, traversing the lofty forests, or loitering by the limpid lakes of Michigan, for the proudest musings of the scholar who revels in classic land. It may argue a want of refinement in taste, but I confess that a hoary oak is to me more an object of veneration than a mouldering column; and that I would rather visit scenes where a human foot has never trod than dwell upon those gilded by the most arrogant associations of our race.

What are the temples which Roman robbers have reared,—what are the towers in which feudal oppression has fortified itself,—what the blood-stained associations of the one, or the despotic superstitions of the other, to the deep forests which the eye of God has alone pervaded, and where Nature, in her unviolated sanctuary, has for ages laid her fruits and flowers on his altar! What is the echo of roofs that a few centuries since rung with barbaric revels, or of aisles that pealed the anthems of painted pomp, to the silence which has reigned in these dim groves since the first fiat of Creation was spoken!

I shall diverge from my western course to-morrow a few miles southward, in order to visit a group of lakes, near which a band of Pottawattamies, a tribe I have not yet seen, have their encampment. I will leave this letter open, in order to give you the result of my visit.
Calhoun Co., M. T., Dec. 23.

I write to you from a little cottage in a beautiful grove, not far from the banks of the Kekalamazoo, where two young gentlemen, recently from the east, have made their home in this land of enterprise. It is amusing to observe how little singularity people here attach to a mode of life which, in older countries, would be looked upon as highly eccentric. My entertainers are both young lawyers, liberally educated, and unused to privation; and yet the house in which I am passing the night, with every article of furniture it contains, is of their own manufacture; a saw, an axe, a woodknife, and a jack-plane being their only tools. It would amuse you not a little to look through the window, and see our group at this moment. One of my companions, whose axe and rifle are suspended by wooden hooks to the rafters over his head, is professionally engaged in drawing a declaration at the table upon which I am writing; while the other, having just got through removing the remains of our game dinner, prepared and cooked by his chum, is now sitting with a long pipe in his mouth, watching a coffee-pot, which steams up so fragrantly from the live embers, that no light consideration would induce me to part with the interest I have in its contents. Their house, which has been thus occupied for three months, is a perfect pattern of neatness; though, as it consists of but a single room, no little ingenuity is required to arrange their books, house-keeping apparatus, and sporting equipments, so as to preserve even an appearance of order in such a bandbox. They have already sufficient business, they tell me, to sustain their moderate household; and as the Indians supply them with abundance of provisions, they have ample leisure to devote to study.

It is not very uncommon, however, to meet thus with persons of education, and some accomplishment, under as humble a roof as this in the wilds of Michigan. For so rapid is the growth of society here, that he who aims at a prominent station in the new community must be a pioneer far in advance of the growing settlements. Two years ago the first white man raised his log hut in the county of Calhoun; it has now a population of 1500, and I have passed an evening in at least one mud-plastered cabin, whose fair and elegant inmates would grace any society.

When I see the wives and daughters of men habituated by early education to all the comforts of refined life, thus submitting cheerfully to every privation for the sake of those whose happiness is involved with theirs, I cannot help calling to mind the jargon of novels so often adopted by people of sense in cities, where the terms "excellent match," and "supporting in the station where she has been accustomed to move," usurp all considerations of mutual affection, and capability in the parties united to study each other's happiness through life. I am more than ever persuaded that there are two kinds of refinement in life, which bear but little similarity to each other; and the one least often met with is that which is independent of modes and fashions, of tailors, milliners, and cabinet-makers,—which does not necessarily lean upon a pier-table, nor repose upon a chaise longue,—which—shall I confess it?—may be nursed without a silver fork. The purest porcelain which the factories of China produce does not require a single tint upon its surface to show the fineness of the texture; but that in which coarser clay is blended is always charged with some gaudy hue to hide the intermixture of the mongrel material. This doctrine, though, is so little in accordance with those taught in those English novels which constitute the modern text-books of elegance, that while the mode of eating an egg is the test of good-breeding, and the art of pattering French phrases the criterion of intellectual cultivation, I should as soon think of interfering with the particular province of a lackey or friseur, as of breaking a spear at such disadvantage with the authors of "Almack's" and "Men and Manners—."

But a truce to this prosing. Did you ever see a jumper? A couple of hickory poles so bent that the runners and shafts are of the same piece, with a crate placed on four props, complete this primitive species of sledge; and when the crate is filled with hay, and the driver well wrapped-up in a buffalo robe, the "turn-out" is about as comfortable a one as a moderate man could wish. In such a vehicle as this, with a harness every way suitable, viz. a collar of undressed deerskin and reins of rope (the twisted bark of trees is often used), did I, with one of my present entertainers, the first companion I have yet had in travelling, sally out from Marshall this morning. My horse, who had detained me there a couple of days by a soreness of his back proceeding from the saddle, seemed highly to approve of this new mode of travel: Mr. Osbaldistone behind Tom Thumb, Sesostris in his chariot, or Yorke in one of Brower's new omnibuses, could not have dashed off with more glee than did we with our merry jumper along the dimpling waters of the Kekalamazoo; when, lo! just as we had crossed a bridge of unhewn timber, and were under full way through the oak openings, our frail bark struck on a rock hidden by the snow, and we were capsized and wrecked in an instant. Fortunately, though both were pitched like a couple of quoits from the machine, we were neither of us hurt; and my companion returning to the settlement to borrow a horse, I mounted mine, and leaving the remains of my crank establishment where chance had thrown them, I rode on, while he overtook me in time to introduce me to his friend, and make me so pleasantly at home in their dwelling as, you must observe, I now am. Good-night; I will tell you to-morrow evening how we dispose of our time till then.

December 24th.

The air was mild this morning, and large flocks of snow-birds twittering among the burr-oaks, with jays screaming from the woods, and packs of grouse rising continually before us in the openings, made our route to the camp of Warpkesick, a Pottawattamie chieftain, more like a ride in the spring-time than a winter excursion. I was accompanied by my companion of yesterday; and as we were both well-mounted, we galloped over the openings towards Lyon Lake, at a rate that brought us in a few minutes to the white sand-beach which fringes that beautiful water. The marks of an Indian trail were here easily discernible; and following the foot-marks dashed in the yielding sand, the frequent print of moccasins soon led us again away from the shore into a tall wood beyond. A morass, that shook for yards around as our horses' hoofs encountered the sagging peat, was next to be crossed; and then passing between two small lonely-looking lakes, where a tall pine or two lifted its sweeping cone above the tapering tamaracks around, we struck at last into a dense forest. Here the numerous deer-runways, with the flocks of wild turkeys, and innumerable tracks of rackoons, wolves, and bears, showed us that we were upon a favourite hunting-ground of the Pottawattamies. As for the wolves, they are little disturbed by the Indians, who consider them fair hunters like themselves, and privileged to go unmolested. They generally abound around a hunting-camp; and soon grow fat on the offals of game slaughtered near it. But bears, though the successful hunter invariably takes his dead quarry by the paw, calls him his grandfather, and asks his pardon for killing him, "being compelled to it by necessity," are hunted with great avidity; and you generally find a tamarack swamp, the favourite covert of these animals, in the vicinity of a hunting-camp.

We had ridden for about a mile through the heavily timbered land, when reaching the banks the Nottawaseepe, a branch of the St. Joseph's, I heard the sound of children's voices, and descried two or three red urchins wading through the shallow stream on stilts, while others of a similar age were amusing themselves in shooting bows and arrows on the opposite side. We immediately forded the stream, and making our way into a swamp, where the horses sank to the knee at every step, came unexpectedly upon a piece of firm ground, some eighty yards in diameter, and found ourselves in the middle of the camp of Warpkesick. It was composed of three or four wigwams only, but they were large, and probably contained several families each. They were constructed of mats, arranged precisely in the form of a tent, and supported in the same manner, an opening being left in the centre for the escape of the smoke, and a blanket suspended over a hole cut in the side, supplying the place of a door. The day being mild for the season of the year, the indwellers of these simple habitations were, at the moment of our arrival, variously occupied in several groups on the outside. Some of the men were cleaning their weapons, and others were arranging a bundle of muskrat traps; while one old fellow, whose screwed-up features, peering from under a mass of grizzly locks, indicated the cunning of the trapper, rather than the boldness of the hunter, was occupied in flaying an otter but just taken. The women alone, however, appeared to be assiduously engaged—the men having all a lounging air of indolence, incompatible with the idea of actual employment: pressing skins was the occupation of the former; and they sat grouped each like a hare in its form around a collection of boiling kettles, over which the skins were suspended.

A tall virago of fifty, whose erect stature, elf locks, and scarlet blanket floating about her person would entitle her to flourish as Meg Merrilies in the frontispiece of Guy Mannering, stood up in the midst; and had it not been for some tolerably pretty faces among her junior collaborators, might have been taken for Hecate herself, surrounded by the weird sisters of the caldron. A pack of wolfish-looking curs, about twenty in number, completed the assemblage; which, when you take into consideration the variously coloured calico dresses and wampum ornaments in which the females had arrayed themselves, with the white, blue, red, and green blankets in which the men were wrapped, constituted about as motley a collection as ever followed Falstaff to the field. Warpkesick himself, the chief of the gipsy band, issued from his lodge while I was thus studying the appearance of his adherents. He was a young man, not more than thirty, with a handsome though somewhat voluptuous cast of countenance and remarkably fine eyes. His stature was rather below the middle size; and though the upper part of his person was extremely well formed, with a deep chest and broad flat shoulders, one of his legs, whether from deformity or misfortune I did not like to inquire, was so twisted under his body as to be worse than useless. He supported himself upon an ashen staff about eight feet in length, and terminating at the bottom in a round ball, to prevent it, probably, from sinking too deeply into the earth while in rapid pursuit of game; the chief being, in spite of the unsightly encumbrance he is compelled to drag after him, when bounding like a stricken panther on his prey, one of the keenest hunters of his tribe. He received us courteously, but remained standing; while several Indians gathered in a few moments around him: after shaking hands with them all in succession, I took up a loaded gun, and by way of breaking up the formality of the meeting, desired an eagle-eyed young Indian to make a shot with it. He hesitated for a moment to comply, and immediately all the others, from some whim or other, insisted that I should shoot. Our conversation being altogether in signs, it was some moments before I understood their gestures; and I confess, that having but little practice with a single ball, I was any thing but unembarrassed when I came to understand the purport of the request they were proffering with so much animation. A small blaze that was instantly made with a tomahawk in a sapling, forty or fifty yards distant, left me no excuse for pretending longer to misunderstand my worthy acquaintances; and placing the gun to my shoulder, I was as much surprised at putting the ball within a couple of inches of the centre, as if the tree had screamed when thus pierced by my random bullet.

Having met with those in Michigan who will drive a rusty nail with a rifle at this distance, and shoot leaves from each other's heads at six rods, I could not account for the degree of approval manifested by the spectators, till my companion informed me that the Indians, owing perhaps to the inferiority of their rifles, which are of English manufacture, are but indifferent marksmen at still objects. "Tai-yi," cried the women, "Neshin," said the chief, and "Nesheshin," echoed his attendants; while the blankets of the lodges were now for the first time raised, and entering, we stretched ourselves on mats around the fire. A youth of nineteen sprang to his feet as I removed the dingy curtain which formed the door, and revealed a face and form that might be the model of an Apollo. Being ill at the time, he was but half-dressed; the purple blanket dropping from his shoulders setting off a neck and chest of the finest manly proportions. His features were copied by Nature from a Greek model; while his shaven crown, with the single chivalric scalp-lock tufted with a heron's feather, would, in its noble developments, have thrown the disciples of Gall and Spurzheim into ecstasy. The peculiarity of his head-dress, with the beautifully beaded leggings round his ankles, revealed to me at once that the young gentleman was an Indian dandy—a Pottawattamie Pelham in an undress; and I assure you that Mr. C— never schooled any of his New-York rivals to wear their Spanish cloak with a better air than was exhibited by my red friend Mitosway-Coquatchegun, or Ten-Garters, as he gathered the folds of his blankets about his person.

Pipes were now lit, and Ten-Garters, who was too unwell to smoke himself, politely, after a few whiffs, tendered me his, while my companion, who could partially speak the language, was supplied from another quarter: we were soon perfectly at home. I had picked up from the floor of the lodge, on entering, a rude musical instrument—a species of flute, of imperfect tones, but having a rich mellow sound—when, as I was trying to squeeze a tune from the gammutless [sic] pipe, Warpkesick rose abruptly, and stating that he had to start at once on a trapping expedition, signified that we should take our departure. An Indian pony stood at the door, and leaping at one bound into the wooden saddle, an immense bundle of steel-traps was handed to the chief by a by-stander; and accompanied by an Indian on foot, almost as sorry-looking as the miserable beast he rode, our abrupt host disappeared at once into the woods. I was lingering behind to purchase the flute, and had conciliated the squaws wonderfully by tearing out the silk lining of my frock-coat, and giving it in shreds to their children, when my friend, being already mounted, told me we had better move off. I had barely time to cross the saddle, when a whoop rang through the woods, which, while it made my horse spring almost from beneath me, would have wakened Rip Vanwinkle from his twenty years' doze. The piercing cry from the forest was echoed with an exulting shout from every wigwam. A dozen dusky figures leaped through their flimsy porches, with as many rifles gleaming in their hands. He of the heron feather was the first that caught my eye, and as his gun pointed in the direction whence the first whoop came, immediately behind me, I could not help, in spite of the undesirable propinquity of its muzzle, admiring the eagle-eye and superb attitude of the young warrior. Not a soul advanced three paces from the covert whence he sprung. There was a dead silence. The children held their breath, and "Meg Merrilies," who had stepped on a fallen tree at the first outcry, now stood so still that her eldritch form, were it not for the elf locks streaming over her scarlet blanket in the breeze, might have been mistaken for a figure of stone. Another whoop, and the cause of all the commotion at once appeared. A noble buck, roused from his lair by Warpkesick, comes bounding by the camp, and buries his proud antlers in the dust in a moment. A dozen scalping-knives pierce his leathern coat, and the poor creature is stripped of his skin almost before he has time to pant out his expiring breath.

I rode home reflecting upon all I had ever read of the want of vivacity and fire in the Indian character, and concluded that I would rather have witnessed the spirited scene I have just attempted to describe to you, than double all the knowledge I have hitherto laid up from such sources.

I leave this comfortable house in the morning, and it will be long before I reach again one half so agreeable.

Letter XVI

Prairie Ronde, Kalamazoo Co., M. T., Dec. 26.

"Stranger, will you take a cocktail with us?" called out a tall athletic fellow to me as I was making my way through a group of wild-looking characters assembled an hour since around the fire by which I am now writing. There was a long-haired "hooshier" from Indiana, a couple of smart-looking "suckers" from the southern part of Illinois, a keen-eyed leather-belted "badger" from the mines of Ouisconsin, and a sturdy yeoman-like fellow, whose white capot, Indian moccasins, and red sash proclaimed, while he boasted a three years' residence, the genuine wolverine, or naturalized Michiganian. Could one refuse to drink with such a company? The spokesman was evidently a "red-horse" from Kentucky, and nothing was wanting but a "buck-eye" from Ohio to render the assemblage as complete as it was select.

I was in the midst of the first real prairie I had ever seen—on an island of timber, whose lee, while making slow headway for the last two hours, with a biting breeze on my beam, it had been my whole object, aim, and ambition to get—a comfortable bar-room, a smoking "cocktail," a worshipful assemblage (Goldsmith's Club was a fool to it) had never entered my dreams! Could I refuse to drink with such a company? The warm glass is in my frozen fingers. The most devout temperance man could see no harm in that! It is touched smartly by the rim of the red-horse,—it is brushed by the hooshier,—it rings against the badger,—comes in companionable contact with the wolverine,—"My respects to you, gentlemen, and luck to all of us."

Here was a capital commencement with just the sort of sallad of society I have been long wishing to meet with, having as yet only tasted its component parts in detail. But auspicious as was the beginning, I nearly got into a difficulty with my new acquaintances a few moments afterward, by handing the landlord a share of the reckoning; and I took back the coin forced upon me, with many apologies upon my part for having presumed to pay part of a "general treat," while labouring under the disqualifications of being a stranger. Room was then civilly made for me by the fireplace, and accepting a pipe proffered by one of the company, a few whiffs made me sufficiently sick and at home to lay it by without further ceremony. "There's a smart chance of cigars there in the bar, stranger, if you'd try some of them," said one of the hooshiers.—"Yes," echoed the other; "and they are a heap better than those pipes."—"I allow," rejoined another of the company; "but I wish that fellow would shut the door; he must think that we were all raised in a saw-mill, and then he looks so peert whenever he comes in."—"Poor fellow!" ejaculated one who had not yet spoken, "he is considerably troubled with youngness."

"From the eastern side, stranger?" said another to me, "I am told it's tolerable frog pasture. Now here the soil's so deep one can't raise any long sarce—they all get pulled through the other side. We can winter our cows, however, on wooden clocks, there's so many Yankees among us," &c.

A scattering conversation was kept up in similar quaint expressions for some time; but as Mr. Hackett has already given the cream of western phraseology in his whimsical caricature of "the Kentuckian," I will not tire you with enumerating more of those which fell under my observation.

These unique terms, indeed, were poured out so copiously, that it was impossible for one's memory, though elastic as a pair of saddle-bags, to retain them. At last a train and a couple of carioles drove up to the door, and I discovered, upon their bundling merrily into these vehicles, that the whole company were bound for a wedding. "Jim," cried one driver to another, snapping his whip, "let our horses run near the silk." Jim cracked his snapper, and the light carioles taking the lead, the more humble train skimmed rapidly after them: their dark shadows were soon lost upon the moonlit prairie, and the sound of their bells died away in the distance by the time I had regained my now solitary seat by the fire.

I have had but a sorry time since leaving the agreeable company I spoke of in my last. To-day, indeed, the weather, though cold and windy, has been clear. But on the two previous, I rode for the whole time through alternate snow and sleet, which the wind at times blew so directly in my face as to make it almost impossible to proceed. In one instance, while making my way through a dense forest of twelve or fourteen miles between the openings, without a cabin by the way, my horse stopped suddenly, and looking about ten paces ahead, I saw a couple of deer standing immediately in my path; but my fingers were so numb with cold that I was unable to cock my gun, while the timid creatures slowly retired within the depths of the forest. The Kekalamazoo wound through this wood, but the under-growth of timber was so very heavy that its waters, though within a few yards of me, were rarely discernible; and their ample flow, when seen as now swollen by the troubled current of Battle Creek and other tributaries, though capable of bearing boats of considerable burthen, possessed less charms for me than when I first struck the slender rill as it leaped unsullied from its virgin fountain, and went singing on its course. Still it was with regret, when at last ferried over the Kekalamazoo, so long my only companion, that, on turning my horse's head to the south, I took leave of its Arcadian banks for ever. I passed the previous night at the little hamlet of Comstock, where an enterprising young gentleman, after whom the place is called, having the advantage of a good mill-site, is creating a flourishing establishment around him; a frame-store and several log-cabins, with two or three mills, already giving some importance to the situation in a new country. My ride of to-day, having started late, brought me, about sunset, a distance of twenty miles, to the verge of Prairie Ronde; the intermediate country consisting partly of burr-oak plains, broken sometimes by the short round hills I have before described, and partly of broad grassy meadows, running sometimes into marshes, and occasionally watered by some clear stream, whose sandy bottom would contrast strongly with its low sedgy brink. The ground became higher and firmer as I approached Prairie Ronde; and then, after riding for a few miles through the openings, when I expected to descend upon a broad meadow, somewhat resembling the many I have seen in Michigan, fully answering to my preconceived ideas of a prairie, I came suddenly upon an immense piece of cleared table-land, some fifty feet above a pretty lake in its vicinity. The scattering houses around its borders, with the island of timber in the centre and the range of six or seven miles of prairie on every side, assured me that this was Prairie Ronde; while the piercing blast which, as the sun sunk redly on the opposite side, rushed out from his western resting-place and blew the snow-drift in my teeth, made me eager to cross the waste as rapidly as possible, and sufficiently accounts for the pleasure with which I entered this hospitable inn. The collection of houses which stand sheltered by this wood is called "Schoolcraft." The wood itself, though only five or six hundred acres in extent, has a small lake in the centre, and the village, if not the whole settled part of the prairie, is distinguished by the number of fine running-horses, blooded dogs, and keen sportsmen it has in proportion to the population. Fox-hunting on horseback, with full packs of hounds, is the favourite sport; though wolf, bear, and badger-baiting have each their active followers. The soil is so easy of culture and so generous in its product, that the settlers, after attending to their necessary avocations, have ample leisure for their many recreations. Prairie Ronde, though, like all parts of Michigan, in a great measure settled by emigrants from the State of New-York, is said to count a still greater number of its residents from natives of the south and west. The population generally was, perhaps, fairly represented at the assembly to which I so unceremoniously introduced you at the opening of the letter.

Niles, Berrien Co., M. T., Dec. 28.

I have been now for two days in St. Joseph's county, considered among the finest in Michigan; having, since I wrote the above, traversed the counties of St. Joseph and Cass, watered by the St. Joseph's river, which is the most imposing-looking stream I have yet seen. A ride of fourteen miles from Prairie Ronde brought me first to its banks, which, rising occasionally fifty or sixty feet above the water in a sudden bluff, look higher than those of any river I have yet seen in the peninsula. You must already have gathered, from my attempts at portraying Michigan scenery, that neither the grand, the picturesque—hardly even the romantic—are to be numbered among its characteristics. "The beautiful" comprehends them all: and yet you can readily imagine that, that beauty is neither tame nor monotonous which can shine through the dreary months of winter, and make the half-frozen and solitary traveller almost forget its rigours. It is true, that one brought up in a more rugged and broken country might often miss the mountain-tops leaning against the sky,—might sigh for the sound of a cascade, and long once more to plant his foot upon a cliff; and yet, where would the eye more delight to wander than through these beautiful groves, which in summer must stretch their green arcades on every side? Where rest more happily than on those grassy meadows on which their vistas open? These streams, too, that sparkle so brightly over their golden beds, are they no substitute for the rushing torrents of more mountainous countries? or does the lichen-covered crag tempt one's footsteps more than this teeming soil, when nature has carpeted it with the myriad of wild flowers which the summer's sun calls forth? To no scenery of our country that I have yet seen is the term "Arcadian" more applicable, than to the rich and fairy landscape on the western side of the peninsula, watered by the Kekalamazoo and the St. Joseph's.

The latter stream, when I first beheld it was filled with floating ice, which the deep and rapid tide brought down with such force, that my horse recoiled with affright when I attempted to urge him into the current, at a point where an old woman told me was the usual place of fording. A rope-ferry, a quarter of a mile farther on, removed the difficulty; and finding my way along a rich bottom, where the trail was so encumbered with vines that it was difficult, even at this season, to keep it, I hailed a grim-looking Charon, with a shock head of hair, attired in a green hunting-shirt, who was standing in the doorway of a cabin on the opposite side, and crossing for me in his scow, I was soon conveyed across the wintry torrent. The country now became gradually more populous as I approached the village and prairie of White Pigeon. I had ridden fourteen miles in the morning without seeing the sign of a habitation; and as one meets with neither travellers nor emigrants at this season, there is some company even in the smoke of a chimney, though you do not stop to warm your fingers by the fire beneath it. I expected long before this to have fallen in with a most agreeable companion, in a gentleman of the country whom I met with at Detroit, and who is a considerable proprietor on the St. Joseph's. Having a fine taste for natural scenery, and being one of the best rifle-shots that I have ever heard of, I anticipated much pleasure and advantage from his company and guidance through the western part of the peninsula. But my journey through Michigan is now nearly finished, as it began, entirely alone. At White Pigeon, where I found quite a pretty village of four years' growth, I seemed, in getting upon the post-route from Detroit to Chicago, to get back once more to an old country. I found a good inn and attendance at Savary's, and discovered, by the travellers going north and south, that travelling was not as yet completely frozen up. There are a great many English emigrants settled upon this prairie, who, I am told, are successfully introducing here the use of live hedges instead of fences in farming. They are generally of a respectable class, and seem to be quite popular with the American settlers.

The morning was fine when I left White Pigeon to-day; and as the sun shot down through the tall woods, nothing could be more cheering than my ride among the beautiful hills of Cass county. The road, which is remarkably good, meanders through ravines for a distance of many miles, the conical hills resting upon the plain in such a manner as barely to leave a wheel-track between them, except when at times some pretty lake or broad meadow pushes its friths far within their embrace. A prairie of some extent was to be traversed on this side of these eminences, and the floating ice on the St. Joseph's was glistening beneath its shadowy banks in the rays of the cold winter moon when I reached its borders, and arrived at the stage-house in this flourishing town of Niles. Mine host, who does not seem to be the most accommodating person in the world, has refused to provide supper for myself and two other gentlemen at so late an hour, assigning as a reason that "his women are not made of steel,"—an instance of cause and effect which I merely put upon record as being the only one of the kind I have met with in all Michigan. My fellow-sufferers appear to be both agreeable men; and as we are to travel in company to Chicago, the sympathy arising from our present melancholy condition may ensure a pleasant intercourse under happier auspices.

The county of Cass, through which I have passed to-day, has a population of more than 2000, and contains seven prairies of six or eight miles in diameter, besides many smaller ones. They produce, when cultivated, from thirty to eighty bushels of new corn, or forty of wheat, to the acre. The mode of planting the former is to run a furrow, drop the corn in, and cover it with a succeeding furrow, which is planted in a similar way, and the field is rarely either ploughed or hoed after planting. There are several pretty lakes in this county; but it is not so well watered as St. Joseph's, through which I passed yesterday, which for local advantages of every kind, as well as fertility of soil, is generally considered one of the best in the peninsula. I like Kalamazoo county, however, as much as any part of Michigan I have seen. I am now within eight or ten miles of the Indiana boundary, and some twenty or thirty only from the shores of Lake Michigan, having described nearly a semicircle in my tour through the peninsula, including, with some deviations, the counties of Wayne, Monroe, Lenawee, and Washtenaw on the east, Jackson in the centre, and Calhoun, Kalamazoo, St. Joseph's, Cass, and Berrien on the west; and I have not met a resident in that whole range but what was pleased with the country, and I may almost say attached to its soil. The females indeed will sometimes murmur; and in some remote places I have heard those whose conversations indicated that they had not been brought up with the most ordinary advantages, complain of "the want of society!" But even these would love to dilate upon the beauties of the country when the flowers were in bloom. Others again, who had been more gently nurtured, would sigh at one moment for the comforts and elegancies of their maternal homes, while their eyes would kindle with enthusiasm the next, when speaking of the appearance which the woods around their new dwellings wore in summer. Small communities form but slowly in a country where the settlers, instead of gradually pushing their way together into the depths of the forest, as at the Eastward, drive their wagons in any direction a hundred miles through the openings, and plant themselves down a day's journey apart, just where their fancy prompts them. This will account for my so often lighting upon a pleasant hamlet, after a day's travel through a perfect wilderness.

The river St. Joseph debouches into Lake Michigan in this county; and as a steamboat will probably run the next season from the town rapidly growing at its mouth to Chicago, a railroad from Detroit to this steamboat-harbour is only wanting to bring the visiter of Niagara within a few days' travel of Chicago, and carry him through the flowery groves of Michigan to one of the most important points in the Union, and what may be termed the central head of the Mississippi Valley. Delmonico may then stock his larder with grouse from the meadows of Michigan, and Gassin try his skill upon the delicious fish that swarm her lakes and rivers (would that I could at this moment witness some of their curious orgies); while sportsmen will think no more of a trip hither than they do now of an excursion to Islip, Rayner-South, or Patchogue. In the mean time I have secured you the seeds of more than twenty varieties of wild flowers, which I shall send to their destination as soon as possible, lest, from the rapid increase of internal communication, they may lose half their value from ceasing to be a rarity.

THE ONTONAGON BOULDER

Henry R. Schoolcraft

In May, 1820, Governor Lewis Cass of Michigan led a party of scientists and soldiers on a three-month, 5,000-mile voyage around the perimeter of Michigan Territory, which then included Wisconsin. Henry R. Schoolcraft, a geologist from Albany, New York, accompanied the expedition as a natural historian. The party journeyed into Lake Huron, across Saginaw Bay, and stopped briefly at Mackinac Island, Sault Ste. Marie, and then traversed the Michigan coast of Lake Superior. By June 27 the party had reached the Ontonagon River—known then also as the Copper River—the reputed location of an enormous copper boulder. On June 28, Schoolcraft, Dr. Alexander Wolcott, the party's physician, and Captain D. B. Douglass, the expedition cartographer, found the boulder partly submerged in the water some thirty miles upstream. Cass, exhausted by the rigors of the voyage, did not accompany the party that found the boulder; his guide got lost and he wandered in a circle most of the day.

Schoolcraft was somewhat disappointed with the boulder: "It has been greatly overrated by former travellers, both as to size and mineralogical character, but it is, nonetheless, a remarkable mass of pure copper, and well worthy of a visit from the traveller who is passing through the region." It was in fact the largest mass of pure copper ever discovered.

In 1822, Schoolcraft was appointed Indian agent for the tribes of the Lake Superior region. In 1832 he took part in another expedition to find the sources of the Mississippi River. During his career, he published many scientific papers and works on American Indians. The following excerpt from Schoolcraft's *Narrative Journal of Travels Through the Midwestern Region of the United States* (Albany, New York: E. & H. Hosford, 1821), pp. 119–28, discusses the discovery of the Ontonagon Boulder.

XXXV Day—(June 27 [1820]). The river Ontonagon, (or 'Tenaugon, as it is frequently pronounced,) enters the lake in north latitude 46°52'2", as determined by Capt. Douglass, and is one of the largest of thirty rivers which are tributary to Lake Superior on its southern shore. It is estimated to be a hundred and twenty miles long, and has a width of two hundred yards, with eight feet depth at its mouth. Indians say they generally walk to its head in three or four days, but on account of numerous rapids, it is only ascended in canoes about thirty-six miles, and a portage then made to its source, which is in a small lake called Vieux Desert. This lake has also an outlet into the Menomonie river of Green Bay, and another into the Chippeway river of the Mississippi, by means of which the country is traversed in canoes by the traders and Indians. The lands along this river are generally rough and mountainous, until within three or four leagues of its mouth. Its waters have a reddish colour, like those of the Arkansas, and are moderately turbid; among its forest trees pine and hemlock predominate, but its most remarkable character is the copper, which is found along its banks. This has been known from the earliest times, and is noticed by all the travellers of the region. La Hontan, Charlevoix, Henry, Carver, and McKenzie, have successively published accounts of it, which have served at various periods, to arrest the public attention, and to confer a notoriety upon the country, which it had otherwise certainly lacked.

But amid a great many surmises respecting the extent of the mines very little has been with certainty known. To ascertain how far these accounts are founded in truth, and to examine the mineralogy of the adjacent region, was among the primary objects of the present expedition, and on reaching the mouth of the river, the Governor determined to lose no time in exploring it. It was past three o'clock in the afternoon, when we entered the mouth of the river. The expedition was immediately encamped, and Indian guides procured at the neighbouring village, and at six o'clock, we proceeded in two light canoes up the river, leaving the greater part of our force encamped at the mouth. Our party in this excursion, consisted of Gov. Cass, Dr. Wolcott, Capt. Douglass, Lieutenant Mackay, Mr. Doty, and myself, with a sufficient number of engages to conduct our canoes, and four Chippeway guides. A broad river, with a gentle current,—winding course, and heavy wooded banks, with the dark green foliage overshadowing the water, rendered the first part of the tour delightful.

At the distance of four miles we reached a Sturgeon fishery, which the Indians have established in the river by means of a wier extending from bank to bank. This wier is constructed of saplings and small trees, sharpened and drove into the clayey bottom of the river, with an inclination down stream, and supported by crotched stakes bracing against the current. Against the sides of these inclined stakes, long poles are placed horizontally, and secured by hickory withes, in such a manner as to afford the Indians a passage from one end to the other, and at the same time allow them to sit and fish upon any part of it. The sturgeon are caught with an iron hook, fixed at the end of a long slender pole, which the Indian, setting [sic] on the wier holds to the bottom of the river, and when he feels the fish pressing against the slender pole, jerks it up with a sudden and very dexterous motion, and seldom fails to bring up the sturgeon. On one side of the wier, an opening is left for the fish to pass up, which they do at this season in vast numbers, but in their descent they are hurried by the current against the hooks of the savages, who are thickly planted on every part of the wier. The number of sturgeon caught at this place is astonishing, and the Indians rely almost entirely upon this fishery for a subsistence. What is not wanted for immediate consumption, is cut into thin slices and dried or smoked. Canoes pass up through the opening left for the sturgeon.

Five or six Indians were employed in fishing at the time we passed through, and we stopped some time to observe the sport, and had the satisfaction of seeing several brought up, one of which was presented to us. The sturgeon are generally from two feet to four feet in length, and these may be considered as the minimum and maximum size, as they are seldom seen smaller than the former, or larger than the latter. They appear to me to be of the same species as the small sharp-nosed sturgeon of the Hudson; the acipenser oxyrinchus of Mitchill. This fishery is of great importance to the Indians of the region, and appears to have been known to them from the earliest times, and has been constantly resorted to without any apparent diminution in the quantity taken. Henry says in 1765, "that a months subsistence for a regiment, could have been taken in a few hours time." There is a rapid at the spot fixed upon for the fishery, so that the water is not over four feet deep. We encamped two miles above on a sand bar. The musquitoes here gave us great annoyance.

XXXVI Day—(June 28).—We embarked at four o'clock in the morning. The river is bordered with a rich alluvion covered with a heavy forest of maple, elm, and walnut, and with a luxuriant growth of vines and underbrush. At the distance of ten or twelve miles from the lake, a chain of highlands shuts in upon each side of the river, cutting off the bottom lands of the lake, and increasing in altitude as we ascend. Here also the river becomes narrower and has many rapids. At seven o'clock our guides stopped the canoes, and told us that the river above that place, had a great many bad rapids which it would be very difficult to ascend with all the men in the canoes, and that by landing there, we might proceed by a near route through the woods, and reach the mines much sooner than the canoes could by water. Accordingly eight of the party, including myself, determined to proceed that way, while the Governor with the canoes, now lightened of half their burden, went up the river to meet us at the mines. We were accompanied by two Indians as guides, who led us over lofty ridges, gulfs, and ravines, covered with brush or shattered rocks, for a distance of fifteen miles, when we fell into an Indian path leading to the copper. Here our guides sat down to await the arrival of the Governor and party, who were to pass that way. We had thus far followed them with incredible fatigue, owing to the swiftness of the travelling, the roughness of the way, and the extreme heat of the weather.

It was one o'clock in the afternoon when we arrived at this path, and the thermometer stood at 90° under the dark shade of the forest. We had not been seated a great while, when the other party approached, and we continued our way to the mines; but the Governor was so much exhausted by clambering up the hills, which skirt the river, that he was compelled to return to the canoes. We found the remainder of the way, (about six miles,) no less sterile, mountainous, or fatiguing; and reached the great mass of copper, the chief object of our excursion, at an early hour in the afternoon. It lies on the edge of the river directly opposite an island, and at the foot a lofty clay bluff, the face of which appears, at a former period, to have slipped into the river, carrying with it detached blocks and rounded masses of granite, hornblende, and other rock, and with them, the mass of copper in question.

The first feeling was that of disappointment. It has been greatly overrated by former travellers, both as to size and mineralogical character, but is nevertheless, a remarkable mass of copper, and well worthy a visit from the traveller who is passing through the region. The copper, which is in a pure and malleable state, lies in connexion with a body of serpentine rock, the face of which it almost completely overlays, and is also disseminated in masses, and grains, throughout the substance of the rock. The surface of the metal, unlike most oxydable metals, which have suffered a long exposure to the atmosphere, presents a metallic brilliancy; which is attributable either to an alloy of the precious metals, or to the action of the river, which during its semi-annual floods, carries down large quantities of sand and other alluvial matter, that may serve to abrade its surface, and keep it bright. The shape of the rock is very irregular—its greatest length is three feet eight inches—its greatest breadth three feet four inches, and it may altogether contain eleven cubic feet. In size it considerably exceeds the great mass of native iron found some years ago upon the banks of Red River, in Louisiana, and now deposited among the collection of the New-York Historical Society, but on account of the admixture of rocky matter, is inferior in weight. Henry, who visited it in 1766, estimates its weight at five tons; but after examining it with scrupulous attention, I do not think the weight of metallic copper in the rock exceeds twenty-two hundred pounds. The quantity may, however, have been much diminished since its first discovery, and the marks of chisels and axes upon it, with the broken tools lying around, prove that portions have been cut off, and carried away. The author just quoted observes that such was its pure and malleable state that with an axe he was able to cut off a portion weighing a hundred pounds. Notwithstanding this reduction it may still be considered one of the largest and most remarkable bodies of native copper upon the globe, and is, so far as my reading extends, only exceeded by a specimen found in a valley in Brazil, weighing 2666 Portuguese pounds. Viewed merely as a subject for scientific speculation, it presents the most interesting considerations and must be regarded by the geologist as affording illustrative proofs of an important character. Its connexion with a rock which is foreign to the immediate section of country where it lies, indicates a removal from its original bed, while the intimate connexion of the metal and matrix and the complete envelopment of individual masses of the copper by the rock, point to a common and contemporaneous origin whether that be referable to the agency of caloric or water. This conclusion admits of an obvious and important application to the extensive strata of serpentine, and other magnesian rocks, found in various parts of the globe. From a point below the mass of copper, looking up the river on each side appears a lofty range of earthy bluffs, which have caved into the river, throwing down their trees and imbedded rocks into heaps of ruins along the margin of the stream, and exposing their bare surfaces to view. These bluffs may be considered one hundred and fifty feet in perpendicular height, and are capped by a forest of pine, hemlock, cedar, and oak. On the right hand, partly immersed in water, reposes the copper rock; on the left the little island of cedars divides the river into two channels, and the small depth and rapidity of the water is shewn by the innumerable rocks which project above its surface, from shore to shore. The masses of fallen earth,—the blasted trees, which either lie prostrate at the foot of the bluffs, or hang in a threatening posture above,—the elevation of the banks,—the rapidity and noise of the stream, present such a mixed character of wildness, ruin, and sterility, as to render it one of the most rugged views in nature. . . .

One cannot help fancying that he has gone to the ends of the earth, and beyond the boundaries appointed for the residence of man. Every object tells us that it is a region alike unfavourable to the productions of the animal and vegetable kingdom; and we shudder in casting our eyes over the frightful wreck of trees, and the confused groups of falling-in banks and shattered stones. Yet we have only to ascend these bluffs to behold hills more rugged and elevated; and dark hemlock forests, and yawning gulfs more dreary, and more forbidding to the eye. Such is the frightful region through which, for a distance of twenty miles, we followed our Indian guides to reach this unfrequented spot, in which there is nothing to compensate the toil of the journey but its geological character, and mineral productions. Indeed these are traits which are generally found to increase in interest, in proportion to the increased sterility of the soil, and the impoverished growth of vegetable life. And here also the effect of climate upon the productions of nature, presents a remarkable exception. Trees and plants of particular species, are only found to vegetate in certain latitudes, and to be confined to particular soils, whose chemical constituents are congenial to their growth. Every modification of climate has its peculiar plants and predominating trees. Animals also, particularly the herbiferous species, have, in all countries, more or less confined themselves within the cycle of certain species of vegetable productions,—to the grasses and buds of trees to which they are particularly attached, or, they are impelled in the search of herbs necessary to their health and vigour. But the inorganic masses of the earth are confined to no particular latitudes, and are uniform in their composition. The granites, the limestones, the spars, and the metals, exhibit the same characters, whether picked up within the arctic circle, or under the torrid zone. The mineralogist discovers the same external signs and appearances, and the chemist finds the same mineral constituents combined in the same proportions. It has, indeed, been asserted, that metals are confined to particular latitudes,—that gold and silver, and precious stones, are productions peculiar to the southern hemisphere; but there is nothing in the theories of the formation of mineral strata, the laws of crystallization, or in the known influence of climates upon mineral bodies, to justify such a conclusion;—there is no reason that can be drawn from philosophical investigations to prove that these substances may not be abundantly found in the climates of the north, even upon the banks of the frozen ocean. The fact that these productions are more abundantly found within the higher latitudes, does not appear capable of explanation, on a supposed effect of climate, but is probably wholly independent of that circumstance. On the contrary, there is reason to presume that the precious metals may be found in the northern regions of the American continent. Nothing appears more improbable than that the veins of silver ore, which are so abundant in Mexico, and the province of Texas, are checked in their progress northward into Arkansaw [sic] and Missouri, by the effect of climate. This metal is known to be found in association only with certain limestones, schists, and other rocks, and where these cease, is in vain to be sought. Other metals and minerals have their particular associations, serving as a geognostic matrix, and hence rock strata may be considered as indexes to particular metals, minerals, and ores; and the geologist is thus enabled to predict, with considerable certainty, from the examination of the exterior of a country, whether it is metalliferous, or not. Until such examinations are made, we must be permitted to say, that there does not appear any thing to forbid the hope of finding the precious metals in the regions of the northwest, while there are several facts to prove that it is highly probable. It is here that the stinted growth of vegetation, and the rocky and elevated nature of the country, leads us to look for those treasures in the mineral kingdom which nature has denied in soil and climate. In various places have lead, iron, and copper already been discovered, and the beauty of the carnelian, the agates, and the chalcedonies, picked up along the shores of Lake Superior, prove that the hardy regions of the north are not unfavourable to the production of mineral gems. But it is chiefly, so far as actually known, in the abundance of copper that the mineralogy of this region claims particular attention, and the more so, as it is found in the native form. Pieces of this metal have been discovered in various parts of the region, from the banks of Muddy river, in Illinois, to the mouth of the Copper-Mine river, which enters the Frozen ocean. At the latter place, Mr. Hearne found it in his visit to the Copper-Mine river, in 1771, and represents it as in common use for knives, trinkets, &c. among the Esquimaux, the Dog-ribbed, and the Copper-Mine tribes, who inhabit that inclement region. It has also been found in various parts of Illinois, as at Harrison, and old Piora,—at Dubuque mines,—Winnebago lake, on the St. Peter's,—St. Croix,—Sauteur, and other rivers,—but most abundantly upon Lake Superior, and particularly upon the river Ontonagon, where the large mass which is the object of our present visit, has long attracted attention. It is, indeed, notwithstanding the exaggerated accounts, a wonderful mass, and viewed in connexion with the mineral appearances of the surrounding country, leaves little doubt that extensive mines of this metal exist in the vicinity. But to explore it with any degree of satisfaction, a week or a fortnight affords a very inadequate period, while the extent of the route to be performed, and the danger of so large a party's getting out of provisions in a country almost wholly destitute of game, forbids even the devotion of a few days to that object. Having, therefore, examined appearances, and taken such notes, and specimens of the metal as time and circumstances would permit, we returned to our canoes, which had been left at the distance of six miles below. On reaching the canoes, we were alarmed on finding that Gov. Cass, from whom we had parted at the Indian path, at two o'clock, had not yet reached the camp, nor any of the attendants who were with him,—among whom was one of the Indian guides. Some idea of the rugged nature of the country may be formed when it is stated, that they had lost their way in attempting to reach the river, notwithstanding that they were only distant three miles, and led by an Indian acquainted with those parts generally. Night was rapidly closing around us, and after firing repeated signal guns, and sending out in all directions, nothing could be heard of them. The feelings of the party may be imagined upon this occasion, seated, as we were, in the midst of one of the most awful solitudes, and in a region which had impressed every individual with an indescribable feeling, that was manifested in a general anxiety to depart from it. I was perhaps alone in the wish to continue our examinations. At length the lost party were discovered by a canoe sent up the river, setting [sic] upon the shore, and exhausted with fatigue, and their arrival restored tranquility to our camp.

XXXVII Day—(June 29). At five o'clock in the morning we commenced our return. On descending eight or ten miles, our Indian guides stopped on the east bank of the river, to examine a bear-fall that had been previously set, and were overjoyed to find a large bear entrapped. As it was no great distance from the river, we all landed to enjoy the sight. The animal sat up on his fore paws facing us, the hinder paws being pressed to the ground by a heavy weight of logs which had been arranged in such a manner as to allow the bear to creep under, and then by seizing the bait, had sprung the trap, and he could not extricate himself, although, with his fore paws, he had demolished a part of the works. After viewing him for some time, a ball was fired through his head, but it did not kill him, the bear kept his position, and seemed to growl in defiance. A second ball was aimed at the heart, and took effect, but he did not resign the contest immediately, and was at last despatched with an axe. As soon as the bear fell, one of the Indians walked up, and addressing him by the name of Muck-wah, shook him by the paw, with a smiling countenance, as if he had met with an old acquaintance, saying, in the Indian language, he was sorry they had been under the necessity of killing him, and hoped the offence would be forgiven, particularly as Che-mo-que-mon had fired one of the balls. This animal measures five feet in length, and would probably weigh three hundred pounds. The head is small and narrow, with a long pointed nose, and covered with glossy black hair all over the body, except some spots of brownish yellow upon the cheeks and throat. It appears to be the common black bear of naturalists, (ursus niger,) which is frequent in the United States. By the joy which was evident upon the countenances of the savages upon this occasion, it is a rare occurrence among them to kill a bear. But perhaps this animal is never killed without exultation, as it is universally considered the noblest object of the chase. Some difficulty has arisen among naturalists as to the character of this animal, which, although provided with canine teeth, is supposed to subsist principally upon vegetable food. It is, however, certain that it is also carnivorous, and will prey upon hogs and other animals when pressed for food. The Indians say that it is very fond of all sorts of nuts, esculent roots, and wild honey, and frequently attacks their corn fields. It will travel a great way from its den into the pine ridges to feed upon whortle berries, and is also very fond of mulberries, blackberries, and all sweet flavoured and spicy fruits. They add, that it is only in the utmost extremity that it takes hold of animal food, and in a region where its favourite fruits are plenty, will pass by the carcass of a deer without touching it. On the same account it never attacks men, unless wounded, and too hotly pressed, when it turns upon its pursuers with the fury of a lion. On such occasions one stroke of the paw is sufficient to kill their stoutest dogs. The Indians hold this animal in the highest estimation, not only on account of their great fondness of its flesh, but because there is no part of it which is useless. The carcass, the skin, the claws and head, and even the intestines, are all turned to account. The fleshy part of the claws is considered a very great delicacy,—the claws themselves are cut out, strung together upon a deer's sinew, and worn as an ornament about the neck. The oil, is, however, considered the most valuable part, whether kept for use, or for the purpose of selling to the traders. They rub their bodies with it to protect themselves from the bite of the musquitoe. It has the singular property of destroying lice in the hair, and if occasionally used, of preventing their appearance altogether. They also rub their joints with it, believing with the Romans, that it renders them supple. A singular fact is mentioned by Pennant, that the female bear is never killed with young, and it is explained on the supposition, (for the fact admits of doubt,) that the male possesses such an unnatural dislike to its offspring, as to kill and devour the cubs. On this account, the female retires before the period of parturition, into remote woods and clefts of rocks, and does not return until the cubs have attained a certain growth.

In passing down the river one of the Indians had promised to discover another mass of copper near the river, but after landing and hunting sometime, pretended he could not find it. An Indian afterwards brought us a lump of copper weighing between eight and nine pounds, which he said was picked up upon the banks of the Ontonagon. This specimen was covered with a green crust, and not in so pure a state as the great mass above. On reaching the lake we found the wind directly ahead, and were detained the remainder of the day. In the afternoon a council was held with the Indians, and presents distributed among them, and one of the number, who appeared to merit it, constituted a chief by being invested with a flag and silver medal. In the evening, they danced upon the sand for our amusement. I have already spoken of Indian dancing and music. It is perhaps all we could expect from untutored savages, but there is nothing about it which has ever struck me as either interesting or amusing, and after having seen these performances once or twice, they become particularly tedious, and it is a severe tax upon one's patience to sit and be compelled, in order to keep their good opinions, to appear pleased with it.

XXXVIII Day—(June 30). Detained by head winds. There is very little in the appearances of the country in the vicinity of our encampment, to compensate for our delay. A sandy plain stretches along the shore of the lake as far as the eye can reach. The highlands of the Ontonagon are visible towards the south, and the Porcupine mountains at the distance of thirty miles west, appear to rise out of the lake, and imprint their lofty and rugged outlines upon the distant clouds. Towards the north there is an interminable expanse of water, without a solitary island to variegate the view. Letting the eye fall upon the immediate vicinity of our camp, the Indian village appears on the opposite side of the river, and we are surrounded on all sides by a bed of loose sand, which the wind is continually drifting into heaps. There is not a pebble upon the shore, nor a stratum of rock within a dozen miles. Occasional strata of iron sand, very pure and black, are found. An Indian brought me a number of specimens of iron ore, procured at Point Keweena, near the portage, where he represents it to exist in large quantity. The specimens consist of red hematite and iron pyrites. Both these substances are said to occur in quantity on Iron river, which enters the lake fifteen miles west of the Ontonagon. While encamped here, pigeons have been very plenty, and vast numbers have been killed, some with sticks and stones. The Indians have also supplied us with sturgeon from the fishery, both fresh and dried, and with a part of the bear which they entrapped but the latter, being in poor order, and a male, has not possessed that flavour for which young bear's meat killed in the proper season is generally relished.

The weather since our arrival upon the banks of this river has been clear and warm, and during the middle of the day, oppressively sultry. The wind which blew fair from the E. N. E. on our arrival, shifted to the north west on the following day, and has blown steadily from that point without change. The thermometer stood at 91° on the 28th, at 94° on the 29th, and at 89° on the 30th, and the mean heat as deduced from three daily observations has been 80°. During the same time the mean temperature of the water of Lake Superior has been 66°, and of the water of the Ontonagon river 73°.

PART II.

THE GREAT MIGRATION

A SPECULATOR'S DIARY

John M. Gordon

John Montgomery Gordon, a Baltimore banker, accompanied by Clement Biddle, a relative of his wife, travelled to Michigan in July 1836, at the height of the land rush, bought thousands of acres, and established a considerable fortune. He kept a diary—which now reposes in the Maryland Historical Society—from July to December 1836, when he travelled from Baltimore to New York City, up the Hudson to Albany, then to Buffalo, across Lake Erie to Detroit, and then by horseback across to Lake Michigan through the southern part of the state.

Gordon kept the diary in the hope that it "will form a connected narrative of the successive steps towards the formation of an opinion, will shew to my posterity the lights I acted under, whether successfull or unsuccessfull in any Land purchases and will be a convenient mode of informing my friends of the state of that North West country should any of them wish to invest in it." The diary does indeed achieve its purpose; it is an indispensable source for an understanding of Michigan at the height of the land boom. Intelligent travel accounts, of which Gordon's is a prime example, are among the most useful primary historical sources.

Gordon was born in Virginia in 1810; like many sons of socially prominent southern families, he went north to college, graduating from Yale in 1830. After his marriage in 1833, he moved to Baltimore and began a career in banking and law; his wife was a member of the Biddle family, which was prominent in banking and politics. Major John Biddle, the head of the federal land office in Detroit, naturally received him graciously. Gordon's diary, alas, is incomplete. It begins with a copiously detailed account of his travels to Buffalo and Detroit; the edited portion below includes most of his adventures in traveling through Michigan. The later parts of the diary have been lost.

As he forayed across Michigan on horseback on the Territorial Road, little escaped his notice. We find detailed analyses of land forms, travel accommodations, mishaps, all kinds of people, including the Indians. He was present at Grand Rapids during the distribution of payments to the Indians under the terms of the Treaty of Washington of 1836. Of greatest value to the historian, however, are the discussions of land speculation, speculators, and their role in the soon-to-be state of Michigan. Gordon was only one among many land speculators who descended on Michigan during the land rush of the 1830s. Although a speculator himself, he was ambivalent about his own speculations. In 1836, the year of Gordon's visit, the astonishing total of 4,189,823 acres of public land were sold in Michigan. This figure represented more than one fifth of all public lands sold in the United States since 1789, when public land sales began. So many speculators were buying land in Michigan that President Andrew Jackson issued his famous "Specie Circular" of July 1837, which ordered that only hard money (i.e., specie) be taken in payment for public lands. Since many speculators had been buying up public lands with highly fluctuating paper currency issued by state banks, the Specie Circular had a dampening effect on land speculation in Michigan. While Gordon was aware of President Jackson's decree, its effects were obviously not felt until several months had passed.

The diary does indeed convey a sense of the speculative craze that pervaded Michigan at the height of the land boom. Wherever Gordon went he asked what lands were selling for; 100% was considered the minimum return anyone would consider for an investment. The government price of $1.25 an acre seemed ridiculously lower than its true value. Gordon prospered as a result of his investments. He died in 1884.

Modern readers will recognize that "Ann Harbour" is in fact Ann Arbor (the origin of the name is in controversy). "Jacksonburg" is of course one of the early names of the city of Jackson; "GoGwack" refers to Gowagiac. Gordon's spelling and usage have been preserved; some paragraphs have been broken up for easier reading. As mentioned, the original diary reposes in the Maryland Historical Society; the excerpts here are taken from the version edited by George S. May and Douglas H. Gordon in *Michigan History* 43 (March, June, September and December, 1959). By permission of *Michigan History* magazine.

Detroit Monday 12 at night Octr. 3rd: Arriving here at 6 P.M. we put our trunks into a cart and rode in it to the Exchange Tavern, which being full to overflowing we drove on to the American where with much difficulty we obtained a room in an adjoining shed. Having purified ourselves I sent my letter to Major [John] Biddle, who lives in the next house, and waited on us immediately and carried us home to meet a small whist party, consisting of some dozen military & legal gentlemen. . . . The Society of Detroit to judge from what I saw this evening, must be very good. I like the tone of its manners if I have apprehended it rightly, and I attribute it to the fact that D[etroit] has always been a military post. At Major B[iddle]'s I saw a Miss Biddle, a daughter of a gentleman of that name, at Mackinaw, by his full-blooded Indian wife, who is a Chippeway [sic] by birth and disdains to profane her lips with the language of white men. She is an interesting girl of about 16 and is receiving a good education. Her father is a fur trader which class of persons often intermarry with the tribes from motives of merchandize & because white women are not at hand nor suited to their style line.

Tuesday Octr. 4th. Breakfast this morning with Major B[iddle], with whom I passed several hours in conversation. He has been a Land register at this place for some 16 years. The several L[and] offices in Michigan all deposit their receipts here which under the system of specie payments have to be brought down in ox carts over roads barely passable. Drafts on Philadelphia banks he thinks can be cashed for me at par. But the difficulty will be in transportation to the land offices, at which I may take up land. Major B. thinks investments at $1.25 cts. [per acre] are entirely safe, but does not anticipate as large profits as most persons do. He is of the opinion that speculation may retard the growth of Michigan & that the stream of migration may be diverted. But to this it may [be] conclusively objected, that the Lakes & Erie Canal have a natural monopoly of travel for the N. York and N. England redundant [surplus] population. If it is diverted it must pour into Ohio, Indiana and Illinois, which are already thickly settled, or into Wisconsin which is farther in a straight line west & much inferior in commercial and agricultural advantages. With regard to speculation, if it keeps large bodies of land out of cultivation, then those which are in market will have more ready sale.

But mere speculation, generally speaking, cannot hold on for any length of time. If they have bought on borrowed capital, then their investments are not permanent. But in truth every actual settler is a speculator to the extent of his means and buys for the purpose of sale as many acres as he can lay his hands on. And again if speculation is to retard the growth of the state it is only in those parts where it has been ripe and therefore such as are chiefly occupied by settlers must improve faster. In this view it will be my aim to get into the column of immigration and make my location in its track. The Govrt. price of land $1.15 (which should be considered only as the office fee) is so much below its intrinsic value and settlers will so readily give the first purchaser a few dollars advance (having sold their lands at home for $20, $30, $50, & $75) that when the public Domain is exhausted in Michigan, that which is in second hands will quickly be consumed by the increasing demand of an increasing population accompanied with a decreasing supply. . . .

The surplus population of the free states will always migrate to the free states, and they are the finest race of men the world affords for the settlement and rapid development of a new region. They go to the west to plant themselves and their posterity ever & for this reason the growth of the country they inhabit is progressive, destined to run no race of renovation and decay. The population being free may be multiplied to any degree of . . . [concentration]. Having vegetated on the bleak rocks of N.E. they find the climate of Michigan genial to their constitutions and its soil a Delta, and being prepared to make the most of it, in their hands it becomes as productive as the cotton and sugar plantations of the south. The staple products of the North western states make a better return to the Earth. The southern states having a mixed population, most obey a limit in its density. They work upon the system of killing the Goose which lays the golden egg. The mass [southern settlers], regardless of posthumous wealth, strive only to create a fortune for their own enjoyment, and having no tap roots in the soil, are eager to abandon it when the object of their cupidity is attained. They are destined to run the course of the old slave states. Ohio, Indiana, Illinois, Michigan and Wisconsin are to supply them with food and become the grain growing states of the country. Their geographical position, their soil & population destine them to this end.

The population of Michigan in 1834 was 87,263 which is nearly triple the number of 1830. It is now estimated at 150,000 and will doubtless in a few years reach one half million. Ohio is now well charged with inhabitants containing, at a low estimate, 1,200,000, Indiana 500,000 and Illinois say 300,000. Emigration will probably flow into Michigan until something like a level is found and, as I think, even after that. Because of its great commercial facilities, it being a great Atlantic Western state, combining the advantages of both. It has natural channels of commerce radiating as from a common centre and commanding the Atlantic through N. York, the Canada, the southwestern states through the tributaries of the Mississippi, & being surrounded by navigable Lakes has the advantages of the Mediterranean coasts, add to which it is deeply penetrated by navigable streams from every coast which can easily be connected by canals, and the surface of the country in every direction is so level that rail roads may be constructed with but small cost of graduation.

The region North of the Grand River & west of the Saganaw has not been brought into the market, not having yet been surveyed. That which lies below these rivers is represented to be, for the most part, of great fertility, well covered with timber, well watered and healthy. The upper half of the peninsula, as far as it is known, is not favorably described, and, probably, will be settled slowly. Hence a strong cause for the more rapid improvement of the southern half, which likewise being contiguous to Ohio received a large share of her redundant population, for even that infant state has already become, in its turn, a mint shop of nations. Upon the whole I look forward to the progress of Michigan in the race for improvement to be as clear as the sun in its daily course. Other views might be here suggested but I leave them to be noted down as they are proved and corrected by my own observation; those which have been presented shew the tendency of lands in Michigan to attain an equilibrium with those of adjacent states. Improved farms in the western part of N.Y. sell for $50, 60, 70, to $100 per acre, wild lands from $20 to $50, that is, of a choice quality such as now may be taken up in this state. During the morning I held a conversation with a Mr. Misner, a land agent here and gathered from him information relative to the country on St. Clair River, in which he is prepared to make locations. My impressions upon the whole are not very favorable of that part of the state, & I shall take care to be well informed before taking any definite steps. Major B. calls in a few minutes to carry me to see Haskell, land receiver at Saganaw. This has been a very wet day & the mud in the streets from late rains is knee deep.

6 P.M. I saw Haskell. He has come down from Sagana [sic] to bring specie for Deposit in Detroit. There is much fine land, he tells me, still to be taken up in his district, whence I can go to the Grand River by sleeping out one night. He thinks well of the sections watered by the Shiawassa, the Cass & the Tittebewasse; which were likewise recommended to me by Caroll of Washington. I prefer a more

southern part of the state, though Govern. [Lewis] Cass, is of the opinion that Sagana will be the seat of Government as the state is settled. . . . I am still undetermined which land office to visit first. KeKalamazo is said to have been very much culled. Grand River has been the favorite of speculators and Sagana has not so large a stream of settlers setting towards it. Tonight I shall converse with Deacon and determine, upon the information derived from him, upon the route we shall pursue. Grand River I shall certainly visit. . . .

9 P.M. Spent the evening at the exchange with Deacon upon the best route to pursue. He is very intelligent & familiar with the Country, in which he has resided since the Black Hawk war, and does the business of a general land agent for the location of lands. . . . There is still, he informs me, much good land to be had in the Kalamazo [sic] district, which he prefers to any of the others, on a/c of the lower latitude, the denser population[,] the small portion held by speculators, & the excellence of the soil. He will undertake to guide me through the woods in the selection of a quantity not less than 4000 acres, and inasmuch as he will be a most agreeable companion & I shall be able to obtain much information from him, I shall probably come to terms with him, after ascertaining more about him from Major B. and his other acquaintances. He is the son of a Capt. in our Navy, handsome & about 23 years of Age.

Wednesday Octr. 5th. Noon[.] We have determined to go hence to the Kalamazo district with Deacon and shall proceed tomorrow or the next day to Bronson, the place of the Land office (often called Kalamazo) on horseback, from which point we shall direct our course up the St. Joseph. From the K. district we shall direct our course up to Grand river and down it, if possible, across Lake Michigan into Wisconsin thence Home via the Miss. We have been looking into the stables for horses but can find none as yet to suit us. The road west is so bad at this season that it is desperation to attempt it in the stage, or rather wagon. The passengers walk most of the distance and are repeatedly upset, beside which applications must be made for seats a week ahead. Another wet day. I do not feel my zeal for a long ride at all abated.

10 1/2 P.M. Spent the evening at Genrl. Brady's, with the party I met at Major B's. I made the acquaintance of Major Whiting and several other gentlemen. In the afternoon I called [on] Meredith (a college acquaintance) & Bush, whose sister he married. (Her property like that of every one else has risen greatly in value.)

Thursday Octr. 6th. 2 P.M. I bought a very good looking young

Roan this morning for $92. He is a spirited animal though I fear a little young for hard riding and harder fare. He is a good walker and has a perfectly sound back, an important quality for one's steed in making a journey west. I purchased likewise an India rubber over coat and some other necessaries to protect my person from the weather. An umbrella I discarded. We shall set forth tomorrow if the day prove[s] good. Our route will lead us through Ann Harbour [sic], leaving Ypsilanti on the South. Biddle has likewise furnished himself with a horse and trappings. . . . Our saddle bags are packed and ready for an early start.

Friday Octr.7. 1 1/2 P.M. Gurley's [an inn] 14 miles from D[etroit]. We left D. at 9 1/2 and have stopt here to dine. There was quite a crowd to see us off at the tavern door as is usual at the departure of travelers like our selves. Our equipment, mackinaw great coat, &c were quite a sight. The day rose fair but became cloudy & raw, our horses performed well, however, and the country had too much of the charm of novelty to me to make the ride unpleasant. At leaving Detroit we followed the banks of the [Detroit] river for several miles, along the road which leads to the fronts of many small oblong farms of the old French settlers, which are a few acres wide & run back several miles. On some of them I noticed orchards of fruit trees, particularly some ancient pears, which must be a century old. Turning our faces west after proceeding 5 or 6 miles we struck the River Rouge, a most melancholy looking stream, and traced its course for some miles crossing it occasionally on very precarious bridges. Here I would think the New England migrant might enjoy the ague & fever nine months in the year & the bilious, for the other three. Our general route thus far lay through a level & wet country, in geological character very much like the "Marsh" in Fauquier Co. Va. but much more fertile. It is clothed with a very thick and heavy growth of timber, is well settled & the soil appears to be adapted to grass, in an eminent degree. The road, which was very bad, was thronged with travellers from the neighbourhood, and Emigrants. One Inn Keeper told me that 40 wagons stopt at his house daily with an average of 100 immigrants, chiefly bound for Illinois and Wisconsin. I conversed with most of those whom we overtook and ascertained their departure and destination to be from N York & N England & to Michigan & the two states named above. Wayne C. contains about 25000 inhabitants, being the oldest settlement & the most populous county in the state. I should suppose it to be unhealthy.

Plymouth. 6 1/2 P.M. 26 m. We have just reached this little

viliage [sic] which is situated at 4 cross roads, contains about 50 or 60 houses, 300 inhabitants and is 7 years old. For the distance of 20 miles our route led us over the worst road imaginable, what to the emigrant must be a "slough of Despond" and through the same level, heavy timbered land described this morning. The soil contains a large proportion of clay and while it holds water on its surface long, has no inclination to give current to its streams. . . . The soil, as may be supposed, is admirably adapted to the growth of grass, which springs up spontaneously in great luxuriance when the trees have been cut away, and, near the road, several of the cultivated species are to be discovered, which have doubtless been transplanted in a measure by the food & manure of horses. . . .

The country has been settled some ten years and land near the road is worth, improved $20 to 25, and wood $10 to 15. Six miles from this place, we left the heavy timber and passed into a sandy soil with light oak woods. The soil is like the Rappck. [Rappahannock River in Virginia] bottoms, of fair quality, but with too large a dose of sand, perhaps. . . . The settlements on the road are quite frequent. I was informed to day by an intelligent man, with whom we rode for an hour, that he took up public lands [at $1.25 an acre] 5 years since, nine miles from Ann Harbour (which we pass through) and now would not be willing to sell them under $30 per acre. We had delicious potatoes and butter for our supper. Opposite me at the table I recognized some emigrants who were passengers in the Michigan. They are going to Chicago & take out with them improved breeds of cattle, hogs, fowls, to establish a grazing farm. The stock go around by steam boats. . . . Few get through without accidents to their wagons or horses. The women and children walk the greater part of the way. We passed, six miles from Detroit, a young man & wife travell[ing] in a covered two horse wagon, who were laid up by a broken wheel. . . . They were very young, just married, of highly respectable and refined appearance and were giving up a comfortable life & agreeable establishment in N. York (city) for a farm near Chicago. . . . I saw not one stone of any size between this place and D, the want of which will render Turnpikes very expensive, if not impracticable, though on the other hand the perfect level of the Country adapts it to the construction of Rail Roads. It is to become the Goshen of Michigan. A rail Road is under construction from D. to the mouth of St. Joseph's River, of which 30 miles are to be in operation next Spring. This will be a great facility to the traveller. The country immediately around this place is heavily wooded. Lots in the village of 1/4 acre each sell for $100 to

$500. Every person with whom I converse tells me that govrt. lands well selected must rise 50 to 100 percent per annum. . . . The timber we saw today consisted of oak, walnut, hickory, wild poplar, sugar tree, &c &c all of very large growth and clothed with the resplendent hints of autumn. Henceforward we traverse the region of Oaks which now becomes the predominating tree until we reach the Lake.

Satr. Octr. 8th. Prays [an inn] 6 miles. We arose at 5 & have stopt here to breakfast. I slept last night in an open garret under a crack and awoke with a stiff neck. Cloudy. We have had bad roads again and passed through a region heavily timbered, with frequent clearings on the road. Oaks of the circumference 9 to 15 feet abound in the forests. Such are their dimensions generally to Detroit. I remarked this morning some of the largest Black Walnut I have ever seen. The soil appears to be very fertile and a little more clayey from its proximity to a water course. Having stopt at a farm house to procure a glass of new milk (the water is all Limestone and creates a thirst) I was informed by the owner that he had bought the 80 acres on which he lives 2 years since at $15 per acre. It has few improvements but has been cultivated some 15 years and seems to be very rich. Marl abounds through the county and state generally of so pure a quality that it is used for lime. We have seen very little stone yet. The surface of the earth is becoming more rolling. This Inn is full of Emigrants and their children are crowding around me while I write with the rabid curiosity of genuine Yankeys. The men are prying into my saddle bags & the pockets of my Mackinaw. This is a substantial 2 story brick house, a rare thing in the interior, as the soil contains lime which when burnt slacks and destroys the Brick. Hence, being without stone likewise, the architecture of Michigan must in great degree be confined to wooden materials. The Land lord tells me he entertains about 50 emigrants a day and lodges about 30. Taverns occur at short intervals and there is another main route west parellel [sic] & a few miles south of this, on which the travel is reported to be greater. These data will enable us to form some idea of the amount of Emigration pouring into this part of the state. Beside which there are other streams setting up to Grand River and Sagana. When the obstacle of impassable roads (at certain seasons) is overcome by rail roads and canals, what an inundation of population will sweep over the state? A National Territorial Road is under construction from Detroit to the mouth of the Grand River, commenced by the Genrl. [i.e., federal] Govrt. It will be a fine highway when finished, and the canal which is projected from the falls of that River to D. will bring all that fine country under rapid settlement. . . . Land here is worth cultivated $20 & woods $10. Settlements had penetrated but a few miles from D. and the belt of wet land described had given a character to the whole interior, which with the ignorant and unfavorable account of the Indian traders prevented emigration from extending westward. No sooner how[ever] was this barrier passed and the excellent quality of the soil beyond it ascertained than a torrent of population poured in, which is rapidly covering the whole face of the state.

Lima[,] 17 m. from Prays 3 P.M. Stimson's[.] We dine here. This house is kept by an Englishman and was a favourite stopping place to the traveller whose daintily fed horse could not eat prairie or wild hay he being the only cultivator of tame grass, this side of D. 3 or 4 years since. He still keeps up the sign "English Hay." . . . We passed through Ann Harbour, where we stopt 1/2 hour. The country to that place is a little rolling for the first few miles from Prays, and then the Oak openings begin. They are clothed with a thin growth of large Brash White Oak, & some Burr Oak at long intervals (say 30 or 40 feet) with an undergrowth 5 or 6 feet high which has the appearance of being annually burnt down, as I am informed it is. This periodical burning of the woods produced what is called "oak openings" on the beauty of which the Western tourist is so fond of enlarging. The larger & hardier trees being alone spared and all the dead wood & undergrowth consumed, it assumes the appearance of a grove carefully kept near a gentleman's residence and it is difficult to divest yourself of the impression that you are approaching a stately mansion through a stately forest. It thus has the charm of inviting the traveller still on, and if he has a lively sensibility to the softer beauty of natural scenery he may wander from rise of moon to set of Sun in these arcadian regions in groves of Oaks. . . . The Burr Oak is a variety I have never seen before. . . . It is very like the pear tree about the same size, an excellent wood for burning & agricultural purposes and when constituting the sole growth is an infallible indication of the very best quality of soil. They are preferred to any other species of Land and are hard to be obtained now, having been generally taken up. Oak opening grow at wide intervals, like a regularly planted orchard; they generally have no undergrowth, except grass, though doubtless the ground must be full of rootes, whose tops are kept down by the annual fires, and hence, when guarded from conflagration, having such a strong hold in the soil, these invisible and well grown rootes soon spring up into fine timber. This process I am informed is going on, as emigration keeps the fires in check, and regions which now are scarce of wood will soon have an abundant supply. On each side of Ann Harbour the soil is of an excellent quality light, a little sandy with lime and resting on clay. The settlements on the road we passed to day are very thick, being in farms from 80 to 200 acres. The buildings are good, consisting chiefly of wood framed Houses one & a half stories high, with good out buildings, all presenting an appearance of comfort and neatness which indicate the occupants to be Yankeys. The travelling today, independently of mere emigrants, [is greater] than in any part of the interior of Va. with which I am acquainted. We passed some dozen respectable looking men on foote, who informed us they were going to Kalamazo to take up land and bring out their families. The country back from the road is as thickly settled, I am told, as that immediately on it. The region of oak openings in which we now are, runs North some distance and west to the Lake. It presents certain facilities for agriculture. The trees are belted in the fall with little labour and the ground being slightly plowed and harrowed yields from 20 to 25 bush. wheat, other grain proportion, and 300 or 400 bush. potatoes. In this vicinity, land is worth improved $25 to 30$, wood $10 to $15 & the settlements are thick in farms of 80 to 200 acres.

Ann Harbour is the county seat of Washtenaw Co. and contains 3000 inhabitants (the county say 20,000). It has sprung into existence in the last 4 years. The Huron which runs by the town affords good water power with which 10 acres sold four years since for $100—last spring $10,000 & could not now be had for less than $20,000. A farm near the viliage sold last spring for 50$ per acre. . . .

Jacksonville. Rose at 4 1/2 oclock, which was before light, and have come to this place to breakfast. It is Sunday morning and the bar room in which I write is crowded with tavern frequenters. I am writing and conversing with them at the same time, putting down such answers to my questions as shew the state and progress of the country. This viliage is three years old, is the county seat of Jackson County and contains 500 inhabitants. It is situated on one of the head waters of the Grand River, which is navigable by boats to the main stream, and carried on a good deal of commerce in flour &c last spring and summer down the river, to Ionia, Grand Rapids, &c. . . . A large farm near the viliage, lately sold for $30 per acre, and cannot now be had at double that price. Improvements are going on at a rapid rate. The country we passed through this morning is rather more rolling than that of yesterday and appears to be more fertile. It contains more lime and we saw many Boulders in spots. Settlements are not so thick along the road now and many of them are in the first state of rude log cabins and we saw, in one or two instances the emigrant & his family, who had just reached their lot. The wagon was drawn up to one side in the woods, the children were gathering the bright flowers of autumn, the mother looking around on the wild woods in which she had been set down and the father and his sturdy sons were making the finest trees for the logs of their cabin. There is something wild and pleasing at thus finding oneself on the frontier of settlement. One of these immigrants informed me that he had purchased his lot (80 acres) last year for $9, all of it in wood without a clearing, but lying on both sides of the Road. Wood land in this vicinity is worth from $5 to $10 according to quality. We had a scant night's rest after the ride of Yesterday. I slept on the floor and contrary to expectation has a very comfortable bed which the Landlady had given me after a little coaxing.

Some of the soil we saw in cultivation this morning was as black, as light and mellow, as an asparagus bed. Such indeed is the general character of that which we saw in this morning's ride. The constituent of lime in the condition of small pebble and sand, by slacking when the sod is turned, gives the soil a very dark colour, which continues to acquire a deeper hue, with several years cultivation. This is the source of great fertility, add to which the quantity of vegitable [sic] and ashes deposited by the annual fires, . . . and you have a deep & rich loam which will grease your fingers, and feels in the hand like a finely granulated brown sugar. I have rarely seen a richer tract of country than that which we are now traversing. . . .

The most communicative & intelligent persons I meet at the Taverns are the Doctors. They lounge in the Bar rooms to converse with travellers, are familiar with all the concerns of the county from their practice, and are thoroughly conversant with its growth and development. Being sociable and in want of the society of persons better educated than their patients usually are, they seize upon an intelligent traveller and ask as many questions as they are called upon to answer. Upon entering an Inn, if I have half an hour to spare, I always look around for the Esculapius of the neighbourhood who is not tardy in presenting himself.

Smith's T. 13 miles f. Jacksonburg. 2 P.M. We left Jacksonburg at 10 1/2 and have come only 13 1/2 miles to dinner. I[t] began to rain 7 miles back and we used our Indian rubber overalls for the first time, which proved to be an effective protection from wetting. They are almost too warm over the Mackinaw. The country continues to wear the same general features, slightly rolling, without anything like a mountain or even a hill. Settlements are perhaps a little thicker. The houses in the second stage of advancement are generally framed and about 25 feet by 20 in dimensions, neatly finished, and in good order. Almost every one is a tavern from the necessity of the case and the regular Inns are at intervals of a few miles only.

I was told by a young physician, at the Inn where we stopt to put on our overcoats, that Jackson Co. has been settled 5 years, and as thickly everywhere as on the road. All the good Lands are taken up. Improved sell for $20 to $25, wood from $5 to $10. The Population, which consists chiefly of Yankeys & N Yorkers (there are few Irish, Dutch, or Swiss) is now about 8000. It is increasing very fast and has received an accession during the last year of about 1000. In 1834 its population was 1865. For the last six miles the soil has assumed a very black appearance and appears to be inexhaustibly rich. It is slightly undulating & covered chiefly with a thin growth of Burr oak openings, which as before stated indicate infallibly the most fertile lands. The undergrowth is a low scrub, the young shoots doubtless of old rootes, which render the ploughing at times not a little difficult and sometimes it has been found less labourious to clear and break the heaviest timber land. . . . Heavy timber land has one advantage, that it can be cultivated in corn or potatoes the first year by merely scratching the surface without penetrating the sod. With this trifling preparation of the ground the most abundant crops are produced. The Burr oak soil has been found to improve upon cultivation and is better the 7th than the first year. It grows blacker and more mellow at each turning, by the operation of the lime. No one has yet thought of manuring. The dark complexion [of the soil] pervades the whole tract south of the Grand River and westward to Lake Michg. owing to the presence of a great quantity of vegitable matter and ashes. We have passed in the last 20 miles many natural meadows more or less rich, some with small Lakes in the center, varying in size from one to one thousand acres, and covered with a tall coarse grass. They are very numerous now, and increase as we approach the heads & tributaries of the western streams. They are often connected in a long stream at intervals of 1/2 mile or more, by springs which run out of one into another and finally discharge themselves through a common brook into some river or lake. The Lakes discharge themselves in the same way and frequently alternate in the chain of meadows. Their surface is a water level, the texture of the soil is spongy & springy as black as lamp black and has somewhat the appearance of a fungus. The sod is tough and will bear a horse or wagon for some time, but when broken through, you sink almost beyond extrication. They are composed probably for the most part of vegitable matter & natural loam with the deposit from the Lakes of which they are bottoms, or which, in many instances, may have been filled by beaver dams. Hence they are easily drained and become exceedingly productive of all kinds of grain and grasses. Timothy soon takes roote and is tenacious enough to drive out the natural vegetation, thus affording great facility to the farmer in the first preparation of his farm, by a supply of Hay & Grass at all seasons for his cattle. The convenience of placing their houses near them, for the use of the springs as well as meadow, which is a universal practice, is doubtless a great cause of the intermittent fevers which prevail to some extent among the first settlers. "Prairie" is a term often applied to these low grounds. Such as are above described are called wet prairies. When they have no outlet, the moisture passes of[f] slowly by evaporation. The soil is friable and inexhaustibly rich. For some time, the wetter class were not much esteemed, but they are now growing more in favour and will doubtless in time become among the most valuable Lands of the state. There are like wise the heathy or bushy prairies which have springs and are covered with small shrubs, bushes, grape vines, &c. and are more common in Indiana, Illinois, Missouri & Wisconsin than Michigan, and the dry rolling prairie, generally destitute of water and almost of all vegetation but grass. These are the most common and extensive; the traveller may wander for days in these vast and nearly level plains, without wood or water and see no object above the horizon. These are the grazing grounds of the Buffalo, of this character is a large part of Illinois. Hence a great obstacle to their rapid settlement. Of the Heathy Prairie we have as yet seen no specimens, but shall as we advance farther West. The dry rolling kind, I understand is not found in Mich. All the accounts which settlers give me of the state must however be taken with many allowances for their imperfect sources of information. They are too much occupied with the urgent wants of the day to speculate or enquire much beyond their own farms, or the adjacent sections of land on which they have placed their eyes as a future addition for a son or daughter. . . .

Marshall, Calhoun Co. 9 P.M. Sunday, 17 miles from Smith's. We have made more than double a sabbath's day journey this day, 49 miles, the quickest riding we have done yet. Part of it was performed in the dark. We are in a comfortable Inn, our horses well stabled (I always look to them first) and while supper is making ready I write up my journal. From Smith's to within a few miles of this place, the settlements are thin. The soil continues to be very fertile, a black loam about 18 inches deep, reposing on a bed of clay. Three years since there were no settlements 6 miles this side of Smith's. Now there are houses every 1/2 mile and farms on the road are worth from $15 to $20 [per acre]. But little land remains unlocated in this county which is 24 by 30 miles and contains 720 square miles or 460,800 square acres. Marshall contains about 1000 inhabitants, is two years old and is rapidly improving. Town lots of 4/5 acre sell for from $100 to $500. The Detroit and Maumee railroads are to pass through it and the citizens expect it will be the seat of Government, for that reason, & because it is nearly the center of population. I have not seen the viliage except on the street by which we entered, it being quite dark at our arrival. It appears, however to be finely situated on a plain, and is on the Banks of the Beautifull KeKalamazo. The County of Calhoun contains upwards of 3000 persons having doubled in population last year. Taken generally, its soil is better than Jackson County. This afternoon I saw a prairie Hen, sitting on a bough of the tree near the road a[nd] was able to examine it for 5 minutes. A flock of a dozen afterwards flew from the woods over our heads to the level ground near the KeKalamazo, while we were standing on a bridge across the stream which we had dismounted and turned the road to cross. The waters of the river at this point were beautifully clear, 40 feet wide or more, 2 or 3 feet deep, and quite rapid, affording probably good water power. Deacon says that purchases of farms second hand are better than Govrt. land to one residing on the spot, because they can be turned over often in a year and are a cash article always. When situated on or near the road, there are numbers of emigrants who from various causes, fatigue [sic], sickness of families, despondency of wives at the toil of a larger journey, &c &c are ready to fix themselves on a farm which is partly under way & they will pay a few dollars per acre more, rather than go farther with the uncertainty of supplying themselves so well or so soon with a home. . . . Few Emigrants were on the road today, being Sunday. They stop to refresh their horses, as well as to observe the sabbath, which is so strict a regulation in N. England. Land hear here is worth with the usual improvements, of log houses, from $25 to $30, and produced 20 to 40 bushels of wheat to the acre and the other crops in proportion. A Market for everything exists on the spot and will until this immense stream of emigrants ceases. They pass through like an army of Locust[s] and eat up everything before them. I must retire after supper to prepare for an early rise; tomorrow we shall reach Bronson. . . .

Monday Octr. 18th[.] 8 1/2 A.M. 7 miles from Marshall. The first 3 miles of this morning's ride were thinly settled, the last four, more thickly. . . . The [oak] openings present great facilities for roads especially rail roads, and indeed you may at almost every point drive a coach & four for miles through them in every direction. They embrace a large part of the western half of Michigan, extending to the shores of L. Michigan with occasional intervals of heavy timber & northward to Grand River. How much farther they run in that direction is not ascertained.

There are three main Roads through the state E & W. viz, that which we are travelling, the one which is parallel & pass through Ypsilanti to Chicago and the territorial road, which is to terminate at the mouth of the Grand River, beginning in Detroit. The worst part of all of which Roads is that passing for 20 miles through the Belt of wet timber land which runs North and south of the length of the state and skirts Detroit. . . . 2 P.M. 15 miles f. Breakfast[.] The country for two miles after Breakfast was rolling and of equal fertility with the region behind us. We crossed the KeKalamazo where there is a mill race to conduct the water to Battle Creek. They have a fall of 7 feet which is very valuable. On this side of the river in the bottom I noticed the colour of the soil and the wet places, indications of Iron ore. On ascending the high ground a beautifull view, took us by surprise; Prairie Gogwack lay before us in our path. Deacon had not apprised us that we were near it; It is the first dry prairie we have seen and is of a regular shape, one mile long and 2 wide, a dead level and fringed with beautifull oak openings. The whole is under cultivation, being laid off in half a dozen farms. The soil is black, as rich as fat, and light and friable as an old asparagus bed. . . . Only four years since it was taken up and cannot now be bought under $25 per acre. Deacon tells me, it is too rich for wheat which it does not produce as well as the Burr Oak openings, but throws up the most luxurious crop of straw. It is however the best of all soils for corn, potatoes, oats, &c. It seized upon my imagination more than any place yet seen and I drew up my horse and lingered half an hour to admire it and cross question a farmer who was ploughing near the road. These prairie farms often produce a second & even third volunteer crop of wheat which yield as much as the fair sowing, & without any cultivation. . . . I have no time to say anything about the origin of these prairies; farther than to say that they are, in my opinion made by fires. They are numerous in the western part of the state, south of Grand River and East [sic] of Jacksonburg. . . . They are the first lands taken up from the facility with which they are cultivated and their great fertility; though some emigrants prefer heavy timber, the soil of which they think is good, and the timber will [be] very valuable when it comes to be scarce. Near Bronson are Gull and Grand Prairie, and not far from the s.w. corner of Kalamazo county is situated Big Prairie Round, containing some 10,000 acres, surrounded with fine timber, containing in its center a body of 600 acres in wood the center of which again is a small clear lake full of fish. Of this prairie, or little Prairie Round near it, I have recd. the following account. When Emigration began to discharge itself some few years since, into Kalamazo & adjoining counties, two emigrants were informed by the Indians, that there was a large prairie about 30 miles back in the woods. (These prairies were the grounds on which the Indians raised their corn.) They started on horseback in search of it & having proceeded as far as they could go in that way spauseled their animals where there was good grass, put bells on them and continued on foot. In a few days they discovered the prairie and secured a large slice of it (by squatting with their friends, I suppose).

From GoGwack we passed into oak openings again of the most beautifull growth & finest quality of soil which continued to this place. One mile back we passed a school selection of very fine quality, which I am told is the character of all of them. It is somewhat singular and the fact is no mean proof of the excellence of the soil of Michigan in general. It seems that the General Government gave to the state every 36th section for a school. The counties are laid off into townships 6 miles square, and these again into miles square, which are numbered from 1 to 36. No. 16, the center section, belongs to the school fund and what is a most singular and fortunate coincidence there is hardly a number 16 in any of the counties which is not first rate soil, although located at random. Beside this liberal provision for education, the Genrl. Govrt. has given to the state 70 sections (first choice) for the founding & endowment of an university, all of which have been judiciously located by the commissioners, on prairies, town sites, meadows, &c and at present prices are estimated to be worth several millions of dollars. Twenty sections remain to be located. . . .

Bronson. 6 1/2 P.M. 11 miles from Earl's & 132 from Detroit. We made 32 miles today. We put up at Hawlys. For the distance of two miles from Earls our route lay through Oak openings, undulating, but of an excellent quality and thickly, though newly settled. We then crossed the Kalamazo where it was about 15 yds wide & came to a small prairie stretching along the Banks of the river & containing say 500 acres of a dark mellow could many inches deep, level & capable of the easiest cultivation. After passing the prairie we came through a fine piece of level timbered land and along the side of Comstock's farm which contains 1200 acres, was located by him four years since & would now sell for $30 per acre. It has water power and lies along the Kalamazo. . . . From his farm we followed the banks of the river to this place. Bronson is now the site of the Land office for Kalamazo district which was transferred from White Pigeon 3 years since and at the same time had another carved out of it which situated in Ionia Co. on the Grand River.

Tuesday Octr. 11th. 8 P.M. Rose early. After breakfast we walked around the town and looked over the maps with Deacon who pointed out the parts of Van Buren & Berrien Counties to which we shall direct our attention particularly. I have provided myself with a set of maps for Kalamazo, Jackson, Van Buren, Berrien & Alleghan Counties. These maps are printed on a large scale being copies of the actual surveys of the counties, and shew the sections, small runs, lakes, ponds, marshes, &c; so that by knowing your position in the woods, you readily ascertain by an inspection of them, what obstacles you are to encounter or what Land marks you are to meet in any one direction. These surveys however are made in the winter & thus much bog & swamp being frozen escapes observation. However they are correct for all usefull purposes. In the after noon I went to the registers office and got the Clerk to mark off, as he is in the habit of doing, all sections of land and parts of sections which are located, that I may examine such only as are not taken up. This he does in red ink with the letter S for sold. The sections are divided first into quarters[,] these into halves[,] which make Eights, and the Eights again in halves which make sixteenths which last is the smallest subdivision containing forty acres. But none but an actual settler can enter less than one eighth[,] i.e. an 80 acre lot. By overlooking the Clerk in the operation, I got a good idea of the run of the settlements & state of the counties and thus became more familiar with these Points, than a week's conversation would have made me. Beside which, I thereby, picked up many hints from the cause of why certain districts are more or less cut in upon. I sat with him 3 hours. He is to copy for me the surveyors notes of all the sections and parts of sections unlocated, by aid of which I shall obtain very accurate information so far as their observations can be relied on, as to the quality of soil, growth of timber, level, water &c. I brought letters from Major Biddle to the Cashier of the Bank at this place and to the Register & Receiver, Messrs. Edwards & Sheldon. The C[ashier] thinks I can raise specie [i.e., coin] or its equivalent by a draft from Detroit on the receiver here. I have $8000 in treasury receipts. I had a long conversation with Sheldon last night. Like every one else he thinks things are in the full tide to fortune and investments in Public Land certain in a few years for 300 or 400 pr. ct. He himself has made a large fortune. Hammond is the name of the cashier, who I find has just been appointed and came up the lake with me from Buffalo. This place has been settled three years and now contains 1500 to 2000 inhabitants. Land in this vicinity is worth $15 to $20 in farms. We are lodged in a small room with two beds, Clem & I together. Our tavern is two stories, and 7-feet long with a proportionate depth. The stabling is good. We shall leave in the morning for the mouth of the St. Joseph looking at lands on the Right & Left as we go and return from which I shall make my selections. My maps enable me to see at a glance what lands are vacant and we have only to ride over and choose those which please us. The Land office at each place consists of two departments, the Register who enters your name & numbers & the receiver who takes the pay & gives you yr. duplicates which you hold as evidence of title until the patent issues. From the accumulation of business they are said to be three years behind at Washington in the business of the Land Department, but a late reorganization of it by Congress will soon bring up the patents to the pace of sales. . . .

Freeman's. 8 P.M. 26 miles from Bronson. Left Bronson at 10 A.M. taking a snack of arrow roote & milk at Fayette 16 miles from B. About 6 miles from B. we passed through a body of Land containing 4 or 5 sections which are still unlocated in Town 2 N of Range 12 West viz sections 31, 32, 33, 34, 27, 28, 39, 21, part of some of which have been entered. The road passes through [section numbers]. . . . Heavy timber may be had within a few miles on the Pawpaw. I am partial to heavily timbered land and have a good deal before me to make selections from. We examine these sections farther on our return. There is good water power at Fayette (a city in the germ) on the Pawpaw, which stream waters some fine timbered Lands. . . . We have put up for the night at Freemans[,] a log hut, of three rooms on the edge of a beautifull sheet of water, with a gravelly shore, and luxuriant border of wood, and abounding, as my host informs me, with a variety of good fish, a sweet position for a house. The canoe has floated off else we would have had a trial at spearing fish, the usual mode of catching them. . . . The vicinity has been settled about one year, and wood lands are now held at $5 per acre as our Landlord informs me. I tasted the Lake white fish to night salted, of which such quantities are caught and cured at Detroit, Mackinaw, &c. It is very white, of a most delicate flavor and in every respect superior to our shad of the Potowmack [sic] & Rappahannock. I have a nice mahogany table on which to write my journal while Deacon is talking to one of the neighbours, a late settler who having no family boards with Freeman. He states that the neighbouring forest abound in game, deer, Turkeys &c. Tomorrow we diverge from the road north and south to look at some unlocated sections. Clem has had a raging tooth ache all day and suffered much from the ride. . . .

I have not yet mentioned my equipment for travelling. In my saddle bags, I carry my wardrobe consisting of 3 shirts, 1 do flannel, 1 pr drawers, 3 do socks, 4 hnks, shaving apparatus, medicine, spring lancet, bandages, lint, . . . maps, 1 pack of playing cards, a pound cannister of arrow roote, some cakes of cocoa &c. I wear a coarse hair cap, a Blanket great coat, stout trousers & bootes, gaiters, and indian rubber over all, very light and strapped behind the saddle, likewise a small tin cup to boil my arrow roote in. In my pocket I keep a screw top inkstand, hair brush & comb, and blank book. In a second fob I carry my compass, an indispensable article in the woods. By the By mine is a very bad one, there being none good in Detroit and I neglected to take one with me which I had bespoken in Baltimore. These particulars may be amusing to my posterity at some future day, should my investments turn out well, and I am inclined to think that the foundation of a fortune may be made now, as was in the settlement of Va., on a small capital, with this diff. that it ripens to maturity in a few years in Michg. &c whereas several generations passed away in Va. before those large bodies of land were productive to the holders.

There is a party of half a dozen wagoners eating supper in the room where I write who have just come in and are discussing prices &c. There was no road along here a twelve month since & the first wagon which came in to St. Joseph across the country was looked upon as a great curiosity. The accession to our party for the night has made the sleepers outnumber the Beds and our landlord has inquired of Biddle whether he objects to sleeping upstairs with a strange gentleman who has retired & whom he will find very agreeable. Had Clem been a maid he would not have felt or expressed more astonishment at the proposition. We arrange the matter, however, by having a bed spread on the floor for Deacon & Clem & I [to] sleep together.

I have not mentioned . . . how one finds his position in the woods and identifies the section he wishes to locate. It is thus. The state is surveyed & laid off into square miles, which are designated by townships running north and south of a base line passing through the center and by ranges running East & West of a certain meridian. The meridian & base line are equivalent to a parallel of latitude & meridian of Longitude and a particular section is read thus, viz. Town 1 North of Range 2 West section 25—and so on of the subdivisions of each section. The sections are numbered from one to 36 which compose a Township of six miles square. The 4 sides of sections are marked by blazed trees and the corners, where of course 4 sections meet, have 4 trees numbered within the Range, Town ship & Number of each section respectively—so that by following a line to a corner, reading the numbers on each tree and comparing them with Yr. farmers map, or map got at the [land] office, you ascertain your latitude & longitude. . . .

4 P.M. St. Joseph. . . . We arrived here at 11 1/2 A.M. Our route lay through heavily timbered land and in part through Oak openings. The road was muddy & deep in some places, being still quite new. Along its edge D. pointed out some bodies of woods which has been taken up and are owned by a person named Johnson from Connecticut, a young man, on which he could now realize an advance upon the cost of several hundred percent. All the land on the road has been taken a year since. As we approached the St. Joseph River, we passed through an extensive meadow over a corduroy road. The meadow is owned chiefly by the university [of Michigan] and will some day be valuable for its Hay which will find a market in the Town of St. Joseph or can be readily shipped to the town on the Lake. It lies between the Pawpaw & St. Joseph [rivers].

On the edge of the woods, sitting on the blasted top of a huge oak we saw a pair of gigantic Eagles which I endeavored to approach, but found the ground too wet to bear my horse. These enormous birds, probably, often cross the lake, 60 or 70 miles wide, at a flight and visit now and then the distant shores of Lake Superior. We cross the St. Joseph in a ferry boat. A bridge is now going up, on which the Detroit Rail Road is to run. The view of the Lake is charming, being still rough from the recent storms, which swept every sail from its surface, it chafes the shore like the ocean at Nahant or Long Branch. We are in a very good hotel on the Hill (the town is situated in part on a high & level Bluff) and see below us on the beach the steam Boat Milwaukie (I think) blown high and dry, and another large vessel aground within a few yards of the shore, but within the mouth of the river. After dinner at the Mansion House where I met some persons (whom I was introduced to in New York) we walked down the bluff

1/2 a mile to Deacon's cottage which he keeps, merely for the use of a private room and a bed, for the months that he remains here. The viliage, it is to be observed, is laid off into lots for a mile, perhaps, back into the original forest. About 150 acres, perhaps, are cleared, on which many very comfortable two story frame houses painted white & in the New England style are built or finished. D. has a beautiful Turkey carpet on his floor sent to him by his father, Capt. Deacon of U.S. Navy, and a good glass of wine to give us. We sat an hour discussing a glass or two of it and examined our maps and the surveyors notes with a view to laying down some general plan by which to shape our course when we start into the woods again which will be in a day or two. . . .

After making our memoranda, we walked down to the shipping part of the town which lies under the hill and visited a steam saw mill & freight boat, which were both built by Deacon within 2 years. He has sold out his interest in the latter, and 9/10 in the former. The Boat is a huge scow with wheels worked by a boiler, is now owned by a man named Porter, a merchant, who informs me that it yields a profit of 75 per cent on its cost, about $2000. The mill is supplied with timber from Deacons woods on or near Pawpaw Lake. The last sale of a share was at the rate of $80,000 for the whole. D. assures me that at present prices of lumber it nets a profit of some 300 per cent per annum on its cost, such is the demand for lumber. So scarce is it in the west, that lumber is carried now from the sources of the Allegheny river in New York to St. Louis.

Such is the growth of the west & so large an extent of the country is to be supplied with timber from those sections which possess it, that Pine Lands, for instance, contiguous to navigable streams, must be worth what would appear to be an exorbitant price to one who has not these data in his calculations. I am assured by many intelligent persons that the profit on a saw mill is 3 or 4 hundred per cent per annum. Pine, Poplar, Hickory, walnut & Bass, are the trees chiefly used for lumber, maple and wild cherry for cabinet work. . . . The viliage contains some 50 houses more or less and about 1000 inhabitants. Several vessels are now lying in harbour and there is a good line of wharves on the other side of the river. The Harbour, which is deep, but has an obstruction by a sand bar at its mouth, is to be improved by a government appropriation and an Engineer of the U.S. Corps [of Engineers] is about commencing a survey of it. It is proposed to carry the river straight out by piers, but as it makes a curve at present just before emptying into the Lake, such a plan would throw many valuable water lots in the background on dry land & bring the opposite dry land down to navigation. This is of course advocated or resisted as the interest of the land holder of his friends may be affected. . . .

Saturday[.] 3 P.M. Octr. 14th[15th]. Clem and I mounted our horses after breakfast and galloped 3 or 4 miles down the Beach, which is a fine hard sand but not so good as Nahant for a ride. The road to Chicago lies along the Lake shore and is in some places under water for several miles so as to render the traveli[ng] difficult if not hazardous during the prevalence of certain winds. At this time there is no conveyance to Chicago other than in small vessels which are unsafe at this season, and the road to Galena from Chicago is said to be so bad that I have altogether abandoned the idea of going further west.

The navigation of Lake Michg. is in the present state of things very perilous. The sailors have no skill, the vessels are badly built and when they are overtaken far out by a blow and those ugly short waves, they make one plunge, and go down to the bottom without a moment's warning. There have been many wrecks of this kind within two years. When the vessels happen to be near shore, there is little danger, for the beach being smooth & sandy, in such position when a blow comes the crew run directly for the shore & drive the vessel up high and dry. But, I am told that is a case of constant occurrence for a vessel to put out of harbour just before a storm & never to appear again by the slightest trace. Lake Michg. is very deficient in Harbours, and hence the importance of the few good ones which exist. The mouth of the St. Joseph is of this kind and the town will doubtless become a place of importance. A few years will cover the Lake, like Erie, with Steam boats & vessels of all classes and the borders of Wisconsin & those states which have a footing on the Lakes will begin to [be] filled with a most thriving population. These shores have all the advantages of a Mediterranean coast and it is worthy of remark that nature has made these great Lakes to bend & turn so as to afford the greatest convenience to the greatest extent of country. Add to this the tributaries of the Lakes and their facility to be improved by canals, &c and Michg. in particular from all her advantages of soil and position is to be one of the Granaries of our country. When the rail Road to St. Joseph from Detroit is finished, immigrants will pour in, and the improvement of the former advance with rapid strides thence forward. The first 30 miles of this Road will be completed next spring, if the work goes on as fast as expected. Some ten or 15 years will present the anomaly of a population of labourers with landed estate, all with property of value and no paupers. This is already happening in the southern states, but their prosperity, from the nature of their staple, the character of the people, their kind of labour, &c &c is always liable to sudden checks & great retrogradations. The free states, on the contrary, may be arrested but are not so easily put back in the race of improvement.

The lands at which I shall look near Pawpaw Lake I consider valuable from their proximity to this place. They are some 15 miles distant, have navigable water to the lake and will have a market in the town as it improves, or else a good harbour for shipment. All the lands nearer are taken.

4 P.M. I have just heard from Dr. Abbott, one of the owners of Abbotts Mills, a report that the president has ordered all the land offices to be closed. He heard it at Niles from a passenger who had just come in from Detroit. I do not credit the rumor, but if it be true I am completely sewed up with my Treasury receipts, they are unavailable in every respect. . . .

Sunday Noon[,] Octr. 15th[16th]. Just arrived on our route back. In crossing the Pawpaw, in the boat, my young horse became frightened by the flapping of the sails and was with difficulty prevented from jumping into the River. At this place we take a snack and then diverge from the road on the left-hand into the woods in T4S Range 17 W section 20 (which we are now in) and examine sections 12 and 13 and thence proceed up to town 3 S to look at some sections on and near Lake Pawpaw, on the edge of which we shall lodge. A Rail Road is talked of from this point to St. Joseph as a branch of that laid out to Detroit, the direction of which, however, is not altogether concluded upon yet. We saw at St. Joseph Mrs. Abbott, wife of the Dr. and relict of Captain Helen who was with a body of regulars massacred under the walls of the fort at Chicago, by the Indians, in the last year. She escaped by the protection of an Indian chief who took her into his arms and ran into the river beyond the tomahawks of his warriors whom after much persuasion he prevailed upon to save her life. She has seen many bloody scenes during the last war and has been so affected by them that she is never seen to smile. She is a middle aged[,] fine-looking woman, with a masculine face deeply furrowed by scenes that she has been through.

Sunday Evg. 9 oclock Keyes[.] We are comfortably housed for the night at the cabin of a settler named Keyes who has been here for one year. He is living some 3 miles from the St. Joseph road and has very easy access to it by a road of his own through the woods. A storm is coming on of wind and rain, and I felicitate myself in having a shelter over my head to meet it. Leaving Davis about 1 P.M. we entered the woods and proceed[ed] to sections 12 & 13 which we examined by first running the line between them. They are finely timbered and both of excellent quality. The growth is large poplar, oak, Elm, Hickory, &c some pine. Level & dry but well watered. The soil is doubtless deep as indicated by the growth of forest trees, above enumerated. I shall apply for both sections. They are about two miles from the Road[.] We intended proceeding as far tonight as Abbotts Mills, but a cold rain coming we retraced our course for a mile and are in section 11 near 10. The old man has kindly given us a kind reception, a good supper of milk[,] potatoes and fresh eggs & has turned his horses out of the stable to admit ours. He has cut his hand very severely with an axe, a grievous misfortune to a settle[r] who has everything to make for himself. However he has several sturdy sons, who seem to be smart and industrious. A daughter of about 16 is really a beauty. Indeed I have seen a great deal of that exotic in Michg. They go among the settlers by the name of prairie pigeons.

Deacon has given the old man a story about his being lost one night in a prairie among the saux [Sauk] Indians, and he is now telling, in turn, the adventure of a young man who was lately lost in this neighbourhood, I put it down as he states it. A short time since about day break he heard a knock at his door. It being an unusual hour for any one to be stirring so far in the woods from the main road, he asked who it was before opening the door. Receiving an unintelligible answer, he took down the bar, opened the door & saw a young man of haggard appearance with his clothes much torn by the bushes, & muddy, standing before him. "How are you sir," says Keyes. "How are you sir,"says he. "I see you don't know me." "No. I have never seen you before, but come in stranger and warm yourself by the fire. The young man walked in and began to talk in a style which shewed his mind was wandering. I waked my wife up and made her cook some breakfast for him, which he eat very greedily. After a while he got sickish & faint and we put him in our bed where he laid several days delirious. We attended to him the best we knew how and after a while he came to his right mind & remembered how he came to my door. He said he had gone out 3 or 4 miles with a party into the woods on Black River hunting land. By some chance he was seperated [sic] from his companions and having no pocket compass or map soon became lost and confused. He walked on all day following the surveyors' lines until night when he slept on the ground. The next day he lost the lines, and then he walked on in as straight a direction as he could shape his course. He was now very hungry and eat such berries as he could find. It then began to rain and continued to do so for several days. He had no fire and walked as long as he could to keep himself warm. In this way he continued to wander in the mazes of the woods, shouting at times in the hope of being near a house or some party in the forests, often deluded & led astray by the Echo of his own voice. . . . [He] lost his recollection and has no memory of any thing until the morning when about daybreak he heard the crowing of a cock which he remembers following until he reached the door and then he had no consciousness until he found himself lying in bed. Keyes thinks he must have come 60 miles through the woods over bogs, streams, &c &c [.] The last night he slept out he was within 100 yds of the house, which he could not see through the woods. I stop here to talk to the family. The wind is blowing up a storm. How awful to be in the woods on such a night, with the largest trees falling all around you.

Monday[,] 7 A.M. We slept in the loft last night with the Boys. I closed my eyes at a late hour without serious fear at being awakened or killed, possibly, by the falling of a tree on the roof. It blew a tornado around midnight and, this morning I see many trees with their limbs or tops twisted off. It is very common in this part of the state to have what are called wind falls. That is, something like a whirl wind, descends upon a forest and cuts a path for itself like a scythe through a field of wheat. I heard a gentleman say he was out one night in such a blow, and he was dodging large trees all night which were falling around him, somewhere in this part of the state. Our Host, this morning, would receive no pay. We have contributed a sum which Deacon is to lay out in a dress as a present to the pretty daughter. Keyes has just taken me into a field to show the change of colour in the ground caused by ploughing. The line of the plough may be traced as distinctly as a black mark on the edge of the soil which has not been turned as yet. He is anxious to sell in order to buy more land at Govrt. prices & as I think he has his eye on 11 or 12 which join him. I stop to saddle my horse.

Monday[,] 6 P.M. Beningers[.] We are in the shed of another settler in Range 17 W T. 3. S. section 21. Leaving Keyes, after breakfast, we reached Abbotts Mills (where we took snack) in 2 hours over a very bad road. Abbott & Smith have some 50 hands employed in building a mill &c. They own a large body of land about the Lake which they expect to be the site of a town. The labourers will leave him in a year or two and probably settle themselves in the vicinity. Hence another advantage to adjacent lands in their chance of speedy settlement. The mills are on Pawpaw River and have a considerable water power. Hence too a great advantage to those lands, I am to look at, in the convenience of cutting their timber at the saw mill. After our snack we rode down here and leaving our horses with Beninger walked say 1/2 a mile to the head of Pawpaw Lake, where we found a canoe and paddled 1 1/2 mile over to the point in section 15. The water is very deep and clear and abounds in fish of several varieties[,] viz. bass, mullet, perch, pickerel, &c. The lake is three miles long and 1/3 mile wide in some places 30 fathoms deep, by measurement, and in others said to be unfathomable. After landing we went up into section 10 and followed the creek & line between 10 and 11 up to the corner of 2 & 3, returning diagonally through 10 back to the head of the lake. The land is sugar timber, with large wild poplar, cherry[,] oak &c and thick undergrowth. Even and dry. The soil has every appearance of great fertility. The fractional parts of 10 and 11 lying immediately on the lake have been taken. In them the growth of Sugar Maple is very gigantic and the spot has been the resort of the Indians from Grand River every spring to make sugar. Many of their wigwams are still standing some with all the implements packed away for the next "sap." The trees are deeply wounded & many of them killed by the process of drawing off the juice. A sugar ground is always the sign of good land. The one of which I am speaking has a great advantage from its proximity to the lake which affords a supply of fish & the woods abound with deer. It can be visited in Boats from any port of Lake Michg. up to the Pawpaw; & thence into the Lake through the mouth or strait which connects them. In [section] 21, the head of the Lake approaches within 1/4 a mile of the river with which [it] may easily be united by a canal affording 18 feet fall. Deacon commands this "water privilege" by owning a 40 acre plot through which the nearest & easiest route of communication runs. The shores of this Lake will probably be thickly settled.

Abbotts Mills will create a villiage [sic] around them and to some extent a home market, for produce and lumber. No. 16 a school section has been leased by Deacon for the timber which is floated to the steam mill at St. Joseph. Most of it has been cut down. It was covered with very fine pine, a rare timber in this part of the state. D. pointed out to us 3 or 4 acres immediately on the Lake from which he had been selling pine trees for the manufacture of shingles and had reced. in one year from his share of them $350. There are several cabins within a stone's throw of us on the river, of a very inferior style. That in which we are, is the worst I have yet seen; there is but one room; it is very open & the night is cold. However we have a blazing fire in the capacious hearth and a frank and hospitable reception from the owner who, with his wife[,] is from Monroe County, Virginia. Over the door hangs a gigantic pair of deer horns and under them swings a polished rifle. Beninger informs me that he is a saddler by trade. He emigrated from Va. to Indiana and thence hither 3 years since. On his arrival he had but $2 in the world & the second day ague and fever. He worked on his well days with the lumberers on the Lake at the wages of $1 per day, until he has laid up enough to buy himself a lot. When he finished a house, he was persuaded by his old employer to board some of the labourers, which he did and never received a dollar's pay, being thus cheated in the beginni[ng] out of $275. The produce of three hogs brought him in two years $400. He has lately sold his 80 acre lot at $10 per acre and is about to move. . . .

My feete [sic] are nearly frozen and I must stop and thaw them before going to bed. We are now on the frontier of settlement, there being no cabins to the west & north in this part of the State. The N W 1/4 of 13 in 17 W. 3 S. Beninger tells me contains iron ore. This I shall make a strong effort to get.

Tuesday Morning. We slept three in one bed last night, most uncomfortably, & I awoke with a sore throat and the rheumatism in my Back. We heard the wolves last night howling around us in the woods. They are a great nuisance to the settler in the destruction of pigs[,] poultry[,] &c. Beninger tells me that there were great numbers of them here a year since until the neighbors set seriously to work to destroy them by shooting and traps. Not long since he secured a very large one alive and fastening a chain about his neck dragged him to his house where the neighbors children mustered all their dogs, & set them on the poor creature to worry it. Having amused themselves with its sufferings until they were tired, they left the wolf lying on the ground as if dead. About midnight, however he revived, broke his chain and was heard running by one of the cabins with it dangling about his heels. One settler happening to be up ran out and gave chase following him into the deep woods where the wolf finding himself losing ground & impeded by the chain turned round & in turn gave chase to his pursuer who had quickly to betake himself to a tree. In the meantime other neighbors, having been roused by his cries, came to his rescue and recaptured the furious beast which was forthwith dispatched with a rifle. . . .

Keelers[,] 7 P.M. We have had an insight into the woods today as well as the mud. After passing Abbotts Mills we ran the line between 24 & 25 in R 17 W. 3 S. until stopt by a small tamarack swamp which we went around & struck the dividing line of 25 & 30, following it nearly to 31. . . . The Growth is white wood, oak, ash, maple, &c. No[.] 30 is magnificent Land and the timber, viz, wild poplar, walnut, hickory, oak & beech gigantic. It has a thick undergrowth of grass on which our horses were glad to make up for the deficiencies of their morning's feed. We walked most of the way with their bridles swung over our arms. In 30 & 31 we followed for some time and [sic] Indian Trail, which, by the by, are observed generally to run through the best lands as if the route were selected on account of the deep shade of enormous trees. On these sections the Timber is as thick as it is heavy. The largest trees often touched. . . . The ground was covered with a thick tuft of grass the rootes of which were so matted together as to afford pretty secure footing to our horses though at every step the foundation trembled for yards around. We soon found it impossible to move forward in a straight line and had to pick our way as it opened before us.

After winding about at all points of the compass for 1/2 an hour, we were pleased to discover the tracks of horses, which supposing to be those of some one who had crossed the bog we determined to follow which under the idea of being thus guided by the best route, but having done so for some time we were mortified to discover that we had made a circle & were retracing our own steps. We were brought up at the point where we entered the swamp, on the banks of a small run, in crossing which Clem dropt his saddle bags and got them filled with water. Stopping for a few moments to ascertain our departure & diff[.] of latitude, we took a course due East. For 200 yards we passed through a trembling marsh covered with grass several times as tall as our heads. About mid way we started a Deer. On reaching its edge, we found a creek to be forded. Deacon dismounted and with some misgivings forced Fox, who was very reluctant, to put his sore feet in. He went down almost to the withers & at the same instant his hinder feet sunk through the Bank and thus the poor steed was, as we feared completely and hopelessly mired. The sagacious animal lay perfectly still; had he struggled, he would have sunk out of sight, for we afterwards stuck down branches in trying the Bottom 6 or 7 feet through the quagmire.

We stood for a moment in breathless anxiety at a loss what to do and our sympathy for poor Fox was heightened by the cries of a pack of hungry wolves which at the instant commenced howling around us as if already scenting the poor creatures carcass. It was now growing late & cloudy and no time was to be lost whether we saved Fox or made a cabin for the night. Deacon having first unbuckled the girths of the saddle and encouraged his horse by a pat on the neck, seized the reins of the bridle and pulled his head around towards the Bank with all his force, he plunged and struggled and after a series of the most desperate efforts we succeeded in getting him on the bank again. I would hardly have felt more joy at saving a human being than in thus seeing a fine horse rescued from such a miserable death. Retracing our steps again by a deer path, we were fortunate in hitting the stream a little lower down where it had a sandy bottom and the fording was entirely safe. A few minutes brought us upon terra firma in a fine body of Oaks and we quickened our pace to reach the main road ere night fall. We crossed section 9 nearly diagonally. Just before reaching section 16, riding at a rapid pace, Clem & I being ahead; we came to another small run which having a sandy bottom, we crossed at a trot, and spurring up our horses we had not proceeded 10 yds before both plunged in a springy place up to the shoulders & Clem and I were thrown over their necks. Clem alighted on his head which stuck in the mud & was nearly struck by the feet of his horse as the frightened creature floundered through. We got both through however with no other damage than a full suit of mud. . . . In three miles farther riding we gained the road and pulled up before Keelers. A hard rain has now set in and though the House is full of guests and we have every prospect of sleeping 3 in one bed, yet how much more comfortable than sleeping in the woods without tent, food, or fire! Our route through the woods today was not more than 12 or 14 miles. Sections 10, 11, 25, 13 in Town 3 S. 17 W and 12, 13 in 4 S 17 W. . . . I shall put in for.

Bronson[,] P.M. Octr. 19. It rained in torrents last night and snowed at intervals and though we slept double in a thin bed, I thanked my stars, when I saw them about day break through the roof, that we were not lying in the bushes. At ordering our Horses this morning Clem's was discovered to have cut the sinew of his ankle very badly and to be unfit for riding. Upon consultation we decided to leave him [the horse] behind and to hire another in its stead from Keeler, which we did; but it was so poor a creature than Clem fell behind & has not yet come up. He has stopt I suppose at Freemans or Fayette. From the latter place we came hither by the old road which leads through the Grand Prairie. Having understood that the land office opened tomorrow we hurried on and left a note for Clem at Dodges explaining our leaving him behind. In 18 we entered Grand Prairie which contains some 3000 acres and has a soil in every respect like other prairies we have seen. A large portion is owned by the university. It is all settled by purchasers, or squatters, who gain an easy subsistence by cultivating small farms. . . .

My horse was very jaded this afternoon and could not be whipt out of a slow walk. From the time of leaving Keelers it rained and snowed without intermitting and we had a most uncomfortable ride. My feet were like icicles and could be kept from being frost bitten only by jumping & running by the side of my horse, who in turn was much relieved thereby. The Old Road is more thickly settled than the new. . . . I have not shaved since we left Detroit. . . .

Bronson[,] 20 Octr[.] 5 P.M. Deacon and I were bed fellows last night, the tavern being too full to admit of sleeping by ones self, a luxury rarely met with in this part of the state. This morning we made a copious note of such Land as I shall apply for. I have down about 10,000 acres. . . . Clem has not come up, & I am a little uneasy at his delay. Judge [Epaphroditus] Ransom informed me to day, that marl of a pure kind is to be found in large formations in low Bottoms. In some places it exists in very great bodies, and at one point near Clinton, from which the water has been drained there are 100 acres constituting a bed of pure lime. Prairies he thinks were made and cultivated by the Indians and have, since being abandoned by them, been kept in their present condition by annual fires. We had venison today and magnificent cauliflowers, which grow in the natural virgin soil to the size to fill half a bushel. My horse foundered today!

Saturday[,] 8 P.M. Octr. 22[.] Bronson[.] Clem arrived yesterday as Deacon and I were driving out of town in a wagon to look more particularly at those unlocated sections about 6 or 8 miles south of this place through which the St Jo. road passes. . . . We shall go to Ionia in a day or two and I shall take a portion of my treasury certificates with me, leaving in the hands of Sheldon, funds to an amount sufficient to pay for all the Lands I take up here. . . . This morning Clem and I . . . walked to Grand Prairie to shoot grouse. We borrowed very good double barreled shotguns from some young men in town. For the first hour we hunted without success & had despaired of seeing any game when upon entering the edge of a corn field we put up 50 in a flock which rose up like thunder and lit again within 100 yds. The first three or four shots I only made the feathers fly, but upon increasing the charge I was more fortunate and had the pleasure of bringing down 3 in succession. We followed them up until they took shelter in the woods. On our return we stopt at a tavern and had a bird broiled for dinner, substituting the tongs for a gridiron. The woman refusing any pay I distributed among the children some 5 cent pieces which I got at the mint and which have served to gladden the hearts of many children at the house we have stopt at. There are some Virginians squatted on Grand Prairie. Having no water, the farmers use wells entirely, which require to be sunk some 80 feet. We shall leave for Ionia on Monday. Our Inn is crowded to suffocation and the sitting room filled with stage drivers and citizen boarders, smoking pipes & playing eucher, the national Game of Michg.

Octr. 23rd[,] 6 1/2 P.M. I rode to Grand Prairie again this morning in pursuit of grouse and saw but two, one of which I killed. My horse has recovered from his stiffness and is again in condition to travel. . . . 1/2 of this villiage was sold yesterday for $12,000 (i.e. of the remaining vacant lots.) The Site was taken up a few years since at $1 1/4 per acre and this price would seem like wild speculation. The point however is an important one, on the head of boat navigation of the Kekalamazo. It is the land office, central in its position, where population has some thousand souls added to it annually. If one considers that Michg. has now none or few towns, that its population is pouring in at the rate of 50 thousand a year, that they have been accustomed and must have their villiages, that the soil is of excellent quality generally, it will be perceived that these town speculations have a real basis of intrinsic value & are not like investment in town plats in old states, where the wants of the people have been supplied in this particular gradually with their slow growth. Suppose New York without towns and villiages tomorrow, that they are all sunk by an earth quake. The wants of the people would soon build them up again with great rapidity—such, on a smaller scale, is the process of town manufacture now going on in Michigan. However I shall invest nothing in Lots.

Octr. 24th[,] Monday[,] 5 P.M. Yankey springs[,] 30 miles from Bronson[.] We left Bronson at 7 1/2. Clem on a hired and I on my own horse. The country for 10 miles, until we reached Gull Prairie was oak openings of very good quality. The Prairie contains about 6000 acres of Land[,] 2000 of which are owned by the university. In most respects it is exactly similar to those which we have before seen. . . . A settler near the edge at whose house we dined, stated to me that from his own experience he preferred openings to prairie, that the old farmers on the latter think they begin to perceive a slight deterioration of soil by cultivation, whereas in Washtenaw Co. for instance, some parts of which have been settled 12 years the openings have continued to improve with every crop to the present time. Such observations have been likewise made in Kalamazoo Co., which as likewise as Berrien & Van Buren Counties have been chiefly taken up by settlers.

Grand River District is understood to have been much infested by speculators. In 3 or 4 years my informant thinks, that all the good land in Berrien & Van Buren cos. will be worth & sell for readily $10 per acre. After leaving the Prairie we again passed through oak openings to this place, some very beautiful and rich, but for the greater part more or less rolling, and holding in its bosom many clear lakes which were alive with Geese & Ducks. We have had a delicious day. On dismounting here I had the pleasure of meeting Major Whiting, to whom I was introduced in Detroit, and who is on his way to Grand Rapids to make a payment to the indians north of Grand River on account of their lands the title to which has lately been extinguished by the Genrl. Govrt. It is to be a meeting similar to that held last month at Mackinaw and composed of such as could not visit that remote point. He proposed to turn us aside that far out of our way to witness the spectacle, which we readily agreed to, as we hereby see Grand Rapids[,] a place reckoned of great importance & shall not lose much leeway. Whiting . . . is travelling in an open wagon with the specie which he does not hesitate to mention in the bar room of the tavern. Such is the security from Robbery in Michg. . . . This place is called Yankey Springs by a French settler named Moreau, an indian trader who lives near here, and has given the stand that name in spite of the loss of the custom [of trading with the Indians]. He likewise keeps an inn. . . . Barry County in which we are, will probably become a great sheep pasture; it is too rolling for cultivation. Whiting has a person named Trowbridge with him to assist in paying the Indians, & drive his wagon for him. A drunken Irish Taylor is making a most disagreeable growling while I write & talking to Clem & me whom he takes for speculators, a race particularly odious to emigrants, and justly so, for no sooner has a settler established himself than all the lots around him are taken up by these persons who when he desires to enlarge his farm charge him 3 or 4 prices. It is very cold. I met here an old Gentleman . . . from some part of the state of New York whom I saw in Bronson and who tells me he has been waiting here several days for the arrival of Monroe, a Land Hunter who is to guide him in his explorations in Barry Co. He has already, he informs me, selected about 7000 acres about Bronson and intends applying for about as much more. . . .

Robinson's[,] 2 P.M. Octr. 25[,] 39 miles from Yankey Springs. We are at the junction of Grand River and the Thornapple near an indian villiage, the inhabitants of which, however, are absent at Grand Rapids to receive their pay. There are but few houses in it & those small and dingy, shaped like an inverted funnel. Every tribe varies the style of their wigwam architecture. These resemble tents. They are made by sticking poles in a circle & drawing them together near the top leaving open a small orifice for the smoke to escape. They are covered with bark so closely as to turn the water. There is some fine bottom lands immediately about us. Such sites are usually selected for villiages as their rude architecture is thus more conveniently carried on. The se[c]tions which embrace the mouth of the Thornapple, the villiage and all the fine open land around containing say 1000 acres, have been squatted on by Robinson & his kin, the eldest brother having married a squaw and thus gained the confidence of the poor savages, whose possessions he is already grasping at before they have relinquished them. He lives, usually, at the house we are stopping to dine at, but is absent just now at Grand Rapids to collect his debts from the Indians when they are paid off. His wife and children are with him. Last night we slept in the loft with some 20 persons, land agents, speculators, foot and horse passengers, labourers, carpenters, &c &c[.] Clem and I monopolized one bed. We had clean sheets and I slept very well except being awakened by a cat, about midnight, walking over my face. We started this morning at 6 and reached Leonards at 8 to Breakfast a few minutes after Major Whiting had left. Leonard gave us a good meal which our ride and his very pretty daughter who waited on us made us relish vastly. I have several times had occasion to remark on the beauty of the Michg. Girls. Indeed we have scarcely seen a single young face which can fairly be called homely since leaving Detroit. Our route to day lay through Oak openings of a very good quality with a few rugged points at intervals. Indeed, you hardly see any other kind of tree to any extent, and in a ride of 2 or 3 hundred miles it finally becomes wearisome to the eye. . . . We came upon Major Whiting four miles back. In fording the Thornapple the last time our horses nearly swam. Clem got very wet and I lost my whip. Moreau, the French indian trader (who was of the Whitings party and had rode ahead to prepare the boat for him), stood on the bank of the stream and directed us to the shallowest way else we had got beyond our depth.

We learn here that the Ottawas have been waiting a month, encamped outside Grand Rapids, in daily expectation of the arrival of the Govt. agent. The poor creatures have no other divisions of time beyond seasons, viz. the time of planting, corn eat[ing], Roasti[ng] ears, gathering it ripe, and snow & ice. So they are often a month out of calculation . . . . Grand Rapids[,] Octr. 25. 7 P.M. 40 miles from Lewis' at Hinsdale's Boarding House. We got in after dark and upon much solicitation were squeezed in here. A bed has been rigged up for us in the store. From Robinsons hither we passed through oak openings of very good quality, all of which have been taken up, being highly valued on account of their proximity to Grand Rapids, which, every one thinks, will become a very important point. All the Lands near the Grand River are entered from its mouth to its source on the south side. Those which lie north are in possession of the Indians whose title was extinguished at the last session of Congress. The territory thus acquired embraces some 8,000,000 acres extending north to Mackinaw, most of which is thought to be of a very inferior quality, though very little is known of its true character. It has been explored hitherto only by the Indians who range through every corner and section of it in their hunting expeditions.

Major Whiting and Trowbridge called this morning to accompany us over the river to witness the payment of money and distribution of goods to the Indians. We crossed the rapids in a Keel boat at a point where they are 250 yds. wide and 4 or 5 feete deep. The land immediately opposite the villiage on which we are to put ashore is a high bluff extending for miles up and down the stream and back 4 or 5 hundred yds. to the Forest. A little to the south is an indian villiage containing 200 or 300 inhabitants, who consist chiefly of the flock of Mr. Sater, the Baptist missionary. He has been living near them in a cabin some 10 years and during a greater part of this period had communication with no whites but the inhabitants of Detroit and with them by means of pack horses through the woods by Indian Trails once or twice a year to procure necessities of life at periods of scarcity. His wife continued with him all this time. They have several children. He has learnt to speak the Indian dialect and preaches to them every Sunday. Many of the old men, he informs me, have been baptized and have good ideas of Religion. Slater is a very modest man and of a weakly nervous constitution, yet he has evinced the courage of a lion in thus planting himself, in the midst of savages, hundreds of miles from thick white settlement, without understanding their language and undertaking to teach them a new religion and reclaim them from their Barbarous life. To a great extent the villiage[s] have turned themselves to agriculture, being supplied, latterly, with the implements by the whites.

The high level bluff described above seems once to have been entirely under cultivation. I noticed much marl in the soil, so that, by a kick of the foot it could be turned up at any spot. Along the bank of the river for some distance up were arranged the tents of the indians & temporary wigwams of all who had come from a distance to receive their shares in the general distribution. Some were from the mouth of Grand River, the Thornapple, Flat River, the maple, the looking glass, near St. Joseph[,] &c &c all arriving finally by canoes through the Grand River. We first directed our course to the house of Mr. Slater (which is a good log cabin,) and were conducted by him to the meeting house in which were all the goods arranged in bundles for distribution. None of the Indians having assembled on the spot, Major Whiting dispatched a crier to give notice that he should begin the division in two hours. In the meantime Trowbridge[,] Clem and I strolled up the banks to examine the camping ground more minutely.

There were some 200 temporary huts, tents, wigwams, &c arranged in groups of 4 or 5 near the water, with their beautifully finished canoes drawn upon the sand. Some were crossing at the moment with squaws who used the paddle as dextrously as a ducks foote and passed over the rapid parts of the current as easily as two strong men could pull it through the stiller water below. Others were crossing the shallows on their little ponies riding double and triple. We peeped in the wigwams to see what was going on. The inmates were generally squatted around their half extinguished fires, eating their breakfast of pumpion [pumpkin?] or hominy, boiled. Some were arranging themselves in their gayest attire for the occasion. Several we saw already decked out in all their finery, high crowned hats with cockades & feathers, cloth hunting shirts, rings in their ears & noses, in some instances a chain of them hanging from the forehead down over each eye to the cheekbone, silver bracelets from the wrists to the shoulders & the ankles to the thighs, blue tights, mockasins, much trimmed & ornament[ed] with beads & porcupine needles, a belt around the waist. Their faces painted as if for war. Such as were in mourning for a relative had their features marked with black streaks. The proportion of children seemed great. These latter were playing with bows & arrows and some drew back in sport & pointed them at us when we approached their tents. Near one group of wigwams I observed a long pole planted in the ground with a dead puppy tied to the top, which is perhaps a religious ceremony. Trowbridge seemed to think it was perhaps intended for food as the Indians are notoriously fond of the flesh of this faithful animal. T. has seen much of this tribe, having assisted in paying them for many years. He informs me that they eat all kinds of unclean animals, which they boil in one common pot; often when making maple sugar they will throw a dog into the caldron [sic] and cook their food day after day, thus mingling two operations. He was once in the woods, he tells me, for a day or two without food and came by chance to an Indian camp. Their dinner was boiling at the time in one pot. It consisted of a puppy, a polecat & muskrat. Being half famished he made a hearty meal of this revolting Salmagundi. Many of the Indians knew him and shook his hand with much cordiality. At passing they would salute us with their "Bon Jour" a term picked up by them from the French Trader.

About one mile up we came upon the frame house of [Rix] Robinson, the Indian Trader, which is his store. He was selling tobacco and other articles to some dozen Indians. I have already made some mention of this personage. He is a man cast in the mould of a Giant: well framed, active & erect as a hunter, about 50 years of age. For some 30 years he has been the agent of the North Western Fur Company for the purchase of peltry. During this time he has been stationed at various points remote from the frontier of white population an[d] in the bosom of the Indians over whom he has obtained and exercises great influence. He has taken a squaw to wife, a thing absolutely necessary in his mode of life if one wishes to be married, for a white woman could not exist under the privations of a rude wigwam in a winter of great rigor. He speaks the dialect of the Ottawas, fluently. Near his store was his tent, in which he sleeps, and about it 4 or 5 of his half breed children. His woman was young and very pretty, dressed in the aboriginal style with a half dozen yards of fine blue cloth thrown gracefully over her shoulders. Indeed the squaws give even to blankets, some times, the ease & grace of drapery on a statue, holding it on their shoulders with a lightness & security which a white woman might in vain seek to imitate. Robinson has squatted on an 80 acre lot opposite the Grand Prairie opposite the Grand Rapids under the expectation of securing it at Govt. price by means of a future preemption Law. The water power which it commands will, with its adaptation to the site of a town, make it very valuable. I am informed that if put up for sale the 80 acres would bring $1000 or $1500 per acre. He has planted a brother (of whom he has six) at all the best points from the mouth to the sources of the Grand river, with the view of gaining the title by occupancy. One is the mouth of Grand River, one of the best Harbours on Lake Michg., another is at the mouth of the Thornapple a good point for transshipment, a third at the junction of the flat & Grand, a fourth, I believe, at Maple River &c. all of which are tributaries of the Grand and will become towns or places of transshipment. Independently of these prospects the Elder Robinson is said to have accumulated a fortune of about $100,000 by traffic with the Indians.

At our return to the meeting house we found most of the Indians assembled and the distribution of good[s] begun. Mr. Slater acted as crier, holding in his hands a list he called each one by name in his turn and handed him his share tied up in a blanket. It contained broad cloth, calico, cotton, thread, needles, yarn[,] soap, fish hooks, cooking utensils, such as one bell metal boiler, tea pot, tin pans[,] &c and a few tools and agricultural implements, a coarse shot gun to the men & a $10 rifle to the Chiefs. The savages were arranged around the house in family groups[,] some reclini[ng] on the Ground, others were seated on benches. The children of the Chief were distinguished by more silver rings & bracelets & a better style of dress than the lower class. The majority presented a miserable and squalid appearance, with few clothes except a blanket and in some cases without mockasins. I noticed one old woman who had nothing on but a small thin blanket worn to shreds & patches. Some of the girls, however, were very pretty[.] All had delicate & well formed feet, which their tight trousers shewed off to much advantage. Of the Chiefs there were some noble looking men. He whose appearance struck me most was named Shiawas, from the mouth of the Grand River. For several years he has been victim to rheumatism, which has chained his Herculean frame to the ground. He lay on the grass all the time, and his limb[s] which were cast in the strongest mold rested in the most graceful repose. His features were strongly marked, played as if a little volcano might be slumbering under them. In height, I should suppose him to be six feet one inch. I was informed that he was a great hunter and warrior and was at the massacre of the River Raisin. Around him were arranged his family. His wife was decently clad and possessed a very matronly air. She fed him during the day with boiled hominy and pumpion from a large Gourd with a wooden spoon. Her daughter of about 14 years of age was quite a beauty as she sat combing her black hair which was parted exactly in front. . . . A very pretty squaw was pointed out to me by Trowbridge, who had been the wife [of] a trader or merchant in Grand Rapids, and lived in a comfortable house like a white lady. Upon her husband's death 2 years since she broke up house keeping & returned to her friends & tribe in the woods and now dresses like them.

The next finest looking man to Shiawas, was Win-de-go-wish, about my height and size, a beautiful figure and a hundred times more elastic. He was about 50 years of age. The Orator of the Tribe and noted among them for his singular modesty & diffidence. He had lost a finger. Next was Muc-cut-o-quit, a little inclined to corpulancy and very unaboriginal in his figure, but possessing withal a countenance most strikingly benevolent. I was so much impressed with this characteristic expression of his face as to be induced to enquire particularly into his character. Trowbridge, who has known him for many years, informed me that he was noted for this trait among his tribe, by whom he is reverenced as the best man among them. He suspects him to be the son of a white man, probably some French Trader. During the morning I had occasion to see his kindness of feeling developed. A poor blind Indian was called upon to receive his share of goods and stumbled forward without support amid the shouts & laughter of the whole assemblage (for the Indians are fond of a coarse joke)[.] Some were preparing to play tricks upon him, when Muc-cut-o-quit stept forward silenci[ng] all around him by a look, assisted him with his bundle and led him out of the crowd in the most considerate and benevolent manner. I must not omit the name of His Turkship Cob-e-moo-sah, a sharp featured keen eyed chief of moderate stature and exact proportions[.] He has three young wives, sisters whom he espoused on the same day, and who have presented the uxorious hunter with three young warriors apiece. . . . He has had other wives now dead, whom he probably removed by the sinister influence of arsenic or some other favourite drug to make room in his wigwam for the "sisters three." . . .

I derived much amusement from examining the costume and features of the various chiefs and their families. There was a great and very obvious variety of feature, generally stampt with the strong trace of Character. The wonderfull elasticity of their frames struck me forcibly. The oldest men squatting themselves on the ground would spring to their feet with the bound of a boy. The women were made to perform the offices of pack horses in carrying off on their shoulders their husbands' bundles. . . .

Thursday[,] Octr. 27[.] The site of Grand Rapids was located as long back as seven years by several settlers in small lots and has lately passed through several hands. [Lucius] Lyon obtained a part of the water power from an old French Trader. He has sold 1/2 or a smaller share of his interest to Sargeant, a shoe maker in Detroit, for $6000. Sargeant sold out last spring to Judge Carroll of New York for $80,000. Thus do town sites change hands. . . . Villiage lots are now selling at from $500 to $5000, but its rapid settlement has been somewhat retarded by the circumstance that nearly the whole of Kent County has been taken by speculators who hold up their lands at from $5 to $20 per acre and thus throw back or divert the stream of migration, and on the north side of Grand River about 300 settlers have squatted in consequence thereof. Some of them have gone so far in improvements as to put up mills. They are said to keep a land office of their own in which each squatter's name & section or lot are entered as evidence of title when Congress passes another pre-emption Law, and all persons coming among them are required to join the association. They have caused surveyors of their own to extended the lines across the river of the old survey, so that each man makes a description of his location as exact as those kept at Govrt. Land offices. They doubtless, by this early and close combination, have ulterior views of enforcing Lynch law in case it becomes necessary thus to assert their claims. The Lands on & near Grand River, which they have a thus monopolized, are said to be of very superior quality and, if put on public sale, would bring from $5 to $50 and at some points $1000 per acre. This Point is the County seat and if we consider the navigation and the water power, she is destined probably to become a second Rochester, or a Greater than she. The fall is some 20 feet produced by a stratum of limestone crossing the river at this point. The Rapids are shallow & steam boats will be compelled to pass around them by locks & a canal. . . .

Trowbridge wishes to make an investment in town lots here and will inform me if any favourable chances offer. We again spent the day on the other side of the river with the Indians. They number about 1000. Clem and I assisted Major Whiting in Counting the money which was paid them, in all about $8000, which with the amount paid out at Mackinaw and the value of the presents, makes perhaps the sum of $75,000; this is all they receive for the remainder of their Michg. Lands, in extent say 8,000,000 [acres]! The lots on Grand River alone would bring thrice, nay ten times that price. The Chiefs received $500 and $250 according to rank, as of the first or second degree. The men and women from $2.50 to $50, according to the number of persons in their families. By the terms of the Treaty they are to occupy a slip of land on Lake Michg. some 60 miles long north of the mouth of the Grand River for 5 years and then to incorporate with the inhabitants of the state or be removed beyond the Miss. Slater has prevailed on his immediate flock to remove to the Kalamazo River on which he proposes to purchase a few acres of public Land at Govrt. price and fix them at agriculture. In a few days, he tells me that most of those who are now paid a few silver dollars will have spent or been cheated out of all. . . .

Trowbridge, who is my Cicerone on this occasion, pointed out several chiefs this morning and gave me partial sketches of their lives and characters. Most of them had been present at the massacre of the River Raisin. Among these old Cu-gi-as-cum interested me most. We gave him the cognomen Spread Eagle on account of his roman nose and Eagle eye. His age was about 80 though apparently not more than 60, about middle stature, a face of the sternest aspect marked with a more than usual degree of savage Gloom, with a very compact though active figure. His features were much scarred with wounds. He was decidedly the noblest Roman of them all in his bearing, form & countenance. For many years he was the leading Chief of his whole tribe whose favour he sacrificed by a treaty with the Genrl. Govrt. for the sale of their Lands in the southern part of Michg. The Indians, always averse to a sale, had unanimously resolved in full council, to shoote the first man who signed the Treaty. Cu-gi-as-cum was intimate with Govr. Cass who persuaded him (with the promise it is said of an annuity of $500) to step forward in the face of this threat at the hazard of his life and affix his signature. The other Chiefs were soon induced to follow his example and the lands were sold. Old Spread Eagle soon became obnoxious to many attempts upon his life by poison, a favourite mode of removing an enemy among the Indians, and all his family were destroyed in this quiet way. The Old Chief however escaped all the messes prepared for him and still lives in the daily apprehension of his being daily removed. He has lost cast[e], and seems to hold intercourse with none. His wigwam is near the mouth of Flat River (30 miles above) in which he was nearly drowned lately by some of his persecutors, who left him for dead upon the Beach. The Govrt., it is said, gave him his annuity for a year or so, but now it has been stopped. He did not come in for a full chief's share at the distribution of the money. The census or roll, was made out by Robinson, and many have been omitted by him by mistake, design or misspelling their names. I saw an old woman, whom I mentioned yesterday, with nothing to cover her aged limbs but a worn out blanket. Her name was not down and no bundle had been sent for her. She was a widow without children and thus left to meet the rigours of a Michg. winter without clothes[,] food or any thing. We made a contribution for her on the spot, and Major Whiting threw in an extra blanket and small articles of various kinds. . . .

We shall leave in the morning for Ionia. Trowbridge goes with us. From the window of the house where I am writing, I see by moon light, far across the Grand River, the ancient forests, hitherto the domain of the roving Indian & untrod but by him and the game he pursues. They are soon to yield to the axe of the whites and bear on their cultivated bosoms half a million of civilized men. The wild Indian in his native greatness, roaming the woods, is a sublime sight, but how infinitely more sublime the spectacle of civilization on its march, softening every thing with its plastic touch and raising new life into nations of intelligent and happy beings. Yet it still excites a feeling of melancholy to think that those thousand fastnesses untrod but by the hunter, those profound seclusions, the ancient empire of solitude herself, must be broken by the strokes of the axe, and the monarchs of the forest, "those murdered Banquos," be brought to the ground to build the hut of some squalid settler. The surveyors are already rattling their chains and two years more will bring the whole region within the grasp of the speculator. Trowbridge and I have been offered some town lots at about $500, which he & his friends here, think cheap. I am disposed to make a little investment, but time presses, & perhaps upon the whole good farming Lands @ $1.25 are a better purchase.

Memo. (Major Whiting informs me). The National road from the mouth of Grand River to Detroit is to run through Oakland, Livingston, Ingham, Clinton[,] Ionia & Kent Counties, passing near here and so on west. I[t] was begun three years since by the Genrl. Gvt. and is in part completed. Congress made no appropriation last year. Whiting has had the management of it lately. When finished it will be a thoroughfare to the state and much enhance the price of lands near which it passes. The other National roads are to Fort Gratiot, Saganaw, and Chicago from Detroit. These are not to be turnpikes but are to be made in the best style the materials of the country affords. Twenty one years ago all that was known of Michg. was the strip settled about Detroit on the water. None had then penetrated the woods farther than a mile or two, except Traders and an expedition 30 miles up into Oakland was considered a great achievement. . . .

A ZION IN THE WILDERNESS

Edward W. Barber

Edward W. Barber came to Vermontville in Eaton County with his family in 1836 at the age of twelve. His memoirs, published in the 1890s, are a fine example of what became a kind of cottage industry in Michigan—the recording of the experiences of early settlers. Every family had its own tale, told often to all who would listen. Since New England Yankees were persons for whom Scripture was a living reality, analogies between their adventures and those of the Children of Israel were not overlooked. They were proud of their place in history and determined to preserve the record of their accomplishments for posterity.

But there were other reasons as well for the rash of pioneer histories, a genre of which the Barber and van der Veen essays are fine examples. By the 1870s, the pace of social and technological change quickened; almost overnight the pioneer period ended and the Gilded Age slipped in. A wave of nostalgia for the old days resulted in the formation of the Michigan Pioneer

Society (later the Michigan Pioneer and Historical Society), as well as county and municipal pioneer and historical societies. Old timers remembered the tradition of pioneer hospitality, the cherished evenings by the firelight, the joy with which even strangers were received, and the high degree of community cooperation.

Barber felt that "modernization" created social distinctions that did not (he thought) exist in the pioneer period. He regretted the passing of the old simplicities. The Vermontville colony was an attempt to recreate a New England village in the Michigan wilderness. Vermontville was noted for its high level of cultural life; Robert Kedzie, one of the famous early professors of Michigan Agricultural College, and one of the founding fathers of scientific agriculture, lived in Vermontville; his son, Frank Kedzie, who served as President of Michigan State University during the early twentieth century, grew up there. Each family had a village lot as well as a farm site. Since the population was not dispersed as in most other Michigan pioneer settlements, interaction between individuals and families was intense. Barber became a newspaperman; later he served for years as Reading Clerk of the United States House of Representatives. But for all his nostalgia Barber was not an uncritical historian; his anguish over the destruction of the hardwood forests of lower Michigan has a very contemporary ring.

The following excerpt has been adapted from two of Edward W. Barber's essays in the *Michigan Pioneer and Historical Collections:* "The Vermontville Colony: Its Genesis and History, with Personal Sketches of the Colonists," vol. XXVIII (Lansing: Robert Smith Printing Co., 1900), pp. 197–265, and "Recollections and Lessons of Pioneer Boyhood," vol. XXXI (Lansing: Wynkoop, Hallenbeck Crawford Co., 1902), pp. 178–226.

Among Michigan towns and villages with an interesting early organization, not another one was more unique in its genesis, settlement, and history than Vermontville. Founded by an organized colony of Vermonters, with Michigan, a church and a school in their minds, the land was purchased of the government in the names of selected trustees under a written compact, which set forth the plans and purposes of the colonists. Only one person, the minister and leader, had ever seen Michigan. It was an ideal town and village, with a written constitution duly signed by each of the proposed colonists before the land was bought and its location known by any of them. They made the venture at random in an entirely unknown region, but they were men and women who believed in the guiding hand of Providence, and although more work than wealth fell to their lot, they builded even better than they knew. . . .

My father, Edward H. Barber, came west as a land looker, with other Vermonters, in the spring of 1836, and in May of that year purchased about twelve hundred acres of government land in the present town of Vermontville. . . . In the fall of 1839 the family moved to Vermontville—father, mother, and four boys—arriving there in the evening of October 9, a moonless night, in a drizzling rain, and environed by pitchy darkness, following a lumber wagon drawn by a yoke of tired oxen and driving a brindle cow; and there and then the experiences of pioneer boyhood, at the age of eleven years, commenced. My mother died in 1838, her sickness delaying coming to Michigan a year or two. . . .

We started from Benson, Vermont, on Wednesday, September 18, 1839, and were twenty two days making the journey to Vermontville, Michigan. The first part of it was by wagon to Whitehall, N.Y.; the second, by the Champlain and Erie canals to Buffalo; the third, by the steamboat Lexington, Captain Root, to Detroit; the fourth, by oxen and wagon to Vermontville. The trip from Detroit occupied eight full days, with seven nights' experience in Michigan taverns and some familiarity with bedbugs and other vermin. Each day, from early morning to night, the slow moving wheels revolved. There may have been some laughter, but none is remembered. It was a solemn journey, like going into the unknown. Now it is made in four hours. . . .

My earliest recollection of anyone anticipating Horace Greeley's advice by going west was the packing up and moving from Benson to Illinois, of an uncle, John Barber and family, in 1832, when I was four years of age. He had the "Illinois fever," and he moved before making a visit and seeing the country, but no doubt, having heard from the lips of a Vermonter a description of a the wonderful prairies, ready for the plow, and obtainable for $1.25 an acre. He went from Whitehall to Buffalo by canal, thence by the schooner Austerlitz around the lakes to the mouth of the Chicago river, where he landed, loaded his household goods on wagons, forded the south branch of the river, at a spot known as Barber's Corners, according to information furnished me by his son, Royal E. Barber, an attorney of Joliet, Illinois. United States surveyors had not then run the section lines, and subject to the earlier incoming of some other settler and squatter he had the choice of a farm in that region of the country, so he turned a furrow around a tract half a mile square, squatted on it, and commenced living. When the surveyors ran the lines his furrow was very near to the section and quarter lines, and then his purchase was made of the government. Land grabbing was not as fierce then as it is now.

In 1835 the "Michigan fever" caught my father and he came west on a prospecting tour in the spring of 1836. He was a member of the Vermontville colony, having signed the organization papers, and in May of that year he made his purchase of land in the township. The same year he made a visit to his brother, John Barber, in Illinois. After telling about the fine timber land he had bought in Michigan, John asked this question: "Edward, why didn't you come and locate here, where the soil is rich and the land already cleared?" Yankee like, Edward replied by asking another question: "Why, John, what are you going to do for timber?" "Buy it," John replied. "You will spend the best part of your life chopping and burning timber in order to raise crops, while we go to work at once and raise crops to buy all the timber we need." Because men differed in their opinions as to practical questions some settled on the prairies of Illinois and others in the wilderness of Michigan. . . .

My father made a second and third trip to Michigan in the years 1837 and 1838. The stories that were told about the Great Lakes, about the wonderful richness of the soil which only needed to be tickled with the hoe to make a bounteous harvest, had a stimulating effect on my boyish imagination. It was another life, and one could picture it as he pleased. The part of Vermont in which we lived had been settled a little more than fifty years, and had an old look; the hills had been stripped of their forests, the streams had begun to dry up, and for a number of years families had been moving away, first to western New York, then to Ohio, and next to Michigan, Illinois, and Wisconsin. The advantages and disadvantages, the future probabilities and possibilities of different western localities were freely discussed. The Clinton and Kalamazoo canal—from the mouth of Clinton river in Macomb county to the mouth of the Kalamazoo river on Lake Michigan—had been surveyed through Eaton county and Vermontville along the Thornapple valley; and work had been commenced of the east end of this public improvement; the Erie canal had been a great success, though the west part of it had been constructed through a wilderness, and from what was known the location seemed to be a very desirable one. The heads of families who came west in those years saw better opportunities for themselves and their children than in the east; they desired better land; they had ideals of religion and education; but to their children it was a journey into the unknown, a realm of the imagination rather than of reality. The after-lessons were those of experience.

In September, 1839, we bade adieu to the old Vermont home. There were tears and farewells; ties were severed never again to be united on earth; hands met in a final clasp. None of the grandparents were ever seen again, and but a few of the boys who had played together, fished in the brooks, or learned to read, write and cipher at school, ever saw one another thereafter. It was a wide separation. Railroads were in their infancy. The household goods were loaded upon two wagons and hauled to Whitehall, New York. As the head of Lake Champlain and the initial point of the canal, it was the common starting point for the emigrants from western Vermont for the west. The next day the family of six took passage on a line boat for Buffalo.

There were at least four grades of canal boats in those days. The packet carried no freight, but only passengers and ordinary luggage, like the passenger trains on railroads today. They made fast time, some six miles an hour, and were fitted up in comfortable style, with dining rooms, staterooms, and other accommodations for first-class travel. The line boats were intended especially for families and their household effects. They had bunks for sleeping, a room for eating, a storage room for goods, with trunks and some boxes on deck. Their speed was three miles an hour and it required more than a week to make the journey to Buffalo. The freight boats and the scows made up the list of vessels for the canal. Horses and profanity were the motors; the packet horses going on the trot, the rest at a steady walk unless there was a race to see which boat should reach a lock first. The three classes of boats named—the packets for passengers with a small amount of baggage, the lineboats that were patronized chiefly by movers with their household goods, and the freight boats and scows—give a good idea of the most convenient and swiftest modes of conveyance for the pioneers of two thirds of a century ago as they moved westward to make new homes for themselves and their children. It was a continuance of the westward movement in which our race has been engaged for centuries, for more than double the time that has elapsed since the beginning of the Christian Era. . . .

The locks along the canal were great curiosities for one who had never seen an engineering work more difficult than a mill dam. Crossing to the Hudson River at Albany in making the change from the Champlain to the Erie canal was a notable event of the journey. . . . The canal was for all its wonderful results only a narrow ditch, a stretch of 363 miles of commercially mudded water, connecting the Hudson River with the great lakes of the northwest. All honor to DeWitt Clinton, who, seeing its necessity as far back as 1812, was able to influence his state to commence work on its construction in 1817, saw it opened in 1825, at a total cost of $7,602,000. . . . The canal part of the journey consumed little over a week; at Buffalo we boarded the steamer Lexington.

After leaving Buffalo a severe storm arose, lashing the lake into a destructive fury, and the captain deemed it prudent to turn into the harbor at Erie, Pennsylvania, and wait until it subsided. It was a tedious and seasick trip. Early Sunday morning the boat entered the mouth of Detroit river; the sun shone brightly, seasickness disappeared, passengers thronged the upper deck. The boat stopped at Malden, Canada, for a few minutes, and a British soldier in the regulation red coat was the only object that made an impression. . . . The boat docked at the foot of Woodward Avenue in Detroit, and the household goods, with a new lumber wagon brought from Vermont, were unloaded on the wharf, and boyhood pioneering in Michigan commenced. . . .

Father hired two teamsters to take most of the goods from Detroit to Vermontville. He also bought a yoke of oxen out of a drove of cattle on the commons a short distance northeast of the hotel, as ox-power rather than horse power was required for the work of making a new farm in the wilderness. In a logging field a team of horses would be as out of place as an old fashioned stage in competition with a modern railway. A yoke went with the oxen, and they were driven down Woodward Avenue to the wharf, the wagon was put together, and the team driven back up the avenue to the hotel; this was my pioneer ride in Detroit. . . . On October 2 we took the territorial road out of Detroit for our destination, about one hundred and forty miles distant by the highway. It was beautiful Indian summer weather; a purple haze hung over the forests; squirrels chattered by the roadside or leaped from tree to tree; the hum of the partridge was often heard; the chirping of autumnal insects filled the air with music, and wild pigeons were abundant. Slowly we moved along, making about two miles an hour, or an average of seventeen and one half miles a day. Log taverns were frequent. The territorial road had been a great thoroughfare for immigrants, but in 1839, owing to the panic of 1837–8 and the consequent hard times, the tide of travel had slackened. . . . On Sunday, October 6, about noon, we passed through Jackson as people were going home from church. Brought up among New England Puritans, with their strict Sabbatarian ideas, by whom all work, except salting sheep—Vermont then was a sheep state—was tabooed on Sunday, even the reading of a newspaper being strictly forbidden, and not a loud smile or the least play being permitted, to be seen traveling on the Lord's Day by persons going home from the meeting house, was not in harmony with conscience as educated, and so made a lasting impression on my mind . . . .

North of the village of Bellevue for about a mile the trees had been cut down for the four rods width of highway; the stumps were green and stubborn; the trunks lay stretched on the ground; and the tops formed brush fences on each side of the road next to the standing timber; while the wagon track wound its tortuous way among the stumps and the butts of the fallen trees. To make a miry place passable logs had been cut, about fourteen feet long, and hauled in across the track, rolled together as closely as they would lie, and over this primitive causeway, or "crossway," as such an improvement or betterment was called, the wagon jolted and twisted, and the oxen walked doubtingly as if fearing that their feet might slip between the logs. Such was the beginning of road making in this heavily timbered land. . . . After leaving the chopped out highway a mile north of Bellevue village, the rest of the journey was through a dense forest, with here and there the underbrush and a small staddle cut away, and blazed trees on each side so as to indicate the driveway—scars that the axe had made on the trees at short distances for the guidance of travelers on their way in and out of their homes in the forest. The marks were needed, as the leaves had already commenced to fall, and in many places the track was not visible. When, occasionally, some settler drove out to Bellevue to the gristmill, or to buy a few necessities at a store and call at the post office for the mail, was all the home travel the highway received, except for that of the incoming pioneer family. It was a region of great trees, beech and maple, elm and ash, basswood and cherry, with scattered oak and black walnut, a thick undergrowth of saplings; and where the land was low by some swamp or stream wild grape vines, as if seeking the light, climbed to the tall tree tops. It was near the close of Indian summer that year. No wind stirred even the topmost boughs of the giants of the forest, and scarcely a sound broke the spell of loneliness that gave to pioneering a new experience. Talking to and guiding the oxen hitched to the lumber wagon, driving the brindle cow, and watching for the scars on the trees that mutely pointed the way, we moved steadily deeper into the forest, at the average pace of one mile an hour. Animated nature was represented by wolves, bears, deer, wild turkeys, partridges and black squirrels along the route, rather than by human beings. . . .

As already mentioned it was on a dark and rainy evening that we arrived at our destination. The rainy spell that is apt to come at the close of Indian summer had set in, and the next day was cold, drizzling and disagreeable. My father's family was the last to arrive of the twenty two families, members of the colony, that settled in the village and owned farming lands round about it in different directions. Not an acre of cleared land did he own, but some twelve hundred acres that were covered with heavy hardwood timber. Looking at the somber sky only small spaces of which were visible; at the little areas of landscape dotted with stumps and fallen trees that could be seen; at the village highway, also full of stumps and logs; at the dense woods out of which a living must be hewed; at the rude log houses with their contracted accommodations, shake roofs and mudded interspaces of the logs to keep out the cold and keep in the warmth; at the soggy earth and big tree trunks and poles that were fences in front of many residences—the enchantment lent by distance disappeared. The Michigan of imagination had suddenly become a reality. Hearts were warm, welcomes were cordial, great fireplaces made of mud and stone with stick chimneys mudded on the inside made the evenings bright and cheerful; assistance was gladly rendered in getting settled, without expectation of reward. The human feature of the beginning of pioneer life was much more attractive than the promises nature afforded; and yet it seems as if to the early settlers as much of joy and as little of sorrow, with all the hard work, came as falls to the lot of any other class of people in the struggle to live and get ahead.

Realistic pioneer life in the wilderness had come, and the halo of romance faded away. The log house had one room below and another up stairs. The lower story was kitchen, sitting room, parlor and bedroom. There were valances around the bed in one corner of the room, and in another corner was an open space in the upper floor and a ladder on which to climb above, where three more beds were established, two for the four boys, and a spare one for company about which drapery of some sort was hung. Boxes and a trunk or two to store things in helped to complete the upstairs' conveniences. In the living room was the cook stove the pipe from which reached through the roof; shelves for crockery were made by boring holes in the logs and driving in pegs horizontally to support the boards that were placed on them; chairs and table and light stand, with six regular occupants, left but little room to spare for cat or dog or visitors. The cellar was a hole in the ground at the center, into which potatoes were dumped for family use during the coldest weather, most of them being buried, the piles covered with leaves or straw and dirt, out of doors. The supply for the first winter was bought for a shilling a bushel. When winter came and the sleighing was good, father yoked the oxen, hitched them to a rough sled, drove to Marshall, twenty-eight miles distant, purchased a load of wheat at forty-four cents a bushel, had it ground, and was home again in four days. . . .

The first implement to become familiar with was the ax. The red man had his tomahawk and scalping knife; the white man who succeeded him introduced the ax and the carving knife. The change signified a good deal. . . . The woods had to be cut away, and food cooked and carved and served in a more civilized fashion. . . . When moving west, on the Erie canal, father bought two boxes of axes made by Isaiah Blood at Hoosac, New York, and the first thing to learn in the line of practical education, to meet the requirements of the time . . . , was how to chop. A beaver knows how to fell trees by instinct, but man has to learn the art by experience and he needs, to do it well, the ax, muscle and judgment. It is his mission to improve natural conditions. Those axes, and the different makes of axes, their temper and their faults, were more freely discussed in Vermontville at that time than the telephone system today. . . .

Ax helves and the proper weight of the ax for effective service were more frequently and fully talked over than politics or religion. Each member of a family old enough to swing this first implement of civilization in a wilderness had one of his own and kept it bright and keen. Mine, at twelve years of age, weighed three and a half pounds. During the first winter education with the ax was confined to cutting wood for the house. The method of getting it was primitive; some one would go to the woods nearby, cut down a tree of the desired kind and size, generally sugar maple, trim off the brush, chop the trunk into two pieces if necessary, hitch the yoke of oxen to the butt by a logging chain and haul the stick to the house to be chopped the proper length for stove or fireplace, and split for use. Patience, perseverance, and some other virtues were called into exercise in building a fire of this green wood. . . . If a fire went out at night, the only alternative was to take a shovel or pan and go to some neighbor's house for live coals, which was occasionally done. Lucifer matches had not come into general use, though invented in 1829. Pipes were lighted by picking up a small piece of coal with the tongs and placing it on the tobacco, or by poking the bowl into a bunch of coals and getting one at random. . . .

In the spring of 1840 education with the ax commenced. Not far from the house, on the adjoining Hoyt lot, was a small wild cherry tree. No thought of Washington's mythical hatchet and cherry tree was in my mind. One day, when alone, so that no person could see the pioneer effort, the ax went with me to the cherry tree, and we haggled it down. If there is such a thing as cruelty to a tree this one suffered. However, it furnished an opportunity to begin a new branch of education. The cherry tree was sacrificed in the desire for practical knowledge. Father thought it was not exactly right, when he learned of the transaction, to chop down a cherry tree on another man's land. The matter of trespass in the case had not entered my mind. Trees stood in the way of progress and learning to get rid of them was the first plain duty in sight. The ax then was the friend of progress and civilization, but now it is the enemy of agriculture, horticulture, and prosperity. Slaughtering the forest then was the primal work of preparation for civilized society; saving them now would conserve its true interests. Conditions often change more rapidly than do the thoughts and habits of men. They act from habit all the time, and from judgment only when they are exercising it. New circumstances—environments—bring new duties. . . .

That summer of 1840, father concluded to build a sawmill on the Scipio [Creek] at a point about a mile and a half from where we lived, with no road or blazed trees through the woods to guide one's footsteps. Having selected the place for the milldam, and having learned from the wood chopping and cherry tree experience of my willingness to use an ax, we would start out every morning, except Sunday, soon after breakfast, with our dinner, axes and a bush-hook, to cut the underbrush on the bottom land above the proposed dam and mill site. The thick undergrowth of bushes and vines was slowly cut down and piled in windrows for burning on several acres, and the large water elms left standing for the water of the pond to kill in good time. Without water they could not thrive; with too much of a good thing they perished.

A mile up the Scipio, Reuben Sanford, a pioneer, had commenced clearing and built a log house, but with this exception, from the source of the mouth of the creek, where it emptied into the Thornapple [River], the sound of the white man's ax, unless in the hands of surveyors when they marked the trees for section lines and corners, had not been heard. It was the boy of sixty years ago who had the privilege and opportunity of learning by experience of the beginnings of civilization in the wilderness, and only the boy of that period is left to narrate the simple story, as all of the pioneer settlers who were heads of families have passed away. No one was near enough those summer days to hear the sound of our axes or came along to give advice. In the silence of the great woods, stretching away for long distances with only here and there a settler, the work of cutting and piling the brush was accomplished, and later on when dry the heaps and windrows were burned, and a new era fairly commenced.

The uplands bordering the creek were very broken and hilly, and were covered with a heavy growth of beech, maple, oak, and other timber. One afternoon, while engaged in this work, the sky clouded over and the mutterings of a thunderstorm were heard low down the western horizon. Getting ready as quickly as possible we started for home. In the haste we forgot our bearings, and soon discovered that we did not know the right way out of the woods. There was neither sun nor star for a guide, the storm was coming on and the wind had commenced to moan in the tree tops. We talked the matter over hastily, but could not decide which way would take us out of the woods so that we could reach home before dark. We knew the right direction was nearly east. Finally father thought of the fact that the moss grew thickest on the north side of trees. Examining a few of them we made up our minds which way was east. Then to avoid traveling in a circle, as men are apt to do when lost in the woods, we took sight ahead for some tree that was as near east as we could determine, made straight for it, then sighted another tree in the same direction, and so on until a familiar spot was reached, when the lost feeling disappeared as suddenly as it came. The drenching storm caught us, however, before we reached the first clearing, some sixty rods from shelter and home. . . .

The sawmill was built, the first dam went out as it was made entirely of earth no brush having been used to prevent the water, under pressure, from working through the treacherous soil and quicksand, but it was reconstructed, a great deal of brush being used, and remains as solid as any dam built by beavers, up to the present time. While that mill was building, [with] Amos Spicer, of Eaton Rapids, superintending its construction as mill-wright, it was a daily experience to carry the dinner to the workmen in two big pails supported by a neck-yoke over the shoulders. A trudge of a mile and a half, with baked beans or a boiled dinner for eight to twelve men, through the woods, with but a road marked out for oxen and wagons, was a toughening experience. The workmen gathered on either side of a newly hewed stick of timber, using if for a table, and with clear spring water that bubbled from the foot of a hill near the bottom land, ate heartily, told their rude stories and enjoyed the repast.

In that sawmill, when finished, another branch of education commenced and ended. It was equipped with an old-fashioned wooden water wheel, with an upright sash for the saw. Helping to roll in the logs, spotting them for the sawblocks, setting the tail-end of the log with a pinch bar and driving the teeth of the dog into the log to hold it in place for the saw, sliding the slabs out of one side and the boards out of the other, like separating sheep and goats, was the extent of my boyhood experience in that line of business. . . . That pioneer enterprise in Vermontville was the beginning of an important transformation—a change from log houses and log barns to frame houses and frame barns—to greater household comforts; though, on looking backward for sixty years, it seems as if the joy of living in the rude log dwellings of the pioneers was fully as great as it is now. There was a great deal of mutual helpfulness then, and a large amount of hope for better times to come as a result of labor. . . .

In the summer and fall of 1840 the first five acres on the farm were chopped and cleared. That furnished the first lessons of the logging field, as after burning the brush the logs had to be hauled together and rolled into big piles for their holocaust. On the uplands the white ash, cherry, basswood and red elm were saved and left standing for rail timber. All the rest of the timber was burned, going off in smoke except for a small deposit of ashes. Generally the ashes were hauled to an ashery and sold for five cents a bushel to be made into black salts, a wagonbox load of thirty bushels bringing $1.50; and the black salts, the first product from boiling down the lye, were hauled to Bellevue and sold to the saleratus factories of that village.

Coon skins and black salts were about the only articles of importance that could, at first, be exchanged for money.

With the log piles and the brush in a dozen clearings on fire in the evening the woods were brilliantly illuminated. Generally the torch was applied at the close of the day so that the heat and smoke would not interfere with the work. In the morning the unburnt portions were tumbled together with handspikes, and then the rolling up of more piles commenced. This work was done mostly in the fall, but sometimes clearing ground in the spring for corn or potatoes had to be done. . . .

Not infrequently some settler would have the ague and fever or be otherwise disabled about the time that his few acres of chopping were ready for logging, and upon the product of these he and his family depended for food for the ensuing year. Clothes could be patched, but the stomach must be fed. Then the neighbors would turn out voluntarily, have a logging bee, roll into heaps five acres of so of timber in a day, set the piles on fire towards evening when the job was finished, and thus enable the sick or disabled pioneer to get in a crop on the new land. These logging bees were quite a common occurrence. Eight to ten yoke of oxen and twenty to thirty stalwart men and boys made ordinary hard work a pastime on such occasions, and when the acres of log heaps were on fire in the evening the light illuminated the sky like a great conflagration, and made the dark background of the forest seem all the darker from the contrast. There was more of such cordial and mutual helping in the early days than there is now. Of official charity there was none, but of personal assistance, backed by hearty good will, there was a great deal. At the logging bee, the good qualities of human nature found an admirable expression. . . .

The fence question is always a serious one. To build fences along the highways, partition fences to separate the farms, and fences to subdivide farms into lots, involves an expense amounting to millions of dollars to an agricultural state. Men are gregarious; they like to live close together, but they want some sort of artificial barrier between them, one side of which says "this is mine" and the other side that says "this is yours." The first fences in the woods were made of brush, logs, poles, and rails. When clearings were made log and pole fences were built along the highway and the sides of the cleared fields next to the woods were generally adorned with a brush fence, made by falling the tree tops near the outer edge of the chopping in a windrow stand next to the standing timber. The chopper would first fell the trees that stood in nearly a straight line next to the timber that was to be left standing, then from the inside of what would be the cleared field would fell all the tree tops that would reach the line of the fence, lop the limbs in place to prevent hogs from crawling through, and let it remain until the timber outside of it was cut away, when it would be dedicated to smoke and ashes. For two or three years such a fence would bar out cattle, but a predatory hog would sometimes find a way through into a corn field or potato patch, and then hard feelings between neighbors might arise, as questions touching the legality of the fence, the right of the hog to be there, even if there was no fence (he was a recognized free commoner in the woods) and if proven a trespasser wide differences of opinion as to the damage done existed and were vigorously discussed. A brush fence was from a rod to two rods wide, and varied in height as well as width with the size and spread of the limbs of the fallen trees. Climbing over one from limb to log and log to limb, made the fence seem unnecessarily wide, but the tree tops would not admit of its being narrower. Coming to one while hunting it was an easy matter for partridge, squirrel or other game to get away into the woods or to find safe shelter among the tangled limbs and brush of the fallen timber; and yet many a hiding spot was afforded to lay in wait for the wild turkeys that would hop and fly from limb to limb to get into the brush protected corn field. Thus all these things had their advantages and disadvantages. . . .

The old settlers, when they had brought a patch of earth face to face with the sun, and had planted their scanty acres of cleared land, had to fence out invaders, both their own and their neighbors' stock. In the woods cattle were free commoners. Sometimes the fence would be made of poles, a flimsy looking barricade against the lofty palisade of ancient trees that stood, as they had for centuries, outside of the "betterments," but this was generally sufficient to keep the wood-ranging cattle out of the field on which so much labor had been expended, and whose green and springing grain was dotted and splotched with blackened stumps and an occasional log that the fire had only partially consumed. The pole fence was laid after the same fashion as the rail fence, but with less regularity. Here and there the trunk of a fallen tree of considerable size was utilized as the foundation. Rail cuts were uniformly twelve feet long, but the size and height of the young trees, and the number of persons engaged in the work, determined the length of the poles used; the whole business was a question of adaptation to circumstances. . . .

After these primitive fences came the rail fence, or snake fence as it was sometimes called from the slight resemblance in its zig-zag shape to the wriggling course of a serpent. Early in this country it was called the Virginia fence, perhaps for the reason that the Old Dominion was the mother of it as of presidents. . . .

Roads were horrible; sometimes impassable; when not raised eighteen inches above the surface by hauling logs across the driveway and rolling them close together, called corduroy, they were two feet below the surface in the mire, and even then not very solid. Often, as "in the days of Shamgar, the son of Anath in the days of Jael, the highways were unoccupied, and the travelers walked through the bye-ways." From Bellevue, through the woods for fourteen miles to the nearest post office, the road was of such character as to make the last installment of the journey from New England to the colony the hardest part of the trip. It was merely underbrushed, trees on each side blazed with an ax to guide the traveler, and passing over many wet and low places, they soon became quagmires by being cut by passing teams. A mile an hour was good time over them. Some families, moving in, were compelled to camp out in the woods overnight, and to accommodate them a shanty was built near a brook for shelter. From this fact the stream got the name of Shanty Brook, by which it is still known. In October 1839, when my father Edward H. Barber, moved in with his wife, four boys, an ox team, wagon and cow, we left Bellevue a clear and frosty morning, before the sun was up, stopped long enough in the woods to eat a lunch, feed the oxen and extract some milk from the brindle cow, and about nine o'clock in the evening arrived at the top of the hill in Vermontville, a rain storm having set in after dark at the close of the day and of Indian summer. . . . For a mile or two north of Bellevue the road had been chopped out four rods wide, and also for half a mile or so south of Vermontville. The rest of the way of the track was through the woods, and sometimes hard to find on account of the fallen leaves. But we made a mile an hour that last one of our eight days from Detroit, and three weeks from Benson, Vermont, and reached our stumpy Canaan at last. . . .

Wolves were plentiful, and it was an easy matter by giving a long human howl in the evening to start a wolfish serenade. In the fall of 1836 Oren Dickenson came to the colony with a horse team, his family not arriving until the spring of 1838, a year and a half later. The road then was but little more than a trail, just enough underbrush having been cut out to allow a team to pass. None of the mucky places had been corduroyed and the mudholes were deep. To drive a team through by daylight was oftener tried than accomplished. R. E. Griswold started from Vermontville early one morning to drive through to Bellevue. Night overtook him while yet in the woods, and in the darkness he could not follow the track, over which but few wagons had previously passed. He stopped the team and endeavored to find the roadway by getting down upon his knees and feeling with his hands for the wagon tracks, but in vain. It was as dark, he once said, "as a stack of black cats." Thinking that he might be within hailing distance of Bellevue he gave a loud halloo, and was answered by a prowling wolf. Again he shouted, and other wolves responded in different directions. They were cowardly whelps and seldom attacked a person, yet none the less these voices of the night were unwelcome music to a lone traveler with a team in the dense woods and darkness. He unhitched the team, tied them to the wagon, seated himself in it, gun in hand, talked to the horses for company, and through the long night watches listened to his serenaders, whose performances culminated in a thrilling wolf chorus in the wilderness. When daylight came the next day the blazed trails on either side of the pioneer highway indicated the route out of the woods.

Such incidents, not being able to make fourteen miles by daylight with a pair of horses and a wagon, show better than words can describe the character of the roads the first settlers had to travel over. In a few years they were so improved that the trip to Marshall, where most of the settlers sold their products and did their trading, could be comfortably made in a day, going there one day and returning the next, though when goods were to be purchased for the winter outfit for the family the trip and trade would consume three days. . . .

Opening roads, not making them, was the first public work that demanded attention. Except a few leading thoroughfares that were established under the direct authority of the state, under a special act of the legislature, the township authorities ordered them and had them surveyed, and the work on them was in payment of the highway tax. Non-residents were assessed the same percentage on their property as were residents, but the latter could work out the highway tax as certified to the pathmasters or overseers of the several road districts, while the former had to pay in cash as part of the general tax, and from this source came the only money that was received for highway purposes, except in cases where the town meeting voted a specific sum for some special purpose. The necessity for opening a new road, when petitioned for, was decided by the three highway commissioners of the town. When a new settler located upon some outlying piece of wild land not on an established highway, a road for him to get in and out was a necessity. The first thing to be done after the survey was chopping down the timber that stood on the legal four rods in width that constituted the established highway. The resident owners of land in the road district were notified by the pathmaster when and where the road tax would be worked out. Axes, hand-spikes, a yoke or two of oxen to haul logs out of the driveway or to some miry place for a causeway, were the chief requisites for opening a highway to sunlight and civilization. Chopping down the timber would begin at the outer edges, and then from the center the trees would be felled in a straight line, their tops making the two jagged brush fences next to the standing timber along the entire length of the opened highway. Straight through the woods the cutting would be made, the small trees and underbrush cut low so that the stumps would not catch the wagon hubs, and the logs chopped off and wheeled about for the driveway where necessary.

The days when the people came out to open a new road through the woods were more like holidays than work days. A number would assemble along a strip of road, the work would be systematically planned and prosecuted vigorously. The sound of axes and falling timber awakened the forest from the slumber of centuries. There was strife among the choppers to see which one could cut down his half of a tree first, and there were no laggards or drones in performing this earliest public service. Every blow struck was along the line of improvement and progress, and this gave mental encouragement and muscular strength. Year by year new roads were opened, and not many years elapsed until there was scarcely a track in a township that wound its tortuous way among the trees of the forest. Such a spot now is a charming relief, a delightful touch of nature, amid the general openness of the country. We long for trees when they are gone, and slaughter them unthinkingly if not unmercifully when they interfere with getting a living from the soil.

Familiarity for more than sixty years with the forests of Michigan and with their disappearance has taught the lesson that their preservation and restoration is now an important problem to the welfare of the State. Already, in the agricultural portions of the State, the percentage of area covered with timber is smaller than in some of the thickly settled countries of Europe. It is not an easy matter for a people who have been forest destroyers to become forest preservers; their habit of thought is all on the side of destruction; men act from habit almost unconsciously all the time, but from judgment only when they are exercising it; and yet history teaches the important lesson that many of the once fairest and most productive regions have been made desolate by the destruction of their forests. Countries once fertile and populous have been thus rendered sterile and tenantless. Every interest, we know, is self-seeking to the extent of its opportunity, and it may seem that the forest destroyers are only dealing with what they exclusively own, but the right to do so to the injury of all the people may properly be questioned; for they are working a serious injury to the farms, the climate, and the industries of the State. Forests obstruct the winds and protect man, animal, and plant. They retard evaporation, absorb the rains and melted snows, and thus feed perennial springs and maintain the constancy of running streams. The forests gone, suddenly floods which follow heavy rainfalls damage the labors of man. Driving winds, unobstructed in their course, do greater harm to vegetation, and it becomes more difficult to grow fruits and grains as the country becomes almost wholly cleared. Carried to excess, the very means which man uses to obtain greater production from the earth, brings him trouble and renders production more precarious. . . . Getting rid of the forests was the work of pioneers with whom my boyhood was associated; but now the preservation of the comparatively few acres of them that are left standing, and the restoration of them on hilltops and hillsides where the soil washes away and leaves the land of little value, should not longer be neglected. To make a region of a country better worth living in than when he found it is the duty of every good citizen. . . .

The first three winters after our arrival in Michigan—those of 1839–40, 1840–41, and 1841–42—were very mild, and caused much favorable comment when comparing them with the severer winters of New England. During one or two of them, in the months of January and February, playing the old-fashioned game of base-ball was a frequent pastime. The small clearings, surrounded by the tall forests, were protected from the sweep of fierce winds. When in the woods chopping down the timber or cutting sawlogs their force would scarcely be felt. Nearly all of the State then was a mighty windbreak, and the forests furnished kindly shelter for man and beast. It seems as if this lesson of experience should not be entirely forgotten. The economic value of groves for breaking the force of cold and cruel winds, and for sheltering houses, barns and stock from their effect, was lost sight of in the indiscriminate slaughter of our arboreal vegetation.

There were no more stately and beautiful forests than those of

Eaton county. Of the land located in Vermontville by my father in May 1836, about three hundred acres of the original beech and maple forest, almost untouched by the relentless ax, still remain in nearly a square form, forming a body of woods from the central part of which one cannot see out into a clearing. Dropped down blindfolded into this patch of woods now, one could realize that the whole region was sixty-five years ago on the first of May this year, just before the sound of a woodman's ax had awakened the forest aisles from the slumber of centuries. . . . Had one third been sacredly reserved as woodland, the remaining two thirds would be worth more for agricultural purposes than the entire acreage denuded of its timber. The winter winds would be less severely felt; the springs and brooks would not have dried up; the drouths would have been less destructive of vegetation, and men would have been less the enemies and more the friends of nature than has been the case. Forest trees and foliage are the lungs of nature, inhaling and exhaling the atmospheric elements, breathing in carbonic gas and breathing out oxygen, and serving a wonderful purpose in the economy of nature. The forest is as useful as it is beautiful, and from every point of view it is one of the most helpful friends of man.

Half a century ago the hilltops were crowned with noble trees, and the hillsides were hidden by the dense foliage of that superb floral growth which gave to Michigan a wide renown and great wealth. Most of it had to be cut away, but much more of it than has been saved should have been preserved, both for adornment and for utility. Many of the hilltops and hillsides are now well-nigh barren fields, the rains washing their fertility into the valleys and the streams carrying it away. In some instances there was a slight temporary gain from cutting off too much of the forests, but the final result is a permanent loss. Too completely shorn of its forest glory and beneficence is the timbered region of Michigan, and for the sake of a paltry gain which reckoned the stately maple, the nut-bearing beech, the strong-rooted oak, the spreading elm, the useful ash, the valuable cherry, the great black walnut, the soft basswood, the massive whitewood, as merchandise to be got rid of and replaced. It was once my experience to drive the team that hauled a load of walnut lumber to Marshall, twenty eight miles, every board of which was three feet wide and over, without crack or flaw, and deliver it to the late F. A. Kingsbury of that city, a cabinet maker, for the slight sum of twelve dollars a thousand feet. Cradles and coffins were cheap in those days. Now such a tree as the one that furnished that lumber would be worth as much as forty acres of cleared land; and yet, of the most valuable timber a net profit of one dollar a tree was not realized; too much of a good thing has been followed by too little. . . .

Religion and education were the ideals of the Vermontville colonists. The Congregational polity was as natural to them as was the town meeting the basis of civil government. Both were government by the people and suited their notions of independence and responsibility. The first minister and father of the colony was Rev. Sylvester Cochrane, from Poultney, Vermont. The first meeting that was held in the wilderness he opened with prayer before the settlers drew lots for the choice of village locations and farms. Though they believed in Divine Guidance, they were nonetheless anxious for a good selection. Cochrane . . . remained in the colony from 1837 to 1842, and afterwards for many years was pastor of a church at Northville, Michigan. The last part of his stay was not all "sweetness and light;" difficulties arose connected with building the Academy, and he never returned to visit the colony he was instrumental in building. Still, after the troubles ended, he was always mentioned with great respect. The early meetings in the log schoolhouse were peculiar to the time. In the summer came barefooted men, in shirt sleeves; wives and mothers in calico dresses, with clean clothes and bare feet, smiling and happy; all assembling to hear the gospel preached twice and during the intermission to talk over various matters of interest to the young community, or if any one was absent to ascertain the reason. The stalwart minister offered prayer, read the Scriptures, gave out the hymn and all joined in singing, those who could keep time as well as those who could not. Martin S. Norton or Willard Davis used the tuning fork to get the right pitch, and then the solid sermon of an hour, as stern and uncompromising as the decrees of fate. While earnest in his ministerial work, Mr. Cochrane did his full share in clearing the forest and raising crops for a living; making maple sugar in the spring, planting corn and potatoes, and doing whatsoever his hands found to do with all his might. I recall an amusing incident. In the spring of 1839, just as the sap began to flow, having ordered a barrel for gathering it, Jacob Fuller, the cooper, who lived at the west end of the village, nearly a mile away, went for a barrel, found it outside the log shop, and the cooper's family being still abed, put a stick in the bunghole, shouldered the barrel and marched home. On his arrival Mrs. Cochrane was getting breakfast, and was surprised to see him walk up to the house with a new barrel on his shoulder. She asked where he had been. "Why, Jacob, don't you know it is Sunday?" Then for the first time it dawned on his mind that he had violated the third commandment, and his sorrow was intense. He went to the log schoolhouse as usual at meeting time, and with tears streaming from his eyes, confessed his fault. Somehow he had lost a day in counting time, and his reckoning, not his intention, was wrong. . . .

The records of church meetings and trials, kept by S. S. Church, clerk for over thirty years, are very full and accurate. He was a model scribe. An examination of these records shows that the Congregational Church was a prominent factor in the life of the young community. Of the heads of original families all but two of the original colonists . . . were or became members. To a greater extent, probably, than any other village settlement in Michigan, the Vermontville Colony was composed of members of the church.

Citations and trials for unbrotherly conduct were of frequent occurrence, though a more orderly community could not be found. When complaint was made for some alleged offense, a committee was uniformly appointed to endeavor to reconcile the militant members. To give an idea of the character of these proceedings a transcript of the record in a case between Martin S. Norton and Wells R. Martin is worth reproducing. The specifications in detail at a church meeting held January 18, 1847 are:

> 1st. Brother Norton charged Brother Martin with lieing [sic] or prevarication with regard to Mrs. Martin's mother coming to Vermontville.
> 2d. With prevarication in regard to a statement made to Brother Robinson, coming from Brother W.J. Squier.
> 3rd. Charges him with a lie in a statement made to Brothers Browning and Norton respecting Doct. Robinson's father, and his, Doct. Robinson's, two uncles.
> 4th. Charges him with making a statement in the presence of Doct. Robinson, Brother Norton, and his son, respecting his wife's feelings concerning a certain piece of property—and afterwards denying statement.
> 5th. Charges him with prevarication in a statement made to Brother Downing in regard to the opinions of his neighbors, touching the matter of Brother Browning's acting as umpire or referee in the case of Brothers Church and Norton.

The last specification refers to another difficulty that came before the church for adjudication and settlement. These matters seem strangely trivial now, but they stirred the little isolated community to its depths and provoked much earnest discussion. With a daily mail and newspapers to keep in touch with the live and throbbing outside world it is not probable that they would have received any attention. They are only important now as showing the relation of the church to the social gossip and feeling of fifty years ago. The details were talked over and stirred the community as much as an embalmed beef court of inquiry stirs the people of a great nation today. None of these things, or the decision in regard to any of them, affected the social standing or business character of any of the parties an iota. They often grew out of unfounded suspicions or family misunderstandings and temporary quarrels. The period of fighting with blows had evolved into the period of fighting with words.

Mr. Martin, the defendant, was acquitted on the first, second, third and fifth specifications and convicted on the fourth. Then, the clerk was ordered to furnish Brother Martin with the decision in his case, and to inform him that the church will require a written confession on the next Sabbath. But the storm blew over. Explanations took the place of recriminations. The sky cleared. On March 26, 1847, W. R. Martin was chosen one of the delegates to represent the church at the Marshall conference.

The extent of these internal troubles is indicated by the proceedings of a single church meeting held May 4, 1847, when committees were appointed to adjust difficulties between brethren, if possible. First, Brothers Sprague and Merrill were appointed to visit Brothers Norton and Church on a mission of peace; second, Brothers Scovell and Merrill were instructed to wait upon Brothers Morton and Martin and their families in the interest of peace and reconciliation; third, Brothers Dickinson and Fairfield were commissioned to call upon Brothers D. H. Robinson and W. R. Martin and try to bring about a settlement of their difficulties; fourth, Brothers W. Davis and Gray were selected to visit the family of the latter. Brother W. Gray was instructed to visit Brother W. F. Hawkins and ascertain his spiritual state, and report to the church. . . . This seems to have been a general house cleaning, or church cleaning, session. Scarcely a male member escaped during the first twenty years. Generally a winter revival would bring discordant members together again, after the confession of some wrong and asking pardon of each other.

All sorts of questions were brought before the church for adjustment. As an example, under date of January 28, 1847, is a minute of charges preferred by Brother Armstrong "against Brethren Church, Norton, Martin, Barber, W. J. Squire, Dickinson and Robinson, that said brethren have wrongfully and unlawfully used their influence to retain and have retained money belonging to school district No. 2 of Vermontville." Besides the appointment of an investigating committee, nothing came of this groundless charge. Nowadays it would be a proper case for a civil court. . . .

The Thornapple Valley was not a land flowing with milk and honey when these pioneers entered it in the last week of May 1836, sixty-one years ago. They found no figs and pomegranates ready to be plucked, nor the blossoms that bore edible fruit save the wild plum, though wild grapes grew along the river bottoms and ripened and sweetened with the autumnal frosts, and there was no milk, but occasional bee trees, the hollow spaces of which near the tops were laden with honey. Finding a bee tree and felling it so as to save the sweetness was quite an event in the young community. There were no prairies or marshes where natural grasses grew for cattle. All the acres were covered with dense and heavy forests. In the spring and early summer the woods were carpeted with flowers; it was dark shade below; but there was sunshine above. When they settled down to the work of a lifetime, clearing the savage woods away, making homes for themselves and their children, and realized how far away they were from railroads, the newly forming highways of the world's activity, with markets for their products nearly thirty miles distant, as they were all thrifty Yankees and wanted to gather in their share of western wealth from the rise in land values and the products of the soil, the prospect was not hopeful or cheerful.

Still, with few exceptions, this little band of men and women, in the heart of a dense wilderness, kept steadily at work until better and brighter days came to them ere they left the scene of their earthly labors and trials and passed to their final rest. They lived close to nature, and this of itself is an education. A home in the country is the best starting point in life. Nature decides against those who forsake her for the more artificial modes of society. . . . But the old days cannot be reproduced or their experience repeated. There can never be another Vermontville. A general characteristic of all its early settlers was their intense individuality. To leave New England, canal it to Buffalo, risk the lake voyage to Detroit, was not the work of effeminate men and women. It required real grit and the stiffest backbone. A man who had the stamina to settle in the wilderness of Central Michigan and hew out of the surroundings of a new life possessed the qualities of both pioneership and leadership. Every individual Yankee who located there was capable of being a directing spirit in larger enterprises. But the greater opportunities, who could discern them? Chicago was little else than a mudhole, and the modern Northwest was not even a dream. Being all leaders, there was a constant locking of horns, and the court of last resort, from which there was no appeal, was the discipline of the church. It was oftener resorted to than the civil tribunal of justice and jury. But if at times they were hot tempered, they were sincere and just, and they helped to lay the foundations of a great State. Their work is ended. Their influence lives. For the preservation of our institutions their children's children will have more serious problems to solve than did those who assisted in their creation. It may be a dream, but none the less it seems a clear perception, that in the rural village, with intelligent cooperation in the cultivation of the soil, using the masterful forces of nature applied to machinery—each working for all and for each other—the practical Christianity of the Master of Nazareth will find complete exemplification, and the noblest types of American manhood and womanhood will be developed. Each higher stage of civilization is an ideal before it becomes real—an aspiration before a realization.

HOLLANDERS IN MICHIGAN

Engbertus van der Veen

The next selection, adapted from Engbertus van der Veen's "Life Reminiscences," describes the early history of Holland, Michigan, a community in some respects similar to Vermontville but also strikingly different in other respects. The founding and growth of Holland, Michigan, by a group of Dutch settlers who emigrated after 1848 is one of the remarkable episodes in the history of Michigan. The idea for emigrating to Michigan and establishing a colony on Lake Michigan was conceived by a charismatic leader, Dominie (or Reverend) Albertus Christian van Raalte. Van Raalte, troubled by religious tensions in his homeland, led his followers to what is now Holland, Michigan, where he sought to create a Christian society in which his followers would become more worthy followers of John Calvin and the important Dutch Christian Reformed leaders.

Van der Veen, who was born in Amsterdam in 1828, lived in Holland, Michigan, almost from the time of its founding; for many years he owned a hardware store. His memoir, written late in his life, conveys the flavor of life in a deeply religious and industrious community. Many of the Dutch immigrants had migrated from Amsterdam and other cities, adding considerably to their difficulties in becoming acclimated to the rigors of life on the Michigan frontier.

This excerpt is taken from Henry S. Lucas, *Dutch Immigrant Memoirs and Related Writings,* vol. I (Assen, The Netherlands: Van Gorcum & Company, 1955), pp. 489–514. The order of paragraphs has been changed.

Those were the good old days when immigrants crossed the ocean in sailing ships; my father sailed with his family in May 27, 1847, to this happy country, America, in the *Snelheid,* under the command of Captain J. J. Gorter. After a voyage of 49 days we arrived in the harbor of New York, and in sixteen days traveled from New York to Chicago, going by steamboat up the Hudson to Albany, by canalboat on the Erie Canal to Buffalo, and by steamboat over Lake Erie and Lake Huron, through the Strait of Mackinac and over Lake Michigan to Chicago. The last part of the journey was made in a sailboat to the mouth of Black Lake, now called Macatawa Park. The vessel came to anchor at the entrance and a yawl landed the passengers with their trunks, boxes, and other possessions on the beach. As there was no harbor the men carried all the goods over the beach to a flatboat lying in Black Lake to take us to the place where Dominie [Augustus Christian] van Raalte had settled. At midnight we landed at the foot of Fifth Street in what was called the City of Holland, really a dense forest of big trees—timber of all kinds. The air was full of malaria caused by the swamp, stagnant water, and dirty waters of Black Lake—a place of sickness and death. The night was dark, so we built a brush fire partly for light, partly on account of the damp air. We could not see how dismal and fearful our surroundings were. The moaning sounds of the western pine, the night birds squawking and shrilly breaking into weird cries, the hooting of owls, and the croaking of a multitude of strange creatures made a painful impression on our family just arrived from Amsterdam, and filled our hearts with dismay. However, the dawn of the first morning was welcome. Slowly the immigrants already settled here awoke from their slumber and made their appearance through the openings of the places in which they rested at night—little square log houses or huts made from branches placed against each other or leaning against falling trees.

Kees de Witt, an old soldier who served in the army of Napoleon I, and his wife, had erected a tent just long and wide enough for two, and so low that they had to creep on their hands and knees to get in and out. Nearly all the people we met had come from the rural districts of The Netherlands. Their dress and appearance were foreign to us who had come from the cities. Their dialects and their habits of speech were new to us. "Oh! oh!" cried mother, "I wish I were back in Amsterdam! Why did we come here?" She took courage, however, hoping soon to leave these miserable surroundings, for she remembered that some gentlemen in New York had told father that Dominie van Raalte's settlement was a large city, well populated, with many homes. She said to father, "First before all else go to the city and rent a good house with a nice lawn, near a brook with running water in which we can wash and rinse our clothes and bleach them on the lawn." So father went to Dominie van Raalte's abode, a plain board shanty, to find out where the city was and learn all the particulars about the location. Meantime mother comforted herself with the thought that she would soon be settled in a good house with everything as pleasant as in Amsterdam.

Father came back with a downcast look, saying that Dominie van Raalte thought we might find a vacant log house among the Indians who had a village near Black Lake on the present Diekema farm. Here stood a few small houses, a log church, and a cemetery nearby in which stood a large cross made of square timbers. Some of the settlers looked upon this cross with suspicion and contempt. On the beach the Indians built their canoes. "Horrid," cried mother in agony. "What! a vacant log house and one that has been occupied by the Indians? O, what shall we do?" A cry of distress sprang from her agonized soul, followed by weeping. We remained in the woods without preparing any shelter, waiting for a boat to come and take us back to our old home across the ocean. We had left our boxes and trunks, all unopened, on the beach, ready to load them upon a ship. There they remained about two months in rain and sun. No ship appeared, and we were left to our fate.

After father came back from Dominie van Raalte, in deep disappointment, the children asked for bread. All we had was dried ship's biscuit. I had been taken sick when on the Erie Canal and came near dying. When we landed at Black Lake I was so weak I could not walk. I had neither doctor nor medicine, and death would have been welcome. But the Lord did wonderfully. On the flat bottomed boat at midnight near the point at Central Park I felt a change and was cured. I had had nothing to eat for many days, but now my appetite returned. I asked for bread, but there was nothing. So we had to wait till something turned up. We did have some beans, however. Water was supplied by a spring, and for days we had bean soup.

After a while father found a vacant house in the woods near the place we had landed. It was built of logs each about eight inches in diameter. The walls were about three and one half feet high, the whole being covered with a peak roof.

Small trees used in place of rafters had been fastened on the logs and thatched with hemlock brush. Into that shelter we moved from our open air abode. This was our first lesson in training for the life of a colonist. My father opened a box containing a large table upside down, unpacked the feather beds and valuable articles such as china and crockery which had been tucked carefully between the table legs. The table was placed in the center of the room; our beds were spread out on the ground, for there was no floor. Water pitcher, bowls, plates, umbrellas, and other objects gave such impression of civilized life and reminded us somewhat of our life beyond the sea. Evening and night came as before and also the strange and unbearable variety of sounds. Again there was that horrid hooting and croaking. We placed an open umbrella in the door of our dwelling to keep any unlawful intruder, man or beast, from walking in. By this time the hemlock branches had dried out and began shedding their leaves which dropped in what we were eating and drinking. Our house looked like a large bird cage because of the chinks between the logs and hemlock branches. One afternoon a thunderstorm came up. The bolts roared like heavy cannon; the rain poured down while father, mother, aunt, and children tried to keep themselves dry under umbrellas. I took shelter under the table. Plates, pitchers, and other objects that would hold water were placed in the beds to keep them dry. But everything was soaking wet, for the rain came pouring in torrents through the brush which formed the roof.

After waiting in vain for a boat or vessel to take us from this place, father opened a box of coppersmith's and tinner's tools—only a few taken from the shop in the old country. We had some tin plate and solder rivets, etc. A fallen tree was chosen for a work bench. The news spread that a tinshop and store had been opened, and so the first hardware store in Holland City was a settled fact. One day while at work seated on our tree, soldering, there came a pretty girl of fifteen, carrying a leaky pail. I repaired it and she paid for the work. I looked at her again, following her with my eyes when she walked away—and she was gone. Six years later we became close friends, and for years thereafter we were each other's joy and happiness.

Marriage customs in those days were interesting. Two Sundays before the ceremony the minister announced from the pulpit before the congregation our intention of marriage. The purpose of this declaration was to enable anyone who had any lawful objections to the proposed marriage to state his reasons. This, according to the custom, was said to be "under the law." No one appeared, which showed we were in good standing; and on Saturday afternoon before the marriage at 5 o'clock, the appointed hour, we were to be at the home of Dominie van Raalte. It happened that I was busy that afternoon making stovepipes for C. Hoffman, who helped me while I worked on them. He wanted me to help him get ready his stove, but before I had finished it my pretty bride came in to see where I was and tell me it was past the time when we were to present ourselves before the dominie. I laid down my tools, washed myself, and changed my clothes—all in a hurry—and we were on our way, walking to the spot where the knot was to be tied. I don't remember what became of Hoffman, his stovepipe or stove—all I know is that we were late, but not too late for the solemn words to be pronounced by Dominie van Raalte who also gave advice and encouragement, closing with a prayer.

Lighthearted and happy, I went with my bride to the house of her cousin Herman Verbeek, with whose family she was staying. We talked and had supper. Not being so well posted as was my bride, I looked upon her as my lawful wife—the dominie had said so—and I thought the ceremony had been duly performed, although I did know that we were expected to come before the pulpit in church on the following day, during the Sunday service, for benediction. But oh, no!—my better half told me that the ceremony on the next day would complete our marriage, and that I would have to go back to my little room over our one-story 12x20 hardware store, to which early in the morning I had said "Goodby, old bed, I won't come back to you again." I told her that if she understood it thus I would wish her good night, and so I went back to the hardware store where five hours before I had been making stovepipes.

All summer, up to the date of our marriage, I had boarded with my friend's cousin, Herman Verbeek, with whom we were to stay for a few days until we began housekeeping. Sunday morning I went to his house for breakfast, and met my sweetheart. We went to the log church near the cemetery, and Dominie van Raalte pronounced the benediction. The soldier Kees de Witt placed the pillows on the floor before the pulpit on which we knelt to receive the benediction. Kees received his tips from the bridegroom and was happy. This was the final part of the ceremony, and now our marriage was in perfect order. Monday evening a few friends, Dominie and Mrs. van Raalte, Mr. and Mrs. Reitsma, Mr. and Mrs. Meengs, Herman Verbeek, and my sisters Christina and Hannah came to celebrate our wedding. My bride had prepared a wedding cake and served it with coffee, and we had a pleasant time. According to the custom no presents were given, which made everybody comfortable and free to enjoy the event. Our clothes were neat and plain. Our furniture was simple—only a cook stove and no carpet on the floor. . . .

About four weeks after our arrival in the woods, while father stood near a tree that had fallen on our tin shop, an old lady by the name of Slag came on a dead run stating excitedly that a man had just come with a drove of milk cows. Twelve dollars would buy one. "Just think of it—30 guilders for a milk cow; she is worth only that much for beef." Father went to see this man, and bought a black cow. It became my duty to feed her. For an hour in the morning, and several times during the day, I led her from tree to tree so she could eat the leaves. At other times we kept her tied to a tree, believing such treatment would be sufficient, But what did city folk know about cows? At best we had two or three scanty meals a day and thought a cow ought to be satisfied with only a few leaves. One morning we looked through the openings between the logs of our hut to see if the cow still was tied to the tree. We saw her rope, but the cow had gone; and so before breakfast I had to go into the woods to look for her. It was not until afternoon that I found her pasturing with other cows near the river. Klaas Hinderman told me that she had been there all day. From that time we let her feed at will. We made a tin bell for her so we could readily find her. She went dry in the fall, and we took her to Mr. I. van Dyke at Port Sheldon, where she died during the winter, and this put an end to our interest in cows.

Not many days after we arrived in Holland Bart Slag and I took a stroll through the woods and walked to the Indian village. When Bart saw the Indians he started on a run, thinking they would kill him. I looked around but was not a bit afraid of Indians. I had a greater fear of wild beasts, and in my imagination, seeing terrible beasts, I too ran away. On one occasion Abraham Slaghuis came running out of the woods. Thinking he had heard a fearful roaring, he believed he had escaped violent death. A few days later he again heard the same roaring and, more courageous than before, went to look for the beast but found it was only a night owl whose hooting had frightened him. Others had similar experiences. Some of the settlers thought they had seen a monstrous black animal, but upon looking a second time saw it was a blackened stump of a tree that had frightened them. On another occasion when people who had been frightened met a bear, the latter quietly ambled away. . . .

The colonists suffered much in the fall of 1847. We had neither food nor money. For days some of our people had nothing to eat but pork. Others had nothing but beans while some had only ship's biscuit. The strong and healthy among the men walked to Singapore or Allegan or Grand Haven to buy provisions, carrying them home for their families. But the weaker and helpless colonists had to make the best of it. Dense forests without roads, low land, swamp, and river made it almost impossible to reach any market with oxen or horses. It was 24 miles to Allegan, 30 to Grand Rapids, 22 to Grand Haven, and 14 to Singapore. One day farmer Anton Shorno, who lived eight miles from Black Lake, came to Holland with some salt pork, and sold all of it at eight cents a pound. Dear old lady Slag bought a small piece of about two pounds, paying eight stuivers (i.e., eight Dutch cents) for it.

Aart Vissers, the baker, managed to buy some flour and made bread which he sold at ten cents a loaf. Father bought all he could, and so we ate bread, soup, salt pork. Mr. Luther ate nothing but pork for three days; others were fortunate if they had anything else to eat. Some merchants from Allegan loaded a scow with potatoes and other provisions and floated it down the Kalamazoo River to Lake Michigan and along the shore to the mouth of Black Lake. There they loaded a yawl with the provisions from the scow and came to Holland with small quantities, thus making the settlers believe their supply was limited. This enabled them to charge a dollar for a bushel of potatoes which at home had cost eight or ten cents. They sold their groceries at the same rate. Everybody, however, was glad to get something to eat and willingly paid any price asked.

A plan was formed to open a co-operative colonial store. All goods were to be bought at wholesale and sold to customers at cost with a small percentage added. A committee was appointed to collect money in the form of a loan, to be returned with interest. Loaning money for this enterprise was considered a noble cause. The sums so collected were entrusted to a committee of two, Bernardus Grootenhuis and Mr. Elias Young, an elder from Grand Rapids, who were commissioned to buy merchandise in New York. They bought a lot of dry goods, groceries, shoes, Yankee notions, and other articles. They paid for some of these things in cash, and charged the rest to "Dominie van Raalte and Company." The first committee purchased a vessel in which to transport to Black Lake the goods that came from Chicago. This vessel also was to transport articles purchased from the settlers by the Company and carry them to the Chicago market. Shingle bolts, bark, oak staves, cord wood, and other wood products would be exchanged for necessaries. The co-operative company secured the sailboat *Knickerbocker*. Ale Stegenga and his son Wipke were placed in charge of the vessel; Jannes van de Luyster Jr. acted as local agent. The harbor at the mouth of Black lake was choked with sand. When the vessel came in from Chicago, she dropped anchor off shore in Lake Michigan. One of the crew was sent ashore in a yawl. A messenger was sent to the local agent in Holland. The goods had to be transported over the sand choked entrance and loaded in a boat and brought to Holland. Whatever the committee had bought from the settlers was shipped to Chicago by the same means. The local agent was busy managing this business which included sending scows to the mouth of the lake. . . . Grotenhuis was manager [of the store], Verhorst and Jim Westveer clerks. The committee was handicapped by lack of funds. Their management was without system, and the cooperative enterprise incurred expenses which made the goods exceptionally expensive.

Binnekant and Houtkamp then started a general store, accepting shingle bolts, staves and bark in exchange for store goods. This store was located at the foot of Second Street, near the Lake. Stores also were opened by Henry D. Post and others. With such competitors the colony store could not flourish, and the enterprise was a failure. The *Knickerbocker* was sold; and the remaining store goods were distributed among those who had loaned the money. The balance due was charged against Dominie van Raalte who was burdened with this debt for a long time. Finally, the brethren in the east helped him out of these difficulties.

The strange climate, malaria, moisture in the woods and swamps, stagnant water in the pools, improper food, and lack of shelter undermined our health, and many died. My sister Anna was seriously ill. Dr. J. J. M. C. van Nus who had just arrived from the old country was called. He gave her some medicine which did not help her, father remarked that he gave only a small dose. The doctor replied that this was true, saying he had only a limited supply and had to ration it that everybody might have some. My sister died along with four others that same night—and there was not a soul available to help the sick, for nearly everybody was suffering. . . .

Father sent me to Dominie van Raalte, as his house was headquarters for everything, to tell him that my sister had died and to ask of he knew where we could obtain a coffin. The good man made ready to go with me, but first took a bowl of fresh milk. It was early in the morning and we walked through the woods until we came to a brush shed occupied by a carpenter who had a few rough boards from which to make a box. Two men carried the box on their shoulders to our place. After placing my sister in a sheet, they laid her in the box and nailed on the cover. This done, they carried the coffin on their shoulders and, followed by my father and myself, buried it near Fourth Street and River street, without any ceremony whatever.

The settlers grieved deeply, for they could not bury their dead decently. Thus when his wife died, unable to find materials for a coffin or anyone to help him in his bereavement, Notier de Reft had to dig a hole near his hut, wrapped his wife's body in a bed sheet, and buried it with his own hands. There were others who buried their friends and children in the same manner.

Several doctors came to Holland, but they were not the best. Their intention was to fill their pockets. When their ignorance became apparent they went away. My father also fell sick, and the doctor gave him a teaspoon of brandy every hour until father refused to take any more. He felt he was becoming intoxicated. Soon it became clear that the physician was only a horse doctor. Another doctor came to Holland bringing with him a lot of sheep, for, as he said, he cured the sick by giving them mutton. He sold his mutton at a good price, collected handsomely for his services, and want away with his pockets well filled, after which other doctors also came and went.

Our never-to-be-forgotten Dominie van Raalte was loved and trusted by all. His untiring zeal and readiness to help comforted the sick. Every morning he received patients in his house, administering medicine with a tablespoon. Around him were bottles of quinine, blue pills, and rhubarb. The log kitchen served as a waiting room; the sick sat on a long board bench. In turn they went into the room where the dominie dispensed his medicine and gave advice; and this went on day after day. I have often wondered if he ever received any pay for his medicines.

Whenever anything unusual happened such as the arrival of a wagon or a boat with something for sale, the fact soon became known. One day a boat loaded with fresh meat came to the landing place, and many hastened to the spot. Everybody was eager to buy, but the owner of the boat insisted on providing the sick before selling anything to the others. Those who had sick folk in their tents secured fresh meat at a high price. The rest who were in good health went home happy that they had actually seen fresh meat.

After a short while we moved into a small house made of rough boards, owned by Jannes van de Luyster. The house had one room with a low ceiling. A ladder thrust through an opening gave access to the room under the rafters. The little room on the ground floor was occupied by four families with their children. The upstairs under the rafters served as sleeping quarters. Our beds were spread out on the boards, and the four families laid down side by side with their feet towards the opening. It was my good fortune to lie near Boudewijn Dertro and his wife Maria. Their evening dialogue was not amusing. Maria had no trouble in falling asleep, and soon snored to beat the band. "Quit that snoring," cried Boudewijn, "or I will kill you!" Then he would give her a vigorous shaking. But Maria did not like being interrupted. When she again began snoring there was another verbal barrage. Maria often talked to me and told me how much fun she had when as a young woman she went to circuses and dances. Poor soul, she died before New Year's. Her husband thanked the Lord openly, saying "I thank you, Lord, that I am delivered of her." But his joy was short lived, for soon after he also closed his eyes, never to open them again.

There was much amusement over our scratching which began with the plague of Egyptian lice. The woods and huts were all filled with the pests, and no remedy could be found so long as we lived herded together. The lice had been brought by the immigrants. When in spite of the vermin we began to fall asleep, we found comfort in dreaming of the past in our fatherland. Only when in my imagination I was back in Amsterdam, could I find joy and comfort. Then I saw the royal palace, bands of musicians, soldiers on horses, infantry marching through the Kalverstraat to the Dam. Again I walked in the Pantoffel Parade in the Keisergracht, again I was in the Boter Market where I saw the Jew Smoel with his tray full of cookies and Sara with her can of pickles. Once more I heard drums and trumpets. There at the Duivelshoek I again saw the dog shows. And there was the Munt, the famous old tower. There I found my friends, old chums, and told them I had lived in America—in the howling wilderness, shut off from civilization—and how happy I was to be back again! In my dreams I kicked the very stones in the street, to be sure I was not dreaming, and that I was back again in my beloved Amsterdam. But when I awoke, great was my disappointment, for it was only a dream! The night birds could scream, the owls hoot, and the surroundings looked so desolate that I felt as if I had been banished from my friends, robbed of the joy of life.

Five of the first settlers—Dominie van Raalte, Jan Binnekant, Jan Rabbers, Jan Stegman, and Jan Koolvoord—each bought on contract eighty acres of the land which originally had been intended for the use of the city and its surroundings, for pastures, vegetable gardens, etc. Four of these men intended to speculate and make a little money. "No," said Dominie van Raalte, "it was understood before we bought this land that no person could buy more than eighty acres of state's land, and that this land should be reserved as colony land, for the benefit of the settlers." At first they objected, but finally they turned over the land they had bought over to five trustees selected by the people at a citizen's meeting. My father was one of these trustees.

As soon as the trustees received the money from the sale of the land, they bought more land on contract, paying a little down in order to secure all of the land for miles around to distribute to the immigrants who were arriving each week. Thus, it was hoped, a large Dutch settlement would come into existence. All this caused Dominie van Raalte much labor and no end of trouble. The state lands in Drenthe, Vriesland, and surrounding country also were secured, at least so thought the dominie. But certain speculators who dug the canal in Grand Rapids received from the state land warrants which had been appropriated by the legislature for the payment of the canal. Seeing the immigrants settling on the choice lands of the region, they hurried to the state Land Office in Ionia. They selected the lands for which the dominie had repeatedly visited the Land Office. This caused Dominie van Raalte much difficulty and expense, all of which afterwards raised the purchase price of the land. The dominie empowered lawyers, and traveled from place to place to obtain information, but with no result. The land officers obliged their countrymen; the Hollanders lost the land. Finally, however, the dominie succeeded in securing title to the disputed land.

Meanwhile the city had to be surveyed and platted, a job given to Mr. E. B. Bassett from Allegan. With compass and chain he laid out the blocks, lots, streets, and public market places. First he ran a line through Eighth Street from east to west limits and platted the city north from that line to First Street—after the model of Allegan, and unfortunately without making provisions for alleys. After he finished this part of the city he became ill and went home, but soon sent Mr. John Dumont to survey and plat the south part from Eighth Street. After he laid out the streets and blocks, he sold his compass and chain to his helper Ben Grootenhuis. With the help of a man named Van Dam, Grootenhuis surveyed the lots in each block. The surveying finished, the plat was brought to the county clerk's office where it was registered as the village of Holland. The five trustees sold the first house lots for $15 each, but soon raised the price to $48 for corner lots and $38 for the lots between. The money thus received was divided among three funds: One for the salary of a minister and for church expenses; another for constructing a harbor and to encourage navigation; and a third for the improvement of the corporation and payment of its debt.

The trustees, knowing what benefit factories brought their communities, started a shingle mill. They had little success, however, for they were without capital, had no acquaintance with markets, and lacked the means of transporting their product. A good many settlers, however, made shingles for their own use. Henry D. Post and Dominie van Raalte started an ash factory to make black salt for the Chicago market. Mr. John Littlejohn and other citizens of Allegan talked against the Dutch settlers, wishing they would move away. They feared heavy taxes to support such a crowd of paupers. No! and again, no! Mr. Littlejohn! Although you are considered an intelligent man, little do you understand the history and character of the Dutch, a people zealous, enterprising, and persevering. Our ancestors by hard work converted the bottom of the sea into fertile fields. Over land and sea they are known as daring and patriotic people with deep appreciation for statesmanship. Should their children eat paupers' bread provided by the citizens of Allegan? No! As true children of the old Dutch stock they possessed the courage and perseverance to transform this land covered with timber and interspersed with soggy marshes into a countryside dotted with farms, villages, and factories, and now blessed with railroad and steamboat lines which bring our products to market, and all this by the grace of our God! To Him be the praise!

The principal motto of Dominie van Raalte was "My fellow countrymen, unite in form, and elevate yourselves; aim at a lofty standard of life; cultivate knowledge; lay an adequate foundation for your colony according to a well developed plan, that you may be a great people among the other groups of this land. Be diligent in educating your children; don't hold a calf in higher esteem than our own child." Before this settlement was organized into school districts, the promoters of education hired a Yankee school teacher, Mr. Hoyt from Kalamazoo; paying him a salary of $30 a month. The children went to school in the log church on the cemetery grounds. The older children, and also some of the younger, went to school in a room in Mr. Houtkamp's house on East Eighth Street. This house was built for Mr. Houtkamnp by Mr. R. Schelleman in the winter of 1848. The teacher was a Methodist who commenced his daily task with prayer. Our textbooks were Bibles, on each page two columns—one in Dutch, the other in English. We had to read in English and, by looking on the other column, tell the meaning of what we were reading.

The principles to govern our life in a consecrated Christian common wealth as laid down by our leaders were: to educate the young, build seminaries and common schools, organize local government, establish factories, open navigation, construct a harbor, and build roads. Town meetings were the order of the day. These gatherings were held in Binnekamp's home and hotel on the northwest corner of Eighth and River Streets. The first was s simple beginning, for the colonists had nothing; and sacrifice and labor were needed to start the wheels of our common life. Here young and old met on a basis of equality to discuss all questions of local importance. The consistory, composed of the elders and deacons, constituted the highest court, chiefly to maintain discipline.

The French and Yankee settlers on Point Superior who had vacated the place in 1836 had left a few empty houses. Jan Binnekant moved one of them to his lot on the corner of Eighth and River Streets, and this became the first hotel. . . . Binnekant, the landlord, himself asked grace before each meal which was closed by all singing a psalm in chorus.

This hotel, as we have noted, was the place for public meetings, and many an enterprise had its birth in this building. Everybody had the privilege of bringing new propositions before the meeting, which were disposed of to the best interests of all. At first meetings were held in the open air, and always opened with prayer. Committees were appointed for different tasks. Volunteers were asked to open roads, cut down trees in the schoolyard and public square, and open the harbor at the head of the lake by digging out the sand bar. The first public worship was held in the open air near the dominie's kitchen. The men had to stand up, but women, children, and the physically weak sat down on logs and fallen trees. The dominie stood and preached on a rude platform. Everyone came to these meetings unless something serious prevented. It was the only place where all the people could meet each other in common friendship after a week of hard physical labor. The boys and young men came to see the girls, to hear a sermon and join in the worship; but the older people longed for the words of truth and the communion of saints. Through the week, evening services were held at Binnekamp's hotel, Bible study at the dominie's house, and prayer meetings in the little red schoolhouse on East Eighth Street. The settlers were sincere Christians, God loving men and women. The Lord's house was their joy—a fountain to fill their hearts and minds with strength from above, encourage them to persevere, and do all things charitably, trust in God who would give them better day, and crown their affairs with success. Dominie van Raalte's preaching proved a blessing, the tie that bound men's hearts in love and caused them to place their trust in Him that He would care for them and help them.

The trials, exertions, and severe physical toil during the week caused many an exhausted person to fall asleep at Sunday services, but the resourceful dominie knew how to rouse them. Whenever it rained, we worshiped in the dominie's log kitchen. Occasionally, the Old Country students Jannes Van deLuyster and Cornelius van Malsen preached. . . .

During the summer of 1847 the settlers built a log church on the cemetery grounds. Gerrit J. Kroon was the architect. By the close of autumn it was so nearly finished that a room in the front of the building could be used for worship. Two old-fashioned cookstoves—Premium No. 9—were set on each side of the room, their stovepipes being passed through the side walls. While being transferred, the two cross plates which supported the covers were lost. Father made two new ones out of sheet iron but these soon warped from the heat, and so the room filled with smoke. But the room was warm and the smoke mattered little. First comers occupied the seats nearest the stoves, hugging the stove between their legs and remaining in that position throughout the sermon. The dominie stood on a little platform which had been erected near the partition. In the morning he preached a sermon; in the afternoon service he asked questions from Scripture. By the next summer the entire building was finished, with pulpit and pews according to custom. It was a satisfaction to have order in our worship. The first communion was celebrated out of doors behind the dominie's house, the communicants standing in a circle with the dominie and elders in the center. It was a solemn sight—in the midst of the discomforts of our life to remember the death of our dear Saviour and partake of His holy sacrament. How they testified that the Lord was good! The new church was provided with communion tables, children were baptized in front of the pulpit, and when marriages were solemnized with benediction—usually on the Sabbath—Kees de Witt, the janitor, laid the pillows before the pulpit for the couples to kneel on. Most everyone rewarded the good old man with a tip.

On New Year's morning we went to church to hear the New Year sermon. How well I remember the dominie preached on New Year's

Day of 1850 in that old log church from the gospel of Luke, 16, 2. . . . "Give an account of thy stewardship, for thou mayest no longer be steward." The dominie preached with great earnestness, warning his hearers to take these matters to heart. To me the truth came with great force—it seemed a matter of life or death itself. From the depth of my soul I cried out, beseeching the Saviour for mercy. I went home penitent, meditating upon my sins and upon the redeeming love of the Saviour to save souls of such even as me.

In the afternoon of that day we had a meeting of a different nature. It concerned the renting of pews. In front of the pulpit a table had been set, boards placed upon carpenter's horses. Elder Aldred Plugger took the chair while C. Hoffman acted as clerk. The consistory managed the affair. Deacon Teunis Keppel acted as auctioneer. Standing on pew he asked, "How much for a seat in this pew?" "Six dollars," offered three persons. "Who will pay more than six? Who?" "Seven dollars!" "Who more than seven?" The lucky person had to appear before the chairman and pay the money. Everybody knew that the amount had to be paid at once, but with the consent of the consistory purchasers may pay their sums later to the treasurer, Aldred Plugger, in his store. Sometimes the bidding became lively and some of the bidders were swept away in the excitement. So Lambert van Dis, Dirk Maurik, and others were loaded with seats at a high price. For the young people who had little recreation this was pleasant amusement, as to them any commotion was welcome. Yes, those young men were not as careful as they ought to be, for over the church door was written the admonishment, "Beware of your feet when you enter the House of the Lord."

The spirit of the Massachusetts Pilgrim fathers ruled the settlement, and many felt the sting of discipline as severe as any inflicted by the Blue Laws of Connecticut. The dominie and consistory exercised extensive ruling power, settling disputes, applying justice, rebuking people. Mrs. Fanny D. had gossiped about a neighbor woman who complained to the consistory. The penalty was public confession in church. I felt sorry for her. An elder had noticed a young lady, Sesine S. who improperly exposed her neck, so a cloth was placed over the offending neck and thus modesty was restored. Mr. Hermanus Doesburg published an article in the newspaper about the dominie and the consistory. The article was headed The Pope and his Cardinals. Doesburg was punished by being denied admission to the Lord's Supper. The time came for Holy Communion when according to custom all sat near the table. An elder stood at each end to keep unworthy persons from sitting down and prevent infractions of the regulations. One of the elders who did not know a reconciliation had been effected with the consistory saw Doesburg take his seat among those who intended to receive Holy Communion. Taking Doesburg by the shoulders with much patience, he requested him to leave the table, which created great commotion. Doesburg became very excited, stood up and declared he understood that on the day before all had been forgiven. Thereupon the members of the consistory corroborated his statements; and peace was restored whereupon Doesburg was permitted to sit down.

In the 1850's, perhaps it was in 1855, a circus came to our city and spread its tents in a vacant lot opposite the Grand Haven House, Mr. C. van der Veer's hotel on the corner of Sixth and River Streets. What a great scandal this was, violating the morals of the community and insulting its Christian charter! The elders, J. Labors and Teunis Keppel, stood near the entrance of the tent to note all who went in. Those who entered could be sure they would be required to make a strict accounting. The children were interested in the circus, but their fathers told them that it was a sin to see the performance. The circus men wandered among the stumps, swearing and using vulgar language, saying "What a d——d hole this is."

Our life was plain; even in church on Sunday the clothing of the people was simple. No one went thirsty during services, for a pail full of water with a dipper in it stood ever ready at the door. The dominie's two sons Bertus and Ben brought to church an Old Country jug filled with water. The churchgoers brought with them their noonday meal, consisting mostly of bread. This they ate in the church, washing down their frugal repast with water from the pail.

In 1854 our people began the building of a new church on the corner of College Avenue and Ninth Street. Jacobus Schrader was the architect. . . . The sills, crossbeams, and heavy timbers were hewn in the woods. The flooring, wallboards, ceiling, and pew boards were planed and matched by hand. For weeks Piet de Vries and others planed the floorboards. Ben Grootenhuis, assisted by his son Johannes, painted the structure in 1856. When the new building was finished we moved from the log church in the cemetery. Thus the members, who belonged to the Reformed Church, built this church with great zeal, with cash earned by hard labor and saved by rigid economy. The church was dedicated, but the members failed to incorporate the church body according to law. Tunis Keppel, an old settler, and his followers, immigrants of later years, never paid a cent toward expenses. They took advantage of the fact that the church body had never been incorporated, and seceded. They told the minority they should leave the church and surrender the building. Keppel and the rest of the consistory held the keys; they were determined to keep the structure for their own following, forgetting, as men of common sense would not, that the consistory were acting as trustee for the members. But according to law, inasmuch as the members were not incorporated, they were only a religious society and the majority ruled. Keppel was ambitious to perpetuate his own name. The consistory and the majority of the members, in the interests of purity of doctrine and peace of conscience, separated from what they declared was the wicked church in the East. . . . Thus they expelled a minority of their own brethren without refunding them a cent of their hard earned money, without a church building of their own, to drift, for themselves. Time came for the Classis to meet, according to the minutes of the latest session—that is, before Keppel's secession. Its sessions were to be held in our historic church, but Keppel and his followers said the church was theirs. On the morning of the day the Classis was to convene, the consistory locked the double door with a logging chain. The leaders, Van den Berg and Derk te Roller, one on each side of the doors, stood like sentinels guarding the entrance. Other members of the consistory, supported by a group of their faithful, stood within calling distance. By their gestures they showed themselves ready to resist any attempt to open the church door. Keppel, dressed in his best, walked inside the church yard from the gate to the church door, up and down, looking excitedly in all directions, his fists clenched as if ready for combat. . . . Seeing no agreement could be reached, they organized a classis then and there and adjourned to the Third Reformed Church. I went home, leaving the scene with a heavy heart, saddened so see how selfish men could act in the name of Christianity.

Tunis Keppel kept the church keys; and when the janitor, Dirk Sluiter, had to ring the bell he went to Keppel who accompanied him to the church, opened the door, and kept watch lest the ejected members should claim their church. After the janitor had rung the bell, Keppel locked the door. How well did Solomon declare that "the evil doers fear even when there is no pursuer."

In one of the public meetings held during 1850 in Binnekamp's hotel, it was resolved to purchase a bell for public use. A subscription list was opened and money was pledged to secure the bell we desired. The bell, bought in Troy, New York, arrived in good condition. A committee constructed a frame about ten feet high and set it up in the woods at the corner of College Avenue and Tenth Street. Gerrit Alberts, the watchmaker who had served as a soldier under Napoleon I, cast the metal sockets for the yoke because, as he claimed, he could construct them in such a way as to permit the bell to swing freely. To Hermanus Doesburg was assigned the task of ringing the bell. He was required to ring it on Sundays before church time, throughout the week for town and church meetings, in case of fire and burials, and four times each day at 7, 12, 1, and 6.

When the church was completed in 1856 this bell was placed in the tower. That faithful bell still rings out in silver tones from that old tower, reminding me of the days gone by and filling my soul with emotion. And that old copper rooster on the steeple—how I did work on it, making a good pattern and constructing in its bowels the apparatus that would enable it to respond to the winds from every direction! . . .

Work on the harbor and opening roads was on a voluntary basis without pay. We cut trees although we had never seen an axe in our lives. We chopped around tree trunks thinking that the best way to fell them. This was dangerous, for a tree standing on the center of a stump might fall in any direction, endangering the lives of the choppers. The roads were made just wide enough for a team of horses. If two teams happened to meet, they turned out into the woods the best they could. In low places logs were laid side by side across the road, such a construction being called a "log bridge," or "corduroy road." Riding over such a bridge in a lumber wagon drawn by oxen was a severe trial. The shaking made me sick in my stomach. I chopped down trees on my father's property on the southeast corner of College Avenue and Eighth Street, where we intended to build a house. I began chopping a dead hemlock tree two feet six inches in diameter, which had no limbs. Like others, I chopped around the trunk. As the outside had rotted and was soft I soon reached the center of sound wood only a few inches in diameter. The tree began to sway a whip lash and I started on a dead run. Fortunately, it fell in another direction. On another day I chopped a green birch tree 16 inches in diameter. To my horror, when it began to fall, I saw my brother Christian coming. I shouted with all my might. He thought I wanted him to run toward me. Fortunately, the tree lodged in another tree and my brother was saved from certain death. Trees standing near houses were dangerous, and cutting them down was entrusted to Indians and Yankees who knew how to fell trees in any direction. A large tree stood close to the house of John Kolvoord on Eighth Street near Columbia Avenue. Mr. Gerrit Wilterdink thought he had acquired the art of felling trees, but the Kolvoord family, not trusting his skill, stood outside the house to watch him while he worked. Bart Kolvoord, John's brother, looked at the tree and said, "It is a dangerous thing to chop down so big a tree." He was right, for Wilterdink failed to drop the tree away from the house, and it crashed through the roof crushing the stove and furniture.

A resolution was adopted to open a road between Holland and Zeeland to be done by volunteers. Trees were cut down in mid-winter during a heavy fall of snow. Fires were built which enabled us to keep warm while we ate our frozen bread and drank water from the streams. The Cedar Swamp east of the city limits was filled with water and cedar logs were piled in the road to make it passable. Next was hewn a road leading through the low land across the brook to the log church. This likewise was accomplished by volunteer labor. Everybody turned out whether he knew how to chop down trees or not. I chopped down a tree near the brook, about 12 inches in diameter. The tree was crooked, and when it came down, the lower part swung around my head and I escaped by a hair's breadth. Once Kees Kuit, brother in law of G. and Jacob van Putten, was chopping down a tree when a man cried, "Look out!" Kuit dropped behind a big log and the tree fell over him. Jacob van Putten scolded the man for his thoughtless shouting, for he should have waited till the tree started to fall before giving his warning. I remember that the dominie's team of black oxen, driven by Cornelius van Herwijnen, pulled logs and stringers which were needed to make a firm road bed. Thus was finished this important road, the one over which so many of the settlers went to church for worship, to be married, or to carry their dead to their final resting place.

Step by step the settlers built their town in accordance with their ideas of comfort and happiness. Eighth Street was the first thoroughfare to be opened. Trees were cut down and piled high in the Public Market, or Fish Market, by the church, or in the school yards. These piles of logs and brush burned readily during the dry weather of the following summer. A fire started in the woods and, whipped by a strong wind, spread to the woods everywhere. The pine and hemlock trees were aflame to their very tops. This was on a Saturday morning, and everybody turned out to keep the fire from spreading to the few dwellings already standing. People carried water and covered their possessions with sand. Hermanus Doesburg and I were asked to keep watch during the night to keep the log fences around the schoolyard from catching fire. All Sunday the people fought the fire, so there was no public worship that day. People carried their clothing and furniture into the streets and open spaces, thinking things would be safer there than in the houses. But in spite of the fact the fire raged on all sides, the Lord's protection was marvelous. The fire burned the brush and wood around the houses and even swept under the house belonging to Mr. V. Verhorst, situated near the City Mills, but not one house was lost. Finally it began to rain and the fires were extinguished. We were very thankful for the fires because the town looked much better than when the brush and logs covered the ground on all sides.

The first water-driven sawmill in the Colony was built at Groningen, three and one half miles northeast of Holland. This neighborhood was named Adam and Eve after two settlers everybody knew at that time. But in Holland Jacobus Schrader erected the first windmill to be constructed in the colony. It was built according to Old Country models. . . . This mill was situated near the Grand Haven Bridge on River Street, but it never sawed much lumber.

Oswald van der Sluis arrived from Arnhem in the summer of 1848. He erected a sawmill near the lake on Fourth Street. This mill, which operated a one-frame saw, produced a good deal of lumber. Mr. Bosdijke, a gentleman of rank, came from Amsterdam by way of Canada. In 1849 he installed two sets of small millstones with which to grind wheat and corn. This was our first flour mill but its operation soon came to an end when Bosdijke returned to the Old Country. One time the dry logs, brush, and rotting wood which still lay in great quantities near the houses, caught fire. A wind rapidly spread the blaze, endangering the mill. I heard a voice near Binnekamp's Hotel, and saw Mrs. Binnekamp ringing a dinner bell shouting "Fire! Fire! Van der Sluis' mill is burning! Help! Help!" Everybody rushed with ropes, shovels, and pails to put it out. A pail brigade was formed, a successful way of extinguishing the flames. . . .

On at least one occasion were the blue laws applied. Instead of going to church one Sunday, Joos ver Planke and Kees Dok played in the woods and broke the windows of the orphanage. Deacon Keppel, made a complaint before Justice of the Peace Henry D. Post. The court—the first jury trial in Holland—was held in a small house next to Binnekamp's Hotel, and Old John Trempe served as chairman of the jury and I was one of the jurors. As we talked about the case, one of the jurors said he had been told someone had heard that, while the boys were in bed, Kees had said to Joos, "I'll whip you if you tell what we have done." This settled the case. "Guilty," said the foreman of the jury. Joos being too young to be sent to prison; the judge made his father pay a small fine. But Kees was sent to the county jail in Grand Haven for thirty days. When the sheriff and his wife heard the grounds on which the boy had been sentenced, they laughed heartily. No lawyer had been employed to defend him, and it as only a jury's verdict that had sent this young villain to jail for thirty days, on account of the crime of breaking a pane of glass seven by nine inches. The sheriff entertained the boy as a member of his family until the thirty days were finished.

Our Indian neighbors were very good people so long as they trusted our honesty. . . . One spring morning a young brave, all trimmed up in Indian style and accompanied by a young squaw, came into our store. They bought a cook stove and paid for it in gold, telling me they would call for it. From time to time the Indian came to look at the stove until, late in the fall, he took it away. One Sunday our dominie announced from the pulpit that a chief had complained that the settlers had taken away their sugar troughs, and that the Indians were revengeful. He demanded that we punish the guilty persons and that the troughs be returned. The dominie told him that this had happened perhaps by mistake or through ignorance. After the announcement the dominie advised that those who had taken the troughs should return them. The people had taken them home for feeding their hogs. One day a family chanced upon a dressed deer hanging on the limb of a tree. They took the venison home and salted it in a keg. When the Indians noticed that their deer was gone, they came to the house. The Indians opened the locked door and found the venison. They seemed to be able to recognize their property. When the family came home they found the door open and some of the venison on the table, cut into little pieces. The family understood this meant revenge, and without delay hastened to settle with the Indians.

The majority of the first settlers were Christians, but yet imperfect, which showed itself in many ways—on one occasion especially in a political election in the township of Zeeland which had been organized in 1850. The southeastern part of the township at Drente was known as Statesland, while the country beyond from Forest Grove to Jenison formed one township. The first town meeting in Zeeland Township was held in the log church at Zeeland. Early in the morning of the day of the caucus Dominie van Raalte, accompanied by such as had the right to vote and also by some friends and boys, went to Zeeland, walking the entire distance, climbing over fallen trees, and wading though water. They arrived in time for the meeting. Dominie van der Meulen was in the pulpit acting as chairman. Soon there was great excitement, and Dominie van Raalte stood on the pews appealing to the men, saying "Brothers! Brothers!" The Zeelanders, supported by their friends form Statesland, wanted all the offices to the exclusion of the men from Holland. The dominie's exhortations calmed the spirits just in time to prevent hard blows.

After the caucus we went home in a body. Some of the office seekers were angry and jealous, complaining that the Zeelanders had captured the best offices. Pieter van den Berg had said, "Holland is ignored." Others said: "Well, well! that old Jan Hulst from Statesland, justice of the peace! That man with such a rebellious character! He is more for war than peace!

The Zeelanders and the Stateslanders were angry at the men from Holland. They declared that the Pope and His Cardinals of Holland (Dominie van Raalte and the consistory) had come to Zeeland to impose their rule, and that they were selfish. The expression "Pope and his Cardinals" was frequently employed by malcontented spirits, especially in the editorials of *Die Nederlander*, a weekly paper published for a short time by men who gloried in publishing vicious articles.

The last day of the year always was a happy holiday. A society had been formed to raise a fund to help needy people in the Old Country to emigrate. Members paid their weekly assessed amount into a fund. On the last day of the year they drew lots to determine who might have some friend of family come over with all expenses paid. Persons so helped would refund this sum which in turn would be used to help others. The drawing took place in Aldred Plugger's store which was filled with fragrant odors coming from the bakery in the kitchen in anticipation of the evening festival. At this gathering we saw happy faces, much in the spirit of the old custom in the fatherland. What a comfort it was to see everybody in good spirits when New Year's Day drew near! Everybody behaved modestly. We had no saloons to make us unhappy. Will we ever behold the day when the evil saloon is banished from our land? May the Lord Grant it! The first building lots were sold on the agreement that no saloon was ever to be built upon them. Of course there were people who had whiskey at home; when friends called they were given drinks which made them merry. There were too many people of this sort, but there were no saloons.

The homes of Toon van der Wal, Captain Gerrit J. Havekate, and old Bongars, and the blacksmith shop belonging to Hindrikus Stokking were resorts of the thirsty ones; and everybody knew this. One time a smart fellow told Jan Kroll a butcher and friend of the bottle, that after the vendor had delivered a deed the purchaser was free to do as he liked with the property. The agreement not to open a place for the sale of liquor was not binding and could not be enforced, he stated. So Knoll opened a saloon in the second story of his house on Central Avenue between Seventh and Eighth Streets. Jan Vissers opened the front room of his bakery on the southeast corner of Central Avenue and Eighth Street for the accommodation of church-going people who wanted to smoke and drink on Saturdays. The room was always full of good Christians who smoked, drank beer, and talked about sermons, the Bible, and Christian comfort. The more strict called this place the "church saloon." These brethren came to see the sinfulness of their ways, which resulted in breaking up the "church saloons."

Dominie van Raalte preached against places of temptation and deeds of wickedness. He was an eloquent and pious minister, his sermons were powerful and instructive. And although not perfect, he was a wise and loyal leader, serious, inspiring courage, and ready to give advice to all who asked for it. He was the first to donate cash to promote any good cause in the church. May his name and influence long be a blessing to the community. The first sermon the dominie preached in English was at the funeral of Abraham Cahill in the house built by Jan Slag on the lot where the present Engine House no. 1 is located. . . .

The settlers stretched as far as possible what little they possessed. For our narrow circumstances demanded careful use of money. From tin plate I had on hand I made, among other articles, a square basin supported by three small legs and provided with a little handle, to hold live coals when placed in a wooden foot stove, following Old Country style. One day Mr. Hindus Stokking, the blacksmith from Drenthe, called on mother and stated that he could sell some foot stoves if I would make some. So one day early in the morning, accompanied by Elder Broek, I set out for Brenthe, carrying a lot of basins and tied together with a rope over my shoulder. We walked through the woods, climbing over fallen trees, traveling up and down hills, wading through low land and brooks, and crossing large streams until at last, late in the afternoon, we arrived at the home of a widow, the mother of a number of children. They were friendly and glad to see us. Mr. L., an old widower, was visiting in the house, and seemed to take a leading part in the household affairs. He was sweet on the widow and must have had some understanding with her which afterwards resulted in marriage. The girls were busy—some churned, others came in with the cows, and everybody worked. The cows, the house, and even the air out of doors carried the odor of wild leeks, a green plant which grew plentifully in the woods during springtime. The milk and butter, in fact everything, had the unpleasant taste of leeks.

It was spring and the evenings were long. The front door of the cookstove was open and the glow of fire lit the room. We ate by the light of a candle, and, as soon as we had finished our supper, Mr. L. suggested that instead of reading a chapter from the Bible we should sing a psalm. Next came a prayer of thanksgiving during which for the sake of economy the candle was put out because, as he said, we would not need any light. The evening passed pleasantly. "Good night," said one of the daughters and, lighting the candle, she mounted the ladder to go to her bed on the second floor. Thinking the girls would let the candle burn longer than necessary, Mr. L said, "Girls, blow out the light." "Yes, yes," they replied, and all was dark. After that we went to bed, and, being young, I soon was in sweet dreamland. It was dark when I awoke but the rooster's crow announced the dawn. How often in life's journey—in dark hours of sorrow, in trouble, and in trial—the Lord has given His children the faith to see the signs of glorious morning! This is only a part of our experiences; hitherto the Lord has helped us, 1903.

LIFE IN THE COPPER COUNTRY

John H. Pitizel

In the fall of 1843 a Methodist minister, Rev. John H. Pitizel, began a nine-year stint of missionary duty in the vicinity of Lake Superior. He worked in many parts of the region, including a year at Sault Ste. Marie, three years on the Keweenaw Peninsula, which he called "Kewawenon," and one year at the Cliff Mine, where he observed the great copper rush of 1843–1846. His descriptions of the copper mines and social life among the miners is one of the valuable documents of the pioneer period.

The "Michigan Conference" to which Pitizel refers was an annual meeting that coordinated the missionary activities of the Methodist Church. This conference was organized in Mansfield, Ohio, in 1836; its missionary area included all of the then territory of Michigan. After each annual conference, ministers were sent over a wide area. "In the Fall of 1843," he wrote many years later, "it fell to the lot of the writer to take part in this missionary work. For nine successive years he was subject to its discipline and duties. One year at the Saut [sic] Ste. Marie; three years at Kewawenon, on the southern shore of Lake Superior, two hundred and fifty miles from the Saut; one year at the Cliff Mine, with Point Kewenaw for his field; and four years superintendent of the Lake Superior District, residing at the Saut."

In the third year of his Methodist "itinerancy," Pitizel began working among the miners of the Lake Superior area. Years later he recalled that "this circuit, as it might be called, is over two hundred miles in extent, counting the zigzag trails across Point Kewenaw. This made it necessary to travel more or less almost every day, and often twenty-five or thirty, and even more, miles a day, carrying a pack weighing from twelve to twenty pounds. It cost me, in all, about twelve hundred miles traveling, nearly eight hundred by foot, and the rest by water. Such are the characteristics of Methodist itinerancy in this region."

Pitizel's memoir describes not only the hazards of missionary life in Michigan's Upper Peninsula in the 1840s but also the social life and even the technology of copper mining. The "copper rush" had peaked about 1846; the Cliff Mine Pitizel described had already become a capital-intensive operation. The national publicity about the removal of the Ontonagon Boulder in 1843 and the discovery of rich copper deposits in the Keweenaw Peninsula led to a copper rush, which peaked in 1846. The Pittsburgh and Boston Mining Company opened the Cliff Mine in August 1845 with an investment of about $110,000; before the mine closed, it had earned more than $2.3 million in profits. In this mine were huge fissures of pure copper, weighing in some cases a thousand tons.

The following is an excerpt from John H. Pitizel, *Lights and Shades of Missionary Life* (Cincinnati: Western Book Concern, 1857), pp. 131–74.

The Michigan annual conference met this year [1843] in Ypsilanti, on the 15th of September. It was more than a month after before we heard any thing about our appointment, and, even, nothing official. We had never been so comfortably fixed to winter at that station as now. On account of our new church, which had progressed thus far under our supervision, and some other matters not so easily managed by strangers, we had hoped to remain another year; on other accounts we had no special reason to regret a change.

It was near the close of October, when blustering winds and occasional snow squalls warned us of the near approach of a long winter, that a breeze from a warmer clime, chilled in its long passage over the lakes, reached us, uttering, in language not to be misunderstood, "Arise, for this is not your rest." But many and formidable were the obstacles in the way of removal. The lateness of the season, the dangers of the Lakes, rendered appalling by late and serious disasters, particularly that which happened to the steamer *Julia Palmer*, which for sixteen days had been at the mercy of storms—all these, aggravated by a report directly from Point Kewenaw that, in consequence of the great loss on the *Julia Palmer*, many of the miners were almost exposed to starvation, and that provisions were not to be obtained; added to the fact that our own funds were nearly exhausted—these and other circumstances gave a gloomy appearance to our future prospect. But while reflecting on this aspect of things, I was rebuked by that passage from the Savior, "Behold the fowls of the air, for they sow not, neither do they reap, nor gather into barns, and yet your heavenly Father feedeth them." This is enough. Will God feed the birds and not his children?

The want of religious society in our prospective field was a serious drawback on our feelings. But we had always made it a matter of conscience to go, if possible, to an appointment; and, therefore, resolved to venture our all on the goodness of the appointing power, and, at least, throw our length that way.

For a long time we had looked in vain, for some vessel to bring winter supplies to the mission. For nearly two months, up to the sixth of November, we had lived on borrowed provisions, and yet none came, and no way seemed to open for us to get away.

The schooner *Fur Trader* was expected by the 10th of November, on her way from the *Saut* to the Ontonagon. We put all things in readiness, and awaited her arrival with great solicitude. November 10th came, and true to her expectation the old schooner came in sight.

Night had just dropped her dark brow over the face of the sky, when a rap was heard at the door of the mission. Who should be there? Who but one of the hardy pioneers of Lake Superior, who knew not what it was to shrink from toil and danger? Yes, it was a missionary, brother P. O. Johnson, and his delicate wife, who had come just about two hundred miles, in a bark canoe, to labor in the place of the old incumbents. This did not look like an assertion I saw some time ago in a Catholic publication, that Protestant missionaries did not penetrate into this country till "*feather beds*" etc., have been provided for them. No missionaries have labored in the true spirit of sacrifice more than some of the Protestant missionaries of this region. I need not say that they came unexpected, as it was the first hint we had of the new arrangement, only so far as we were concerned.

November 11. The *Fur Trader* came to anchor opposite the mission. But imagine our disappointment when we learned that she had been driven out of her course by adverse winds—had been to the Ontanagon, and was on her downward course for Saut Ste. Marie. The only alternative now left us was to coast. We were now subjected to a series of perplexities and disappointments in procuring men, a canoe, etc., which it would be tedious to name.

By the evening of the 15th of November we succeeded, with the blessing of a kind Providence, in finding a good bark canoe, and two able-bodied *voyageurs*. Now our goods, which had been packed for shipping, must be overhauled, and the bare indispensables packed ship-shape for a canoe, and the remainder packed and left till spring. The whole constituted no great bulk, as we had no furniture of any kind. What little we had was disposed of on leaving the work below. And whether we could get chairs, bedsteads, tables, stoves, crockery, etc., was a question that it would not do to try to solve. The truth is, means should have been sent us from the start. The Missionary Society had appropriated one hundred dollars toward our support on condition we failed to get our pay from the miners. But had the rigors to which we were constantly exposed been fully known, the appropriation, small as it was, could have been subject to no such contingency. With eight dollars loaned to us by a friend, after a rough journey of four days, in which we were buffered by the elements, having, in one place, for some distance, to force our way through ice which had closed up Portage river, we succeeded in reaching our new home, adoring that kind and merciful Providence which had kept us and guarded our way in every step.

Our New Field

After being very uncomfortably situated for some time, for want of a house to live in, a place was at length provided for us by the Company. This would have been ready for us on our arrival, but our long detention at Kewawenon led the Company to think that we were not coming, and all the buildings had been leased. On the 29th of November, much to our comfort, we took possession of our new home. This was a cabin built of round logs, a story and a half high, divided below in two apartments by a board partition, with a wood-shed made of rough boards. There was no cellar, or other conveniences about the concern, except what were included within the building. During the winter, when a large body of snow lay on the roof, as was often the case, the heat of the two stove-pipes, passing directly through the roof without chimneys, and the rarified air under the roof, caused the snow to melt, and the water running down the walls on the outside became congealed, which, on thawing, often forced its way inside, and made the house wet and uncomfortable. Our utmost vigilance could not wholly guard against this difficulty. But our cabin was a much better one than some of our neighbors had, and we have always felt grateful to the Company for giving us possession of such a home. It is simply mentioned here as a specimen of backwoods life. Added to the house, the Company kindly furnished us with a cooking-stove and other heavy furniture, which we were to use free of charge, and return when done with them. They also filled our bill of supplies in the provision line, and charged to my account till it could be cancelled. Mr. Taylor, of the Albion Mine, kindly loaned us a box-stove and some crockery. Thus all our wants were met in a way we had not anticipated.

The scenes surrounding us were different than any to which we had before become accustomed. Mining must go on day and night, the constant din and bustle of which is often annoying to one unused to such business. If you retire at nine o'clock, the bell ringing for a change of *shifts*, at ten o'clock, will awake you. This will be accompanied by the bustle of men coming from the mine, and fresh hands taking their place. Perhaps before you are fairly asleep again, you will be aroused by a car rumbling on a track, from the mineral shed to the stamp-house, where the mineral is precipitated into a large box, the bottom of which is an inclined plane, and thus conducted to the stamps. And then here are these six ponderous stamps, propelled by steam, which are crushing the mineral all night. Meanwhile you may hear the hammer and anvil and the incessant creaking of the old *whim*—a machine for raising copper from the mine—and the retort of an occasional blast like that of a cannonade. All these things make some noise, but the frequent fighting of several mules in a barn near our dwelling, added to all the rest, completes the "confusion worse confounded." Such, in substance, were our impressions penned on the spot.

In the period of a year, matters had materially changed on Point Kewenaw. The two previous years, the "copper fever" had raged to a great extent. The country swarmed with persons who were exploring it, and "laying permits," or "making claims." If *trap rock* could be found in any locality, having veins of *quartz* or *spar*, with or without copper, it was thought to be a "good indication," and forthwith a permit was laid, a company formed, and the stock divided up into shares, and these were thrown into the market for the highest bidder. Sometimes gentlemen from the cities, a little flush with money, but green enough, as it regarded the geological formations of that region, at the sight of a few rock "*specimens*," without ever having seen the prospective mine, would eagerly catch the bait thus thrown out. Perhaps, on more close inspection, the mine which presented such "good indications," was located in some cedar swamp or lake.

But in many places the prospect was sufficiently flattering to induce the proprietors to erect buildings at considerable cost and prosecute mining. But these prospects, becoming overhung with doubt, such locations had, in many instances, been abandoned. The ill-directed attempts of persons who came there and expected to grasp an immediate fortune, without either capital or labor, and the extreme into which speculation had been carried, were now reacting, most severely, upon the interests of the country. So much so that many persons abroad seriously thought mining operations on Lake Superior to be all a "humbug," undertaken on purpose to swindle men out of their money. This change in the condition of the country tended materially to circumscribe the sphere of our missionary efforts. Several locations were visited at different times during the year, and meetings held among the miners as opportunity offered. I made one trip about mid-winter to the Kewawenon mission, and administered the ordinances to the people at the request of the missionaries, neither of whom was ordained. In my absence Rev. J. W. Holt, from this mission, supplied my place. These trips were all made on foot, as was the customary mode of travel by land. Excepting those occasional excursions abroad, our efforts were mostly confined to the Cliff Mine and vicinity.

The mixed and unsettled character of the inhabitants was not very favorable to evangelical effort. The English miners were principally from Cornwall, England, and were familiarly known by the title "Cornish." Their dialect, though not so barbarous as the Yorkshire, is so different from the Anglo-Saxon of our own land, that an inexperienced ear is often at a loss to determine what is said, especially in rapid speech. The letter h, especially, is so much in the habit of straying away from home that he is seldom found where he really belongs. He usually finds about the following connections: "*Hi will give the orse some hoats and ay.*" In a school which I taught at the Cliff, during the winter, there were some scholars that I could hardly make give the simple sound of i, without the h going before. This must serve as a specimen of the manner in which the Queen trains her subjects to "murder the King's English."

Many of the miners were German and Irish. Among the former a few were Lutherans; the others, with the mass of the Irish population, adhered to the Romish Church. There were also a few French who were Romanists. Several of the agents, clerks, or employes were our own countrymen, and, in general, were well educated and shrewd business men. To make money was the object which induced most of the inhabitants to forego the blessings of home, in a better land, and endure the privations and hardships of the wilderness. Many favored the institutions of religion as a matter of policy, as connected with mining, who, so far as their own life and practice were concerned, lived in entire neglect of their spiritual interests. It is tacitly acknowledged, even by the most skeptical, that without the moral and religious restraints of the Church, it would be hard to control such men as are generally employed to work the mines.

Many of those miners had families in a distant land, some across the great Atlantic, whose society they had not enjoyed for years. A few knew what it was to rejoice in the liberty of the Gospel. But several had found their way into that region who had once tasted of the sweets of redeeming love, but like the prodigal had left their Father's house. In this wilderness many snares were but too successfully laid for their feet. The influences around them tended to harden them into their career of backsliding. Some abandoned themselves to drinking and gambling, hunting and fishing, and other amusements on the Lord's day. To such the warning voice of the Gospel seemed lifted in vain. Vice and wickedness of various kinds and degrees obtained here a luxurious growth.

Our religious meetings were conducted with great inconvenience for want of a suitable place. The only place we could obtain at the Cliff was a small school-room. The class formed the year before had been broken up by removals. Soon after our arrival we collected another class of about a dozen members, with whom, during the year, we enjoyed many precious seasons. Our public meetings were often seasons of interest and profit; and, in the midst of a far too general neglect of divine things, we have reason to believe that the efforts put forth at that station, in the name of the Lord, were owned by him to the edification of his people and the advancement of his cause. . . .

During my residence among the miners we found many large and warm hearts to throb under the rough exterior. And while the facts compel us to speak of many evils, many things were found worthy of high commendation. For frankness, warm and generous sympathy, and liberality to relieve the suffering, to support the Gospel, to aid the cause of Sunday schools, or the missionary cause, we have seldom known this people to be excelled. They have been trained to acts of liberality and hospitality from children. Convince them that a noble charity is in want, and it will here find a ready and generous response.

One practice as connected with the public worship of God among them we could wish was generally in use; that is, congregational singing. No people in the world are so familiar with the Methodist hymns as our English brethren. And they nearly all sing. The praises of God as thus sung by the whole congregation, in which the several parts are generally well sustained, come nearest to our notion of the anthems of heaven of any thing we can conceive. Some of the singing we have heard at the Cliff Mine is often brought to our remembrance. With those dear brethren we hope by and by to sing "the song of Moses and the Lamb."

Eagle River is an inconsiderable stream, except at its mouth, emptying into Lake Superior about twenty-five miles west of Copper Harbor. It derives its name from the Indian—*Me-ge-zeh*—an eagle—and *se-beh*—a river. The small town at the mouth bears the same name. The site is an immense sand-bank and has no attractiveness. The special want is a good harbor, as it forms the depot for the Cliff Mine and several others, is a central rallying-point for all parts of the Lake, and necessarily a place of much business. A good pier, built at great expense, supplies, in a measure, the want of a harbor. Here is a regular preaching-place; but no society has been formed, and no immediate prospect of one. Mr. Atwood kindly opened his dining-hall for religious worship, and, with his family, has shown us many marks of favor. A mile and a half upstream is what is called Eagle River Diggings. Here are the Lake Superior Company's works—now abandoned—our place of residence.

From the Lake, going nearly south to the cliff, we ascend gradually till we reach the top of the hill, five or six hundred feet above the level of the Lake, two and a half miles inland. A road has been constructed at much expense—still very rough and uncomfortable. The wet places are bridged with round logs, technically termed *corduroy*. The hill-side is stony and uneven. From the top we have a fine view of Lake Superior to the north. When the atmosphere is clear, Isle Royal can be seen, at a distance of fifty miles. The land is heavily timbered with birch, maple, hemlock, etc., and well watered with numerous springs. The soil is alluvial, and adapted to farming purposes. Many people get their living by farming in as rigid a climate and on poorer soil. Still it is granted that farming can never become a cheap source of industry or revenue in the Lake Superior region.

Passing through a defile, we gradually descend, by means of a road which winds around the side of the bluff, to the south. The natural scenery is here highly picturesque. As you descend, to your left is a deep chasm, which forms the valley of Eagle river. Here you look down on the tops of tall trees, and far beyond the land rises to view in mountainous ranges. Here a cold spring gurgles from the cliff, and crosses the road; there a delightful little stream tumbles down the precipice, and makes music on the ear. To your right, the Cliff now rises above you in majesty and grandeur. At the works the top of the Cliff is two hundred and twenty feet above the west branch of Eagle river. Here one would suppose that nature in one of her freaks, had attempted to shake down the mountain; for in every direction lay broken masses and heaps on heaps of the trap rock thrown down from the top. Some of these masses are as large as good-sized cabins, and have lain in their present position sufficiently long to support the growth of good-sized trees. As you look up to the masses which crop out to the summit, you would naturally imagine that some were just ready to leap from their fastnesses. And should they do so, woe betide whatever was beneath them.

On the side of this convulsed and rocky cliff, in the midst of some of these rocks, are situated the houses, shops, and works of the miners. There is here no appearance of pleasantness for a village, environed, as it is, with lofty woodland, which intercepts the view in all directions. The office and store joined together is a pretty good building. Some of the dwellings are tolerably comfortable, but not built with regard to convenience, or external neatness or order. Necessity has been the rule, and was a good one to begin with. But the Company has opened on a rich treasure, and will probably be disposed to bestow more taste on their future improvements. On our arrival here we found one hundred and forty persons at work on the Cliff Mine, seventy to eighty underground, and about sixty *grass hands*—a miner's term for surface workmen. Captain Jennings, a master at mining, was Agent, but succeeded the next summer by Mr. L. Hanna, a gentleman well qualified for so important a charge. Captain J. still managed the principal mining operations, while Mr. H. took a general oversight of the whole business.

The workmen are generally robust and hardy, but rough in their appearance and manners; yet, under their rough exterior, are some noble minds and generous hearts. To get a good view of them, as they issue from the mine, you should be at a prominent place at the ringing of the dinner bell. You may see them coming from the mine, covered with mud and dirt, and often drenched from head to foot. Sometimes they leave their light behind them, but often you will see a small tin lamp fastened to the hat, or a piece of candle in a lump of wet clay attached to the hat—all burning. The workmen now, generally in a single file, make a straight wake for their boarding-house, crossing each other's path in nearly all directions. If one did not know better he would suppose them to be inhabitants of a world where the sun's rays never reached; and they are, eight hours out of twenty four.

The Cliff Mine as Seen in the Summer of 1848

If the kind reader is disposed to take a peek at some of the wonders that are disclosed beneath the surface of the earth, he may please accompany me through the Cliff Mine. But before doing so we will go to the office and form the acquaintance of the Agent, Mr. Hanna, Captain Jennings, and others. Thence you will be desirous to visit the stamps, where you will see a large bank of mineral stamped through the winter, yielding from ten to twenty per cent. of copper. Several persons are here employed in washing copper. The stamps have lately been somewhat improved. They now stamp about two hundred and thirty tuns [sic] per month. In one month, eighty-six barrels of this copper were washed and barreled, ready for shipping.

Let us now go partly up the bluff, into a large mineral shed, where the stamp-work is first burned in a huge fire, then broken to pieces, and conveyed to the stamps. Here are also several men engaged in cutting huge masses of the pure copper into blocks sufficiently small to admit of being transported. This part is attended with great labor and expense. A wagon is driven along side this shed, where these masses are raised by a crane, and thus swung into the wagon, and drawn to the Lake. From eighty to one hundred tuns of copper, including that which is barreled, are taken to the Lake monthly.

We will now go up a flight of stairs to another large level, formed of broken stone taken out of the mine. Here is a machine, worked by two horses, to pump out the mind. Adjoining this is what is called a *whim*—the Cornish say *wim*. This is a large perpendicular cylinder turned by horse power, as tanners grind bark. A large rope is wound around this cylinder, with a large bucket at each end, which connects with shaft No. 1, to raise the rock and mineral. To your right is a blacksmith-shop, used mostly for sharpening drills. To the north is another machine connected with shaft No. 1, called a *sheer*. . . . This machine gives a power sufficient to raise ten tuns weight. With this the large masses of copper are taken out of the mine. A little to the left, overhead, is another whim, which connects with shaft No. 2, twenty-eight yards north of No. 1. You may now turn to the right, and follow a rail-track through another mineral shed, where all the broken rock of a poorer quality is taken, and the precious separated from the vile. As we turn about to see whence all this treasure is taken, you will naturally cast your eyes up the bluff, where you may see a large opening which once contained a great mass of copper. You will notice also a slide of greenstone, dipping to the north at an angle of perhaps 45°. This occasions a *fault* in the vein, in which the mineral ceases.

Before going into the mine we must return to the office to get a change of apparel. If you are at all careful about your velvet or broadcloth, you must doff it before you go under ground. You want a complete miner's suit from head to foot. Then you must have the safe conduct of Captain Jennings or Boss Jones, who will see that each one is furnished with a candle, and a lump of wet clay to put around it, which you must keep moist. Thus equipped, we will now go down into drift No. 1, which is on a level with most of the works we have been viewing; only be careful, in passing by No. 2, not to step off the planks into the depths below. Here you may go in several hundred feet, where not much is to be seen, except the empty space where the mineral has been removed.

We will now return to shaft No. 1, and go below, sixty feet, into the *Adit*. This is a drift extending from the river nine hundred feet north, and is used for draining the mine. Let it now be remembered that we must descend by ladders, several of which are nearly perpendicular, and one quite so. You must now pull off your gloves—if you have any on—and do not be afraid of soiling your hands as you hold on to the muddy rounds of the ladder. As you follow your guide, you must learn this lesson, and not forget it for a moment: "*Hold fast with your hands—never mind your feet.*" As we go down we occasionally come on to a small platform, and, by simply turning round, we take hold of another ladder. But you must not let go one ladder till you see where you are; a single misstep may precipitate you down the main shaft from one hundred to two hundred feet. We now find ourselves safely in the *Adit*. This is called the ten-fathom level, or drift No. 2. The course of the vein is nearly north and south, dipping slightly to the east.

From shaft No. 1 we will now go north, passing over a pit fifteen or twenty feet deep, where the mineral has been removed. Soon we shall reach shaft No. 2, which we will cross on planks, on one side, holding on to an iron bar fastened to the rock on each side. At the north extremity of this drift is a mass of copper which has been thrown down by a sand-blast, which will probably weigh from thirty to fifty tuns. This must be cut to pieces with chisels before it can be taken out. Overhead you will see, in many places, what is called a *stull*, or *pent-house*. This consists of heavy timbers placed across the mine so as to form a scaffold. In this way the *lode* is all approached, and removed from one drift to another, ten fathoms or sixty feet. This *stulling* is often torn down by heavy blasts, and is one source of the danger of miners. In going south we will see nothing very different from what is to be seen north, except that there the lode is not so rich as here.

Finding our way to shaft No. 1, we will again go down sixty feet to drift No 3. The appearance here is very similar to that in drift No. 2. Every-where, you have evidences of an inconceivably rich mine. In places you will find the lode entirely removed; then you will pass huge masses of mineral not yet disturbed. North of shaft No. 2 we will pass a chain-ladder, which, if you are fond of adventure, you may ascend five or six fathoms into a large opening in the mine. A little farther on we cross over a *winze*, which is a communication from one drift to another to air the mine. This is soon to be used for a third shaft. The whole length of this drift, from north to south, is about one hundred and ten yards. If your curiosity is not yet satisfied, we may go down sixty feet further, into drift No. 4. In the extreme end north, after crawling on your hands and knees for some distance, over what miners call *deads*—that is, broken rock—you find yourself in a large opening, where is the appearance of a large mass of copper. The mine in this region is very rich. In this drift, among the many things too tedious to name, we notice what is called the *sump-shaft*. This is only a continuation of shaft No. 1, eighteen feet below the lower level. This, as the others, is to be sunk sixty feet before drifting again. The Captain is much elated with the prospect here, and promises for the next sixty feet to show the richest part of the mine. In what is called the *country*—that is, by the side of the vein—a mass of copper has been taken out weighing fifteen hundred pounds. The material is here raised to the lower drift by a windlass. A short time since I was visiting the mine, and, being desirous of seeing the bottom, my friend J. let me down in a bucket. But the miners, having stopped work, water had collected two or three feet in the bottom. The first warning I had of this was the impression of wet feet as the tub was filling with water. This Boss Jones called *sumpen*.

The most agreeable time to go into the mines is Monday morning when the work commences, or Saturday afternoon after the miners quit work. The mine is then free from smoke. But if you choose to go when all are at work, you will see more. Here you may see a person holding a huge drill, and another with a large hammer, making every stroke tell on the hard rock. There you may see several men, with levers, at work at a mass which has been torn loose by a *sand-blast*. Here you may see one wheeling the rock, and throwing it down through a *mill*, where it is taken by others, put into buckets, and raised to the surface. In different parts of the mine you will hear the blast, the report of which rolls like thunder through the subterranean vaults. A dismal gloom seems to pervade the whole region, and at every turn you will be impressed with the fact that few men are so exposed to danger as miners. But what above every thing else should impress every one is the evidence of the wisdom, goodness, and power of God above, beneath, and all around.

Doubtless you are as ready to leave the mine as to enter it. We have now one hundred and eighty feet of ladder to climb; but, by perseverance, stopping a moment occasionally to take breath, we shall soon be at the top. Now we emerge from a world of darkness into a world of light. We may now return to the office, and assume our own attire, by which time it would be no very strange thing if a good meal would relish well. If the reader thinks this description of the Cliff Mine too minute, it may be a source of relief that this must suffice for all the other mines of Lake Superior—to explore one thoroughly is to see the leading features of all the rest.

PART III.

CREATING AN EDUCATIONAL SYSTEM

PRESENT AT THE CREATION

John D. Pierce

Rev. John D. Pierce of Marshall—one of Michigan's most respected public servants in the pioneer era—deserves the credit along with Isaac E. Crary for the creation of Michigan's public educational system. The state constitution of 1835, whose educational provisions were largely the work of Crary, provided for a Superintendent of Public Instruction. Michigan was the first state to create such an office, and Pierce was, therefore, the first Superintendent of Public Instruction in the United States.

One far-sighted decision that Pierce celebrates in his memoir had to do with the control of the federal grant of section 16 (one square mile) in every surveyed township, the proceeds from the sale of which were to support public schools. In Michigan this amounted to over a million acres. Since Crary was in Congress at the time Michigan was admitted as a state, he persuaded Congress to grant the sixteenth sections in Michigan to the state rather than the townships in which they were located. As a result of Crary's foresight, the state was enabled to use the land-sales proceeds in a fund for the support of education. This arrangement, which applied only to Michigan at the time, enabled the state to build a Primary School Fund for the support of education.

In this document from 1877, Pierce relates some of his experiences as Michigan's first Superintendent of Public Instruction. It appears as "Origin and Progress of the Michigan School System" in *Michigan Pioneer and Historical Collections*, vol. I (Lansing: W. S. George & Co., 1877), pp. 37–45.

When I came to Michigan in 1831, the census of the territory had just been taken, including what is now the State of Wisconsin. It numbered 32,000 inhabitants, where there are now, in all probability, 2,500,000 people. There were then 2,000 in Wisconsin and 30,000 in Michigan proper.

Previous to this period little had been done in this territory for schools. The Legislative Council had passed an act providing for the election of six school commissioners in each organized township for the purpose of dividing the township into school districts, but no provision was made for the support of schools except by rate bills [i.e., tuition payments]. The schools, however, were little else than private schools. But many of the new townships organized up to 1835 had not organized under this system.

In 1834 the census was again taken, and Michigan was found to contain 87,000 inhabitants. Soon after this the Legislative Council authorized the calling of a convention to form a State constitution, and fixed upon May, 1835, for it to assemble at Detroit for that purpose.

It was at this period of our history that the State school system had its inception and origin. Gen. Isaac E. Crary, a graduate of an eastern college and a warm friend of education, was, for a year or two, an inmate of my house. The conditions and prospects of our new State were often subjects for discussion, and especially the schools of various grades, from the a highest to the lowest.

About this time [Victor] Cousin's report of the Prussian system made to the French minister of public instruction came into my hands, and it was read with much interest. Sitting one pleasant afternoon upon a log, on the hill north of where the court-house at Marshall now stands, General Crary and myself discussed for a long time the fundamental principles which were deemed important for the [constitutional] convention to adopt in laying the foundations of our State. The subject of education was of especial interest. It was agreed, if possible, that it should make a distinct branch of government, and that the constitution ought to provide for an officer who should have this whole matter in charge and thus keep its importance perpetually before the public mind.

That gentleman went to the convention and was appointed chairman of the committee on education; drew up an article on the subject; reported the same to the convention; it was adopted, and became the law of the land. It provided what no other [state] in the United States had done, namely: for the appointment of Superintendent of Public

Instruction. This was to be done on nomination by the Governor and joint vote of the two houses of the Legislature.

At the election held in October, 1835, the constitution was ratified. Stevens T. Mason was elected Governor, and General Crary representative to Congress. Members of the Legislature were chosen at the same time. A session was held in November and adjourned over to January. At its session in January—the State not yet being admitted into the Union—the Legislature again adjourned to the July following.

Up to this period, though I had often counseled with Mr. Crary as to what ought to be done to promote the best interests of our State, yet I had not thought of occupying the position provided for by the constitution, being constantly employed in the work of a missionary of the American Home Missionary Society. On his way to Washington, General Crary held a consultation with Governor Mason, and proposed my name for the newly created office. The Governor expressed a wish to see me on the subject, as we were then wholly unacquainted; I accordingly visited Detroit and had an interview with the Governor, about the 20th of July. After discussing the matter at some length, the result was that on the 26th of the same month, in 1836, I was nominated and unanimously confirmed as Superintendent of Public Instruction for the State. I was, therefore, the first that ever held that office in this country under a State constitution. At the same time an act was passed requiring the Superintendent to prepare and submit to the Legislature to be convened on the first Monday in January, 1837, a plan for the organization and support of primary schools; a plan for a university with branches; also a plan for the disposition of the university and primary school lands. This, then, was the first work assigned me to do, and I had five months before me in which to do it. One thing was favorable: it was a day when all was astir with activity and life,—the watchword was progress and improvement. The field was clear; there were no old institutions and deep-rooted prejudices to be encountered and removed. But the condition of the State had to be taken into account. We were less than 100,000, all was wild, and the people were comparatively poor; all was to be created anew.

We had no canals, no railroads; even the old slow coach was scarcely to be found. We had the lumber wagon and the Indian trail. We forded rivers, waded marshes, and when night came, if we found a shanty with a piece of old carpet for the door we turned in for the night, and all were satisfied. But notwithstanding all this, the people then here came mostly from the region of school-houses, and were anxious for schools. I may add, also, that the early movement in this direction aided materially in the settlement of the country.

Soon after I received my commission I went east and visited such men as John A. Dix, Governor Marcy [of New York], President Humphrey [of Amherst College], Governor Everett [of Massachusetts], President Day [of Yale], and others of like character. I was cordially received by all. What Michigan had already done was a matter of surprise, and much solicitude was expressed for our success. I attended also the American institute of instruction held at Worcester, Mass., and the college of professional teachers held at Cincinnati. My object in this journey was information in regard to schools, from the primary school to the university; their organization, management, and support. The whole subject had been committed to my hands. Besides, I had over a million acres of university and school lands to look after. Such, then, was the responsibility and such the interests involved,—interests not only for the then present but for the future. A failure, or even a bad beginning, must necessarily affect the State in its educational interests for a long time. A distinguished gentleman of Ohio, an earnest friend of schools, remarked to a convention of teachers at Cleveland, that their State was fifty years behind Michigan "for the want of such a beginning and such a man" as we had.

After two months' absence I returned and drew up my report. In it the great questions involved were discussed, and the three specified plans required by the Legislature were drawn out somewhat in detail. At the appointed time it was presented, and after a full and free interchange of views and some modifications it was adopted as a whole with scarcely a dissenting voice. Such was the beginning.

But it is one thing to adopt a system, and quite another and very different thing to carry it out. The best laid schemes often fail for want of skill in carrying them out.

At this period in our history there was one question pertaining to our primary schools of absorbing interest, the settlement of which must necessarily affect them for all time to come. The question gave to General Crary, our representative [in Congress] and myself much solicitude, for on its solution depended in a great measure the success or failure of our whole system. But it was a difficult question to manage, because it depended on the action of Congress. That body at that time seemed to be not very well disposed towards Michigan on account of our southern boundary trouble. Hitherto, on the admission of a new State, the sixteenth section has been donated to the township in each and every case. But these sections had been so managed in all the new States by the townships as to be of little worth to the cause of education. Many a section of great value was sold at an early day, and bid in by the settlers for a mere song. Besides, there was no equality in the system,—one section might be valuable, another of little worth. I once sold a section for $31,000, while in the next township the reserved section [i.e., section sixteen] might not have been worth as many pennies. Hence it was deemed of great importance to us that these sixteenth sections reserved from sale should be given in trust to the State, and not to the surveyed townships. How the uniform policy of Congress could be changed, was the problem to be solved. But it was accomplished in this wise: General Crary, our representative, acted with the committee [of Congress] whose duty it was to draft the ordinance of admission. This work was assigned to him, and in drafting the ordinance he so worded it that these school lands [i.e., section 16] were really conveyed to the State, and it passed without question. The change in the form of conveyance of these sections seemed not to have been noticed; had it been,—as he subsequently told me,—no doubt the common form would have been substituted and the lands given to the townships. There was no deception about it; the ordinance spoke for itself, and yet its effect seems not to have been perceived. It infused vigor into our new-born system, and life into ours. Thus, much was gained; we had secured a foundation on which to rear a superstructure, and materials with which to build.

When the system was once adopted and the machinery in operation, it was easy to organize schools throughout the State. The apportionment to be derived from the income of the school funds operated as a stimulus to each and every school district. But here the greatest difficulty was to be met, and it is one not yet wholly surmounted. How and where is an adequate supply of competent teachers to be procured? After discussing the subject in its length and breadth, I proposed that a certain intermediate grade of institutions between the primary schools and the university should be used for qualifying teachers for their work, as well as that of preparing young men for the university course and others for the ordinary business of life. This the [Michigan] constitution required, and it was a favorite scheme of General Crary's. But it was attempting more than the state of the country at that time could warrant. Accordingly the amended constitution left the university free and independent of all other institutions, as it ought always to have been; and the normal and union schools have taken their place and are doing the work that the intermediate grades were designed to accomplish. But these schools at that early day could not have been established, nor yet the duties of county superintendents adopted. The country was too new and too poor; houses were to be built, roads laid out and made passable, bridges and cross-ways to be constructed, mills and mill-dams to be erected, and farms to be laid out, cleared, fenced, and plowed. Outside of Monroe and Detroit we had no cities and villages. So, also, churches and school-houses,—they existed only on printed plats, like the blacksmith's shop. A traveler inquired for such a place; he was told he would find one at Marshall village. He went on and on till, out of patience, he asked a settler where he could find said shop. "Oh," said the man, "you are in the shop now, but the anvil is back seven miles on a stump." Considering the state of the whole western world at the time, the wonder is not that we did so little, but that we were able to do so much.

Soon after the adoption of our school system it was reviewed in the Michigan Gazeteer, and pronounced superior to that of any other State; and yet that it would be found in some measure defective, "not only in practice but in principle." One defect was that it did not provide for the support of a school in every district throughout the year. To have done this at this time was simply an impossibility. Besides, five days a week for forty weeks is as much as any school ever ought to be kept open in one year. I think this is in accordance with the sentiment of all experienced teachers. To have proposed thus early in the settlement of the country to levy a tax to keep the schools open the year round would have defeated the whole thing.

Even up to 1850 we failed to procure the passage of a law for the establishment of free schools, even for three months; and then the best we could do was to make it the duty of the Legislature to establish such schools after five years, and this was neglected for two years longer. The second defect pointed out was in not providing for the appointment of county superintendents, to be named by the State Superintendent. Such a proposition at that day would have been as fatal as the other. The people were not prepared, nor could they afford, to be taxed $1000 or more or less in every county, in addition to their other taxes, to pay a superintendent. Township inspection was our only resort; it was the best we could do. In this connection allow me to suggest that the question with the statesman is not what I may *like* to do, but how much I *can* accomplish. This includes an appreciation of all the circumstances with which he is surrounded. So with the teacher when he enters the school-room. What he may *wish* to do is one thing, what he may be *able* to do is another and very different thing. He must examine his materials, measure and weigh them, before he can decide what and how much he can do. To rush ahead, regardless of circumstances and equally so of consequences, is the peculiar characteristic of your one-idea fanatical reformer,—he can pull down and destroy, but he has no skill in construction. Such an one can never be a successful builder. He makes no account of the difficulties to be met or obstructions to be removed: hence failure is sure to be the result of his labors. The saying is, "be sure you're right, then go ahead." You point the boat in the right direction above Niagara for the opposite shore, but before reaching it you and your boat are at the foot of the falls.

While the sixteenth section in every surveyed township was reserved from sale and given to the State in trust for the support of primary schools—equal to one-thirty-sixth of the whole seventy-five sections—equal to 48,000 acres, to be selected, most of it, from any part of the State, were given as a perpetual fund for the establishment and support of a university. The same amount was given to all the other new States, severally. But from some cause they have each and all failed to create any institution within their respective borders of any marked character. They have no college, no university founded on this grant and supported by its income, of any special note. It was hence reserved to Michigan, by means of like character and no more abundant, to rear up within 38 years from its inception and the location of its site, an institution *rivaling* Yale and Harvard, but outstripping them both. This is now universally acknowledged. The New York Observer says that "the University of Michigan is a marvel. Forty years ago the land—the forty acres that is now occupied—was an unfurrowed plain, whose soil the plow had never chafed, never disturbed; where but yesterday the deer roamed free as air, the wolf howled, and the Indian pitched for the night and kindled his camp fires. You will find in all the history of the past nothing to compare with it in the rapidity of its development and growth."

When the matter of devising a plan for a university was committed to my hands it caused me no small degree of solicitude. It was said that no State institution of the kind has ever succeeded or can succeed. It was proposed to name the several private colleges that already existed on paper, and others that were to come into being, "The University of Michigan," and distribute the income of the fund to them in due proportion. This, or something like it, was the plan, under whatever name or form it might have been presented at different times. This scheme I opposed with all the influence I could bring to bear against it. But it came within one vote of succeeding; and for being instrumental, as supposed, in defeating the measure in the House,—it had passed the Senate,—I was denounced on the following evening, by some of its warm friends, in no measured terms.

Wishing to prepare myself for the contest that I was aware must come, and did come in earnest, I addressed, in the summer of 1837, a circular letter to a number of gentlemen in the world of letters, proposing this question: "Shall we, in the commencement of our career as a State, grant to an indefinite number of private associations the right of conferring degrees, or, for the present, concentrate our energies in one university?"

I received answers from such men as Dr. Wayland, President of Brown University, President Humphrey of Amherst College, President Day of Yale, Governor Everett of Massachusetts, and Bishop McIlvaine of Ohio. All deplored the multiplication of institutions under the imposing name of universities and colleges as unfavorable to sound learning, and advising, if possible, the plan of concentrating our energies on one university. President McGuffy made this striking and explicit declaration: "All that can be said of the universities and colleges of the south and west is that they are well-endowed academies, though some of them are not even that." [The] letter of Bishop McIlvaine expresses . . . clearly and . . . fully the views of all:

> Dear Sir: Long absence from home has prevented my answering your circular letter sooner than the present. It requires but little time to make an opinion on the question your propose. I consider the present multiplication of institutions called colleges, and empowered to confer degrees, exceedingly detrimental to the interests of genuine education. They so divide patronage as to create a competition, which, instead of leading to the result which some suppose must be the consequence,—of elevating the standing of the several institutions,—produces precisely the opposite. . . . Where such multiplications have taken place it is difficult for an institution that wishes to maintain a dignified stand to compete in patronage with others of less conscience in such matters. . . . Other States will supply the little colleges. Be it yours to set the example of a genuine university, a mother of learning, rejecting, not following the opinions of the inexperienced on the subjects of education.
>
> Yours very truly,
>
> C.P. McIlvaine

Notwithstanding the cogent reasons and unanswerable arguments of the ablest men of the land, so persistent and combined were the private and personal interests connected with other enterprises that it was doubtful for a time, even to the last hour when the final vote was taken, and the question settled, how it would be determined. Had the result been different, you would never have heard of the University of Michigan, which is now the pride and crowning glory of the State. The object was to combine in one institution, worthy the name of university, all the worthy elements that could possibly be brought together, and especially the leading Christian denominations of the land. We had the fund and must use it,—having accepted the trust,—not in scattering it abroad, but in accordance with the true intent of the grant, in founding and sustaining a real university. My determination was to prevent, if possible, any failure or perversion. That nothing of the kind may ever be laid to my charge, I trust I may be allowed to present to you my closing remarks on this great question, made in my report to the Legislature of 1838, while the matter was still in doubt and undetermined:

> Deeming the question above discussed to be one of vital importance, the Superintendent has felt constrained, in the outset of that career of improvement on which the State seems disposed to enter, to present to the consideration of the Legislature, his views in an extended form on the subject.
> It is to be borne in mind that the policy now adopted is destined to affect the literary standing and character of the State, not only for the time of the present generation but so long as the republic and its institutions shall be preserved; nay, more,—so long as its name and the memorial of its deeds shall be read in story or in song.

The results of the decision of that day are known and read by all men. It was a triumph that was exceedingly gratifying, and from that day I cherish the fond expectation that Michigan in future years would have a university worthy of the name. But I did not expect to live to see it reach such an eminence as it has already attained. Henceforth let wisdom guide its councils. Let no claim to recognition that may degrade it from its high position be listened to for a moment. As well might the disciples of Paine be recognized as any other class whose presence must destroy its usefulness.

One other question fell to my lot, solitary and alone to decide, the decision of which, for the time being, created a great deal of ill feeling, and brought down upon me a storm of denunciation. Indeed, so intense was the excitement that an indignation meeting was proposed to be called at Ann Arbor. The occasion was this: The Legislature passed an act authorizing the Regents to procure a plan for buildings. They employed an architect from New Haven to draft one; that plan, if approved by the Governor and Superintendent of Public Instruction, should be adopted. The one prepared was a truly magnificent design, and would in that day have involved an expenditure of half a million dollars, if not more. It was accepted by the Regents and approved by the Governor. It was presented to me. Most respectfully but decidedly I refused my assent, and gave as a reason that it would absorb so much of the university fund as would cripple it in all time to come; and urged further that a university did not consist in buildings, but in the number and ability of its professors and its other appointments, as library, cabinets, and works of art. The result was that the Regents receded, and the present plan was adopted, and the university started into being. Twenty years or more after, at the house of Dr. Denton, one of the medical professors, in company with President Morgan of Pennsylvania, the doctor, in referring to my refusing my assent to their plan for the building and the bitter feeling incited against me at the time, remarked that while he was unwilling to give me credit for so much sagacity as that action indicated, yet he would truly say that it was the best thing that ever happened in the State. My reply was that I was just as well satisfied then as now that its adoption would have been fatal to the institution.

There was still another question in which I was called upon to take part. It was my purpose from the beginning to make all our schools free in every case, from the lowest to the highest,—free from rate bills and tuition bills. I assumed the position that the property of the State should be holden [i.e., financially liable] for the education of every child in it. But the wealth of the State has ever opposed free schools, and yet no class is more deeply interested in the education of all. There is no safety in the midst of debased ignorance. It was urged that while our university should be open to all our own young men, we surely were not called upon to admit others without charges for tuition. True, but every young man who comes to our University spends his money here, and there is nothing which gives so much importance and character to a State as an institution of high standing to which young men from all parts of the world can resort. The view taken was that this would be worth more to us than any tuition bill that might be charged, even to a hundred fold. Besides, young men from abroad cannot be expected to come here unless there are inducements beyond those existing in other institutions. This policy was finally adopted, and I think no one at this day can say that it was not the wisest and best course.

It will thus be seen that at an early day we had some important questions to settle, the determination of which has not ceased to have a direct influence on the educational interests of the State. An enterprise so magnificent as the education of a whole people to be successful must rest on a firm basis. After referring to what the Legislature had done in perfecting what might be termed the State school system, I expressed my confident expectation of its success in these words:

> What remains is to carry it into successful operation, making from time to time such modifications as experience shall determine to be necessary and desirable. Most certainly have we laid the foundations for raising a fabric of gigantic proportions and great magnificence; our whole superstructure, when duly perfected, by the wisdom and councils of experience, cannot fail of being the ornament and glory of State in all coming time, and as useful in all its departments, as grand and beautiful in its design. Hence, if we fail—as remarked by a distinguished gentleman at the late session of the college of professional teachers—it will be a magnificent failure, and draw after it consequences of direful import. But we trust, through the Providence of the all-wise, the high and mighty Ruler of the universe, who has thus far so benignantly and prosperously guided the councils and affairs of our State, that the system will flourish and bear much fruit, even long after those who were instrumental in its production shall have returned to the dust of the valleys and gone to their final home.

I may say in this connection that we had in our settlements in that time a large proportion of educated men, and many families anxious for schools of a higher order, ready to engage in any enterprise that promised success. The leading men of that day were the fast friends of education, and hence our success. This was especially true of the members of the Convention and of the first Legislature.

I have thus given you a mere outline of the past of Michigan as far as its educational interests are concerned. No new State ever started into being with so many warm and devoted friends of education as we had. Five of the best years of my life I gave to the work. In it I traveled by night and by day,—on one occasion five whole nights out of eight,—not in railroad palaces, but in lumber wagons and stage coaches, through rain, mud, frost, and storm. But I can truly say I feel fully compensated. . . .

A WOLVERINE SCHOOLMASTER

A. D. P. Van Buren

Anson de Puy Van Buren emigrated to Battle Creek during the 1830s and at the age of sixteen got a certificate to teach in the Goguac Prairie School where he remained for seven years. Later he studied at the University of Michigan and taught in various places for the remainder of his life.

Van Buren's memoir is indispensable for an understanding of the history of Michigan education in the pioneer era. The log cabin schools he describes, primitive as they may appear to the modern reader, were nonetheless on the "cutting edge" of social innovation. Compulsory education and the common school was just coming into being as Michigan was filling up with settlers; the New England Yankees hardly needed prodding by the authorities to provide at least a rudimentary education for their children. Van Buren, looking back nostalgically on the log cabin schools, found much in their favor. He regretted some aspects of "graded" schools and the bureaucratization of the public school system in Michigan.

Van Buren was an active member of the State Pioneer Society and one of the most prolific contributors to the *Michigan Pioneer and Historical Collections*. This essay, dating from 1889, is excerpted from A. D. P. Van Buren, "The Log Schoolhouse Era in Michigan," *Michigan Pioneer and Historical Collections*, 2d ed., vol. XIV (Lansing: Wynkoop Hallenbeck Crawford Co., 1908), pp. 283–402.

The course of empire that took its way westward in the Mayflower carried with it the effects and fortunes of that picturesque group, the emigrant family, which, in their first New England homes, laid the foundation for a new republic in this western world. Later, we find this family leaving their New England homes for still newer ones farther west. And still later, we see the same familiar group aboard the tented wagon or canal boat, again moving westward. They are next seen at Buffalo, where they take a steamer for Detroit, Michigan; and in the early thirties they might have been seen in the canvas covered wagon leaving Detroit for their destination in the interior of the new territory. We can follow this group on its pilgrimage through the wilderness, now putting up at the rude tavern, or farther on, camping out in the woods by their wayside fire. Thus, after a wearying, toilsome journey, over bad roads, impassable marshes and swollen streams, they reach the spot selected for their new home in the unreclaimed wilderness. A log house is soon erected; a log schoolhouse soon follows, in which the schoolmaster, who had "come abroad" with the emigrant family, is installed as instructor of the children in the new settlement. And as he entered that cabin schoolhouse with his baton of power, "the birch," he became the *avant courier* of the common school system in Michigan. . . .

And now, reader, let us lay aside the spectacles of today and look through those of 1838, the period we are considering, if we should see things just as they were then; we shall find human nature the same in both periods, but all else changed. . . . [The first log schoolhouse in which I taught] stood on the north side of the territorial road that ran westward across Goguac prairie, Calhoun county, and was about half way between Deacon Joseph Young's log house and John Stewart's frame house, and on the lands of the latter. It was a small, one story, rude log structure, one of the first outcroppings of the log house epoch of Calhoun county. John and Enoch Stewart had been seized with mercantile aspirations in the early days of the settlement, then some seven years old, and had erected this building for a grocery. But the grocery business proved a failure, and the building, in true pioneer spirit, had indulged in frequent fits of hospitality, for on many occasions it turned itself into a dwelling for emigrant families who had sought a temporary sojourn on the prairie, while prospecting about the region for a permanent home. Such was the previous history of this rough tenement, which, after remaining tenantless for a year or more, was now to lend itself to the beneficent purposes of a schoolhouse.

It was built of oak logs with "cobbled up" corners. The roof was composed of shakes that were held in their places by long poles laid lengthwise over the lap of each course and pinned down at each end. The floor was of puncheon. A fire-place with broad jams was surmounted with a stick chimney which ran up the outside and east end of the building. There was but one door, and but one window, on the south side. The door swung on oaken hinges, and was fastened by and answered to a wooden latch that was raised by the accustomed latch string. The logs were "chinked and mudded up" and the building was considered fit for winter use. There was not a nail or a particle of iron about the house. The glass was secured in the sashes by little wooden pegs, and the cross-piece over the fire-place was a wooden support.

Our schoolroom furniture, like the building, was of the most primitive kind. Holes were bored into the logs, some three feet from the floor, on the sides and west end of the room into which long pegs were driven: boards were secured on these legs slanting inward, for desks. Rough boards on wooden legs ran parallel to the desks for seats. Slabs with shorter legs constituted the seats for the smaller children. The schoolmaster's table was also of pioneer make. On it, in early morning, he wrote the copies in all the writing books, and mended all the pens, which in those days were all quills, and put each into its own book which was kept in a pile on the table till writing time, when they were distributed to their owners, and after that exercise, they and the pens were returned to the master's table again. In the drawer of the table the school roll and cherry ruler were kept. At the close of each day's exercise the roll was called, and to each parent's or patron's name was noted the number of children who were present. To the schoolhouse, then, on Monday morning, of the last of November, in the year of grace 1838, I wended my way. And, as I pulled the latchstring and entered my new home, I began to feel the responsibilities of the teacher weighing upon me. Here I am, thought I, at the foot of the "hill of science" up which I am supposed to lead this troop of aspirants for knowledge. Or am I to lead, persuade, and whip some up, if they ever get up at all. For despite Dogberry's saying that "to read and to write comes by nature," some don't take them that way. It was thought in those days that art must be supplemented by the use of the "birch" in educating boys and girls.

School was called by rapping upon the window sash with the back of a book. School bells were not in vogue then, neither was the blackboard or any of the modern facilities in school teaching. The teacher was equipped with his cherry ruler, whip and penknife, a writing book made from foolscap, in which was a Holland quill.

The morning exercises began by hearing the first class, composed of the best scholars, read in the old English reader. The second class, composed of the second grade of pupils, then read from the same book. Both classes read twice round. The third class read from the elementary spelling book, and then came those little "freshmen," the a b c darians. These little beginners took but shallow draughts at this Pierian fountain of knowledge, two or three times in the forenoon and afternoon. The teacher used the papspoon, so to speak, giving them a letter at a time. It took from three to six weeks for one of these little neophytes to master this alphabetical column, this key to all knowledge. Then it was put to the task of learning to master simple syllables of two letters. Beginning with b-a ba, b-e be, b-i bi, b-o bo, b-u bu and so on to the end of the chapter. It then began on simple words, where it soon broke loose from "leading strings" and commenced to read alone.

Writing came in the forenoon immediately after reading. All who wrote engaged in the exercise at the same time, the teacher in the meanwhile looking over their work, giving directions as to position, and holding the pens when he was not mending them. The pupils wrote twice a day. The pens were made of the goose quill imported from Holland, in bunches of 25 or 50, bound with the accustomed red cord. The writing book was made at home of foolscap paper, six or a dozen sheets sewed together, covered with coarse paper, and the pupil's name written on the cover. The book was kept scrupulously clean, the pupil regarding it as his duty to keep it so. The schoolmaster was at least a good penmaker. He was supposed to have graduated in a school of penmanship where legibility predominated to such a degree that you could easily read every word of one of his copies. It did not require an expert to make out the meaning of his writing, or that of the people of that day. The schoolmaster was usually the penmaker for the whole district or settlement. Pens were often sent him by some resident of the district to be mended, and quills to be made into pens. But the old quill pen and the use of the old penknife have long since gone out of style.

The classes spelled once in the forenoon and once in the afternoon. Each half day's school closed with the spelling of the first class. A credit mark was given to the pupil who was at the head of the class at the close of each afternoon's spelling, and the next morning he took his place at the head of the class. In spelling a word every syllable was pronounced. Thus—incomprehensibility was spelled: i-n in, c-o-m incom, p-r-e pre incompre, h-e-n hen incomprehen, s-i si incomprehensi, b-i-l bil incomprehensibil, i i incomprehensibili, t-y ty incomprehensibility. This we called spelling. Spelling is properly arranging letters into their syllables and these into the word. Merely rattling off the letters in a word, as is done today in most schools, is not spelling. Letters are to the word as the word is to the sentence.

Our fathers and mothers learned to spell from Dilworth's spelling book, and they did it thus: I-n in, there's your in, f-a-n fan, there's your infan, t-r-y try, there's your infantry.

There was no particular lesson given (for we had no class) in arithmetic. Each pupil was urged to go on in this study, as fast as he could, understandingly, learn all the rules, which he alone recited to the teacher, "work out" all the examples, and, regardless of any other pupil, get through the book as soon as he could. In those old days no special system or plan regulated the daily work in the schoolroom. The word "grade" was in the dictionary; it was reserved for a later day to see it work wonders in the schoolroom. We let the pupils grade themselves. That always mysterious process by which, in mind as well as body, boys and girls expand into youths, and mature into manhood and womanhood, cannot be regulated by any one special system, grade or plan by educators, however wise it may be. Had I attempted to put the class restraint upon those bright boys and girls, and forced them to move on with the slow pace of the dullards, I think they, becoming restive and impatient, would have broken loose and pushed on alone. I do not think we were ready for the "graded system" then. At any rate, we were neither helped nor hindered by it.

My charges and I got along well during the winter. I early learned that the surest way to keep my pupils interested in their studies was to keep interested in them myself. You will find that the pupil's dislike of study is often brought about by the lack of interest manifested by the teacher in the pupil's progress.

During the winter the school inspectors, Dr. Wm. M. Campbell and Judge T. W. Hall, of Battle Creek, paid us a visit. It was a new thing, both for pupils and teacher, to go through our accustomed recitations under the critical observation of the school inspectors, but a few helpful hints concerning the lesson recited was all we got from them. The writing books were all placed on the table for their inspection. Writing was then considered one of the primary branches to be taught in a common school. The three r's, reading, 'riting, and 'rithmetic, were the radical basis of an education, and it was well laid out in the old . . . schools. Those old copies in the writing books yet sound familiar as we, in imagination, look over the inspector's shoulders, and read: "Learn to unlearn what you have learned amiss," "Money makes the mare go," "Lawyers houses are built with fools' money," "The lawyer who pleads your case may have a fool for a client," "Many men of many minds, many birds of many kinds," and so on, to the end of the chapter.

It was always an interesting study for me to contemplate, that ambitious neophyte, the young writer, as he sat bent over his task holding that instrument, mightier than the sword, the gray goose quill, clumsily between thumb and forefinger, with its feathery top pointing upward over his right shoulder, while he, with distorted face and strained muscle, was striving to write as well as the copy. An interesting study, because I had only to go back a few years to see myself in that way. I was then but seventeen years old; many of my pupils were older. As I have said, in another place, my teaching at that age was a matter of necessity; there was no other teacher to be had then; it was a marked exception to the prevailing rule as to the age of the teacher. . . .

The spelling school, or spelling matches, the quilting party, the evening frolic or "bussing bee" and various other social amusements then in vogue were a natural outgrowth of the times. The frolics and "bees" above referred to answered their purpose, but something more than the social was wanting; there was a desire for some higher recreation, and as we seldom had any preaching, lecture, or concert or like entertainments, the spelling school supplied the want in affording a kind of intellectual tournament for the whole settlement; hence they were very popular. On such an occasion the log schoolhouse afforded a kind of arena for a rare contest between the pupils of a school, or between different schools, as competitors. The parents of the children, or patrons of the school, in fact everybody, both old and young, came either to witness this battle of words or participate in it. It was a kind of spelling book tournament in which that well known knight, "Webster's Elementary," challenged the whole list of competitors for the prize. In this list there was many a little "belted knight" that broke a lance in some close encounter with an older foeman; and, what would seem to be passing strange in other contests, here many a woodsy demoiselle "touched the point of her spear against the shield," in entering the lists with her chivalrous competitors for this wordy prize, and many a passage at words between these fair rivals and their sturdy brothers was the scene of the most enthusiastic applause.

The teacher had but to announce to his pupils, "There will be a spelling school here this Friday evening," and the glad news soon spread through the district and surrounding settlements. When Friday evening came the oxen were hitched to the sleigh or sled, which had been rigged for the occasion with the wagon box upon it, seats thrown aside and the bottom of the box covered with straw. Into this the young people were snugly packed side by side. On the route to the schoolhouse they stopped at every settler's cabin, stowing away the accessions to the load till it was packed as thick as a box of Jamaica figs, with a border of boys hanging to the outside of the sleigh. Meeting one of these merry loads gliding along the winding snow track through the woods, singing some popular song, ditty, or catch, one would think it a wandering singing school on runners.

All assembled, the school was called to order. The old folks would be given the honorary seats on the desks, with their backs to the wall, where they sat as honorary members, while the orthographical scrimmage was going on, in which the pupils wrested with the supreme difficulty of Webster's Elementary. Two boys or girls, or a boy and a girl, volunteered, or were appointed by the teacher, to "choose sides." These leaders taking a central position against the back seat alternately chose a scholar, who, as his or her name was called, took seat where chosen. The teacher then announced the rules that were to govern the contest. Strict order was to be observed by all in the room. The teacher, who was umpire, with the Elementary Spelling book in hand, took his stand in the middle of the room. He would pronounce the word but once, the pupil was to spell it but once, and to pronounce each syllable as he spelled the word. If he missed the word or the pronunciation of a syllable the teacher would say "next," and the one who missed was to sit down. The other side was not to hastily catch the word missed and respell it, but were always to wait until the teacher said "next" before they spelled the word. Thus, the preliminaries being settled, a tallyman chosen, the parties rose to their feet, and the contest began. The first word is pronounced; all is silent; the contestants and spectators listen with eager attention as word after word is given out and spelled, or if missed, how breathlessly they listen to hear whether the opposite side spells it correctly, or perchance to hear the teacher cry out "next," and repeat it again and again. How intently all now watch the contest, and glance along the lists, as the very sound of the word "next," like a fatal bullet, drops a pupil at each utterance, leaving long gaps in the ranks of the spellers. But this is a battle where thorough discipline and sharp attention to the business in hand win. The parties, watching their comrades drop, are aroused to new exertion, and with ears alert they watch every articulation and motion of the teacher and speller, eager to profit by the slightest mistake, as they hear the ominous "next" uttered and reuttered, as word after word is missed, and pupil after pupil drops, until the one who "spells down" the school stands alone in his glory.

The spelling match was a most excellent discipline for my pupils, and I am sorry that it has gone out of fashion in the common schools of today. These matches were often brought about by a challenge to us from some rival school, to meet them in their schoolhouse and dispute the championship of spelling with them; and we were naturally willing to accept the challenge. . . . The winner, who would vanquish one after another of the last five or six would be honored by shouts and applause from the whole schoolroom. Was this not a proud occasion for the hero or heroine of the evening? Those who won the palm as the best spellers in these matches were not only the proud victors of that evening, but their names came down from school to school, and they were remembered as the best spellers of that day in their different school districts. At least, after fifty years, their names are yet familiar to me. . . .

My pupils studied their spelling lessons for these contests out of school, hence no time was taken from their studies during the day. The interest that everyone took in these schools made them popular, and there was no difficulty in keeping good order, for all came to spell or to listen, and consequently all were interested in them, and benefited by them. At any rate, these contests, with the aid pupils got in the day school, developed the good speller, an important thing in a pupil's education. The boy who, having missed a good many words in a spelling school, and, being rallied on it, said: "The trouble is, I have not got the hang of the schoolhouse;" this boy must have belonged to a later period than the one I am writing of, for the boys of that day, in the first place, "got the hang" of Webster's Elementary so securely that it made no difference after that what schoolhouse they were in. They had the knack of spelling so well in hand that you could put them through the Elementary, "from a to izzard," and many of them would not miss a word.

The old school text-books, though we used to get tired of them, were really our best friends and advisers. In the by-gone days when it was sometimes the penance, and sometimes the pride of the school boy "to speak a piece," the "English Reader" and "Columbian Orator" and the like were not infrequently the means by which the taste for literature was first awakened. Books were then so scarce that we committed to memory passages admired, for fear we should not see the coveted volume again. We are half inclined to think that the old school readers made better lovers of literature and better critics than the over-free facilities of the present day. There was surely less misquotation and probably less misunderstanding of the things read. Says an old school boy: "For the sake of those old dog-eared volumes often read in semi-stealth, under the desk lid, instead of the more appropriate arithmetic, we have a kindly feeling towards every such compilation—albeit considering professional oratory and elocutionary reading as one of the plagues mercifully spared Egypt by the modern visitation of the frogs." But when the young mind in these days of many books first gets hold of a story, and first enters or gets "astray in the wilderness of literary delight," then a guide is needed—a mentor. But in those days, the boy or girl with a taste for reading was in no danger from embarrassment in the great number of books to read. Charlotte Temple, The Children of the Abbey, Alonzo and Melissa, The Scottish Chief, Thaddeus of Warsaw, Robinson Crusoe, Fairy Tales, Arabian Nights Entertainment, and Nursery Tales were about all the story books or reading we had then. The age of cheap books had not set in; periodicals, children's magazines, Youth's Companions, and books and publications of that ilk were not thought of. No constant stream of fresh literature as there is now, when every newspaper, from the little village gazette to the great metropolitan journal, has a story in it. But the boy could not go amiss then, except that he got lost in some intricate sermon or theology. He could get no books but what were worth reading. . . . But now among the great number of good and bad books the case is different; in passing through this garden of literary sweets, the unguarded youth is captivated by "the song of the siren," as Ulysses was in passing the islands where the nymphs dwelt. There is no other way to safely lead the young past these dangerous allurements that surround their path, than by giving them the best books to read. But this is not a very easy task. It is very easy to advise as to the best books, and to insist on reading them, but to create an interest in them is another thing. To get the young to read Scott and Pope's Homer, instead of the dime novels, to read Todd's Student's Manual or Tom Brown of Rugby, instead of the Boy Pirate or the Young Brigand of the West, is a thing to be most desired. Graham's and Godey's magazines were the first popular periodicals we had . . .

The books we read, the songs we sàng, and the stories we told fifty years ago! We read what history we could. . . . The only history our family had was Hale's United States History, . . . [and] we read that threadbare. . . . Of newspapers there were none save an occasional Free Press or Advertiser from Detroit, and this was devoured eagerly regardless of politics. One of our neighbors had several old numbers of the Philadelphia Evening Post. I remember that its stories and select reading were like novels to us, and in reading one of them we were so choice of it that it was handled with the utmost care and returned when read as if it had been a valuable book. This was fifty years ago, and since then I have ever the kindest remembrances of the Saturday Evening Post. One of the old time readers says, "If I had a book I was never lonesome. I wouldn't thank anyone to entertain me if there was anything to read." What a contrast to the young people of today, who are dying of ennui, even in the sight of a well-filled library. The songs of the Revolution and the late war were then popular. "The Dying Sergeant," "Perry's Victory," "James Byrd," "Billy Burlow," "Will the Weaver," and other old songs and ballads that we learned of our parents were sung at the time. There were many good singers and story tellers, on and about Goguac prairie. Among the best was Wm. Michael; he was also a humorist and mimic. . . .

Even the Negro songs, like the lay of the last minstrel, are numbered with the things of the past. The frolics and husking bees developed a love of stories and story telling. Then each pioneer family, whatever else it brought from the old home in the east, did not fail to bring its own family traditions, or stock of legends or stories; besides, they had interesting narratives of their trials and experiences in coming west, to enliven the long hours of the winter evenings. Thus each settler's family had its own history, legends, and folk-lore, as abundant resources to draw from in conversation, or to weave into interesting narratives, on any special occasion. And as there were few books and no newspapers to read, the father and mother related to the children the experiences and stories of their early lives, and those their fathers had told to them "in the times when there was many a brave fellow, and many a bold feat."

The old schoolhouse, to a certain class of pupils, may be said to have been a sort of penitentiary, where they were confined under the abhorred thralldom of "books, birch, and knowledge." Under the old school regime, it was stoutly believed that knowledge could only be made accessible to the child by means of the "birch," that "sparing the rod would spoil the child" was devoutly believed by parent and teacher. It was thought that whipping never came amiss to the boy; that he had done, or that he would do, something to deserve it; hence it was always safe to whip him. His case was similar to the Irishman's when he said of our country: "They have no good weather in America, for when it does not storm, every fair day they call a weather breeder." So it was with the boy. If he was not already in some scrape, he was supposed, in his most quiet hours, "to be brewing mischief." The boy of the old days was considered a convincing illustration of the Calvinistic idea of total depravity.

It is not with any degree of pleasure that my pen lingers over this subject; but rather, with feelings that shrink from it, and denounce it as a wrong, do I attempt to describe that period in the past, when the pedagogic inquisition was in use in the schoolroom. Most of the punishment inflicted in the school then, if it was not torture, was cruel and barbarous. The teacher was the adjudicator of all the difficulties that transpired. This was a time when he had the rare opportunity to enforce good morals, a love of truth, honesty and all that tends to develop a noble character. He ought to have been a clear headed, honest and good man. No one had so many opportunities to do so much good to the young. He had them with him all during the school hours of the week, while the minister had them only an hour or two on Sunday.

For slight offenses the boy was ordered to go and sit with the girls, or the girl to sit with the boys. Some took this as severe punishment; they would hide their faces in their arms and cry like babies; but now and then a boy would stand a good deal of such punishment, and, though feigning to dislike it, would enjoy it hugely.

Those pupils who through inattention or sheer idleness did not study, were made to wear the "dunce cap" and sit upon the "dunce block" till they made amends for past idleness. The split quill or stick, placed astride the ear or nose, and the victim to it made to stand before the whole school, was another mode of punishing a pupil. Parents would have thought such punishment at home ridiculously absurd, yet they allowed it to be inflicted upon their children in the schoolroom. It was a species of schoolroom torture that I once have been guilty of, but could never be again.

There was another mode of torture that was called punishment, which compelled the pupil to stand on one foot, bend over so as to point and hold his finger within an inch of a mark on the floor. He must not touch the mark, nor let his finger vary half an inch from it; if he did, crack, crack, came the tough beech whip across his back.

Reader, did you ever witness such a scene in a schoolroom and see the poor trembling victim of a pupil, thus poised on one foot, his body bent over, his arm stretched out and finger pointing to the mark on the floor until his head grew dizzy and every muscle in his body, legs and arms quivered with pain? Sometimes, weak from such an exertion and stretch of his muscles, he would pitch forward until his finger bent on the floor; then crack, crack came repeated blows of the whip over his bent back. Such punishment was inflicted on the pupils in the schoolroom some fifty years ago. I thank God that we have outgrown such cruelty in the government of our schools.

Aside from the beech whip, the cherry ferule was the most important instrument for punishing the disobedient or refractory pupil. With this the teacher ruled their copy books in the morning, and feruled their hands during the day. Sometimes he would compress the fingers and thumb of the pupil's hand in his own, and then strike the ends of the fingers with the ferule. This was a torture worthy of the days of the Spanish Inquisition. Feruling the palm of the hand was bad enough; this was cruelty itself. The extended palm was not only feruled till it grew red under the painful blows, but until it was blistered. And if the pupil shrank from the pain inflicted, or threw out the other arm to ward off the blows of the ferule, it came down heavier and edgewise on the interfering arm, till the victim screamed out with pain. Perhaps the thin edge of the ferule would hit the thin bone of the arm, when the pupil would shriek, "Oh, don't, oh, don't, I won't do so again." Or, if the pupil tried to get away, or did shield his hand with his freed arm, the blow would descend with greater force on his head. This was another species of torture in the schoolroom that reminds one of a barbarous age. Let it be said of this day that we have not only outlived but outlawed such inhuman practices in our schools. Keeping the pupils in at recess, or after school, was another means of correcting them. Frightening, by means of threats, was also a method of correcting refractory pupils. I remember that my old teacher, in New York, one day caught a little boy in some mischief, and seizing him in his arms, stepped into a chair, and pushing open a trap door in the ceiling, exclaimed: "I will fill your pockets full of bread and cheese, and throw you out into the world in a cedar swamp!" At the same time, poking the little fellow's head through the opening, he gave him a tilt up, holding him by the shoes. The poor frightened child screamed as if he was really going to leave us all for the "cedar swamp."

There was much, as we have said, that was not humane in the

methods for punishing pupils under the old system. And as a civilized people we claim that the teacher should never go outside the humane in punishing for offenses committed in the schoolroom, or by his pupils out of it. At the point where chastisement begins to be cruelty, the pupil commences to lose respect for parent or teacher, and he naturally hates what he believes to be cruel.

The birch, or beech whips, which were most used in the schools, were the most formidable weapons in the pedagogic armory; they were obtained from the lowlands bordering the stream, where the beech grew tall and slim, and secured in desired quantities for the schoolmaster. He would take them, trim them, run them through the hot ashes of the fireplace to wilt and toughen them, then lay them aside behind the chimney, or in some secure place, where the pupils would not see or get them. In all matters of serious import that came before the teacher for settlement, and involved punishment, the "beech" was the infliction imposed. We do not know when the birch or beech whip was first introduced into the schoolroom. We hear of it as far back as the memory of man runneth, and, in imagination, we can hear its "whacks" over the backs of pupils, and their responsive cries, "Oh, don't," sounding out from the schoolroom all along the corridor of time, till we reach the days of John Calvin, and on to the remoter time of Solomon, who gave the first sanction for the use of the birch in his public saying, "Spare the rod and spoil the child."

It is needless to say, and it goes without saying, that the parents and teachers of the old days believed stoutly in Solomon. We do not maintain that no corporal punishment should ever be inflicted on the child at home or in the schoolroom; but we do maintain that punishment should never be cruel, unjust or unreasonable, and that it should not be given in anger or in unkindness. No one knows quicker than the pupil punished when the teacher transcends his duty in any of these respects. O. S. Fowler gives the following instance of cruelty in the parent most justly rebuked by the child: "The boy was bending over as the father plied the whip across his back; bearing it uncomplainingly until he felt, and knew, that he had been whipped enough, and still finding the blows falling fast and heavy upon his back, he cried out, 'Lay it on, old heathen, lay it on.' " Never was truer and juster rebuke given; and this rebuke should apply to all such instances of cruelty wherever found, in the schoolroom or household. And do you not believe that some of our children, as they read in the Sabbath-school books about the habits of people in heathen lands, are inclined to think that we need to cross the water or go to Bor-i-boo-la-ga to find the heathen?

The teacher who best controls his own temper can best control his pupils. The man of noble impulses and a kind heart, who is stern though just and reasonable in the management of his school, is the safest guide and best teacher of the young. . . . As regards myself, on reviewing this subject fifty years afterward, it seems almost necessary for me to "stick pins into myself to be convinced" that I was the young schoolmaster who had ever resorted to such severe punishment in the schoolroom. . . .

I have written of the common school during that formative period, the log schoolhouse epoch in Michigan, a period of pedagogy which led the way to the development and successful establishment of the system of union or graded schools in this State. I have written of these schools as I knew them in my experience as schoolmaster, giving a plain, unvarnished narrative of the work performed by the pioneer pedagogue in preparing the way for our splendid school system. The pioneers built upon the township meeting, the spelling book and the Bible, and they built for the future. Step by step the historian unrolls the development of the log schoolhouse into the branch university, as well as the development of the mill into the village, the town into the city, and that into a great State.

Our present graded system is perfect. In regard to its organization and regulation, it moves with the perfection of clockwork. We have never had a school system that equals it, and while I say this I have something to say about the prevailing modes of teaching which have not always been the best that could be devised for educating, that is, drawing out the latent energies of the young. How many capable graduates we have known who have passed from the union school or college to find that all their book learning has left them unfit for the first step of the business of life. This is the more to be lamented as there was never any better stuff in the world for the shaping of men than there is in the American boy of today.

As we have said, the graded school is the people's school, and the most perfect of its kind, but we wish to devise some way to better adapt it to our educational purposes, to make it a more natural, efficient means in educating the young. . . . The word "grade" seems to have a talismanic power in modern school teaching. So much so that by it everything is solved in the schoolroom. It is the formula that regulates the daily progress of classes, and is considered so indispensable that nothing can be taught without it. We dislike the word "machine" as it has been made to serve many purposes. But we can find no word that will better express our meaning, hence we use it. The "machine," then, is as conspicuous in the schoolroom as it is in the party convention, or the cotton factory. And while there is no principle or even suggestive thought connected with it, yet it times, and moves and regulates the whole school curriculum. By it the pupils must be put through so many evolutions each day till they reach the end of the book, or end of the term. So many revolutions, or recitation "rounds," will carry them through the first grade, so many through the second, and so many through the high school. It is more a matter of numbers than knowledge, through all of which they march like soldiers to a certain point. No attention is paid to any one pupil's wants and merits, whether he is slow or quick to learn, all must march together in line, each pupil being treated as a part of "one stupendous whole." Little or no individual instruction is given, and as for training, which was once considered indispensable to the development of the true scholars of real manhood and womanhood, it has become obsolete in the educational calendar of the day. No attention is paid to adapting the course of instruction in any school to the genius of the pupil, or to the wants of the people who patronize it. Some minds, like the olive tree, mature slowly; they require a longer time than others do for the development of their powers.

Because a pupil cannot keep up with his class, or stands lower in it than his mates, this does not evince incapacity. If it does, Sir Walter Scott was a dunce; and General Grant, who graduated at the foot of his class, was another. Charles W. Whipple was turned out of his class at West Point for incapacity, yet he made one of Michigan's best chief justices. . . .

Nowadays there are teachers of grades, men and women appointed to fetch a pupil through a certain stage of his education, and then pass him along to the driver of the next. It is quantity that is sought now; the systematizing of the school is such that pupils go over five times more space in their studies during a single term than they used to do with the old school teacher. So great a regard is paid to quantity, amount to be accomplished in a week, a month, or a term, that all that is necessary for the teacher is to tap the bell, the pupils are in their seats, another tap, and they march to the recitation seat. Then a set of questions is asked the pupil; he rises and answers them; another and another rises, and so on to the end of the class. Or certain ones are given an example to solve on the blackboard. Each one explains his example and takes his seat. The next lesson is given and the recitation is over. Now this would do if those who answer the questions or solve the examples always understood them thoroughly;

and most especially, if those who have not asked any questions, or who have not solved any examples, understand the lesson, it is a good recitation. The graded system puts all of one grade in the same classes. Now that is against the nature of the pupil's mental endowments. Some are bright, learn easily; others, though abler, must go slower, must have more time to acquire knowledge, or they must go on with the bright pupils, with what they can catch in the hasty recitation. Others again, in the same grade, have got there by a longer course of study, because duller, and must go slower than the bright pupils. And even parents are often so anxious to have their children get into the higher grade, that they complain bitterly because they are not "advanced," when the teacher assures them that their children are not qualified for the advance. They can't keep time and step with the fast pupils. In other words, you cannot grade intellect that way, and force pupils to learn or acquire the same lessons in the same way, or go through geography, arithmetic and grammar with equal ease and study, by day's marches, in which all learn well the same lessons. It cannot be done. This class recitation, in the graded system, crowds out individual genius and personal quality of the teacher. The same is true of the pupil, he is as much crowded out as the teacher. Thus, when the graded system crowded out the teacher's individuality, his power to teach by personality in the classroom, the old schoolmaster disappeared, and with him went the training of the child [and] the molding of character, the crowning achievements of his classroom labors.

CHAMPIONS OF THE WEST

Henry S. Frieze

The University of Michigan was established 1817 and remained in Detroit until 1837. It moved to Ann Arbor when residents of that community offered forty acres of land; the new campus opened formally in 1841. The university's first decade in Ann Arbor was difficult. For a time its future was threatened by disputes over the role of religion in the institution, the proper mission of a state university, and the degree of legislative control. During the 1850s, however, the university came into its own under the leadership of Henry Philip Tappan, a scholar who admired German ideas about what a university ought to be. Tappan ignored religion in making faculty appointments; he stressed academic excellence and professional competence. By 1860, under his leadership, the university had a reputation as one of the best American state universities.

But Tappan made enemies. He thought of Michigan as an uncouth primitive state; he offended members of the state legislature by his preference for the German idea of a university. The Detroit *Free Press*, a Democratic paper, ridiculed him; Republicans reformers regretted his opposition to the admission of women. In 1863 Tappan, a controversial figure, was forced to resign.

Henry S. Frieze—who became a Professor of Latin at the university in 1854—describes Tappan's personality and impact on the university in the following memoir from his "Reminiscence of the Times of President Tappan," *Palladium* (Ann Arbor, 1888), pp. 113–28.

In the summer of 1854, while teaching in Providence, Rhode Island, I received an invitation to take the chair of Latin in the University of Michigan. The letter officially announcing my appointment I found awaiting me at the post office just after I had dismissed my classes for the day. The hand-writing of the address was new to me—a large and strong hand; one might say, a stalwart hand; such, too, as can be produced by nothing but the old fashioned quill-pen. How the hand-writing on the outside of a letter sets us to guessing! and how inevitably we conclude, at last, that the only way to find out the writer and the contents is to open it. I ran through it rapidly, rather excitedly, and found at the end the name of Henry P. Tappan, President. It was very cordial and urged me to accept the appointment. My old friend and college-mate, Professor Boise, had already become one of the Michigan Faculty, and had given me some information about the prospects of the institution. It had lately taken a new departure, headed by a new President, in fact, its first President, associated with officers recently appointed. The idea of a life in what was then the New West was very tempting, but to me the most powerful attraction was the fact that the State University was expected to be an integral part of a state system of education, and that those who served in it were devoting their lives, not to the interests of some limited corporation, but to those of a commonwealth, destined to have a population as great as some of the entire kingdoms of Europe. None of the old colleges in the Atlantic States had ever held such an organic relation to the general education. Each of them was in some sense isolated, and took little interest in building up the educational fabric as a whole. But this new University was so linked with a great community of secondary and elementary schools, that in its growth and progress it must carry along all these with it. I broke loose, therefore, from long cherished associations, and migrated to what my Rhode Island friends called the far-off wilds of Michigan.

We reached Ann Arbor at midnight on the 16th of September, 1854, and were taken by the omnibus, at that time the one omnibus of the town, to the residence of Professor Boise, on the north side of the campus; the building now used for the offices of the University hospital. In the morning, a Sunday morning it was, we looked forth for the first time on the campus, its few scattered buildings, and upon what could be seen of the town. There were then but few dwellings between the University buildings and Division street.

My first walk was over the fields to the old St. Andrews, a somewhat dilapidated frame building, which has recently been removed from the ground. I was conducted to a seat, and, as it was early, had a moment to survey the surroundings. They were certainly not inspiring. A large part of the plaster had fallen from the ceiling, and there were painful tokens that more was coming,—patches here and there hanging in various stages of suspension, which, I supposed, must keep the congregation also in suspense; though as they gradually came in, they seemed to accept the situation as the normal state of things. My attention was particularly disturbed by the perilous situation of an elderly lady two or three seats in front of me, over whose head hung a formidable fragment, like the sword of Damocles, or like the rock hanging over Pirithous, threatening every moment to fall-jam, jam lapsura. The younger worshipers in our beautiful and solid churches of the present day can hardly conceive of the uninviting appearance of the shaky old buildings that occupied their sites thirty years ago.

The youthful appearance of the congregation I remember as one of the things that impressed me. There were but two or three of those silver-haired patriarchs such as I had been wont to see in eastern churches at the head of so many of the pews. The town was still young, and its population chiefly of young men and women.

And our acquaintance with them began at once. They called upon us, both families of the University and of the town, as soon as our arrival became known, and welcomed us with the warm-hearted hospitality characteristic of the place then and always: —not forgetting to assure us that they had found the climate remarkably healthy, free from malaria and intermittents,—always with the exception of cases brought hither from less favored localities, such as Ypsilanti, Dexter, or from regions still farther west.

One of the first to give us welcome was the President, Dr. Tappan. I need not describe him. Every one has learned from our local traditions something about his noble figure and bearing, and his genial manners. He was every way remarkable; in person, mind, spirit, and character, teeming with ideas and full of enthusiasm. Mrs. Tappan, too, was a lady of strongly marked character; not by any means angular or too pronounced; but happily blending refinement and gentleness with firmness and decision. One of the President's family at this time was the young astronomer, Dr. Brunnow, who had recently arrived from Berlin to take charge of the Observatory, now nearly completed; and who married two years later the only daughter of the President.

At an early day some friends took me about the town in search of a home. Ann Arbor had been passing through a period of depression. It had grown at first a little too fast, and had suffered the natural reaction, and this so much the more as the University during its first decade had failed to meet the public expectation. The town, however, under the new state of things inaugurated by Dr. Tappan, was beginning to recover a little of its former liveliness; and so, instead of finding every house for sale or to rent, I found only one in every two.

What was the University at this time? Externally, or in the way of buildings, it consisted of the two wings of the present University Hall, the original part, or east front of the Medical College, and the four residences, which, with the exception of the President's house, are now used for public purposes. With these few buildings, far apart, the campus seemed quite ample for all future wants. But President Tappan, with larger foresight, regretted that we did not possess all the land from the campus to the river; especially as it could have been purchased at that time for a song. And this regret, indeed, must be perpetual. The campus had been left undisturbed since the last plowing, and had fallen back into the state of nature; covered with its annual growth of clover and wild flowers, and in their season with wild strawberries; the last a delight to the children of the town.

The institution consisted of two Faculties, the Academic and Medical, and about three hundred students. In the Academic or "Literary" Department were the two Professors, Williams and Fasquelle, reappointed from the original Faculty, and the younger corps, made up of Boise, Haven, Winchell, Brunnow, and myself; in the Medical Department, Douglas, Denton, Sager, Gunn, Ford, Palmer and Andrews. To the Literary Faculty, somewhat later, were added Peck and Trowbridge, graduates of West Point, who had recently resigned their commissions in the army, and had accepted chairs in our new Scientific course. Both, however, after remaining on the ground some two years, left the University, to occupy similar positions in the east. At about the same time Dr. Haven also resigned the chair of History and English Literature, and his place was filled by the appointment of Andrew D. White, while the new School of Engineering was placed in charge of Professor Wood. Thenceforward the Literary Faculty remained unchanged to the close of President Tappan's administration in 1863. The Law Faculty, consisting at first of Professors Campbell, Kent and Cooley, was organized in 1859.

The senior member and one of the most interesting personages of our Academic Faculty, was Dr. Williams. He had been the first to enter upon the work of instruction at the University in 1841, and had been identified with the institution from the beginning. He was one of the best of men; thoroughly sincere, absolutely free from all obliquity. His genial kindness, his pleasantry, his ever ready repartee, made him the favorite among all the professors of two generations. But he possessed also traits which are not so generally known. He was a man of earnest piety and of strong religious convictions, and he carried into his life the religion he professed. Perhaps also it is not generally understood that he was something more than an ordinary teacher. He was a profound scientist, and so highly appreciated in this direction by the accomplished Dr. Brunnow, that the latter dedicated to him his volume on Spherical Astronomy, published in Europe in 1865.

Next in seniority was Professor Fasquelle; a French gentle-man so long resident in England, and then in America, that he had almost lost his national character. In scholarship he was exceedingly accurate, precise in his teaching, and conscientiously punctilious in performance of every duty; rather retiring and taciturn, and in manners free from parade. But he habitually looked at the dark side of things, and he had a special dread of the meetings of the State Legislature. This may now seem strange; but at that time the University did not look to the Legislature for help in the way of appropriations. The State had loaned to the institution at the beginning the money for erecting the first buildings and had charged the amount to the Regents; expecting them to pay to the state the annual interest on the loan. But the annual payment of seven thousand dollars would have so impoverished our treasury that the Regents would have been obliged to shut up the doors of the University. Therefore, it became necessary to petition the Legislature at every session to remit this interest for the next two years or until the next biennial meeting of that body. Of course there was always more or less debate in both houses, much questioning about the utility of the "Ann Arbor College," and nervous professors were in dread of seeing the institution swamped, and their occupation gone. And it was good Professor Fasquelle who most of all stood in fear of such a calamity. And so every second year, about the first of January, he was very much depressed, and it was difficult for his friends, especially for me, who lived opposite to him on Huron street, to keep up his spirits. He would say, whenever the time of the legislative session drew near: nun untergehen eine schwere zeit; now we are going to have a hard time. But the danger passed over as regularly as it recurred, and we have lived not only to see the University declared permanently free from this liability, but also to see the Legislature generous in contributing to its support and enlargement.

Next came Professor Boise, the most critical scholar of us all. He exerted a salutary and enduring influence on the scholarship and discipline of the institution. He was rigidly exact, and no one could escape his vigilance. He used to say that he could no more put up with a blockhead than with a shirk. "He is the man who keeps the bars up," was a remark sometimes made by one of my colleagues, with a marked emphasis on the pronoun "he," and with a dubious glance at the conscience-stricken professor of Latin.

Professor Winchell, and also Professor Haven, so long as he was with us, represented the University much more frequently than any of their colleagues in the state assemblies of teachers; exercising an influence in that direction which is felt in the schools and in the University to this day.

Professor White joined us in the fall of '57. To him we owe the higher character and tone of our department of history. His ideas and methods were indelibly impressed upon that part of our work; and, in fact, through the students who went out from his classes, and carried his methods, and also something of his enthusiasm into other institutions, he did much to advance the study of history in all our American colleges. He also had a cultivated taste, and at once took an interest in improving the appearance of the University grounds. He awakened an interest in tree-planting; and to this we owe the most pleasing feature of the campus and of the University avenues. Nothing could have been more uninviting than that whole quarter of the town prior to 1858. The native oaks on the lines of the old farm fences, were all that relieved the bald aspect of the campus, while the avenues were as yet almost destitute of shade trees. This was speedily transformed. The city, as a result of a lively meeting at the court house in the spring of 1858, planted nearly all the trees now on the University avenues. The Literary Faculty planted the elms extending along the whole west front of the campus inside of the fence, Professor White, the double row from the main entrance to the Law Building, and the maples along State street outside of the fence. The Regents planted those which border the walk from the same corner to the Chemical Laboratory; the class of '58, the group around the Tappan Oak; and other classes added groups here and there as class memorials. All this was done in the successive seasons of tree-planting from '58 to '61. The long avenue extending to the southeast corner was added a few years afterwards. During the same period the citizens generally planted shade trees through the streets of the town.

To this enterprise, the work of three years, is due the most attractive feature of the campus and of the city at the present day. Shall I venture to ask whether the public spirit of citizens, faculties, and students would now be equal to the same thing over again?

The Faculty of the old time in some of its ways was quite different from the present generation of professors. One marked characteristic at that time was the absence of bachelors. But I have in mind some peculiarities in their habits of life, and especially their common and favorite practice of spending leisure hours and holidays in country rambles and sylvan sports. The country in all directions still retained much of the primitive forest, and many of the beautiful "oak openings;" tempting some of us by the game in which they abounded to become occasional huntsmen. Our most accomplished sportsman was Dr. Williams, the senior member of the Faculty. His game-bag was sure to come home well filled. I have accompanied him many miles on the stretch through woods and swamps, and over the hills; and he was never the first to give out. He had been in practice from the very beginning of his residence here, for he has found quails and prairie-hens nesting even on the University campus. Indeed, wild fowl of every variety could be found throughout the tracts of woodland, then extending almost unbroken from the campus to the river. In after years the good Doctor used to complain of the impertinence of the new settlers in obstructing his hunting grounds with their barbarous fences, and in draining off all his old duck-ponds.

Immense flocks of pigeons sometimes roosted for the night on the great oak trees near the present home of Professor Demmon. And these same old trees often remind me of the tragedy of which one of them was once the scene; in which three of the professors took a conspicuous part, while the principal figure was a coon dwelling in the hollow of a decayed limb near the top. As these three were taking their favorite ramble through the wood, they discovered the animal stretched out and sunning himself in the crutch of the main limbs a few feet lower down than his hole. He was sleeping the peculiar sleep of the coon, that is, always with one eye open; and it is remarkable that he caught sight of the pedestrians at the very moment they caught sight of him. It is a well known fact attested by the famous Captain John Scott, whose skill as a marksman was only equalled by his veracity as a story-teller, that when a coon sees a huntsman approaching who is noted as a good shot, he instantly comes down and surrenders; wishing, of course, to prevent the waste of ammunition, and to save useless trouble. But in this instance, as the coon saw us entirely unequipped for the occasion, he made his way up to the entrance of his nest and disappeared; and we should have passed on, and left him unmolested; but just then one of farmer Baldwin's boys happened to be coming that way with an axe in his hand and accompanied by a large farm dog of the mastiff kind. The boy and the dog at once took in the situation. The former climbed the tree and commenced chopping at the base of the rotten limb. The mastiff planted himself on his haunches, looking eagerly upward, and ready for action, while the three professors, armed with extemporized clubs, stationed themselves around at equal distances. The poor fugitive startled from his retreat, made his way towards the tip of the limb, and as it cracked and gave way, sprang for dear life. But almost before he touched the ground, he was in the jaws of the enemy. Then you could see the truth of the old proverb: in ludis etiam ostendunt se mores. The Professor of Greek rushed forward, or, as we incontinently now express it, "pitched in," eager to put in his work with the powerful mastiff. But the Professor of History was instantly seized with pity and remorse, threw away his club, and wished the coon alive again. "Let him steal farmer Baldwin's whole corn crop, if he wants it; for hasn't the poor creature pre-emption rights?" But the Professor of Latin stood still, silently contemplating this fresh instance of the caprice of Fortune, who, as Horace says, delights to cast down them that dwell in high places.

Now, as to the students of that generation,—are not students always and everywhere the same?—young men at the transitional and plastic period of life? quickly moved either to mirth or anger; hating injustice; respecting manhood; reverent of solid worth; quickly seizing the ludicrous side of things, and merciless to all hypocrisy and humbug?

And yet in many respects the students of to-day are different from those of twenty-five years ago, and the reason of the change is not far to seek. Treat young men, even full grown men, like school-boys, and they will feel and act like school-boys. Give them the freedom which makes the difference between the University and the secondary school, and throw them upon their manhood, and they will justify their liberty. And this in general indicates the change that has taken place and the cause of it.

The University most unfortunately had been organized at the start after the model of the eastern college—which is not, never has been, and with that organization, never can be a University. Under higher titles and more show of dignity, it is, after all, the school master and the school boy. The former sets the task and holds the boy to strict performance. Teaching and learning are largely matters of routine. Love is not the motive to work, but necessity or rank, and college honors; the parchment and the name of graduate. Antagonism between teacher and taught is quite inevitable. Hence malicious fun—invention of, and more often, repetition of practical jokes at the expense of the authorities. Our students had developed under like influences the manners and customs of the old colleges—modified in no small degree by their greater maturity (for they were generally older) and by their greater earnestness. Yet, partly in imitation of the customs of the old colleges, and partly from the inevitable tendency of the organization, they had taken on many of those ways which would be deemed ridiculous in youths of the same age in any other position—business young men in cities for example. It is only the more earnest tone of the great body of our students, always noticed by those who have had opportunity to compare them with those of the institutions farther east, and the incessant movement we have made in the direction of manly freedom, that have at last caused these traditional follies almost wholly to disappear from the campus.

Has the presence of women had anything to do with this? Well, if we are human, we must say yes. None but the most unkempt barbarian is not improved by the presence of a woman. And yet, old-fashioned college men look back upon the rough sports and practical jokes of the early days with a trace of regret; as if such things, after all, were essential to the life of a well ordered American "college." The custom of hazing and many other puerile follies originated in those hives of mischief and roguery, the "dormitories," an institution common to all the old colleges, and with which our University also was saddled in its first years. They were abolished, indeed, by President Tappan, the very year of my arrival here, but nevertheless the seed sown in them bore fruit for many years in the traditional spirit and customs of the students. In fact, with the abolition of the dormitories and that of the cast-iron system of prescribed studies, pursued in unbroken graded classes, we took the first step towards the individual freedom and sense of individual responsibility, and possibility of individual development, which in promoting true manhood and contempt of puerile tricks and manners are the indispensable conditions of a University life; and it is precisely these that make the distinction between a College and a University. But the change has been gradual.

Another traditional custom, beginning like hazing, in a frolicsome vein, was the publication of "mock programmes" at the time of "junior exhibitions." "A mock programme" afforded large opportunity to those members of the junior class who were not honored with an appointment to exercise their wit at the expense of their more lucky classmates, and of any others, whether officers or students, whom they might wish to ridicule. Members of the Faculty, especially such as had salient peculiarities, and sometimes the President, not infrequently found themselves advertised in doggerel lines to take part in the performance, while the exhibitors themselves were named and characterized in such a manner, and their themes also designated with such absurd titles, that when the poor victims appeared on the stage, the audience being plentifully supplied with the "mock programmes" as well as the genuine, could hardly escape their influence. Many of the officers were indicated in these humorous documents by some nickname; even the venerable Dr. Williams was not spared. But beginning as they did, in a spirit of harmless mirth, just like the practice of hazing, they inevitably took on at last a more or less criminal character, not seldom outraging both morality and decency. For college life cannot avoid occasions of personal enmity, and the college community must always contain at least some base characters; and the influence of both came naturally to show themselves in these anonymous programmes. Playful satire, if it be anonymous, soon becomes malicious satire. Attacking in the dark, in sport, leads to stabbing in the dark. The programme, therefore, like all anonymous writings of a personal nature, tended to breed in the authors of them an unmanly and dastardly spirit. Accordingly these programmes at last became a public nuisance; and President Tappan and the Faculty made every effort to suppress them. This was very difficult because of the facility with which the printing of them could be secured in neighboring towns; and of the ease with which they could be circulated in secret. To be sure the authors in a few instances were detected and expelled, but the temptation to make use of such a congenial instrument for venting malice and vileness from time to time led some of the more reckless to repeat the offense, and it can scarcely be said to have been abolished, until the junior exhibitions themselves disappeared, a few years before the commencement exhibitions were also dispensed with.

I may note in passing that commencement exercises and exhibitions of the early day were held in the primitive churches of the town; first, in the old Presbyterian church on Huron street, between Fourth and Fifth, then in the old Methodist church on Ann street.

The High School Hall afforded the next resort. As this hall was very long, and the stage at first located at one end, the speakers could not be heard by more than half of the audience, there was therefore inattention, impatience, loud talking, and great confusion. At one of the exhibitions at which Dr. Williams presided, a Junior stopped short in his speech, and protested against the uproar. The late Judge Lawrence, then president of the School Board, taking great pride in the new High School building, and unwilling to have the great hall regarded as a failure, arose, and appealed to the noisy multitude in such a felicitous manner as to win attention and good feeling, and then he requested the crowd in the long aisles to seat themselves flat on the floor. They all at once complied, there was general silence, and the speaking proceeded without further disturbance. Before the hall was again occupied for similar purposes the stage was removed to its present location at the side, and continued to be employed for commencements and exhibitions, until the new Presbyterian church, completed in 1862, afforded a more convenient place.

President Tappan, on these occasions, was the central figure, and at the commencements, before conferring the degrees, usually made brief addresses to the graduating class; and these speeches, indeed, were among his happiest efforts. In fact during the whole period of his residence here, from '52 to '63, he was the most conspicuous personage of the town, as well as of the University. He was a born prince. He possessed all the traits of mind and form that characterized the old Knickerbocker families of New York, to which he belonged; a noble figure, dignity of manner without stiffness, a genial spirit, a generous heart, and a strong will; straightforward and outspoken, incapable of dissimulation; impatient of opposition, and quick to resent an injury; unwavering in friendship, full of tenderness for the unfortunate. He was the last man in the world to deal with politicians or to act the politician. In his simplicity he thought that men only needed to be shown the truth; that they would, of course, be honest and conscientious enough to obey it. It did not occur to him that, besides this, they must be conciliated into doing right, caressed, coaxed and coddled. Hence, in his efforts to get important measures enacted at Lansing he was sometimes defeated by those who entertained contrary designs, and who were cunning enough to create an impression that his honest boldness was pride and arrogance; that he was a haughty aristocrat, with no sympathy for common people, and that the University which he was trying to build up in the interest of the whole people, and which consisted mostly of poor men's sons, was an exclusive and an aristocratic institution. Hence, they claimed, there must be a people's college somewhere else. At the same time, we at the University and in this town, were well aware that he was in hearty sympathy with the farmer and the farmer's occupation, and that one of his favorite plans from the very first was to make the University subserve their wants, as well as those of all other classes of citizens.

All of us who were acquainted with President Tappan and his family, recall our social and personal relations to them as among the pleasantest reminiscences of the early days.

The society of the town still retained something of its pioneer character. Every considerable social gathering consisted largely of the first settlers; generally on intimate terms, simple and cordial in manners, and comparatively plain in dress. The Tappans, particularly the President and his wife, did not enjoy what are called "parties," large evening assemblies of a formal character. In fact, I never saw them present on such occasions. They preferred to meet with a few friends at home or abroad, in an unpremeditated way; and the President would not admit that anything else was society in the best sense of the word. He thought that nothing could be called conversation in which there were not at least two consecutive sentences; and found but little satisfaction in remarks "about the weather." He was fond of good music; quite cultivated, too, for a layman, and was never happier than when reclining at a leisure moment on the parlor lounge, and listening to some one playing selections from Haydn, Mozart, Beethoven, or Mendelssohn. Dr. Brunnow was an accomplished student of Beethoven. Mrs. Professor White and Mrs. Brunnow were good pianists also, and at one of our amateur concerts all three of them with myself took part in the programme. The posters announced in flaming letters that Dr. Brunnow, Mrs. Brunnow, Mrs. White and Professor Frieze would perform the overture to Fidelio arranged for eight hands.

Yet our music at that time was not usually of that high order. The people were better pleased with simple songs and old fashioned quartet music, and hardly appreciated instrumental music of any kind.

Our amateur musical club, on which we depended for the staple of our programmes, was made up partly of professors and students, and partly of the ladies of the Faculty and of the town. There was Professor Trowbridge, now of Columbia College, Professor Winchell and Professor Brooks, and among the students, A. K. Spence, afterwards Professor Spence, Byron Cutcheon, now Congressman Cutcheon, and O. B. Wheeler, afterwards an officer on the U.S. Coast Survey. We depended entirely upon "home talent," and did not feel the need of anything exotic. In fact, when it came to the selection of soloists, I found myself not a little embarrassed with the number who were, or, at least, thought they were equal to any emergency. The proceeds of our concerts were appropriated to the purchase of the "Nydia."

Well, the amateur musicians of that day have nearly all disappeared. Some few of us remain to recall the delightful reunions of our club, and smile to think of all our excitements and stage terrors in the presence of our brilliant audiences, the elite of Ann Arbor. And whenever a performance was over, as the (grand) conductor, I always awaited with some little nervousness the verdict of President Tappan. He was usually considerate and generous; but if we had admitted anything into a programme which was more humorous than musical, he was wont to give expression to his disgust in the most unqualified terms.

How remote and foreign all these incidents,—to me so recent—must seem to most of those who read these lines! How totally changed are the personages and the scene! Many of the prominent figures in the town and the University are sleeping the last sleep; many dwelling far away and widely separated, in other states and lands; some few still living here as the link between the present and the past. But some of those no longer here, whether dead or living, are still exercising upon our University, and upon our community, through the work they achieved, and the lives they lived here, an influence which will never end.

I must, in closing again mention three of these absent or departed ones, who, in my judgment, more than all the rest, have left an indelible impress upon the University. Henry P. Tappan, the man of broad and intelligent views, knowing better than any of his contemporaries in this land what a University should be; the man who left here the germinal ideas which are already springing up into a glorious harvest; James F. Boise, the man of nice scholarship, the critical teacher, and unyielding disciplinarian, whose power will never cease to be felt through the long line of classical instructors in the University and in the schools who have inherited more or less directly his accurate habits of investigation and of teaching; and lastly, Andrew D. White, the founder in our University of its rich and varied courses in history; whose broad and philosophical plan of historical studies has furnished to his successors a secure guidance for the conduct and development of this work to its present unequalled standard of excellence.

AN INAUSPICIOUS BEGINNING

Charles Jay Monroe

The beginning of Michigan Agricultural College—now Michigan State University—was precarious. The legislature, responding to demands for practical education for farmers, created the school in 1855; the college opened at its present location in 1857. The first class found a three-building campus set in a gallows orchard of dead trees in a partially cleared field, surrounded on all sides by a vast forest. The new school was authorized to teach "an English and scientific course" as well as "natural philosophy, geology, meteorology, entomology, veterinary art, leveling and political economy, with bookkeeping and the mechanic arts which are directly connected with agriculture."

A circular of December 1856 described the program of the school at the time of its founding. Applicants had to be at least fourteen years of age "and must have acquired a good common school education." Students were to devote "a portion of each day to manual labor, for which they will receive equitable remuneration." The "course of study . . . will embrace a wide range of instruction in English literature . . . mathematics, and . . . Natural Science."

The college soon found itself in financial difficulties. Rising prices depleted its original grant, and small appropriations barely covered costs. Its early reputation was uncertain; to many critics, it seemed that the school was merely a training ground for the pioneer tasks of clearing land, and that agricultural education was suffering. Appropriations were cut even further, and the curriculum reduced from four years to two. Enrollment plummeted; in February 1860, there were only nineteen students.

For a time, the legislature suspended classes while it debated the future of the college. Eventually, the four-year program was restored, and in April 1861, sixty-six students enrolled. But the Civil War intervened, and the senior class was excused to enlist in the Union army. Demands reemerged in 1863, 1865, and 1867 to relocate the college in Ann Arbor; not until 1869 was it clear that Michigan Agricultural College would remain and prosper at its present location. Over time, the institution has made important contributions to the development of agricultural education and related sciences.

The memoir by Charles Jay Monroe, a member of the first class to enroll in Michigan Agricultural College, describes the opening of the institution. It is excerpted from Charles Jay Monroe, "The College and the Students, 1857–1860," in Thomas C. Blaisdell, ed., *Semi-Centennial Celebration of Michigan State Agricultural College* (East Lansing: Michigan Agricultural College, 1908), pp. 61–78.

The College, when I first saw it May 10, 1857, consisted of a tract of mainly timber land, without an acre fully cleared. A few acres had been slashed down and the logs and brush cleared. On every hand were old stubs and partially burned trees. The fire had scorched the timber next to the clearing, so that at every point of the compass to which you turned, you beheld dead and blackened trees which presented a most desolate scene. There are a few pictures in the library which give a faint idea of it.

College Hall, a dormitory, and a small brick barn constituted the buildings. The old dormitory, known for many years as "Saints' Rest," stood a little east of the present site of Williams Hall, and was burned in 1876. These buildings were surrounded by logs and stumps, the carpenters' and masons' leavings, and other rubbish. The roads to the buildings were lined with stumps which had been dug or pulled out and in some cases partially burned.

The road from the College to lower Lansing was fairly good, judged by the road standard of those days. Lansing consisted of three parts, Upper, Middle, and Lower, and the distances and partition woods between them were sufficient to make them distinct towns.

The travel to the College was mainly from Middle Lansing, via Michigan Avenue. This street was usually a mud hole from the hotels to the College, particularly in the spring and fall, and was lined with timber except now and then a small opening made by new settlers. In this connection I wish to call attention to the large stone beside the road with a fair-sized tree seemingly growing through it. As I remember it, the crack was then small and only partly across the stone, and the tree was about the size of a finger. It was the frequent resting-place on the trips to and from Lansing. I suspect that the growth of the tree is largely due to the mud scraped from the shoes of the wayfarers, which furnished soil and water and created a sort of common ownership in the many contributors. I doubt if any boy in subsequent years passes the stone and tree without thinking of college days.

Lansing had no railroads. The nearest were the Detroit and Milwaukee at St. Johns, and the Michigan Central at Jackson. Most of the boys came by these routes. From Jackson to Eaton Rapids there was a plank road, but it had so many broken or missing planks that for a good deal of the way the square edges of the plank made it worse than the round logs of a corduroy. From Eaton Rapids to Lansing it was mainly mud holes. We regarded ourselves as fortunate if we got our trunks through, even by carrying a pole or rail for considerable distances to pry the old stage out of mud holes.

Personally, I did not know as to the road from St. Johns. I only recall that when there was a comparison between those from the north and from the south, one would conclude that both were among the worst in the state. It is fair to state that the vacations in those days were in the spring and fall, and so at the seasons of the year when the roads were at their worst.

The dedication exercises were held May 13, 1857, in the college room usually known as the chapel. This room has been the general meeting-place for all sorts of gatherings for fifty years. At the dedication it was crowded to its limit, and many stood about the doors, both inside and out. With two others I stood in the south center window, the platform being on the north, or opposite, side.

The next day those wishing to enter the College met in this same room as requested by the president. They were required, as I remember, to register their names, ages, residence, and occupation, and state the occupation they expected to follow after leaving college. Then the rooms were designated where they could go for examination. Fortunately for many of us, the questions were easy. The next day we again assembled, and all who had passed were assigned rooms. There were four students to each room, to do their own chamber work. Within a day or two we were again called to the chapel by the president. He stated that for the present he wished to assign the work as far as possible to those familiar with the work designated. A show of hands was asked, for those accustomed to driving horses. Probably four-fifths responded. After a few questions, the teamsters were chosen. Next, those familiar with oxen, a less number, responded. I was named to drive one yoke. The call was continued until nearly all the different sorts of work were mentioned and someone of those lifting the hand would be designated.

The first work, in which nearly all took part, was cleaning up the carpenters', painters', masons', and plumbers' rubbish, and clearing away the logs and brush near the buildings. As I remember it there was not an acre fully cleared on the farm—that is, with stumps out as well as logs and brush removed. Later there were many changes made in the assignments. As for myself, I continued to drive the oxen through the summer of 1857, mainly on the stump machine. In the summer of 1858 I drove the same team as a logging team, and they were extra.

Visitors coming to the logging field who were familiar with that sort of work were sure to notice and admire the team. Those remembering back to the days when clearing and logging were a prominent part of the work in Michigan will realize that a good logging team was highly valued, and their ability to make a log snap was often praised.

I recall an incident which occurred at a near neighbor's. A Mr. Seaver had an extra yoke of oxen of which he was very proud. As I was passing the field with several friends where he was logging, one of the party expressed the wish to drive out and see the men roll up a log heap. I introduced my friends and stated they would like to see a heap made; I also remarked that I was sure they would like to see his oxen draw the logs. He hitched to a long one and waved to everybody to keep away from the switch end, then sprang toward the oxen with raised whip, calling out, "Haw, Buck." This brought the oxen toward him and he, dancing back to keep out of their way, stammered out, "I beg your pardon, I beg your pardon, Buck, I meant, Gee."

In the winter of 1857 and 1858 chopping was the principal work. Over a hundred acres on the south side of the river was slashed into windrows and burned the following summer. We worked in three divisions, two and one-half hours each—first, 7 to 9:30; second, 9:30 to 12; third, 1:30 to 4. The second was expected to be out in time to take the tools of the first, the rule being that the same boys should follow each other in the use of the same ax.

An incident occurred the latter part of the winter which furnished considerable amusement and was made the subject of a very entertaining essay read before the Lyceum. As division No. 2 was leaving the dressing-room (where clothes were changed or overalls put on over the ordinary suit) word was received that a bee tree had been found and that the boys of No. 1 division were having a treat of honey. The boys of No. 2 abandoned the usual custom of marching in Indian style of single file and struck a double quick for the scene of feasting. The bridge was a large fallen tree reaching from bank to bank. Ordinarily it was adequate, but on this occasion when the whole squad were having a neck-and-neck race and all were wanting to cross at the same time, it resulted in several taking a forced bath before the coveted feast. Arriving at the scene, a pitched battle occurred which discounted a college rush. Besides, the bright sun warmed up the bees, and they with natural patriotism sought in a very stinging manner to defend their home and honey. They inflicted a good many wounds which soon became prominent and remained so for several days. Like all great battles the sad scenes came afterward. While none were killed and only a few wounded as above stated, the after effects of the hearty feast of honey mixed with rotten wood proved very disastrous in its relaxing effects, and sent most of the participants to the hospital. Few wanted any dinner and a less number went to the afternoon classes.

The principal work of 1858 was clearing the land, especially that cut over the previous winter. Some corn, oats, potatoes, and garden truck were raised and the old apple orchard was set out. The most notable and impressive event of the season was the fever and ague. The plowing and stirring of a hundred acres or more of new land with all its decaying vegetation turned loose an immense amount of miasma. The remark often made, "that it was thick enough to cut with a case knife," had much truth in it. In the latter part of August and fore part of September there were 70 out of 100 students unable to attend classes, at least they could come only every other day, as the fever was mainly intermittent. That is, one day the patient felt as well as ever, and the next, never felt worse. The main consolation the sufferer got was the frequent assurance that it was only the ague and nobody ever died from it. Classes were greatly interrupted and in some cases suspended for a short time. Many of the students became very impatient at the interruption of classes; some not familiar with fever and ague declared that it was unnecessary, that the boys were just as well as ever part of the time and might get their lessons and not be holding others back. I had a roommate who was of this way of thinking and unwittingly expressed it too freely. As my boyhood home was on the windward side of a mill pond I knew personally of its debilitating effects and still more of it from frequent observations of others, and reminded him it was a more weakening and serious disease than he could appreciate without actual experience. A little later it got hold of him. He was a sturdy, pushing New Englander and fought it off bravely, keeping up his work and study. One morning about 10 o'clock I came in from work and found him behind the stove doing his best to keep his knees from shaking, his chair from rattling, and his teeth from chattering. He put up his hand imploringly and said, "Don't say a word; if I ever get over this I'll never say another thing about anybody, as this is the meanest disease I ever saw."

The principal work of the winter of 1858–1859 was chopping, only instead of slashing it down we cut a large amount into four-foot wood, which was drawn to a long shed just east of the old boarding-hall. This furnished us rainy-day work or entertainment, fiddling it up with a bucksaw.

About a dozen of us remained through the spring vacation doing chores, cutting wood, etc., and four of us were able to recall in the Lincoln campaign that we had been rail splitters. A pleasant event of this vacation was our invitation to and attendance at the marriage of our Professor Tracy to Miss Sessions, professor of mathematics of the Michigan Female Seminary, of which I shall speak later.

The summer of 1859 the College can fairly reckon as its first year in which the production of farm crops and garden truck was the principal work of the students. All of the ordinary farm crops were raised and the quality and quantity compared favorably with those of the best farms in this vicinity. The garden in variety, quality, and quantity was by far the best up to this date and added greatly to the pleasure, comfort, and economy of living at the College.

The late Professor Prentiss of Cornell, who was a classmate, had the superintendence of the garden and directed the work in the afternoon, and it was my pleasure to assist him by having charge in the forenoon.

As the work of the four previous terms had been mainly such as I had been accustomed to in the childhood home—it being heavy timber and the clearings commenced about the time I was born—I got little that was new or helpful, except as the continued doing of any task makes one more expert in it. But the work, experience, and observation which I had in the two summer terms of 1859, which included the gathering, labeling, and arranging of seeds, I have felt were of great advantage to me, for which I have always been grateful.

I have previously mentioned the "Fem Sem," a short name for the Michigan Female Seminary, at Lansing in charge of the Rogers Sisters. There was some visiting of the girls at their college during the summer of 1858, possibly started and encouraged by the fact that Professor Tracy, in whose charge the overseeing of the boys principally was, was in the habit of visiting one of its teachers, to whom he was subsequently married, as stated above.

The mutual interest and visiting between the two colleges were greatly increased in October, 1858, when the M. A. C. boys were invited to a husking bee at the "Fem Sem." A field of several acres of corn, as I remember, stood just east of the buildings, now used for the School for the Blind. The night was lighted by one of those brilliant harvest moons and also by the smiling faces of the "Fem Sem" students who acted as partners in the husking. The number of red ears found was quite remarkable, in fact so many and so well scattered over the field were they, that they occasioned a good deal of querying, some declaring that the planter must have had foreknowledge as to the future huskers. When the corn was all husked and picked up, and the stalks bound and set up, we were treated to a bountiful lunch and then to a jolly social time, not soon to be forgotten. We were allowed to linger into the small hours, probably on account of the good work done.

In passing, I cannot help remarking that this was more than a pleasant event to the boys and girls for an evening; it was an important event for the colleges and especially to M. A. C., situated as it was three and a half miles from Lansing in a sparsely settled neighborhood. There were no seniors, juniors, or sophomores to introduce the new comers. For a year and a half about one hundred boys were deprived, except at the short vacations, of the companionship of mother, sister, or friends. The visits of the boys to the "Fem Sem" and of the girls to the College were of great benefit. I feel sure that memory serves me right in recalling the improvement in personal appearance, the greater attention to dress and address, the more frequent care of rooms and of the college premises, and an elevation of the moral tone. It was the assuming of a normal condition in the mingling of the boys and girls, with mutual advantage to both.

There was always plenty to do for busy heads and hands in study, reading, farm work, the care of rooms, and the mending and care of our clothes. Our sports were mainly of the country sort, "one-" and "two-old-cat" ball games, running, hop-step-and-jump, "pom-pom pull-away," tag, and leapfrog. Some of them were not very dignified; still there were no smashed noses, cracked heads, maimed limbs, nor any killing.

The principal event of general interest, and of special interest to those taking part, was a public exhibition at the close of the term, November 16, 1859. Nine students took part, besides a quartet which sang. The exercises were similar to those of the better class of district schools, and consisted of original orations and essays, interspersed with music. The old chapel was crowded to its fullest capacity, the larger portion of the audience coming out from Lansing.

The College was a typical Michigan pioneer in starting in the woods, in opening up roads, in logging and burning green timber, much of it in the wet season of the year, in the pulling of green stumps, and in ditching where an ax was as important as the spade or shovel. It was hard work for the boys and expensive for the College. I recall one large oak stump with a large tap root and a mass of others needed to sustain the tall sturdy tree, cut from it. It was only a few feet from the front door of the boarding-hall. Digging away the dirt and cutting off the roots required about ten days' work. Then it took the stump machine to roll it out and two yoke of oxen and four span of horses a half-day to draw it to the river bank near the president's house, costing about $20.

I have also a distinct recollection of some of the ditches. One between College and Abbot was in places one and two feet deeper than the height of the boys. The dripping from the dirt thrown out and the spatter of the water from the chopping of the roots made the boys look as though they had taken a mud bath.

The administration was frequently criticized for this extensive work, but the legislature which fixed the limit of the location of the College and those who selected the site should share the responsibility.

I have imperfectly and hurriedly mentioned a few of the happenings of the six college terms ending November, 1859, and can now simply add that about two hundred acres had been cleared, four residences, a barn, and a small toolhouse had been erected, the lots well fenced and in condition to produce good crops, and a creditable garden and a greenhouse were well started. Better than all this, I believe the boys generally had reached that point where they appreciated that the work helped pay their way, gain health and vigor, and assist rather than hinder their studies.

I mentioned the dearth of female society during most of the terms until partially supplied by the girls of the "Fem Sem." I would not have it understood nor leave it to be inferred that the wives of the officers were not thoughtful and ready with kindly assistance; but they lived in Lansing until the latter part of the period covered and so could do little. I am sure those at the College, when the steward and all his help left and the boys for a considerable time did the housework, recall how Mrs. Williams came daily to the College and gave generously of her time to assist us. Nor did we forget the many acts of kindness rendered by Mrs. Shearer who naturally left with her husband. For her motherly care and numerous helpful services in previous terms she will ever be held in grateful remembrance.

FIRMNESS OF PURPOSE

Franklin Sawyer, Jr.

State public educational systems were relatively new in the second quarter of the nineteenth century. John D. Pierce, the first Superintendent of Public Instruction, understood well that it was one thing to establish an educational system but quite another to assure quality. In 1838 Pierce began a *Journal of Education* as a means of communicating with all persons involved in the state's far-flung educational system, which consisted of about a thousand school districts. The journal, which was published for two years, sought to promote compliance with the state's school law and to encourage high standards of teaching and learning. Governors of the period—concerned with improving the effectiveness of the state's schools—often discussed the quality of teaching and other educational issues in public statements. "The chief obstacles to the realization of all the benefits of our noble school system," Governor Alpheus Felch told the legislature in 1847, "are found in the want of punctual attendance on the part of scholars, and deficiency in the qualifications of teachers." The role of teacher, Felch continued, "demands high qualifications. . . . His employment should be considered the most honorable, and his efforts [should] be seconded by every friend of the rising generation."

In 1841 Franklin Sawyer, Jr., who had succeeded John D. Pierce as Superintendent of Public Instruction, reported to the legislature on the duties of school inspectors and teachers, and even the human qualities essential for success in these roles. "They must possess . . . great firmness of purpose . . . and a moral courage that will not shrink from the performance of duty." Sawyer regretted that teachers too often were not treated with respect: "He is seldom taken by the hand in the friendly grasp of equality, seldom permitted to participate in the social intercourse of his district. . . . In the street, his presence only evokes ideas associated with ferrules, raw-hides and other instruments of torture for unruly boys." Sawyer's report throws an interesting light not only on the educational philosophy that guided Michigan's growing system of public education but also on some practical problems that arose in the state's endeavor to assure and maintain quality in its schools.

The following is an excerpt from the "Annual Report of the Superintendent of Public Instruction, Ann Arbor, 1841," from Michigan Legislature, *Senate and House Joint Documents,* no. 7 (Detroit: Bagg & Harmon, 1842), pp. 240–64.

While the mere spiritual teacher is treated with the high respect due to his holy office, and the village attorney, the physician, the merchant, the mechanic, the farmer, with all those nameless acts of civility which common politeness and common sense require between neighbors, the school master is looked upon, in too many instances, with disdain and contempt. He is seldom taken in hand by the friendly grasp of equality, seldom permitted to participate in the social intercourse of his district, seldom visited in school with any other feeling than merely to see that the amount of labor exacted is accomplished, and never at his boarding house, where his heart, by unburthening itself of its long pent up griefs, might find the sympathies so essential to its assuagement. In the street, his presence only evokes ideas associated with ferrules, raw-hides and other instruments of torture for unruly boys, his mode of government as master and not of discipline as teacher being uppermost in the mind. In short, the parents referred to, regard the teacher as a mere servant, hired to do a job that no body else can do, and fit for nothing else, morally, intellectually or socially; and when the two or three months for which he was employed expires, he is at liberty to "quit" as soon as he please.

The effect of such false, unjust, abominable, semi-barbarous notions, upon the district school, can hardly be estimated. Children imitate parents in habits of thinking, modes of expression and actions; and the age of puberty will hardly have been passed without bearing along with it the vicious consequences of such example. The child begins to be supercilious in school, and soon his contempt for the school master ripens into a contempt for his authority, and then breaks out into open disobedience. Other children follow the lead thus given; the standard of rebellion is boldly raised, the master is dethroned, and the school, sustained in its lawless acts by this very class of parents whose own example has occasioned the trouble, is for the time triumphant and the district is in a state of disorganization. It is not presumed that extreme cases of the kind are very common in our districts.

2. Duties of an Inspector: The reports under this head embrace three sets of duties—visitation, examination of teachers and scholars, and suggestions to teachers. The questions in the circular were intended to elicit full information on each of these divisions. That point, to a certain extent, had been gained. As a general thing, inspectors do not visit the school; or if they do, only once or twice a year, and then seldom examine the scholars or make any suggestion to the teachers. In some districts, they have not been near the school during the past year.

There are, however, many gratifying exceptions; and it is an important fact, one that delinquent officers cannot dwell upon too thoughtfully, that whenever these official visitations have been frequent, and the examination of both pupil and teacher thorough, the schools have sustained a better character than where no such visitations and examinations have taken place. It is true, faithful officers sometimes meet with virulent opposition in their laudable efforts, and sometimes personal animosity haunts them in their retirement; but mere opposition and mere abuse should drive no public servant from duty.

A brief sketch of the legal and moral responsibilities of school inspectors may not be out of place. It is their *legal* duty to divide the town into districts, to apportion the public money, make out and transmit to the county clerk all the statistical information furnished by the several districts, and, most important of all, examine candidates for teaching "in regard to moral character, learning, and ability." They have, then, high and responsible duties resting upon them. In the eyes of the law, they are the guardians of our common schools and ought therefore to be selected with great discrimination. Themselves the judges of what constitutes qualifications for teaching, their own moral character should be stainless, their own learning adequate to the task imposed, their own ability undoubted. Otherwise, they cannot estimate such sterling qualities in those they examine. They must possess, too, great firmness of purpose—a moral courage that will shrink from the performance of no duty, whether in the exact line of their own predilections or not, which is demanded by the educational interests of the town. If a candidate for teaching come before them, they have no right to recognize him in any *other* capacity for the time than *as* a candidate, and the only *questions* they are bound to answer satisfactorily to themselves, are such as regard his moral character, learning and ability. If his habits are bad, he should be rejected at once; for the pure heart of youth should not be exposed to the contagion of evil communication or vicious example. Any known vice should be deemed a disqualification. If the candidate be intemperate, sooner keep children in ignorance for a while than subject them to so pestilential an influence. An attendant upon grog shops, or even a dram drinker at home, may do to train brutes, but never, never can he educate the human soul. Here, then, is a field for the discerning and severely scrutinizing mind of the inspector. Immorality, in any or all of its protean shapes, however specious may be its semblance of virtue, merits no quarter. It should be cut off at once from all hope of success. With the *religious* views of the candidate, the inspector has no legal or other right to meddle. He may place high his standard of morals; practical virtue should be one test of fitness; but the teacher's *creed*, or the embodiment of his faith upon paper or within the deep recesses of his soul, is something which only Divine wisdom can deal. The question is not whether he is a Protestant or a Catholic, a Trinitarian or Unitarian, a Perfectionist, Latter Day Saint, Mormon or Transcendentalist; but whether he has such an unblemished moral character as will enable him to impart healthful principles to his scholars and be to them a living example of all that is beautiful and good.

As to the kind and degree of learning required by law, much is left to the examiner's sound discretion. Generally, the circumstances of the school, over which the teacher is to be placed, must govern. College learning, certainly, is not contemplated; for that is hardly wanted in common schools. If sought by any, the university is expected to give it. Nor are the higher branches of academic learning essential, particularly in the present condition of our schools. An elementary school, where the rudiments of an English education are taught, such as reading, spelling, writing and the outlines barely of geography, arithmetic and grammar, requires a female of practical common sense, with amiable and winning manners, a patient spirit, and a tolerable knowledge of the springs of human action. A female thus qualified, carrying with her into the school room the gentle influence of her sex, will do more to inculcate right morals and prepare the youthful intellect for the severer discipline of its after years, than the most accomplished and learned male teacher. The heathen notion, that females have no souls, was exploded with the occasions that gave it birth among the wrangling schoolmen of antiquity. It is now generally admitted that they not only have souls, but souls capable of a high order of intellectual development; while, in the matter of heart and all those holier emotions which give to humanity its crowning glory, they leave the "lords of creation" far in the rear. In most of our common schools, the ages of the scholars require female teachers; and the reports show that the summer and some of the winter schools are kept by them. But the inspectors cannot scrutinize their qualifications too nicely. An unqualified female is less to be tolerated than an unqualified male teacher, because her influence, if wrongly directed, is by far the most dangerous.

But we have schools in which children of larger growth seek to perfect the education which in boyhood had only begun. And as the state increases in population, and the necessities of a pioneer existence give way to the intellectual wants which stated periods of leisure are sure to create, we shall find such schools rapidly springing up. Then comes the test of an inspector's fitness for duty. Then comes the time when the common school begins to assume that high and noble and respected station which is due to it. Then comes the necessity of employing teachers who can supply the mental and moral aliment demanded of them, and thus impel the school onward to the attainment of its purposes among the people.

The ability required, undoubtedly means the power to teach. The inspectors must be satisfied, not only that the candidate has a good moral character, and sufficient learning, but that he is versed in the art of teaching. This is all important, and is dwelt upon for a moment because some districts, in their reports, have suggested such an amendment of the law as would enumerate more specifically the qualifications of teachers. But it is believed that, if the term ability be defined as above, no amendment can be necessary. The annals of school keeping everywhere, show that the purest minds and profoundest scholars do not, always, nor indeed often, understand the art of teaching. If Horace had given the world as rich a practical treatise on this most difficult of all arts, as he has on the art in which he himself excelled, many a rejected pedagogue of modern times would have blessed him.

In some foreign countries—Holland, Prussia and others—the art of teaching is taught like any other art; and such has been the conviction of its necessity in Massachusetts, that no less than three Normal schools, or schools for educating teachers, have been established. The two great objects of those schools say the board of education, in their annual report of 1839, are, first, to impart to the pupils a more correct and thorough knowledge of the various branches required to be taught in the schools; and second, to teach the principles of communicating instruction both in theory and in practice, at a model school connected with the main institution.

If, then, the ability to teach constitutes a qualification, the legal duty of an inspector is not exhausted by one examination, especially if that examination be made before the teacher has opened his school. On such an examination, the power to teach, or faculty of communicating instruction, cannot be tested. It is only by following the candidate into the school; and there watching the gradual and sudden developments of his disposition, his modes of teaching, and the manner in which he disciplines his scholars and otherwise governs his school, that the demands of the law can be met. We all know how easy it is to be deceived in these matters. A candidate may pass a good examination, and theoretically be pronounced qualified; yet in the school room exhibit anything but the traits of a school master. His plan of operations may be as eccentric as that which, to insure punctuality, compelled every tardy urchin to walk a mile with a fool's cap drawn over his head, and one of the punctual scholars to follow at some distance to see that the delinquent did not steal an occasional impunity by tearing off the cap and putting it in his pocket; which, to discipline the intellect, awarded a prize to that boy or girl who, at the end of the quarter and on examination day, should recite with the greatest rapidity, giving each word precisely as printed, all the rules in Adam's arithmetic, all those in Murray's grammar, and the Assembly's catechism from beginning to end; and which, by way of punishment for the minor faults of each hour, forced the luckless sinner to stand upon one foot, with the huge quarto bible at arm's length in one hand and a pitcher of water in the other, while a second law-breaker was stationed hard by brandishing a rattan, that neither burden might be dropped or the balance lost. It is not positively asserted that such a teacher can be found in Michigan, but simply this, that precisely that way of "teaching the young idea how to shoot," might not be inconsistent with a faultless examination out of the school. No inspector, then, should deem his legal duty ended with one examination. Having placed the candidate in school, he should keep his eye upon him; and if practically that candidate belies the certificate he has received, the law says such certificate may be annulled.

Formerly, the law made it the duty of inspectors to visit, at least twice a year, all such schools in their townships as should be organized according to its provisions, to inquire into their condition, examine the schools, and give such advice to such teachers and scholars as they should deem proper. That law has been repealed, and, singular as it may appear, no similar requisition has since found its way into the statute book. The reason of the repeal is unknown. It is thought that the omission of so essential a provision, one bearing with such direct force upon the interests of the common school, must have been an oversight in the legislature. It is hardly possible that the only guaranty furnished by law for the proper examination of schools, should designedly have been abrogated. The result is apparent in the district reports. Not being absolutely required to visit schools, the inspectors stay away from them, leaving the scholars to do as they please, and the teachers to plod along without counsel or sympathy. Yet, notwithstanding the law is silent, many conscientious inspectors have continued to visit the schools. And it is hoped that the moral obligation so to do, will be more generally felt than it has been during the past year.

While on this subject, it is respectfully suggested whether that part of our system which imposes on inspectors the duty of examining teachers, be not susceptible to improvement. Within the past year, the state of New York has adopted a plan of superintendence for her thousands of common schools, which commends itself to our attentive consideration. It is the appointment for each county, of a deputy superintendent, whose duties of supervision shall be co-extensive with the schools of his circuit. To his care are committed the educational interests of the county. He examines all the teachers, visits all the schools, collects all the statistics, sees that the laws are efficiently executed, ascertains their defects, and suggests improvements and otherwise promotes sound education. The suggestion that something of the kind, either a deputy superintendent or a county board of examiners, would conduce to the vigor of our own system, is made with a conviction that the town board of inspectors, as at present constituted, cannot be expected to fulfill the purposes of their appointment. In the first place, the office of inspector is too intimately connected with party contentions to be exclusively in the interests of schools. It is not known that mere political considerations have influenced the conduct of a single board in the state; nor is any thing of the kind intimated. On the contrary, it is cause of rejoicing that, so far as the requirements of the law have been obeyed, neither the fear or favor of this or that party has been permitted to turn the officers from the strict line of duty. The fear is not so much, that the officer, when chosen and duly qualified, will play the partisan, as that the too common plea of availability will operate as potently in this as in other elections, and secure the nomination of an individual better calculated to run than to serve. If each party would select its best men for inspectors, men qualified in all respects for the responsible position, without especial reference to their popularity, the interests of our schools, whichever party succeeded, would be abundantly safe. In the present state of parties, however, such a contingency is hardly within the range of probability.

Again, it is thought that economy favors the suggestion. As the law now is, each inspector is entitled to one dollar for each and every day's service. If he does all that is required of him faithfully, not to mention the incidental duties that a conscientious regard for the character of our public schools will constantly suggest, the aggregate of his per diem compensation at the end of the year will be no trifling sum. No means exist in this office by which to ascertain that sum. But take the simple duty of examining teachers, and the county of Washtenaw as convenient for illustration. Here are twenty towns, each with three inspectors. Of the 215 districts, whole or fractional, 157 have reported that schools in each have been kept during the past year by qualified teachers. To be qualified, the teacher must have a certificate; to get a certificate, he must be examined, not by one, not by a majority, but by all of the inspectors. How much time is requisite to examine the teachers of 157 schools? Suppose, merely for illustration, that these teachers are distributed equally among the towns. This will give nearly eight for each town. In the county, where inspectors live miles apart, it is no easy thing to get the board together. If, when once in session, the eight could be examined, perhaps two hours would be time enough assigned to each. But candidates for teaching in new places do not all come along at once. It is within bounds then to assign half a day for each examination. Then four days for each inspector will be required to go over the list, or twelve days for all, making as many dollars. Twelve dollars for each make $240 for the county; and this too on the supposition that no other or subsequent examination takes place. Add the other legal duties of an inspector that might be transferred to the county board or deputy superintendent, and the sum given alone for the performance of but one of those duties might easily be tripled, if not quadrupled. Should the suggestion thus thrown out be deemed important, it would then become a question, by whom the new officer or officers ought to be appointed, how paid, and how much. By the New York law, the board of supervisors are required to appoint the deputy superintendent. He holds his office two years, subject to removal by the board for causes stated. He received two dollars for each day necessarily spent in the discharge of his duties, but the whole amount in any one year is not to exceed five hundred dollars. One half is paid by the county, the other half out of the school fund.

Such is the New York plan. It is worthy of the "empire state." It is for the legislature to say whether Michigan will do well to adopt a similar plan or rely yet longer upon the present defective means of supervision. It is believed that the change suggested will insure greater efficiency in the execution of our school laws, better teachers, better schools, higher interest and more harmonious action among parents, and greater economy.

3. Teachers, Male and Female: To the interrogatories touching the sex, age, pay, &c., of teachers, between two and three hundred

districts replied. From these, it appears that while the ages of male teachers range from 17 to 40, giving an average of 24 years, those of females range from 14 to 28, giving an average of 20 years. But few of the males make teaching a business. Among them are found represented nearly all the professional, agricultural and mechanical interests. The inducements to teach are—a want of regular teachers in the district, no other employment, the wish to raise means for other pursuits, or, occasionally, the love of it as an honorable and self-satisfying vocation. It is evident from this condition of things that the chances decidedly incline to the side of unqualified teachers. Now and then, perhaps often, a young man or a young woman may sustain the reputation of a good teacher; but is believed that seven out of ten, who obtain a certificate, do not themselves feel really qualified for their task. The necessity imposed by law, of keeping up a school for at least three months to secure to the district an apportionment of the public funds, no less than the parental anxiety to have some kind of a school kept, very frequently and very naturally renders an examination of the candidate merely formal. Many act upon the principle that poor schools are better than none, and it is possible, they act rightly. Yet it is hard to admit that so terrible and humiliating an alternative has been forced upon the people of Michigan. It cannot be that we must either go without schools or have schools that do more harm than good to the rising generation. One thing is certain; nothing short of good schools will enable us to hold our legitimate station in the confederacy—nothing short of good schools can prepare our children to be the capable guardians as well as rightful inheritors of our glorious institutions.

One obstacle to good teaching is its inadequate compensation. Replies to the circular show that the average pay of male teachers is about $15.61 per month, and of females $1.27 per week. In one instance, $30 were paid a male teacher; but generally the price of teaching sinks down to $14, $12, $10, seldom goes as high as $20; while a female seldom gets more than $1 or $1.25. Now, what man can afford to qualify himself in the art of teaching, for $15 a month? What woman for $1 a week? The common school teacher is the most useful—the most indispensable functionary in the community; and yet he is the worst paid for his labor. Why is this? The question is more easily asked than answered. Some reply, that the times are out of joint; that the currency is destroyed; that money cannot be had. These are stubborn facts. But giving full force to such reasons, it so happens that the teacher fares no better in days of uninterrupted prosperity. While the price of every thing else alternates with the alternations of the currency, the demand and supply, the facilities for trade and the hundred other circumstances of daily experience, the price of teaching stands fixed; good, bad or indifferent, qualified or unqualified, the luckless teacher has no change "come o'er the spirit of his dream." Some other reason than the common one of "hard times" must be assigned to give it plausibility. It cannot but be suspected, that the only true reason is to be found in the practical indifference generally felt on the subject of school teaching. If the school master is yet abroad and among us, it is feared he will have to work through his present pilgrimage like many other Christian heroes, and look only for his full reward hereafter.

4. Government of the School: The reports show that the old fashioned mode of beating knowledge into the brain, is yet kept up to an alarming extent. The usual appliances are pinching, cuffing, pulling hair and noses, throwing books and rulers at the heads of unruly urchins, compelling them to stand until fatigued into submission, locking up in dark places to scare away the evil genius that possesses them, shaming and other varieties of torture. Nothing so truly indicates a teacher's unfitness for duty, as a disposition to be thus tampering with a child's capabilities of physical suffering; nothing so completely unnerves the energies of his school as this invariable resort, on the most trifling occasions, to instruments of torture as the only means of enforcing his rules. That extreme cases may occur, where the infliction of such punishment is demanded, will not be denied; but, as a general thing, it is believed to be pregnant with evils of great magnitude and wholly unnecessary. The day for such barbarisms has gone by. The spirit of the age is that of moral suasion, and experience declares that it is right. The more recent annals of popular education in the old states, and even in the old despotisms of Europe, prove that the most unteachable and most ungovernable schools can be tamed and managed by moral means. A man of becoming self respect, a force of character that cannot be trifled with, a stern moral as well as physical courage, will inspire not only respect for his authority, but a regard for the objects of instruction that shall render superfluous his rules of government. In many places, bodily punishments are prohibited; or, if tolerated, only as a last resort in desperate cases. Especially to be deprecated and condemned are all inflictions of blows upon the head. If, as mental philosophy and the anatomy of the brain demonstrate, the head contains the organs of the soul, and those organs are so delicately made up of fibrous and nervous tissues that the least derangement in them disturbs the mind's equilibrium, what amount

of reprobation should be visited upon him who, by his recklessness of consequences, so far forgets what is due to the intellectual and moral nature of man, as to risk its utter subversion merely to gratify the passion of a moment! It is believed that when the science of mind is better understood, and its relations with material organs duly felt, the penal code of schools will be essentially modified.

5. Character of the Instruction: The questions on this head elicit various replies. In some districts, the mode and character of the instruction are unexceptionable. The great effort is, to make the scholar understand what he learns—to teach ideas and words, merely as their signs. But in too many of the schools, the character of the instruction is behind the age. In them, the mind is treated precisely as if memory were its only attribute, and not like a spiritual existence, gifted with the highest powers of reason, and adequate to a degree of expansion conceivable only by the Deity. The consequences of such fundamental error, are monstrous and appalling. If the memory be the only faculty worthy of regard, and the standard of intellectual perfection be made to consist in the degree to which its exercise can be stimulated, we may as well cease to boast of the supremacy of mind over the instinct of the brute; for the latter can retort upon us the boast that he too has a memory that can be disciplined and made to approximate that same standard of perfection.

It is contended that education and instruction, though apparent synonyms, have fundamental differences of meaning. To instruct, is to heap up; to build upon; intellectually, to aid the mind in accumulating certain facts; not to create ideas, but to transfer them. A mind, simply instructed, resembles the granary of a shiftless farmer; full of every variety that heart can wish, but all so jumbled together, that if sent to mill, it would be difficult to designate the grist by the name of any known species of meal or flour. Education means more than this. Its true office is to discipline the mind; to call into action and unremitted exercise the affections of the heart; and to develop and invigorate the physical powers. Of what use is the most gifted intellect, if the heart, which gives it direction, be wrong? How much good would that intellect confer upon mankind, if its bodily frame-work were inadequate to sustain the tremendous pressure from within? Education, like nature, has a taste for the beautiful, and consults proportion and harmony in all its operations. Its first great principle, then, is so to proportion and harmonize the intellectual, physical and moral powers, as to make them co-operate equally towards the designed end. If you educate the mind and body, but neglect the heart, you may raise up a giant frame and a giant intellect, but you do it at the peril of all that's most holy and attractive in spiritualized human nature, and run the risk of elevating to a most dangerous position some moral monster, whose sphere of mischief shall only be limited by his aptitude for it. Then again, if you educate only the mind and heart, you do the grossest injustice both to man and his creator; because, by such an act, you virtually question the necessity of physical organization. From the moment you cease to regard the material covering of the soul as an object of your most delicate and unremitting care, you cease to cultivate, for any practical purposes, the intellectual and moral faculties. So, if you educate the heart and body, but leave the mind to grope its way unaided through the darkness of night, you strike from the human system the very source of man's greatness. You do all in your power to annihilate that sublime attribute of humanity which assimilates him to his creator, and makes him master of a power that eternity alone can fully develop. No system of popular education, which is not thus impartial, in its bestowements, can meet the wants of the present age.

The limits of a report will not permit a more ample notice of this most interesting feature in the condition of our schools; although it is one that cannot be too thoughtfully considered by every citizen of Michigan. It should be mentioned, however, in this connection, that while a certain amount of religious instruction is encouraged in many schools, sectarianism finds no admission. This remark, it is believed, can be made without an exception; at least, such is the tone of all the reports which have reached this office. The extreme sensitiveness on this point, as betrayed in the numerous replies to that part of the circular, calling attention to it, argues a healthy state of public opinion, and ought to banish all fears, if such be entertained by a single individual in the state, that any one religious sect, even if disposed, could successfully carry out a system of proselytism through the medium of common schools. Sectarianism never will infuse its poisonous virus into the great veins of our educational system, so long as the people hold their present views on the subject; and the only fear is, that a natural dread of the poison will exclude much that is wholesome from the schools. One extreme is as productive of evil as the other. A school without moral instruction, lacks the essentials of a right education, as evidently as the school opened to sectarianism exceeds them. No system can be perfect that is not based upon the great practical requisitions of Christianity—"do unto others as you would have others do unto you, and love thy neighbor as thyself."

WOMEN'S PROPER PLACE

Michigan Legislature (1859)

Hardly had the University of Michigan attained its reputation for excellence than the demand grew for the admission of women. Women were of course admitted to the state normal school and to private institutions, but were denied access to the state university. There was support for higher education for women—but in separate institutions. "A want is seriously felt for seminaries in the highest grade for the education of young ladies," Governor Kinsley S. Bingham told the state legislature in 1855. "Their education is an object as intimately connected with our social well being, and as important in every moral and religious point of view, as that of the stronger sex." Bingham did not, however, advocate that women be admitted to the state university.

Other Republican leaders, however, went further than Bingham and supported the admission of women to the university. In 1858 Miss Sarah E. Burger announced that she and twelve other female applicants would apply for admission to the university in June. The request was refused, largely because of the opposition of President Henry Philip Tappan, who believed that admitting women would adversely affect both sexes. Having been rebuffed by the university, the young women petitioned the legislature and the regents of the university for admission.

The legislative report on the admission of women to the University of Michigan is based on the petition of the rejected applicants. The report completely supports the admission of women to the university and disposes of the common arguments of the time against such admission. All the other public educational institutions of the state admit women, the report notes, but in the University of Michigan, "where the advantages of all the others are combined, and to which are superadded studies that can only be pursued under the most accomplished masters . . . the Women of the State are not admitted." The report attributes "the preponderance of opinion among eminent . . . literary men" against allowing women to have a university education to "the habit of their lives to consider men as the only suitable occupants of the higher walks of learning, and the only proper recipients of the most distinguished favors of science." The legislative report on the admission of women to the university conveys a lively sense of both sides of the controversy. Women were finally admitted to the university in 1870.

The report is reprinted from Michigan Legislature, 1859 (Lansing: John A. Kerr & Co., 1860).

Report of the committee on State Affairs relative to the establishment of a Female Department in the State University.

The Women of Michigan claim the right to a free and full participation in all the advantages arising from the expenditure of the literary funds of the State.

They base this claim upon their natural rights; upon their relations to society; the duties they are called upon to perform, and the broad ground of a wise State policy, which should provide in the most ample manner for the perfect education of those whose province it eminently is, to form the mass of mind which is soon to control the destiny and shape the policy of the commonwealth. That the position of woman in enlightened society, thus lies at the foundation of its structure, and gives her not only an important, but a controlling influence, informing the manners, habits, and tastes, and in directing the intellectual movement and progress of the rising generation, is admitted by all. With such an admission, it is difficult, and we may say impossible to demonstrate that the full intellectual development of woman is not of equal, if not greater importance, than is that of the other sex.

It is not sufficient to say that she moves in a different and less conspicuous sphere—that her duties are confined to a more restricted, quiet and domestic field—so long as it is acknowledged that her influence controls in forming the character of the sex upon which she is taught to rely, and in the superior advantages of which she claims the right to participate.

Since the establishment of the educational system of our State, the two sexes have been educated together in all our primary schools, in the union schools, in most of the private colleges, and in the State Normal School. From the co-education of the sexes in all these institutions, no inconvenience has resulted; on the contrary, great advantages have been seen and acknowledged. These advantages have been in the greater economy of the system, in the mental improvement incident to a well regulated social intercourse, and in the additional pride and ambition of the pupils. In all the lesser institutions of learning in the State, no change is asked or desired; all are now admitted to the common privileges. The system has been proved, by experience, to be all that its most sanguine supporters have hoped or promised; and the advantages secured such as could not be anticipated from any change in the system that would involve a separation of the sexes in the schools and colleges to which we have referred.

But the University of Michigan, the highest institution of learning in the State, where the advantages of all the others are combined, and to which is superadded studies that can only be pursued under the most accomplished masters; where alone can be furnished the scientific surroundings necessary to a complete education; and which alone has an endowment sufficient to provide such facilities, the Women of the State are not admitted.

Among the reasons urged for this exclusiveness is that of immemorial usage, the claim that never in any country have women been admitted to establishments of this class, and the fear that their admission to our State University would involve such a change in the management of that institution as would strike at the foundation upon which it is based; that it would be such a diversion of the fund provided for its endowment as was not contemplated by the donors; that any change, so radical in a system so well established, and which has prevailed since Universities were known, and which has received the sanction of the good and wise in all ages and countries, and which is sanctioned by long usage and the common consent of our countrymen, cannot be effected without great danger to the institution in which the change is proposed; and that such change, if it does not involve the very existence of the University, most certainly will impair its usefulness and bring into imminent peril the character and reputation of its students.

It is further urged, that many of the studies pursued at the University are not only unnecessary to the proper education of woman, for her appropriate and destined sphere, but are absolutely incompatible with that character for true delicacy and modesty which are the most pleasing and essential elements of her being; that instead of the admitted and mutual advantages which result from the coeducation of the sexes in all of the less elevated institutions of learning, their union in the University would prove injurious to both, by a loss of womanly delicacy of refinement on the one part, and a proper sense of the dignity of their pursuits on the other.

These, with other objections of similar import, are urged with great ability, and we may say with great fairness and sincerity, by many of the most distinguished and experienced educational men in the country; men who have devoted their lives to the intellectual progress of the age, and who are not enemies, but friends, ardent friends of female education.

Any movement against the remonstrance of such ability and experience, should undoubtedly be made, if made at all, with great caution, and only after the most careful consideration of the whole subject, and upon finding the weight of testimony and experience largely in favor of the proposed change.

The preponderance of opinion among eminent and experienced literary men, against the admission of Women to a participation in the privileges of a University education, which gives to the opposition its greatest strength, may, in the opinion of your committee, be attributed mainly to the fact, that custom has never yet sanctioned such admission, and that it has been the habit of their lives to consider men as the only suitable occupants of the higher walks of learning, and the only proper recipients of the most distinguished favors of science.

Professional men are proverbial for their adherence to established forms and usages, and are almost always the last to yield to progress the respect and support to which, in their opinion, precedent is justly entitled. To them, reform is innovation; progress, revolution; and change dangerous and disastrous.

The influence of early education, and the fixed habits of life of literary men, are well calculated to inspire a veneration for, and adherence to, the usages to which they have been accustomed. And though the experience of thousands, within the range of their observation, should prove the advantages of a system which has not been sanctioned by time, we will seldom, if ever, sanction its adoption until the movement reaches the very domicile in which they have taken refuge. This conservatism is in the highest degree commendable, if not carried so far as to stand in the way of desirable progress. To ascertain whether such is not the case, on the subject under consideration, is one of the objects of the present inquiry.

To the immense weight of testimony to which we have briefly alluded, and to the theory of an entire separation of the sexes in the highest institutions of learning in the State, for it is theoretical only, on the part of those who have advanced these opinions, they never having tried the experiment of a combined system—the friends of the proposed reform, oppose the experience of the past twenty years in our own State, in which time a generation has been mainly educated without, so far as your committee is aware, any appearance of the difficulties or dangers apprehended, and which are urged with so much of power and ability; but on the contrary, the experiment has been an entire and perfect success; advantageous in every instance to all participants, and highly beneficial to the institutions which have adopted and sustained the system.

The united testimony of the teachers, students and parents interested in the success of our primary and union schools, in the private colleges, and in the State normal school, as to the superior economy and advantages of a joint education of the sexes, presents a mass of living evidence and practical experience which neither the arguments, theories, nor doubts of men, however exalted or learned, can withstand.

The Women, as a class, have in no instance, been found inferior in intellect to those of the other sex, enjoying the same advantages; nor have they lost any of that delicacy of sentiment, or refinement and modesty of deportment, which ever characterize the American woman. Nor have the men, with whose progress and education they have been associated, lost that high appreciation of the dignity of their pursuits which is an essential element of the American character.

The joint education of the sexes in the highest institutions of learning, has not in this country been permitted, except at Oberlin and Antioch Colleges in the State of Ohio. In both of these Institutions the experiment has been successfully tried upon a large scale, and it is but fit to quote the language of the eminent men at the head of those institutions respectively upon the subject.

President Mann of Antioch College, says:

> I have long been in favor of the joint education of the sexes, 1st. Because woman has as good a right to an education as man, even better if only one of them could be educated; and 2d. Because both can be educated together not only more cheaply, but much better than either of them can be apart from the other.
>
> I think this is the result of sound theorizing on the subject, but I had had many years of practical observation before I came to this State, though not under circumstances precisely similar.
>
> Since I have been connected with Antioch College, that is, for nearly five years, I have had an opportunity to see the experiment wrought upon a large scale, with students of advanced ages, and under what I should not consider to be more or less favorable, or better or worse than average circumstances. This experience has not altered my view of the general question, but it has made certain collateral or accompanying circumstances more prominent in my mind than they were before.
>
> The advantages of a joint education are very great. The dangers of it are terrible. Unless those dangers can be excluded, with a degree of probability amounting to a certainty, I must say that I should rather forego the advantages than incur the danger.

These dangers consist in their opportunities for association together, without supervision or privately. If these dangers cannot be excluded, I would not, with all my partiality in favor of the object, incur the risk. If, for instance, they must be permitted in a city like yours, to board promiscuously among the inhabitants, I should prefer that the young women of the age should lose the advantage of an education, rather than incur the moral danger of obtaining it in that way.

Strongly, therefore, as I am in favor of the joint education of the sexes, I should first demand, what security can be furnished for moral protection? and until this question should be satisfactorily answered, I should not date vote in favor of my own side of the question.

I should make such inquiries as these: Can the sexes have separate lodgings? Can they take their meals together, and then be separated? for it is well that they should eat together. Can they have opportunity for meeting each other once a fortnight or three weeks, in general company, as people moving in the same circle must meet each other in ordinary parties? This is a great safety-valve, and should be provided for. Can you make yourselves secure against clandestine meetings? and also against clandestine correspondence? reasonably so, for absolute security is impossible. Are your president and faculty in a state of mind to exercise vigilance over the girls committed to their care as conscientiously as they would over their own daughters or sisters?

You may think these are collateral matters. I think they are vital to the generation. We have never had the happening of one of these events mildly called accidents, but it is only because of our constant, sleepless vigilance. Our serenity has arisen from our care. The system works well here, and there are great advantages in it. I ought not to say this, however, without adding that very serious dangers must attend the introduction of such a system, and that its administration should command the highest degree of caution and vigilance. We have conducted the system of five years without a disaster, when, perhaps, and probably, some one of our youth who have been here, would have suffered one at home. But we have succeeded in introducing a high tone of moral sentiment among our students. We have no rowdyism, no drinking, no profligacy. We will not have it. Order, regularity, sobriety, and observances of the decencies and proprieties of life, give an elevation to public feeling and conduct which is a great safeguard and guaranty against the indulgence of passion.

I believe, however, schools of both sexes can be safely conducted; that when so conducted, the intercourse of the sexes is

> mutually advantageous; that daily intercourse with young ladies refines the manners of the young men, and actual association with young men, and a knowledge of character and the duties of life, has a strong tendency to expel all girlish romance, and to exorcise the miserable nonsense which comes from novel reading. We began with both sexes; I can conceive that you might have more difficulty than we had, especially if your young men are not under good discipline now. We also have a boarding house for young ladies. I should deprecate exceedingly turning our young ladies out into the street for their meals.

President Finney, of Oberlin College, substantially corroborates and sustains the opinions and conclusions advanced by the President of Antioch College.

The views of President Finney are based upon actual experience in an institution of long standing, with a large number of students of both sexes, and enjoying in the highest degree the confidence of the public.

These gentlemen are among the ablest educators in the country; their testimony is unequivocal as to the advantages resulting from the system of joint education adopted in the successful institutions over which they respectively preside, and both agree as to the precautionary measures necessary to success—which are, separate domiciles for the occupation of the sexes, a careful and sleepless supervision, a high tone of moral sentiment among the students, and in the community by which they are surrounded, and frequent opportunities for well regulated social intercourse.

These prerequisites provided, and there can no longer remain a doubt of the propriety of throwing open the doors of the literary department of the University to, the women of the State, and providing for their admission to the privileges which their brothers enjoy in that favored institution.

When this shall be done, our State will no longer present the anomaly offering free to the citizens of other States those privileges which are denied to one-half the people of our own. But should this act of simple justice to the Women of Michigan be finally withheld, it is hoped that the policy of levying upon the public treasury an annual tax of seven thousand dollars for the support of the University, will at least be postponed, until some plan can be adopted that will secure the benefits of this expenditure to the people of our own State.

If these prerequisites do not exist, then the time has arrived when the public should take cognizance of the fact. If the tone of moral sentiments in our University is not such as may be prudently and profitably shared by our sisters and daughters, then it is time, high time, that efficient measures be adopted for its improvement and regeneration. The men of the State should no longer be compelled to breathe an atmosphere in our public institutions which is unfit for those who are to become their future companions, and the most effective teachers of their children.

It is claimed that in the University, with its medical and its contemplated law departments, which it is insisted are essential to its complete success, the preponderance of men who will attend its lectures for comparatively limited periods, and around whom cannot be thrown those wholesome restraints which are enforced upon students pursuing the ordinary course of college studies, will be such as to prevent that absolute moral security which is an essential prerequisite to the admission of Women in that institution.

To meet this objection, and at the same time increase the usefulness of the medical department, by furnishing additional facilities to the students, at a diminished public expenditure, your committee recommend the removal of the medical department to the city of Detroit, where it would have been at first established had the interests of the University and of the students been consulted, and where alone the facilities for practical demonstration, so essential to the medical student, can be found. So great is the necessity for these advantages which commonly exist in the large cities, that even now both professors and students are obliged to ask them in the locality proposed.

The removal of this department to Detroit and the institution of admission fees to be paid by all non-resident students, commensurate only with the superior advantages which there exist, would relieve the University of a heavy drain upon its income, and render the medical department nearly or quite self-sustaining.

This, with the continuation of the annual appropriation of seven thousand dollars, which for several years past has been made to the University, would, under proper management, warrant the establishment of a law department which should also be located at Detroit, and for reasons similar to those which have been mentioned as applicable to the removal of the medical department. There the student at law would be surrounded by the constant and varied practice of men experienced in the daily and intricate duties of the profession, and which cannot be gleaned from books or the school-room. There the conflicts of actual life in all the grades of courts recognized by our laws, and the forms and usages which matured experience had suggested and established, may be studied with the greatest facility. And the student will go out from your law department an accomplished and practical lawyer instead of a mere book-worm, as would necessarily follow from his graduation at a place removed from these demonstrative adjuncts incident to a location at the commercial emporium of the State. There, too, the medical class would pass from the study to the hospital, where are congregated the subjects necessary to a practical demonstration of the science they are pursuing, and where may be learned in a single day, more of the progress of disease, the effects of remedies, or the skill of the surgeon, then could be gathered in a year from authors or the lecture-room.

The University, as a whole, will share in the advantages incident to the location of these departments, where superior privileges may be enjoyed, in the higher reputation of her graduates, and in the additional social security and elevation of the tone of moral sentiment, resulting from the removal of these departments to a point where the irregularities of their students, arising from the want of fixed habits and an established residence, will be overborne by the prepondering public sentiment of a populous city; advantages which cannot attend its retention at Ann Arbor, where the social sentiment of the town will be comparatively lost, or controlled by the less settled habits and more turbulent manners of the college.

Your committee are deterred from presenting a bill for the reorganization of the University, in accordance with the views expressed, by the large demand which will be made upon the Treasury for the completion of the highly deserving benevolent institutions now in progress; the expenditure which the proposed reorganization would involve; and the still more controlling consideration that a change so important should not be made except upon mature reflection, and after a free and full discussion of the whole subject by the people of the State.

All which is respectfully submitted.

H. Barns, Chairman.

PART IV.

REFORM AND THE POLITICAL PROCESS

SIMPLE JUSTICE

Convention of Colored Citizens (1843)

The proportion of Blacks in Michigan was small in the pioneer period; most were concentrated in the Detroit area but there were Black enclaves in other places, most notably in Cass County. The antislavery movement had a powerful hold on Michigan, a fact that appears to have energized some Blacks and their white allies, including Austin Blair, who would become Governor of Michigan during the Civil War, to demand full rights of citizenship for Blacks. The fact that Pennsylvania granted Blacks such rights in 1838, and that there was powerful support for a similar step in New York—appears to have been a powerful example for Michigan Blacks, who demanded the same from their state. In Michigan the overriding issue for Blacks in the antebellum period was the fact that they could not vote. They suffered as well from other legal disabilities—they could not serve on juries or attend white schools or use public facilities. While some Michigan abolitionists—including those who published the Ann Arbor *Signal of Liberty*, an antislavery newspaper of the period—supported the Black vote, many did not. It is an anomaly of American history that many antislavery whites were at the same time racists and unwilling to extend civil rights to Blacks who resided in the state.

In 1842 Detroit Blacks formed a "Colored Vigilance Committee" to wage "moral and political warfare" for civil rights, and in 1843 Black leaders held a national convention, which was followed by a convention of Michigan Blacks in October of that year. The convention, which was led by ministers and small-business proprietors, objected to denial of educational opportunity, but placed greatest stress on denial of the right to vote. The document which follows is taken from the minutes of that convention, the *State Convention of the Colored Citizens of the State of Michigan, Held in the City of Detroit on the 26th and 27th Days of October, 1843, for the Purpose of Considering Their Moral and Political Condition as Citizens of the State* (Detroit: William Harsha, 1843).

Call for Convention

Believing that the time has come for us to be united in sentiment and action, and to speak out in our own defence and upon the great cause of Human Liberty and Equal Rights: we call upon you to cooperate with us in this important movement that we are about to make. For as we are an oppressed people wishing to be free, we must evidently follow the examples of oppressed nations that have preceded us: for history informs us that the liberties of an oppressed people are obtained only in proportion to their own exertions in their own cause. Therefore, in accordance with this truth, let us come up, and like the oppressed people of England, Ireland and Scotland, band ourselves together and wage unceasing war against the high-handed wrongs of the hideous monster Tyranny. Come up, brethren, and rally under the banner of Freedom; for since our late National Convention, a new and a bright star had made its appearance in our dark horizon, and has attracted the attention of our oppressors, and caused many to cry out, Go on, thou genius of Liberty, go on! The friends of liberty throughout the civilized world have hailed it, and now standing beside us and cheering us to go on. Then, brethren, shall we not meet together, and consult how we may better our condition? Shall we not infuse into the minds of our young men, and posterity, a disposition to be free, and leave their present low and degraded employment, and endeavor to obtain mechanic arts, and to follow agricultural pursuits? Shall we not meet together and endeavor to promote the cause of Education, Temperance, Industry, and Morality among our people; and by our correct, upright and manly stand in defence of our liberties, prove to our oppressors, and the world, that we are determined to be free?

Yes! yes! let us assemble—let us come together, and pledge ourselves in the name of God and bleeding humanity and posterity, to organize, organize and organize until the green-eyed monster Tyranny, shall be trampled under the feet of the oppressed, and Liberty and Equality shall embrace the feet of the oppressed, and Liberty and Equality shall embrace each other, and shall have scattered their blessings throughout the length and breadth of our land.

Wm. Lambert, Chairman of Convention.

Proceedings of the Convention:

Pursuant to the preceding call, the Colored Citizens of this State, through the Signal of Liberty, at Ann Arbor, and the Daily Advertiser of Detroit, urging people to assemble at Detroit in Convention on the 26th day of October, for the purpose of taking into consideration their Political Standing as a People, and to adopt measures for the improvement of the same; the Fort Street Second Baptist Church was thrown open at an early hour on Thursday morning of the above date, and soon became the scene of the most spirited and manly meetings that have ever engaged the energies of the people in this state.

At 10 o'clock, A.M., about eleven delegates were assembled from different counties of the State, together with twelve who were chosen in the city.

The Convention was called to order by the Rev. W. C. Monroe of Detroit, who moved the appointment of Wm. Lambert of Detroit, as Chairman protem.

An Address to the Citizens of the State of Michigan:

Fellow Citizens: The State Convention of Colored Citizens, assembled in Detroit, October 26th, and 27th, to consider their political condition, in behalf of their people in this State, would respectfully address you on a subject to them of the most vital importance.

We, the oppressed portion of this State, rejoice that we are the native inhabitants of a country that professes to be the land of the free, and an asylum for the oppressed of all nations.

But yet we feel ourselves aggrieved, that we are deprived by injustice of those inalienable rights with which we are endowed by the Creator of the Universe, and incorporated and made sacred to every native born inhabitant of these United States, by the Declaration of the American Independence.

Therefore do we solemnly appeal to you for a just reason, why we should be deprived of our free-born rights, which are guaranteed to us as native born Americans.

For we find ourselves existing in this state, with no marks of criminality attached to our names as a class, no spots of immorality staining our characters—no charges of disloyalty dishonoring our birth-right; yet we are prevented from being participants in those free-born rights and sympathies, that are bountifully guaranteed not only to common humanity of this state, but also to foreigners of whatever clime or language. We find ourselves the subjects and not the objects of legislation, because we are prevented from giving an assenting or opposing voice in the periodic appointment of those who rule us, and are made passive instruments of all laws, just or unjust, that may be enacted, to which we are bound to subscribe, even while we have no instrumentality, either in their formation or adoption, and which in their practical operation act upon us with destructive tendency. By subjecting us to taxation without representation, by allowing us but a scanty and inadequate participation in the privileges of education. For we are deprived of a just and equal participation of the educational privileges of this State, for which we are equally taxed to support.

By shutting us out from the exercise of the elective franchise, a right which invigorates the soul, and expands the mental powers, and is the safe-guard of the liberty and prosperity of a free and independent people, and by being deprived of this right, we are virtually and manifestly shut out from the attainment of those resources of pecuniary and professional emoluments, which an unshackled citizenship does always ensure. These proscriptions in the privileges of the State, we consider to be undemocratic, unjust, and not in accordance with the spirit and political institutions of our republican form of government, and contrary to the first article of our State Constitution, which in the first three clauses of said article, declares that, 1st, all political power is inherent in the people. 2d, Government is instituted for the protection, security and benefit of the people, and they have the right at all times, to alter or reform the same, and to abolish one form of government and establish another, whenever the public good requires it. 3d, No man or set of men are entitled to exclusive or separate privileges. And as we, the oppressed form a portion of the people of the State, and are deprived of all rights and privileges guaranteed to the people, therefore, we enter our solemn protest against the word white, embodied in the first clause of the second article of the aforesaid Constitution, which provides for all white male citizens, the exclusive and separate privileges of the exercise of the elected franchise, of which we are deprived, and which is also contrary, and gives the lie to the third clause of the first article of the Constitution, which so positively declares that "no man or set of men are entitled to exclusive or separate privileges."

For the same here avowed proscriptions in the privileges of the government, did the fathers of the Revolution of 1776, declare these United States to be absolved from all allegiance to the British crown. They published as a justification, a declaration of rights, and an extensive list of grievances, and then established a republican form of government for their future protection, laying its foundation on the broad foundation of those noble principles set forth in their Declaration of Independence; which so nobly declares that all men are born free and equal, and endowed by their Creator with inalienable rights, among which are life, liberty, and the pursuit of happiness; that to secure these rights, governments are instituted amongst men, deriving their just powers from the consent of the governed; that the people are the only legitimate force of lawful political power, and that they have the right to institute, alter or abolish forms of government when they fail to secure the ends for which they were established; and that this right is inherent, inalienable, and supreme.

That the definition of "the people," is all men; that to enable all men to exercise their right to institute government, they should enjoy the right of suffrage. That this right is a natural right, belonging to man, because he is a person and not a thing—an accountable being and not a brute. That government is a trust to be executed for the benefit of all; that its legitimate ends are for the preservation of peace, the establishment of justice, the punishment of crime, and the security of rights. They condemn all Legislation violating the spirit of equality. They are the foundation of a true, and unproscriptive republican form of government and the correct guides in all political action.

For the maintenance of these noble republican principles, the fathers of the Revolution, pledged to each other their lives, their fortunes, and their sacred honors, and thereupon ordained and established the Constitution of these United States, which guarantees to every State in this Union a republican form of government, and explicitly declares that the citizens of each State shall be entitled to all the privileges and immunities of citizens of the several States. In accordance with these glorious republican principles, have we year after year petitioned our State Legislature for the redress of our grievances, and we have received from time to time but little attention.

In the declaration of fundamental principles, set forth by the fathers of '76, we fail to discover anything like a system of exclusion. No! there is not an expression, nor an implied sentiment to be found making a distinction in the rights and privileges of any class of American citizens. But on the contrary, its first infant breath, boldly proclaims that all men are born free and equal, and that consequently life, liberty, and the pursuit of happiness, are inherent in every individual, vested inalienably by natural birth-right.

Had the declaration said that all "white men are born free and equal," then our ancestors would not have been deceived into the belief, that they were included as constituting a portion of the party, engaged in the strife against British oppression. Nor have given occasion to the observation of General La Fayette, when he visited this country, that, during the Revolution the white and black soldiers fought and messed together without hesitation. The records of that period clearly prove that the blacks rushed forth to the conflict, and poured out their blood with as much bravery as their white fellow soldiers, in the attacks made upon what they considered to be their common enemy. The testimony of Generals Washington, Green, and many others, to the valor of our people in the time of our country's greatest peril, shines too conspicuously to be impeached by any enlightened individual.

Yes! fellow citizens,—again in the War of 1812, our people were called upon to repeal an invading foe from out native soil. Regardless of the wrongs that had already been heaped upon them, they immediately rushed forth to the conflict; and under the command of General Jackson in the Southern Army, and especially at the Battle of New Orleans, distinguished themselves as valiant soldiers, fighting in defence of their country's honor. The splendid naval engagements, on Lakes Erie and Champlain, were owing, mostly, to the skill and prowess of Colored men. The fame of Perry was gained at the expense of the mangled bodies and bleeding veins of our disfranchised people. The blood of our fathers is mingled with the soil of every battle field: and their bones have enriched the most productive lands of our country. Yes! in these ever-memorable battles which achieved the Independence, and maintained the honor of our country, your fathers and ours, fought side by side, many of whom were laid low, bleeding and wallowing in their gore, which was the dear price they paid for the Independence of this, our beloved, country, that all their posterity might enjoy the blessings of Equal Liberty.

Therefore, we feel ourselves aggrieved, that blessings obtained by the blood and toil of our fathers, are not administered as equally to us as to yourselves. We feel that our sufferings caused by our being deprived of our Political Rights, should call forth the sympathies of the whole human race, but more especially those of yourselves, among whom we dwell & who are the authors of our calamities. For you have trampled our Liberties in the dust, and thus standing with the iron-heel of Oppression upon our heads, you bid us rise to a level with yourselves; and because we do not rise, you point the finger of scorn and contempt at us, and say, we are an inferior race by nature.

Yes! when all the avenues of privileged life have been closed against us, our hands bound with stationary fetters, our minds left to grope in the prison cell of impenetrable gloom, and our whole action regulated by constitutional law, and a perverse public sentiment: we have been tauntingly required to prove the dignity of our human nature, by disrobing ourselves of inferiority and exhibiting to the world, our profound scholars, distinguished philosophers, learned jurists, and eminent statesmen. The very expectation on which such a supposition is founded, to say the least, is unreasonable; for it is only when the seed is sown, that we can justly expect to reap. But yet we feel constrained to say, we present the curious and acknowledged creditable spectacle of a people bending under the weight of a galling proscription, who yet will not suffer by comparison with more privileged citizens of the same rank, either in religion, morality, industry or general information.

A spirit of intelligence pervades our entire population, keeping pace with the progressive spirit of the age and the continual intellectual progress of the nation. There are but few families in which pen, ink and paper, and books, are not common and necessary commodities. If, then, amidst all the difficulties with which we are surrounded, and privations we have suffered, we present an equal amount of intelligence with that class of our fellow citizens that have been so peculiarly favored; a very grave and dangerous question presents itself to the world, on the natural equality of man: and the best rule of logic, would have placed those who have oppressed us, in the scale of inferiority.

Our condition as a people in ancient times, was far from indicating intellectual or moral inferiority. For, we are informed by the writings of Herodotus, Pindar, Eschylus and many other ancient historians, that Egypt and Ethiopia held the most conspicuous places amongst the nations of the earth. Their princes were wealthy and powerful, and their people distinguished for their profound learning and wisdom. Two thousand years ago, people flocked from all parts of the known world, down into Africa, to receive instruction from those wooly haired and black skinned Ethiopians and Egyptians. Yes, even the proudest of the Grecian philosophers, historians and poets, among whom were Solon, Pithagoras, Plato, Herodotus, Lycergus, and many others, all went down into Africa, and sat at the feet of our ancestors, and drank in wisdom. . . . The code of laws administered by Solon to the inhabitants of Athens shows no inferiority of his black instructors. . . . Therefore, fellow citizens, proscribe us no longer, by holding us in a degraded light, on account of natural inferiority, but rather extend to us our free-born right, the Elective Franchise, which invigorates the soul and expands the powers of a free and independent people. We then would be able to disprove ourselves of inferiority, and prove to the world, that we are worthy of the name of American citizens. . . .

Wm. H. Lambert
Chair of Convention

JUSTICE DENIED

Michigan Legislature (1846)

The Blacks of Michigan used all the legal means at their disposal to obtain voting and other rights, including petitioning the legislature. One such petition asked for a constitutional amendment of the constitution "which . . . shall abolish the legal distinction now existing between white and colored citizens, and extend to all the elective franchise irrespective of color or descent." A joint resolution to amend the constitution to grant Blacks the right to vote was introduced in both houses and referred to committees for reports.

The Senate committee report reflects the prevailing sentiment among whites: "Our Government is formed by, for the benefit of, and to be controlled by, the descendants of European nations, as contradistinguished from all other persons." Representative Austin Blair of Jackson, reporting for the House Committee on the Judiciary, disagreed. "Any other conclusion," he argued, than granting full civil rights is "directly at war with the very spirit of our Republican institutions, based as they are upon the doctrine, that a perfect equality of rights, both civil and political, is the birthright of every man of whatever name or color or nation." Neither house of the legislature approved the joint resolution. Not until the adoption of the fifteenth amendment to the Constitution of the United States did Michigan's Blacks obtain the right to vote.

The following is Senate Document No. 12, *Report of the Select Committee on the Amendment of the Constitution, so as to extend Elective Franchise,* Michigan Legislature, 1846 (Detroit: Bagg & Harmon, 1847). Blair's report appears after the Senate document.

Mr. Howell, Chairman of the judiciary committee, to whom was referred several petitions asking such legislative action for "an amendment of the first section of the second article of the Constitution of this State, as shall abolish the legal distinction now existing between WHITE and colored citizens, and extend to all the elective franchise irrespective of color or descent," submitted the following report:

The committee are unanimously of the opinion that it is inexpedient and impolitic to grant the prayer of the petitioners.

At the same time, that your committee feel constrained from a sense of duty, to report adverse to the prayer of the petitioners, they are frank, to say that they recognise among them many of the most worthy and respected citizens of this state—characterized by sterling integrity and moral worth; and feeling as the petitioners seem, that it is strictly a moral question involving the great principles of humanity and philanthropy, the committee are not disposed to question either their sincerity or their motives.

Did the petitioners ask to have themselves relieved from the operation of unjust or unequal laws, or for the passage of such laws as would secure to themselves as citizens of the state, equal rights and privileges with others; it would be the duty of the legislature, if the evils complained of existed, to adopt such measures as would secure equality of rights without regard to the number complaining: but if, as in the present case, they ask to change a settled and salutary feature in our government, so as to give a separate and distinct race of people the full benefits of citizenship on an equality with themselves, a question for grave consideration is presented.

Our Government is formed by, for the benefit of, and to be controlled by, the descendants of European nations, as contradistinguished from all other persons. The humane and liberal policy of our government at the same time, extends its protection to the person and property of every human being within its limits, irrespective of color, descent, or national character.

When, by the act of a distinct race of people, entertaining mutual views and feelings, they shall ordain and establish a government for their own protection and benefit, neither the dictates of humanity or philanthropy requires them to admit as citizens on an equality with themselves, any other distinct and separate race without the unanimous consent of all interested; especially a race physically and mentally different, and one who, by universal consent, could never be admitted to fellowship in social intercourse or domestic relations. "Self preservation is the first law of nature," and is as applicable to governments as individuals. If, therefore, Michigan should admit all male persons to enjoy the elective franchise, irrespective of color or nationality of character, it would require no great stretch of the imagination to perceive a period, when, by the colonization of the African race, the control of government, by the operation of the ballot box, could be taken from those who first ordained and established it.

The African population of the United States being large, and no other state in the Union holding out equal inducements, their settlement in this state, would follow as a natural result from the adoption of such a policy.

A project has been on foot within the last year, and the contributions solicited, to purchase a tract of land in this state, equal to one entire county, with a view to its colonization by Africans. Should this project be carried into effect, they would undoubtedly be entitled to, and receive the protection of our laws, both as regards their persons and their property, but to admit them to all the privileges of electors, would be an experiment, leading as the committee believe, to an innovation unsafe to the harmony of the government.

No distinct and separate race of people have a greater right to be admitted to all the political privileges of our own citizens, than one individual has to demand the enjoyment of the individual rights and property of another without his consent.

If it be a question of morality and of conscience, as has been conceded, then the moral feelings and conscientious scruples of those opposed to the proposition of the petitioners, are equally entitled to respect and protection with those of the petitioners themselves—and the committee here venture to assume the position, that a large majority of the people of this state are opposed to the proposed change in their constitution. The committee fully recognize the doctrine, that "all men are created equal," and that "government is instituted for the protection, security and benefit of the people;" yet in these broad maxims, they fail to discover either the utility, or the moral or political injunction to allow all "nations, kindred and tongues," to be commingled into one indivisible and inseparable community—it is contrary to all experience, and the dictates of sound political policy.

If we are opposed to the proposition, it is our duty plainly to say so to its friends, for it is hypocrisy of the most reprehensible character to give encouragement to, or trifle with the views and feelings of those to whose opinions we are opposed, and no anticipations of political gain or preference can justify the putting forth views for expediency sake, which do not find an honest response in our own bosoms.

Having, as the committee trust, given the subject a fair and candid examination, and from such examination, arrived at the conclusion that the prayer of the petitioners ought not to be granted, they ask respectfully to be discharged from the further consideration of this subject.

Legislature, 1846. House Document No. 12. Report of A. Blair from the Committee on the Judiciary, upon the subject of the extension of the right of suffrage to colored persons.

The undersigned, one of the committee on the judiciary, to whom was referred a "joint resolution proposing to amend the second article of the constitution relative to the elected franchise," together with a very large number of petitions, very numerously signed by citizens of the state generally, praying such amendment, respectfully reports:

That he has given the subject all the consideration which a very limited time and the various duties of the committee would allow. And though the undersigned is not able now to go into so thorough an examination of this question in this report as he would be glad to do, it is still hoped that a very long continued agitation of the question of the extension of the right of suffrage to all male citizens above the age of twenty-one years, without distinction of color, outside of this hall, and the enlightened advance of public opinion consequent upon it, have rendered lengthy argument unnecessary here. The extension is demanded more particularly in behalf of our fellow citizens of the long neglected (and I think I may safely say long oppressed) African race. In the consideration of this subject, I have had no difficulty in arriving at the conclusion that the prayer of the petitioners ought to be granted. Any other conclusion is deemed to be directly at war with the very spirit of our republican institutions, based as they are upon the doctrine, that a perfect equality of rights, both civil and political, is the birthright of every man of whatever name or color or nation. The constitution of Michigan, which it is now proposed to amend, in the very first line of its first article, as the fundamental proposition upon which all the rest is based, asserts, that "all political power is inherent in the people." Believing as I do, most fully in the truth of this doctrine, I am entirely at a loss for any pretext upon which a large class of the people can justly be denied the free exercise of the right of suffrage. If the word "white" was to be inserted anywhere in the constitution, surely it should have been in this first and fundamental proposition, and then it would have read, "all political power is inherent in the 'white' people"—a principle, the absurdity of which, is too palpable to escape the notice of the most obtuse intellect. There is in this country but one way by which political power is manifested by the people and that is by the right of suffrage.

He who may not vote is as powerless practically as if he were dead or enslaved. How monstrous a wrong then do we commit, when we forbid a portion of our people the ballot box, acknowledging at the same time the inalienable right of all to the exercise of political power. Such is the wrong now done to the colored race—a wrong we venture to say without a reason—without cause or excuse, unless an unjust and wicked prejudice, which is a disgrace to those who feel it, ought to be called an excuse. Our laws require of the colored man that he shall submit to the government we have established, and be obedient to the laws of its making, and more than that, he must pay taxes and take share in the burdens incurred for the support of that government. And yet he is denied any the least voice in the choice of his rulers, or in the making of the laws. What better is this than the oppressions against which our fathers rebelled? If "all just government is instituted for the benefit of the governed," then what opinion must we form of the justice of Michigan towards her colored citizens? To these questions there can be but one answer. Michigan must make haste to repair this great wrong—her people must be free. I would willingly leave this subject here, but feel it my duty to advert for a moment to some of the arguments by which the denial of the right of suffrage to the colored man is sometimes attempted to be sustained. It is said that the race is ignorant and degraded and therefore unfit for the exercise of so important a right as that of voting. This, like every other argument in a bad case, is untrue in point of fact: But suppose it were true, does it furnish any ground for continuing a system which has had such a result? So far from it, that it is one of the strongest reasons why our system, as it regards this race, should be changed at once. If by our unjust laws we have degraded the man and besotted his intellect, it is a refinement of cruelty to make this the pretext of further continued oppression. And that such is the case, so far as there is any shadow of truth in the charge at all, who can deny? We have by the scorn of the community and its oppressive laws driven the colored man in most instances into the most menial employments, (none other being left open to him) and thus has he become a blacker of white man's boots, and a sweeper of white man's chimneys! But who shall say that under a system of just and equal laws—laws which shall strengthen his hopes—protect his rights and elevate him to the right of a citizen, he will become nothing else. All experience in this country has proved that the best way to make a good and intelligent citizen, is not first to strip him of all the rights and hopes of one. But on the contrary, whenever you extend the duties and responsibilities of the citizen additional motives are furnished him to be prepared to meet them, and he has been but a poor observer who has not been convinced by the history of our country of the full ability of man to govern himself. But there is still an easier answer to this cavil. If even ignorance and degradation are a sufficient reason for denying the right of suffrage, they should apply as well to the white as the black man, since neither of these are the necessary adjuncts of any color. If we will drive the colored citizen from the ballot box because he is less learned or less virtuous than we could wish him, then by every rule of right the unlearned and vicious white man should go with him. But we adopt no such rule when the white race is concerned. No degree of ignorance or vice excludes them, come they from whatever quarter of the globe they may.—Is it not a shame then, that in a land which boasts of liberty, a colored man may not be treated with equal fairness? Is it a crime that he cannot be white, that we should thus punish him?

One objection more seems to require a remark and then I have done with the question. It is said that great numbers of blacks will flock to this State as their residence, if the proposed amendment should be made. That this would be the case to any very great extent is doubted. But if it should prove true to the utmost of the fears of the most timorous, then would it indeed be an honor to Michigan, that the justice and humanity of her laws caused the oppressed of other states to seek a home within her borders. Besides, it is yet to be proven that the black man necessarily makes a bad citizen. The very effect of the law which attracted him here would be to elevate him, and the fact that he came would be evidence that he at least had spirit enough to love liberty and respect himself. From such a man most evidently the state has nothing to fear, but very much to hope. And shall it go for nothing that by the adoption of this amendment we take a great step towards the elevation of an oppressed race? Does their common humanity with us give them no claim to the consideration of the state?

Believing most fully that the time has come when the colored men of America should be allowed to assume their rightful position as citizens of the republic, upon an equality in all respects with their white brethren, and especially that Michigan ought not longer to permit in her constitution a word which creates an unjust distinction between her citizens, and denies that great principle which lies at the very foundation of her whole political fabric, I can come to no other conclusion than that the joint resolution ought to pass back to the house the joint resolution referred to them and respectfully recommend its passage; but for the reasoning of this report the undersigned is alone responsible.

All which is respectfully submitted.

Austin Blair

THE MICHIGAN RAID

Levi Coffin

Levi Coffin, an abolitionist and active participant in the Underground Railroad, has written one of the most useful memoirs of that organization. He published the first edition of his memoirs in 1876, at the age of seventy-eight, relying on his personal papers, but admitted that "errors might appear" and asked his readers' indulgence because of his advanced age. Nonetheless, his account of the history of the underground railroad is generally considered accurate.

While there were a few fugitive slaves in their midst, most of the Blacks of Cass County, recent research has shown, were not runaway slaves but free Negroes from North Carolina—people who had been free, in fact, for more than a century. When Cass County was established in 1829, it had not a single Black inhabitant; by 1840 there were 3,305. The Blacks in Cass County lived near a large Quaker settlement located on Young's Prairie, close to the center of Cass County in Calvin Township. A few miles from the Birch Lake Monthly Meeting House was the largest concentration of Cass County Blacks.

It was well known that the Quakers took part in the secret activities of the Underground Railroad. Slave owners sent spies into the area to ascertain the names and whereabouts of runaway slaves. In August 1847, a group of about a dozen Kentuckians—including the sheriff of Bourbon County—set up headquarters in Battle Creek, Michigan. The townspeople, discovering their purpose, forced them to flee to Bristol, Indiana, about an hour from Cass County. On the night of August 16, 1847, the heavily-armed party of Kentuckians descended on Calvin Township with the plan of seizing Black persons on Young's Prairie and restoring them to slavery. Word of the danger quickly spread in the area, a large crowd gathered, and the plans of the Kentuckians came to naught.

Foiling the "Michigan Raid" of 1847 was by no means the only such incident in Michigan in this period; in 1848 one Adam Crosswhite, a fugitive who lived near Marshall, Michigan, was rescued in a similar manner.

The selection that follows is from Levi Coffin, *Reminiscences of Levi Coffin* (Cincinnati: Western Tract Society, 1876), pp. 366–73.

The farther north from the land of slavery that a fugitive traveled, the more friends he found, and quite a number of runaway slaves, thinking they would be safe in Michigan, stopped there instead of crossing over to Canada. At a place called Young's Prairie, in Cass County, Michigan, where there was a settlement of Friends, and a number of Eastern people, all staunch abolitionists, there had accumulated quite a little colony of colored fugitives who secured homes in the neighborhood. Some families owned small patches of ground on which they had erected comfortable little log houses, and by industry and thrift managed to live very well.

But they were not secure in these humble, vineclad homes, for Southern bloodhounds in human shape were on their trail, and had scented out their places of retreat. Spies sent out to hunt for fugitive slaves in various neighborhoods in Ohio, Indiana, and Michigan, discovered the colony at Young's Prairie, and ascertained that most of the fugitives had come from Kentucky. Among these spies was a young Kentuckian who professed to be a Yankee and a staunch abolitionist. He claimed to be an agent for some anti-slavery papers which he carried with him, but his speech betrayed him. A Yankee living in Michigan said: "You are not from New England; you are no Yankee; if you were you would say keow and not cow. You are here for no good purpose, and the sooner you leave the neighborhood the better it will be for you."

Several of the colored families spoken of were from Boone County, Kentucky, and their masters learned of their whereabouts. In that county there was a company organized for the purpose of capturing fugitives, with funds for hiring purposes. A plan was formed to seize the negroes at Young's Prairie and bring them back to slavery; and about thirty men, with several two-horse wagons for transporting the negro women and children, started for Michigan. Part of the company on horseback went ahead of the wagons to ascertain the exact location of the fugitives, and to have all things arranged for a simultaneous raid upon the different negro cabins scattered around the edge of the prairie, and in small groves in the neighborhood. They were to make their headquarters in Niles, a few miles distant, in an adjoining county, and scatter out through Young's Prairie in small parties, under pretense of looking for land to purchase, or buying stock. By this means they could obtain all necessary information in regard to the location of the colored people without exciting suspicion as to their real mission. Then some of the company were to meet the teams, and conduct the wagons to different localities in the neighborhood, where they would camp until a late hour at night. This arrangement appeared to contain all the elements of success, but it did not succeed. Slaves often have friends living in slave States—people whose principles are unknown to the slaveholders. One of this class, a man living in the neighborhood of the Kentucky slaveholders, became apprised of all their plans for capturing the fugitives in Michigan, but was misinformed in regard to the time they were to start. He wrote to a confidential friend in Cincinnati, informing him of the plans of the raiders, but stated the time of their starting incorrectly—they started several days earlier. His friend came directly to me and gave me all the information he had received. I was well acquainted at Young's Prairie, Michigan. I at once set about to intercept their plans. There was a settlement of Friends there, many of whom had emigrated from Wayne County, Indiana, and were among the early settlers of that neighborhood. I had been at Young's Prairie, and visited several of the families of fugitives in that settlement. Friends had established a school among them, and they seemed to be prospering. I decided to send a messenger at once to apprise them and their friends of their danger. At that day, letters were often eight or ten days in reaching Young's Prairie, and I knew it would not do to risk sending a message by mail; it would not reach them in time.

A young man boarding with us, an active and energetic abolitionist, volunteered to go if his expenses were paid. I agreed to pay his expenses, and started him at once. As there were no railroads or stage lines then, we had to depend on private conveyance for the journey. I gave the young man letters to my friends in the various neighborhoods in Indiana, through which he would pass, requesting them to furnish him with fresh horses on the stages of his journey. This was promptly done on his way through Wayne, Randolph and Grant Counties, Indiana, and greatly facilitated his journey to Michigan. But his laborious and energetic effort proved too late; the raid was over. The Kentuckians had started several days earlier than the time named in our informant's letter, and their plans had been put into execution. On the night of the raid they divided their company, and each party made a simultaneous attack on the negro cabins. They seized the unsuspecting inmates as they slept, bound them, and placed them in the wagons. A certain place on the prairie had been agreed upon as a rendezvous, and thither the different companies made their way. In one party of marauders was a Baptist minister, who claimed to be the owner of a negro man and his wife—valuable property. They had leased a piece of land of Zachariah Shugart, a

Friend, and had built a snug cabin in which they had lived for three or four years. Being frugal and industrious they had prospered, and were much respected by their neighbors. The minister and his party approached this cabin and tried to gain entrance at the only door, but it was barred inside and resisted their efforts. They demanded entrance, but the negro man recognized his master's voice and refused to open the door.

The party seized an axe, battered down the door and entered. The negro man made weapons of chairs or anything else he could get hold of and fought desperately, keeping them at bay for some time, but was at last wounded and overpowered. During this conflict his wife, leaving her babe in bed, crawled out of a small window at the back of the cabin and ran to Zachariah Shugart's. Zachariah Shugart mounted his horse and rose as fast as he could to the house of his nearest neighbor, Stephen Bogue, who had a very fleet saddle horse. As soon as he heard the news, Stephen Bogue mounted this horse and rode with all possible speed to Cassapolis, the county seat, three miles distant, to give the alarm and obtain a writ to have the kidnappers arrested.

It was now daylight. A large company of men soon rallied and hastened toward Young's Prairie, to rescue the fugitives. They were headed by a resolute, brawny-armed blacksmith, called Bill Jones, who assumed command of their party. Their company increased rapidly as they entered the prairie, until it numbered about two hundred men. The whole neighborhood was aroused, and hastened to the rescue.

Now to return to the cabin whence the alarm originated. Zachariah Shugart, after carrying the news to Stephen Bogue, went to see what had become of his tenants and to watch the movements of the kidnappers. The negro man, after his brave struggle, has been knocked down, dragged into the yard, securely bound and placed in the wagon. The preacher then rushed into the cabin to secure his other property, but the wife was not to be found, having escaped, as mentioned, through a back window while the fight was in progress. The child was crying, and the minister took it up from the bed. Although it had been born in a free State, he claimed it as his own property, on the plea that the child carries the condition of the mother—the rule in slave States. He carried it out, supposing that when the mother heard its screams she would come out of her hiding-place and run to her child—but no mother came. Young children were worth two hundred dollars in Kentucky—too much to lose.

The minister mounted his horse with the child in his arms, and they moved toward the place of rendezvous in the main road, half a mile distant. About the time they reached the place Bill Jones and his company arrived, and the other company of raiders soon came up. The Kentuckians were all armed with revolvers and bowie-knives, and thought to intimidate their assailants by threats and a free display of their weapons. On one side of the road stood a low stake fence, the kind generally used on prairies. Bill Jones and his company soon stripped the fence of its stakes, and with these formidable weapons, the blacksmith commanded his party to charge, telling them not to leave a kidnapper alive. But fortunately for the Kentuckians, there were several Friend Quakers present, who stepped in between the parties and prevented a collision. The brave Kentucky slave catchers were completely cowed, and agreed to go quietly to Cassapolis, the county seat, and prove their property before the proper authorities, as the law required.

The negroes who were bound were soon released, and Bill Jones seeing the Baptist minister on horseback with the infant in his arms compelled him to dismount and let the child's father, who was bleeding from his wounds, ride in his stead. The minister he compelled to walk and whenever they passed a house, the people were called out to look at that child-stealer, a preacher. When they reached Cassapolis, Bill Jones further compelled him to march up and down the street, and called the attention of the people to this divine, who had been stealing a negro babe, and taunted him so much that he actually cried with vexation. The raiders were here served a writ by the sheriff, arresting them for kidnapping, and were committed to jail where they were kept for several days—until the negroes were on their way to Canada. A fair trial was promised to the prisoners, and they were allowed to send to Niles for lawyers. When the time appointed came, a kind of sham trial was held, and they were dismissed without further punishment than paying costs. These amounted to a considerable sum, and but one man in the company had money to pay the bill. The main object to be gained was the freedom of the negroes. The kidnappers were glad to return to Kentucky without the fugitives, and there was soon a general move of the latter from Young's Prairie to Canada.

After awhile the owners of some of these slaves brought suit for the amount of their full value against those persons who had befriended them. The fugitive slave law visited a heavy penalty on those who befriended slaves, not only fine and imprisonment, but sometimes the payment of the full value of the slaves. The case was tried in the Supreme Court at Detroit. The trial was put off from one session to another, subjecting those who had been sued to much inconvenience and cost in attending court, lawyers' fees, etc. But the slaveholders failed to make out the case against them, and the slaves were out of their reach in Canada.

TAKING THE PLEDGE

A. D. P. Van Buren

The temperance crusade—one of the mid-nineteenth century reform movements that swept the United States during Michigan's pioneer period—had a powerful impact on the state, due in part to a charismatic and flamboyant spokesman, Augustus Littlejohn of Allegan, a brother of Flavius T. Littlejohn, who ran for governor on the Whig ticket in 1849. Littlejohn began his crusade in 1844 in Kalamazoo County with a series of meetings. Many early settlers, especially those with New England roots, hardly needed prodding, since they were already committed teetotalers. Saloon proprietors tried in vain to discredit Littlejohn and his powerful temperance lectures, but with no success. The state legislature approved a prohibition law in 1853; it required a voters' referendum before going into effect. The law was struck down by the Michigan Supreme Court, but the Republican-controlled legislature of 1855 passed a prohibition law, that stood up in court. The law, however, proved ineffective and was widely flouted. It was repealed in 1875.

In this selection Van Buren, himself an earnest supporter of temperance, describes Augustus Littlejohn's fervent—and effective—temperance crusade. It is excerpted from A. D. P. Van Buren, "Temperance in Pioneer Days, with a few leaves from the temperance campaign of Augustus Littlejohn in Kalamazoo County in 1844," *Michigan Pioneer and Historical Collections*, vol. V (Lansing: W.S. George & Co., 1884), pp. 426–33.

The word temperance as used fifty years ago, when the first settlement was made in this county, did not convey as much meaning as the same word does to-day. A man might as well put on a boy's jacket as to undertake to crowd the modern meaning of temperance into the old word of half a century ago. Then the person who used alcoholic stimulants with moderation was called temperate; and he only who drank to excess was called intemperate. Anybody, from a clergyman to a hodman, could take the "occasional glass," and still be considered an exemplary temperance man. Now the word temperance is construed to mean total abstinence from all intoxicating drinks as a beverage. It may be said that, for a time at least, the early settlers to this region were from necessity, teetotalers; as there was neither the manufacture of strong drink, beer, wine, or cider, in this entire border. An unwritten prohibitory law prevailed in this new land. What an Eden for that irrepressible reformer known as a prohibitionist! Here was a beautiful county without a distillery, brewery, cider-press, or a liquor-cellar in it! But it did not remain so long; the spoiler came; for, as the village sprung up, and trade and manufactures started, the "serpent of the still" entered this peaceable happy region, and with it came, in process of time, all the evils of intemperance.

Many of the old settlers yet remember the first distillery erected in this county. And what a resort it was for all who wished a draught from the fountain-head, or to get the "old brown jug" filled with whisky; an article that was considered indispensable at raisings, logging-bees, husking-bees, and all the "bees" and neighborly gatherings of the olden time. But there was another class who loved, still more than the old settler, to wend their way to this inviting retreat. It was the dusky children of the forest. That old distillery was the Indian's Mecca; and their trail leading to it was worn deep and smooth by their frequent pilgrimages thither. Here they came to get their supply of whisky, then trail back to their wigwams, have their powwows, or, in their own parlance, get *squi-be*. This last word is the Indian rendering of the French *usquibae*, or, *scubae*, and from the same, by contraction, we get our word whisky. Whisky was the strong drink of the pioneer days. Bavarian, or lager beer, and the lighter drinks came in at a much later period.

Among the early emigrants to this county there were some staunch temperance men; none, however, who in this respect surpassed Titus Bronson, the founder of the "Big Village." He was a prohibitionist to the manor born. When the evils of intemperance began to appear in Kalamazoo, he was fearless and unsparing in denouncing the sale and use of intoxicating liquors. But as the county became thickly settled, the manufacture and sale of liquor increased, till intemperance in this State became as wide-spread as at the East. A few reformers had been at work in the older States as early as 1828; but it was not until 1840, when the seven Baltimore inebriates, like the patriots of '76, arose in their might, shook off a tyrant's servitude, and in honor of the great leader of those patriots, they called themselves "Washingtonians." Each new reformer felt himself a hero, and went to work to make way for the liberty of those enslaved by rum. They raised the banner of temperance reform, and gave the tocsin of alarm that aroused the whole country to a sense of its danger from the encroachments of the monstrous evil of intemperance. As they went from place to place throughout the land, thousands of hard drinkers deserted the cause of rum, and joined in the movement. The Washingtonian campaign resulted in the first great victory that was ever won over the forces of intemperance in this country. It was a great and glorious reform; one that did not stop until it swept over every state in the Union. This movement lasted two or three years, and then there was a lull—a calm after a storm.

The battle was again renewed in 1844. In that year there came into this part of the state a powerful temperance advocate. He stepped upon our boards no stranger to the discussion of the great temperance question. He was about five feet nine in stature, well proportioned and straight as a Choctaw. He had a face of clear intellectual cast, and an eye so black and keen that you shrunk from its glance. His voice was clear and strong, which he modulated so as to express his thoughts and feelings in all the varied range of emphasis and pathos. He was all activity, terribly in earnest, and at times vehement. His intense love of the cause of temperance had got into his blood and fired his imagination. Hence the dramatic power with which he drew the scenes and incidents in his lectures. His elocution was such that he could make a word mean just as much or just as little as he wished: it could bear a gentle message, or one full of "Greek fire." Having a fine command of language he never lacked the most fitting word, or the aptest illustration. "He was master of a terse and pungent rhetoric," and his wit was lively, keen or satirical. He was at times rash and even eccentric; but you bore with him on account of the great good he was doing the cause of temperance. This man was Augustus Littlejohn, in the role of temperance reformer.

He was of the noted Littlejohn family of Litchfield, Herkimer county, New York; a family distinguished for its talent. He was the sixth child among twelve children; the late Judge [Flavius] J. Littlejohn, of Allegan, was his next younger brother. Bishop Littlejohn of Long Island and DeWitt C. Littlejohn of Oswego, New York, were brother's sons. Judge F. J. Littlejohn was considered, in his best days, a very eloquent man. Senator Charles E. Stuart of Kalamazoo, good authority, says he has heard Judge Littlejohn when he surpassed, in power of eloquence, any man he ever listened to. Yet those who have heard both Augustus and his brother, the Judge, say that the former was the most brilliant, eloquent, and effective speaker of the two. This has reference to Augustus only as a lecturer. In the spring of 1844 Augustus Littlejohn came into Kalamazoo county. A citizen of Climax had heard him lecture at Allegan, and gave such a glowing account of him, that the people on the prairie, led by such men as Judge Caleb Eldred, Dea. Isaac Mason, and Dr. S. B. Thayer, invited him to come and start the work of temperance reform in Climax. He came; making his home with Dr. Thayer. During the while, the enemies of temperance had circulated a pamphlet which they said gave the history of a trial of Mr. Littlejohn by a church in New York State. Deacon Mason chanced to get this pamphlet, looked over its contents, and put it into the stove. There was nothing more heard from that source. The old Methodist church, then standing by "Capron's Corners," was secured, and the work began. It was in the season of early spring, when the roads were breaking up, and, to use a western hyperbole—"the prairie mud was up to the top of the fences." Yet that old church building was the center of an unusual attraction for more than ten miles around. Every evening and a part of each day, for two weeks, it was filled by a throng of people eager to hear this popular lecturer. The crowd was so great that to avoid confusion, at the close of the lecture, the audience was requested to remain seated, and a man was stationed at the door, who, as a team drove up, announced the name of the persons or family that were to go in it; thus party after party would leave until all were gone.

The enthusiasm of the people inspired Littlejohn. He grew stronger as his work increased. We used to wonder at the variety and abundance of his resources on the subject of temperance, for they seemed exhaustless; at his fertility in expedience, for he was ready for any emergency; at his talent for extemporaneous speaking, for without a scrap of manuscript he came before his large audiences night after night, a complete master of his subject the ready, full-equipped impassioned orator.

At the close of his lectures in Climax, King Alcohol was

arraigned before a proper tribunal, and tried for his crimes. Littlejohn acting as counsel for the prosecution, some one for the defense. The charges of murder and other heinous crimes were brought against the old king, and clearly proven. He was found guilty, and sentenced *to be burned at the stake*. The sentence was carried out. A spot was selected for the place of execution, and a pile of logs reared on it. The procession was formed at the church, led by Billy Harrison and Jonas Bailey as executioners, who walked to the music of the death march carrying between them the "old brown jug," filled with whisky, representing the condemned criminal. Reaching the place of execution, a stake was stuck into a pile of logs, the criminal was bound to it, the death sentence was read, the pile fired, and King Alcohol was burned to death.

Littlejohn found a great many hard drinkers in Climax, and left most of them sober men. He was a consummate organizer. He knew just what to do, and the most direct and successful way to do it. Says an old resident: "He had wonderful power over an audience; let him have the topers before him in the crowd, and he would talk all the *intemperance* out of them, and talk so much *temperance* into them, that they would swear off drinking, *and sign a pledge on the spot*." He aroused all the old workers in the cause, stirred up the luke-warm and indifferent, got every influential man and woman to aid in "beating up" recruits, and every good singer to join his choir and help

"Roll on the Temperance ball."

At first the drinkers denounced him. But they soon found that did no good, for the meetings grew more interesting and popular, and everybody but themselves flocked to them. They were soon left alone; grew lonesome, and at the same time curious to know what this man said to make everybody rush to his lectures. So the hard drinkers also went,—to find as an oriental queen once did on a certain occasion—"that one half had not been told them." Neither did they leave, as before said, until they had "struck palms" with Littlejohn over their signatures to the temperance pledge.

"Uncle Billy" Harrison took Mr. Littlejohn, with his horse and buggy, from Climax to Schoolcraft, which was his next field of labor. Remarkable success attended him there. From Schoolcraft he came, I believe, to Kalamazoo. He came not on his own errand; it was in behalf of the people and by their solicitation. The most prominent men in Kalamazoo, such as T. P. Sheldon, N. A. Balch, and others had invited him to lecture in that place.

The first meeting was held in the old Presbyterian church. A great number of people came to hear the new lecturer. To quote the remark of one present: "There were all that could get out doors, with something of a crowd in the house." The lecture was just such an one as Littlejohn knew how to give to start the work in a place. It made everybody eager to go the next night, and the exciting report about it and the man spread over the village, and out among the farmers in the openings and timbered lands, and over the beautiful prairies scattered around Kalamazoo. At the close of the lecture a consultation was had as to where the next meeting should be held; the Presbyterian church being considered too small for the number that would come. It was decided to use the M. E. church for the entire course of lectures. While this matter was under discussion, Edmund Rice, a young lawyer of Kalamazoo, arose and objected to Mr. Littlejohn's lecturing to the people here. He said he had a pamphlet which contained charges against the gentleman; he proposed to read them and give him a chance to refute them; and until they were refuted he should oppose his lecturing in Kalamazoo. At this the audience called for N. A. Balch, who was then prosecuting attorney. Mr. Balch arose and did all he could, in a short speech, to allay the excitement. As he took his seat, Littlejohn's voice was heard from the platform in front of the pulpit; he stated in most emphatic terms that he came there as a temperance lecturer, and as long as he had violated no law, he claimed the right to lecture where he pleased, and would consent to no trial of the kind proposed by Mr. Rice. While these matters were being discussed in the house, we could hear the mutterings of an angry crowd outdoors, and now and then loud threatenings of violence to the lecturer. This came from a gathering of liquor men and their confederates, who came to break up the temperance meeting. This thoroughly aroused Littlejohn. He wished to know if there was any safety for a temperance lecturer in Kalamazoo; and as the noise from the crowd outside increased, he exclaimed: "Oh that Flavius was here!" meaning his brother in Allegan. At this juncture I. J. Babcock, one of the "branch" students, went forward to the front of the pulpit, and said in a strong clear voice: "I see the object of this opposition; it is meant by threatening harm to Mr. Littlejohn, to defeat temperance reform in Kalamazoo; and I call upon the students and young men of this village to come forward and form a body-guard to escort him to his place of residence in safety." This had an electric effect on the audience, for it brought to the front scores of young men, who gathered around Littlejohn, while he in his enthusiastic manner, congratulated himself upon having such a brave Spartan band to defend him in the hour of peril. It is needless to say that he reached his residence in safety that night. The rabble finding so determined a body of young men guarding Mr. Littlejohn, soon dispersed and went back to the Kalamazoo House, where they organized an opposition meeting, which was addressed by some of their able speakers. They held several anti-temperance meetings afterwards, at which Belcher, Dr. Starkie, and Mowyer spoke, with a determination of drawing the crowd away from the Methodist church and breaking up Littlejohn's lectures. But with all the eloquence of their fiery harangues, these meetings ended in a signal failure. This terminated the liquor opposition to Mr. Littlejohn in Kalamazoo.

The next evening the Methodist church was occupied. A few had opposed this, and caused some trouble by keeping the door key. But Rev. James F. Davidson, then presiding elder in this district, and Dr. Cornell, a prominent member of the church, forced open the door. Mr. Davidson, thinking that the liquor rabble might attempt to break up the meeting in this church, as they had the previous evening in the Presbyterian church, exclaimed, as he walked down the aisle, his tall, commanding form and defiant look showing him to be the man for the hour of danger: "Let them come; they will find me prepared; Littlejohn will lecture from that pulpit this evening, and as long as he wishes to stay here!" And he did lecture them from that pulpit, every evening, for some three weeks, and as before stated, no more trouble came from the foes of temperance.

Littlejohn was a master of tactics in temperance reform. He had previously secured the names of all the clergymen, and other influential men in the village; and in the evening, if he missed a prominent man, he would ask the audience: "Is the pastor of such a church here?" If he was not, he would say: "He should be; this is his cause, and he should be here to aid in it." It was the same with other leading men in town. His strictures made them afraid to stay away. He got the "bell-wethers" [sic] to come out, and their flocks followed them. Nor did he stop till he had drawn nearly everybody in the service of the temperance cause. He secured all the good singers he could find outside of the church, and then laid the church choir under contribution. Among his temperance choir, we remember Miss Mary Ann Marsh, her brother Wells R. Marsh, and other members of that family so highly gifted with music; Miss Laura J. Hubbard, Miss Mary Clark, Mr. Plant, then clerk for Clark & Gilbert, and many other excellent singers. The lecturer understood music. He could put more life into a choir, and get more music out of them, than any man I ever saw. An hour before the lecture was given to drilling the singers. They being seated in the front pews of the church, he, having taken off his coat, would say, "Now, all ready!" And starting the tune he would move up and down the aisle with arm extended, beating time; and as he strode along, cry out: "Heavier—heavier there!" And down came his foot; or, "Lightly—lightly now!" stepping slower and softly; thus directing them till they struck the chorus, then throwing his voice and the whole notion of his body into the song—stamp—stamp—he would stride along the aisle, the very impersonation of musical force. He would praise the animated singers, and rally the dull ones, to the latter sometimes exclaiming: "Don't give us that canal-boat singing; do, in all conscience, liven up; your dead level singing will put us to sleep." That was the age of temperance singing. There was reform in those songs. The old Whigs sang "Tippecanoe and Tyler too," into power; the temperance workers of this period sang the reign of intemperance out of ten thousand hearts and homes, and the reign of temperance into as many.

Littlejohn always treated the drunkard as his friend, and ever spoke in the most hopeful manner of his ability to reform. Here was his great power over the hard drinker; he not only made him believe that he *could* stop drinking, but he made him believe that he *must* stop. He used no tricks of rhetoric to captivate his hearers; nor did he turn his lecture into a farce by "acting the drunkard" to amuse his hearers. You would as soon have thought of seeing the minister mimic the sinner from the pulpit as of seeing Littlejohn mimic the drunkard to please the people. His mission was not to "play the orator" before crowded houses at four hundred dollars a night. He was not "starring it" through the country on temperance, and delivering such witty and captivating lectures that his hearers went home so dazzled and delighted by them that they forgot all about temperance and kept on drinking just as before. There was no half-dollar fee at the door to keep out the class that needed his lectures, and let in a class that did not. His lectures were free, and furthermore, the class that were to be the most benefitted by them were there in force. One night, as Littlejohn had got fairly started in his discourse, old farmer Fuller came into the church, and with his hat on his head, staggered down the aisle half way to the pulpit, when, hearing the speaker say, " 'Tis a glorious cause," he stopped, and looking up at him, said: "You're right, Littlejohn, 'tis a glorious cause;" and he walked on to the steps of the pulpit, where he took a two-shilling piece from his pocket and presented it to Littlejohn, saying: "Take it for the glorious cause of temperance." The latter, who had stopped speaking when first addressed by this troublesome visitor, now stepped down to him, and putting his hand on his shoulder, said kindly: "Old friend, just take a seat here in front till I am through lecturing, and then we will have a good talk." He did as requested, and remained quiet the rest of the evening. Whether he came on his own errand, or was sent by an enemy to temperance, it made no difference to Littlejohn; for as the old man grew sober, he, in one of his impassioned outbursts against intemperance, hit the old veteran toper's case so fairly and effectually that he went away not only a soberer, but a wiser and better man.

This is the same farmer Fuller who, at the time when the streets in the village were very muddy, walked across Main street on the shadow of the ash pole the Whigs had erected, thinking it a log. George Torrey, Sen., then editing the Telegraph, saw this achievement from his office window, and the next issue of the Telegraph gave the whole incident, closing with this remark: "I believe the man was 'Fuller' of whisky than anything else." The writer of this sketch can vouch for the truth of this feat of Mr. Fuller's, as he was an eyewitness to the whole incident.

Littlejohn always opened his lectures with prayer. The order was,—singing, prayer, singing, the lecture, then signing the pledge, when singing was turned to great account. It was at the time of signing the pledge that he reaped the full harvest of his labors. Few lecturers could equal him in making converts to temperance. Under his management, it was a temperance revival and the people "experienced" temperance as they usually did religion; it came with a change of heart. This was before the "*feudal* days" of temperance reform. Before the Ivanhoes of License, and the Bois Gilberts of Prohibition, had entered the lists and waged a relentless strife against each other's reform. There were no feuds in 1844, among temperance leaders or workers. All were united. The ancient maxim, "When Greek meets Greek then comes the tug of war," was verified by the union of all the temperance forces brought to bear against their common foe, rum; and they came off victorious. When Greece united under one general, she conquered her foes; when she grew clannish and was commanded by ten generals, her foes conquered her. The cause of temperance is now suffering from the feuds among its leaders.

One evening while many were going forward to sign the pledge a tremulous squeaking voice sounded out from near the door: "*Mr. Secretary, put down Myron Hinsdill, the reformed inebriate of Kalamazoo.*"

This created a sensation; for two-thirds of the audience recognized, in that feigned voice, one of Kalamazoo's sterling young men, and as full of temperance as he was of drollery. "Put it down," says Littlejohn, repeating the name and full title. This was more than the audience could stand. A loud laugh upset all business for a few moments. Littlejohn soon found out who this inebriate was, and had a hearty laugh with him over the incident.

Learning that some of the principal citizens were not present at the first lecture, on account of the slight rain, he said at the next meeting: "God bless the people of Climax, they came through the mud over the tops of their boots for the love of temperance. There were no fair-weather temperance folks, no satin-slippered ladies, no nine-dollar boot men among them."

The personal appearance of Littlejohn at once arrested your attention. His gestures, like his face, had a language intelligent and expressive. Everything about him was earnest and telling. And when he got fairly underway, was fully inspired by his subject, and the stirring tones of his voice had brought his audience to the *qui vive* of attention, you had Littlejohn at his best and felt the full power of his eloquence.

I cannot give a review or synopsis of one of his lectures. I would as soon think of giving a synopsis of a bob-o-link's song. They were stirring, powerful, and most effective appeals for temperance. There was "the flash of wit, the bright intelligence, the beam of song, the blaze of eloquence."

Sometimes a beautiful exordium would preface the lecture on some subject akin to it. Every lecture was a fresh one; he never repeated himself, nor allowed his subject to lack interest; it was always deeply instructive. He knew so many things outside of his regular topic, and how to turn them to use, that he often accomplished more by diversion than others would by direct argument.

The following instances will illustrate his method of adding interest to his lecture. At the close of his discourse one evening, he said: "I will tell the story of 'old Put' at Bunker Hill, to-morrow night." The Methodist church was filled at an early hour the next evening. I wish I could give the story of "Old Put" at Bunker Hill as he told it. There was the old hero, mad with patriotism and love of fighting, beseeching, encouraging, stimulating his men to stand to the work; literally holding them to it by his own bravery. But when he saw they aimed too high, he sprang before them, and cried out, "*shin 'em boys—shin 'em boys—give 'em jessie!*" This was the first time we had heard the phrase *give 'em jessie*. At another time he announced that he would give, the next evening, "a description of the battle of Waterloo." That night the house could not hold all that came. But has any one who heard the description of that battle forgotten it? "Nobody could equal it," said an old citizen. "It was the grandest thing I ever listened to," said another. The closing scene where he represented the distress of Wellington waiting for Blucher was the *coup de grace* of the dramatic. When he knelt down in front of the pulpit before the audience, and wringing his hands in agony, exclaimed, "*Oh, that night or Blucher would come*!" The house burst forth in a storm of applause. It was grander than any stage acting we ever saw.

Littlejohn's course of lectures here was eminently successful. Kalamazoo was never so much excited on any subject, nor took so deep an interest in any reform before or since, as she did in the labors of this powerful temperance advocate. Although, at times, it took all the influence of his best friends to make the people submit to his rashness and eccentricities, yet, by his great power and fiery zeal in the cause, he established a permanent public sentiment in favor of temperance, from which the people have not receded, but on account of which they are farther ahead in temperance reform to-day.

ROYAL FIREWORKS

George C. Bates

The mid-nineteenth-century wave of reform and religious excitement gave rise to several new religious sects, including the Millennialists, Spiritualists, Seventh-day Adventists, and the Mormons, or Latter-Day Saints. The Mormons, led by Joseph Smith, originated in western New York. Since Smith was suspected of practicing polygamy, the Mormons were forced to move from New York to Ohio, then to Missouri, and later to Nauvoo, Illinois, where Smith was murdered in 1844. Smith was succeeded by Brigham Young, who led the flock to Utah, but a small group adhered to James Strang, who had proclaimed himself a prophet. Strang and his followers settled first in Voree, Wisconsin; in 1849 the group moved to the largest of the twelve Beaver Islands in the northern waters of Lake Michigan. Strang "took possession of Beaver Island in the name of the Lord," had himself crowned "King James, Viceregent of God on Earth," and married four additional women.

Bizarre incidents followed. The new king ran the island like a dictator;

he enforced the strict Mormon ban on drinking, profanity, and immoral behavior. Some of Strang's followers managed to get elected to important local offices on Mackinac Island, which was then part of the Beaver Island judicial district. Conflict grew between the Mormons and "Gentiles" in the area, mostly fishermen; murders and other crimes by Mormons went unpunished; the Michigan authorities did nothing. In 1851 Strang, charged with burning United States mails and other federal offenses, was brought to Detroit, tried in federal court, and acquitted of all charges. By no means did this end his career. In 1852 he was elected to the state legislature, where he was highly regarded by his colleagues. In 1856 he was murdered and his followers dispersed.

The following detailed and dramatic account of Strang's arrest, trial, and acquittal by George C. Bates, who served as United States Attorney, conveys a sense of the opposition Strang's movement evoked and the kind of people who supported him. The account argues that while Strang's following was small he controlled votes that might well have tipped the balance one way or the other in a close election. It is taken from George C. Bates, "The Beaver Island Prophet: The Trial in This City of 'King' Strang," *Detroit Advertiser and Tribune*, July 12, 1877; reprinted in *Michigan Pioneer and Historical Collections*, vol. XXXII (Lansing: Robert Smith & Co., 1903), pp. 225–35.

And as the event was one of much interest at that time, being mixed up with the political and judicial history of Michigan, and a portion of the Mormons, it seems an appropriate period to put upon record a correct statement of that event, and so complete the early records of the State—and the object and purpose of this article is to accomplish that end. Strang himself in a series of articles in the year 1853 before his assassination, published in the journals of that day, pretended to give a correct account of the causes that led to his arrest and trial, the manner of such arrest, and his triumphant acquittal in Judge Wilkin's court, on the trial of the indictment for burning the mails, delaying the mails, and other crimes against the United States; a copy of which now lies before the writer hereof, but his statements are in many respects utterly untrue, and in the main are a gross libel on the civil authorities and the people of Mackinac county, wherein these events mostly occurred.

As early as 1847, May 11, a portion of the Mormon people under the leadership of Strang as their king, prophet, revelator and seer, took possession of Beaver Island in the name of the Lord, and commenced a series of acts which finally terminated in the arrest and trial of Strang and a large number of his brother Mormons; and eventuated in his assassination there in the year 1856 by some of the Islanders whom he had persecuted from time to time. By the fall of 1850, this Mormon element had become an important faction in the elections of Michigan then closely contested, as the death of Gen. Taylor had left the Whig party a second time confused and the accession of Millard Fillmore to the presidency had distracted and to a certain extent divided its supporters. The election of that fall under the skillful manipulation of John Harmon, Esq., had eventuated in some 700 Democratic Mormon votes, which in a close contest would determine the success of parties in this State.

During the year 1850, and the early spring of 1851, Strang and his people had by their consolidated Mormon vote secured nearly all the local offices of the Island of Mackinac, to which Beaver Island were attached for judicial purposes; and by means of such power, controversies immediately sprung up between the Gentiles of that island and the Mormon officers precisely as they exist in Utah today, and finally eventually ripened into open war, as Strang described it; and soon in the resistance to judicial process from a Gentile justice of Mackinac, one Bennett was killed, and, as was then charged, his heart was cut out by the Mormons, and exposed to derision and scorn. In a small way, these events are a duplicate of what is just now the condition of Utah, and which may there shortly as here in the year 1851, ripen into open armed resistance to the lawful authorities of the Government. But for all the offenses committed by King James and his infatuated brethren, there was no redress in the county of Mackinac where those crimes were committed, and where the criminals must be arrested and tried, if tried at all. The Mormon voters outnumbered very largely the Gentile voters, and so had secured the election of J. M. Greig as county judge of that Island; and nearly all the other local officers there were Mormons, elected by the Mormon vote, which there as in Utah to-day is a unit. The Governor and State authorities were Democratic, and as the Mormon vote might secure them in power, were not very vigorous in their efforts to bring Strang and his people to trial; and as the entire machinery of the county government could be and was in the hands of the Mormons, there could be no legal means to punish their crimes, unless by an armed force. And so the then Governor of Michigan appealed to the President of the United States to furnish the necessary aid in bringing to an end the disorder, riots and crimes of the Mormon people at Beaver Island. But President Fillmore was President by accident, and was then laying his plans, which were finally fully developed, in the Whig National Convention of 1852 at Baltimore, to re-elect himself; and fully appreciating the fact that the Mormons at Beaver Island might give the casting vote at the next presidential election against him, and in favor of the Democratic candidate, and being a very cautious, cold and calculating man, hesitated and halted for a long time before he could be induced to lend the power and process of the United States to the arrest and conquest of King James the First of Beaver Island, and his rebellious and revolting subjects. Webster was then Secretary of State, and he too was anxious and eager like all the other great men of the nation, to be the party's candidate for the presidency; and he, too, saw and felt that the Mormon vote was worth saving if it could be done, and therefore, the best policy would be to let the Democratic State authorities reduce to subjection their Democratic Mormon brethren, and leave the Whig Presidential candidate of 1852 to have the credit, with Strang and his Christian brethren, of having declined to intermeddle with so delicate a question. Much red tape was cut, many diplomatic notes passed, if we are creditably informed, between the Secretary of State of the State of Michigan, and the Godlike Secretary of State of the United States as to which power should subdue this handful of Mormons in Michigan, but who, small in numbers, might by their 700 votes control the next Presidential election in the State.

At that time there was in the United States Senate a young but brave and honest, outspoken man, who had dealt with Joseph Smith and his Mormon people in Illinois—Stephen A. Douglas—a gallant, true and straightforward Democrat—and who always was a pet and protege of Daniel Webster because he was an honest, straightforward, chivalric politician, and he was called into the councils of the Whig administration by Fillmore, as he was in a more trying period in 1861 by Lincoln, and then, as always, his voice was for war on anybody and everybody who resisted the constituted authorities of the nation. Strengthened by the advice of the brave Douglas, orders were at once issued through the Attorney General to the United States District Attorney of Michigan to commence legal proceedings against Strang and his confederates for offenses punishable in the Federal courts, such as obstructing the mail, delaying the mail, cutting mailbags, stealing timber from the public lands, counterfeiting the coin of the United States, passing counterfeit coin, etc., all of which crimes there was evidence to convict them, and of which they had been guilty. Simultaneously orders were issued from the Navy Department to Capt. Bullis, of the U.S. naval steamship Michigan, to proceed to Detroit fully armed and equipped, and report there to the United States Marshal for orders; to transport him and his deputies and the United States District Attorney to Mackinac and the Beaver Island in order that all processes issued by the District Attorney from the Federal courts could be served with certainty, and that Strang, no matter what his force, could not resist capture, arrest and trial in the courts of Detroit, wherein all United States process must issue. Accordingly, in May, 1851, the United States District Attorney using the evidence of several Gentiles who had long lived on Beaver Island, and whom Strang had persecuted and annoyed, in every possible way, obtained warrants for the arrest of Strang and a large number of his confederates, and embarked on board the war steamer Michigan, with Gen. Schwartz as Chief Deputy United States Marshal, and forty well armed and equipped assistants, bound for the Kingdom of James the First, at Beaver Island.

Of course, it was deemed impossible to arrest these defendants, except by *strategy*, for the island on which they had erected their tabernacle was wholly unsettled save by Mormons, and on leaving its shores, there were several cranberry marshes of large extent, and heavy timbered lands where the larch, the pine, the beech and maple grew so compactly and were so completely hedged with underbrush that they were wholly inaccessible; and when the steamer Michigan left the dock at Detroit, there were many loud jeers and sneers by Democrats, whose political sympathies were strong with Strang, that Whig fools were going on a tom-fool errand, with a big ship to aid their folly. Long ere the Michigan reached Mackinac where the Mormon Judge Greig was then holding the county court, the District Attorney had with the aid and advice of Capt. Bullis's United States Navy devised a plan which as will be seen was carried out to the very letter, and which resulted in the capture of Strang and every defendant against whom a United States warrant had been issued.

It was agreed between the United States District Attorney and the Captain of the Michigan, that the steamer should anchor off the court house at Mackinac, at as nearly half past three as possible, that her guns would be trained directly on the court house, the marines mustered to arms, and as much display of force made as this gallant little iron steamer could show. The vessel arrived precisely at the time named, and let her anchor as near the court house front door as possible, and brought her guns and force all to bear on the door of the building where the Mormon chief justice of the county court was then holding a term, sitting without his coat or cravat on the seat of justice. This done, the captain's gig was lowered away with all the pomp and ceremony of war, the United States District Attorney, the first officer of the ship—the boatswain—a splendid large old pilot of the lakes, and one United States deputy marshal embarked in it, and moved directly to the front door of the court house, which stood open half musket shot from the war steamer and her grinning guns. Reaching the land the United States District Attorney, marshal and boatswain, proceeded directly to the court house, entered it, and advancing to the judge's desk, he was asked, "to adjourn the court, and to consider himself under arrest on a United States warrant," then shown to him by the United States District Attorney, "and to come on board." Being at first taken by utter surprise, he hesitated, and attempted to order the Mormon officers of court to arrest the parties for contempt of court. Whereupon the District Attorney notified his honor "that by raising his eye he would see the guns of the Michigan trained upon him and his court house, and that any hesitancy or resistance to the United States process would result in the destruction of the building and his own death, and that nothing remained for him but to adjourn the court and surrender as a prisoner of the law." Still hesitating, the District Attorney directed the clerk of the court to enter the adjournment, and the boatswain and deputy marshal to seize the judge on the bench and take him to the boat, which was done, the judge in the meantime remonstrating and threatening his captors with every kind of punishment. He was led to the captain's gig, and without coat or necktie, just as he was, was pulled off to the ship, where Capt. Bullis, in full naval uniform, received him on deck and escorted him to the very small cabin below decks. In less than half an hour from the time the Michigan let go her anchor, it was triced up again, and she was steaming gently away toward Beaver Island with the Hon. J. S. Grieg as prisoner, confined below decks, in utter amazement at the coolness and impudence of those authorities by whom he had been taken by violence, as he thought, from the judgment seat of the Kingdom of James the First.

Having thus fastened the judge, the next step in the plan laid was to make him an instrument to secure the arrest of Strang the next morning at daylight, and that was accomplished in this manner: Orders were given to slow down steam so as to arrive in the beautiful harbor at Beaver Island at two o'clock a.m., and then the District Attorney descended to the cabin and there opened communication with Judge Grieg. He commenced by recapitulating the many crimes charged against the Mormons, their constant and successful resistance to the State authorities, he showed the judge a United States warrant for the arrest of Strang, told how the Mormons had boasted that Strang could not and would not be captured, that he would resist if he dared so to do, and if not then to fly to the swamps and morasses of Beaver Island, and finally asked Judge Grieg to give him, United States District Attorney, a letter to Strang, to be delivered in the night, and directions where the king could be found, but the judge positively refused to do so. Sitting then down by his side, he laid before him the orders to Captain Bullis from the Secretary of the Navy, to obey literally the directions of the United States District Attorney and Marshal, and then in the most solemn manner possible pointed him to the yard-arm over the cabin, and told him "that, unless he gave such a letter within one hour, he should swing from the yard-arm as certain as the stars twinkled above it." Having done this he instantly went on deck and reported to Captain B. what had been said and done, and he (Bullis) soon descended to the cabin, where the judge in utter amazement, asked was "the District Attorney drunk or crazy," reported what he had said, and asked Bullis "if he could really hang him, provided he refused the letter." Capt. Bullis, with all the gravity of such an occasion, took out his orders, read them to the Judge, and then told him "that, if commanded by the District Attorney and marshal, he should be bound to swing him from that yard-arm." And on this he yielded, wrote a long letter to King Strang, urging him to come on board at once to save his life, and gave specific and minute directions, with a pen chart, how to reach Strang and deliver the missive ere the morning of the next day should dawn.

As great excitement prevailed among the forty deputy marshals on board the Michigan and they were all anxious to take Strang by a *coup de main,* it was necessary to deceive them into sleep ere we reached the Beaver Island's harbor and Gen. Schwartz was ordered to arm his men completely, then have them conceal themselves below the main deck until called for in the morning by the beat of the long roll and they all retired to their hammocks to await the call of the drum beat to action. Steam was again slowed down, and at about two o'clock a.m. the steamer gently let go her anchor at a place designated by Judge Grieg directly in front of the beach, back of which they had erected their Mormon temple and about a half mile from where Strang and his confederates lived and slept. No sooner had she come to, than the same party as that which arrested Grieg, with the addition of a boatswain's boy and his whistle, each man well armed with Navy revolver, cutlass and a covered ship's globe lantern, pulled with muffled oars to the beach, and, leaving a sailor in charge, marched in Indian file through a circuitous pathway around a cedar swamp, where at last they reached the resting place of the king.

It was agreed before disembarking, by Capt. B., that in case of any resistance the boy should sound the whistle and thereupon the bow gun should be discharged with blank cartridge, then the long roll beat, and the sleeping marshals and marines should rush to the rescue. But this was needless. The capturing party on arriving at the place where Strang usually slept saw a light gleaming from the upper window of a long hewn log building two stories high, with the gable end toward the path, and stationing the big boatswain under the farther end window with orders to capture at all hazards anyone who should seek escape there, and the young boatswain at the front entrance, and unveiling instantly the globe lantern, the District Attorney and the faithful deputy crept quietly upstairs, entered a long low room, where wide berths, heavily draped with stunning calico, shielded beds like the berths and staterooms of steamers, which proved to be occupied by Mormon women, four in a bed, and passing clear on to the light they found in bed a wounded man whose bandaged arm told of its fracture, and whose head covered with clotted blood marked him as one of the men who had been in the fight which resulted in Bennet's murder. He was asleep, and the lamp that burned at his bedside was trimmed with perfumed oil, with which his wounds had been anointed. Having gently awakened him, the District Attorney read to him Judge Grieg's letter to Strang, urging him to come to his rescue before day should dawn, and after some hesitation and parley the wounded man called for "Abimelech," who shoved his head through a trap-door and took the letter for the king. While he was gone the captors studied the book of Mormon, conversed with the wounded man, and looked over this strange home where the Mormons dwelt.

About a half hour before day, Strang, the veritable king, clad with a cotton collar spread all over his shoulders, like a Catholic cardinal, with a lithe form, large blue eyes, heavy projecting forehead, and a swinging gait, shot into the room, demanded to see the process for his arrest, and, with anathemas long and loud, he called for his captor to take him at once on board the ship, where he could see his imprisoned judge, whose life depended on his own surrender there before the dawn of that eventful day.

The noise and excitement on shipboard aroused the deputy marshals below, and, hearing the voice of the king on deck, they rushed forth and were greatly annoyed that they had had no hand in his capture. Having thus secured the king, and the leader in all their crimes, the next thing to be done was to use him as an instrument to bring on board the other defendants for whom the United States warrants had been issued at Detroit, and were in the hands of the deputies on shipboard, so that they might all be taken to Detroit at the same time, and this was done in the same manner.

After a hardy breakfast to Strang and a wine glass of brandy from Capt. Bullis, which he sipped very gingerly, the District Attorney exhibited to him all the several warrants against his confederates, recapitulated to him the crimes committed, the outrages perpetrated, and the constant and open and successful resistance by him, to the process of the State court, the expense and trouble the Federal government had been put to, to capture him and, thereupon he assured him that if he did not send out Judge Grieg and bring in each one of the defendants before the going down of the sun, that he, king as he was, should swing from the yard-arm. Strang appealed to the District Attorney in vain; gave him the hailing signal of distress in Masonry in vain, and then having invited the interposition of Capt. Bullis, who reiterated "that he was ordered to obey the command of the District Attorney and should do so," he finally sent out the Judge and by three p.m. of that day every single defendant complained of and for whom warrants had been issued, was brought in and ere the sun went down in that beautiful bay the steamer Michigan with a Mormon freight of over 100 men and women, steamed out to sea, and in two days landed them at the dock at the foot of Woodward Avenue; and this band of strange people were marched like Jack Falstaff's troops through Woodward Avenue up to the old jail, where that now beautiful library building stands, while the streets were lined with amazed and amused spectators of this motley band of prophets, apostles, disciples and devils.

Immediate preparation for the trial of these defendants was made, and a day in June, 1851, set for their hearing in court, and the defendants were all let to bail on Strang's word and pledge that they should all appear, as they did do. In the meantime, to save expense to the United States and to defendants, it was agreed by Strang and his council, Col. Andrew T. McReynolds, of Grand Rapids, and the court and District Attorney, that William D. Wilkins, Esq., deputy clerk of the Circuit and District Court of the United States, should as commissioner go with the District Attorney and officers back to Beaver Island and there take the depositions of all witnesses for the defendants and the United States, and that such depositions should be read on the trials in Detroit, in June, in the same manner as in civil cases, and that all objection of forms to such depositions should be and then were waived. In pursuance of this agreement, the Michigan returned, carrying back Strang and such of the defendants as chose to go, the United States District Attorney, and Gen. Schwartz as United States marshal, Col. McReynolds, council for the defendant, and this novel court opened soon after in the Mormon temple at Beaver Island, where it sat for several days and took the testimony of some 120 witnesses, mostly fore the defendants. Perhaps a more unique or amusing scene was never witnessed than there on that lonely island in that courtroom, where as judge, W. D. Wilkins sat under the very horns of the Mormon altar, where Gen. Schwartz, as marshal, in undress military uniform, maintained most rigorous order over that motley crowd of Mormons, the ladies in full bloomer costume, Strang in his pontifical robes, and the District Attorney and Col. Andrew T. McReynolds, contesting inch by inch this *cause celebre*. During its progress some of the funniest of events occurred, as per example:

The witnesses were all Mormons and would swear to anything for Strang, and the only mode of impeaching them was to make them testify to their belief in the divinity and prophetic power of this strange man. A witness, Mrs. McCulloch, a very sweet and accomplished lady from Baltimore, whose husband had been a surgeon in the United States army, had joined these people, and the lady was intensely interested in the defense of the prophet, priest and king, and swore most earnestly in his behalf. Her cross-examination brought out these answers to the United States District Attorney:

After her examination in chief by Col. McReynolds, the District Attorney, taking his seat very near, said:

> Question—"Mrs. McCulloch, you are an educated, accomplished lady, born in Baltimore and reared in the very best society. Can it be that you are a Mormon?" "Yes, sir, I have that honor, sir;" she said with decided color in her cheek, flashing of the eyes, and contraction of her lips over an exquisite set of teeth.
>
> Q.—"Madam, will you please allow me to look you directly in the eye, when I interrogate you—I always like to watch a witness when I examine them?" "Yes, Mr. District Attorney, you may stare at me if you choose. I have seen greater men and better men than you are. Go on, sir."
>
> Q.—"Can it be possible, Madam, that so accomplished a lady as you are can believe that that fellow Strang (pointing contemptuously at him) is a prophet, seer, and revelator?" "Yes, Mr. District Attorney, I know it."
>
> Q.—"Perhaps we do not comprehend each other, Madam; what do you mean by a prophet?" "You know well enough Mr. District Attorney, I mean one who foretells coming events, speaks in unknown tongues, one like Isaiah and the Prophets of the Old Testament."
>
> Q.—Ah, madam, how do you know that Strang speaks in unknown tongues and foretells coming events?" "Because I have heard him—and witnessed those events thus foretold."
>
> Q.—"Can it be possible, Mrs. McCulloch, that you are so blind as to really believe that that fellow who sits there beneath you—that Strang, is the Prophet of the Lord, the successor of him who bore his cross among the jeers and sneers of Mount Calvary?"

Rising in great anger with flushed cheeks and glistening eyes she shook her fist in the very face of the District Attorney and screamed out, "Yes, you impudent District Attorney, and were you not a darned old fool you would know it too!" Whereupon the Mormons greeted her with cheers, and the judge, marshal and crowds laughed immoderately at the poor District Attorney, who for the first time seemed utterly abashed at the energy of this accomplished Mormon termagent.

Another witness was then called; a very heavy, soggy-looking man, whose cross-examination was substantially in these words:

> Q.—"Mr. Adams, where were you living before you became a Mormon?"A.—"In Boston, sir."
> Q.—"What was your business in Boston, Mr. Adams?" A.—"I decline to answer that question, sir; it has nothing to do with this case." The court—"Mr. Adams, you must answer, sir." "Well, sir, I am an actor. I did act in the theater in Boston."
> Q.—"What part did you enact?" A.—"Well, sir, if I must answer, I acted the heavy parts in the theater."
> Q.—"Well, sir, what position do you hold in this Mormon church? A.—"I am one of the apostles, sir. I represent in this church the apostle Paul, sir."
> Q.—"Well, do you represent that character in costume when you meet with the other officers of Strang church?" A.—"I decline to answer sir."

Being admonished by the court to answer, with great vehemence, he blurted out, "Yes, sir, when I enact the part of the Apostle Paul in our church I do so in my old theatrical costume of Richard III."

"You may retire, Mr. Adams," quietly responds the District Attorney, and he retired.

On such testimony the trial commenced on or near the 20th of June 1851, before the Hon. Ross Wilkins, district judge, and ended on the 10th of July, during all which time the courtroom was crowded with admiring spectators, and the jury acquitted Strang and his confederates on the indictment for delaying the mail, burning the mail, cutting the mailbags, etc., although the evidence was quite clear against them. But the charge of the judge was very strong against prosecutions for any religion, no matter how absurd, and the jury seemed to have imbibed the idea that these men were on trial for religion's sake. Strang's speech to the jury was very strong, full of bitterness and dramatic points. He compared himself to Christ, his prosecutors to the lawyers and Pharisees who persecuted him, and really seemed to feel as he made the jury feel, "that there was a divinity that did hedge him as a king," and that he was persecuted for righteousness' sake. But the end soon came. In 1856, after he had served two terms in the Legislature of Michigan, he was waylaid at Beaver Island and shot to death by some of his men, whom he had caused to be whipped, and the Mormon people soon broke up and deserted that beautiful island. They ceased to become voters for the Whig or Democratic ticket, and so faded away out of history. . . .

COMPLETE THE ASYLUM

Trustees of the Michigan Asylum for the Insane (1860)

The establishment of the Michigan Asylum for the Insane at Kalamazoo grew out of the national movement for more humane treatment of the insane led by Dorothea Dix. Mrs. Dix visited jails, poorhouses, and other places where mentally ill persons were kept, and personally addressed state legislatures—rare for a woman in this period—to remonstrate for improved treatment. While she did not visit Michigan, her influence resulted in a recommendation in 1848 by Governor Epaphroditus Ransom that "provision should be made for the establishment of a hospital for the insane, and an asylum for the deaf and dumb, at the earliest period consistent with the existing obligations of the State. We are invoked by every principle of humanity to provide for the alleviation of the condition of these unfortunate class of citizens, with the least possible delay."

"Prior to the opening of the Michigan Asylum," wrote Dr. Henry Hurd, "the insane of the State were cared for at home in attics, log pens, or cellars, often deprived of light, air and adequate warmth in winter, or were placed in county houses, receptacles, jails, lockups and strong rooms. If the insane were reputed harmless they were permitted to wander aimlessly and irresponsibly about the country. They slept in barns, under strawstacks, or in unoccupied buildings. Frequently they visited farmers during the night, and were the unwelcome guests of strangers."[1]

The Michigan Asylum for the Insane at Kalamazoo was authorized by the legislature in 1848; not until 1859, however, did its first patients arrive. Because the legislature was slow to appropriate funds for constructing the main building, the institution was not finally completed until 1869, twenty-one years after the institution was established.

The 1859 Report of the Trustees of the Michigan Asylum for the Insane deplores the delay in completing the institution, and argues for the completion of the structure. "When finished," the trustees asserted, "no other institution in our country will be provided with more perfect facilities for the complete classification of its patients, and the entire separation of the sexes." The following is from that report taken from Michigan Legislature, 1859 (Lansing: John A. Kerr & Co., 1860), pp. 1–20.

[1] Henry M. Hurd, M.D., "A History of the Asylums for the Insane in Michigan," *Michigan Pioneer and Historical Collections*, vol. XIII (1889), pp. 292–307.

It is now nearly five years since the Asylum was commenced, and any one who has had experience in building, even to the extent of a farm-house, knows that the policy of making small appropriations at long intervals, is anything but an economical one. No private individual or corporation could afford such a policy. The course hitherto pursued is certainly not a judicious one. A sense of duty and justice compels every thinking man in the State to say that the Asylum should be completed, and the miserable condition of four hundred insane fellow creatures scattered all about us, many in chains and cells, demands its immediate opening. What advantage can there be in delay?

Facts which came to our knowledge almost immediately after entering upon our official duties, convinced us that no time should be lost in preparing at least a part of the Institution for the reception of patients. Letters were constantly coming from the friends of insane persons in almost every county, containing sad tales of the trials and anxieties and dangers growing out of the affliction which has befallen them, all bearing the same inquiry—"When will the Asylum be ready for patients?"

County Superintendents of the Poor, also forwarded communications, representing the serious inconveniences under which they labored in endeavoring to provide for the insane committed to their charge. They had found, that even with every facility they possessed, they could do nothing to cure them, and but little to better their condition. None were discharged restored, a few occasionally wandered away, and death came to the relief of more or less each year, and still the number was gradually increasing. They were anxious to know if something could not be done to lessen this accumulating amount of misery and taxation.

We, therefore, felt it obligatory upon us to do all in our power to meet this necessity, and shaped our course accordingly. The fourth section of the Act under which we were appointed, invests us with the "control and management of the Asylum, and all its affairs in as full and ample manner as the existing Board of Trustees." On referring to the original statute establishing the Institution, we find its early opening evidently anticipated, and with this special view, certain powers and duties delegated to that Board which, by the Act passed at the last session of the Legislature, were transmitted to us.

Until the occurrence of the accident of February 11th, everything was favorable to the attainment of the end to which we were impelled by our duty, both as almoners of the charity of our State, and as citizens whose eyes had been opened to the fearful extent of the sufferings they were expected to contribute in alleviating. By the loss of the center building, very serious obstacles were interposed to the carrying out of our plans for the early opening of the Institution. We found that the unexpended balance of the appropriation would only suffice to replace the loss, and that the Asylum would be no farther advanced, as far as the treatment of patients is concerned, than it was at the commencement of the year. The same balance would also finish the wing for the reception of patients, but leave the officers unprovided for, and in the absence of all arrangements for cooking, laundry work, &c., the Asylum could not even then be used. At this juncture, we directed the Acting Commissioner to communicate with the Medical Superintendent, in regard to the feasibility of arranging apartments for the officers in some portion of the wing, and preparing for the treatment of at least a limited number of patients.

We knew very well how essential the center building was to the convenient and advantageous operation of the Institution. It was planned to fulfill certain purposes, and of course no other portion of the house could be made to answer those purposes as well. We were aware, also, of the many disadvantages under which the Medical Superintendent would labor in carrying on in a partially finished Asylum, even with the center building; and we desired to remove as many of the obstacles to its successful management as we possibly could. At the same time, we felt that any further delay in its opening should be no fault of ours.

Dr. Van Deusen's reply was to the effect, that the first, and second floors of the first transverse division would afford temporary quarters for the officers, and that its third floor, and the portions of the wing to the left of it, would accommodate about ninety persons of one sex; that the re-construction of the center building, and the erection of the chapel containing the general kitchen, and the Infirmary, would render the first longitudinal division, with accommodations for fifty-four additional patients, also available; and thus, that one hundred and forty-four, about half of each sex, could be treated with a fair degree of advantage.

The plan was adopted as the one which the interests of the insane and the State most imperatively demanded, and the balance of the appropriation has been expended accordingly. We now earnestly recommend to the Legislature that it be carried into immediate and full effect.

During the past season, all labor about the Institution has been directed with a special view to the completion of the portions as above designated. To this end, there had been required a large outlay for purposes other than those of erection simply. Gas-pipes, for instance, had to be laid throughout the house previous to the flooring, and the attic tanks procured and riveted before the upper ceilings were plastered. All work of this kind has been well and permanently done, and not a single cent expended for temporary fixtures.

The tanks, three in number, constructed of the best English boiler iron, three-sixteenths in thickness, are placed in the attics of the three-storey divisions. Their combined capacity is about nine thousand gallons. These will be supplied by means of a force-pump from the stream in the rear of the Institution. To serve in case of emergency and accidents, two large cisterns have also been built in convenient and accessible locations in the rear yards. They are of brick, laid in water-lime, thirty feet long, eight feet wide, and seven and half feet deep. Their combined capacity is twenty-seven thousand gallons, and they will be supplied from the roofs. A main sewer, about four hundred feet in length, designed to serve the purposes of the entire Institution, has been laid in the ravine in front of the center building. The branch sewers of the south wing have also been finished and put in connection with the main trunk. They are furnished throughout with the most approved traps, constructed of the very best material, and in the most durable manner.

In the rear of the center building, there has been erected a one storey building, one hundred and seventy eight feet long and twenty feet wide. In the extreme rear is the room for the reception of the boilers to be used in generating steam for laundry and cooking purposes, and for warming the Institution. It contains, also, an engine, laundry, drying and ironing rooms, and a carpenter's shop. Its external and division walls are of brick. The roof is covered with slate laid in mortar, and ventilating towers with louvre sides, are placed over all the rooms where such provision was required. A large brick flue extends from the boiler to the fan-room, in the extreme front, for the passage of the steam-mains and service pipes. An underground air-duct, eight feet wide and two hundred and twenty feet long, has also been constructed, to connect the fan-room with the distributing chambers, beneath the building.

Messrs. Nason & Dodge, to whom our predecessors awarded the contract for heating and ventilating the Institution, are now engaged in putting in as much of the apparatus as will be required for warming the portions of the building we propose to occupy. Upon this contract there will soon be due $5000 less twenty per cent. reserved in accordance with the requirements of the statute. The proportionate expense of warming the portions designated is, of course, greater than the entire contract would seem to require. This apparent disproportion is explained by the fact that the steampump, mains, &c., are of the full size which will be required for the whole building. Here, as elsewhere, we have studiously avoided all expenditures for temporary fixtures and expedients.

The interests of the State, in every point of view, would undoubtedly have been far better subserved had the first appropriation been sufficient to construct the entire Institution. Contracts for labor, material and transportation, could obviously have been made on more advantageous terms. The Asylum would now have been in operation, and we might even in this report have been able to present a gratifying account of high purposes fulfilled, of great good accomplished, of misery alleviated, of reason restored, and of afflicted fellow-creatures returned to themselves, their families and the world. The past, however, cannot be recalled, and it is only left us now to advise that course which its experience has suggested, and which the present condition of the Institution, and the insane in our State, demand.

First, as regards the insane and their condition. That it is the duty of the State to make special provision for this afflicted class, all will admit. Whatever may be the social position of the patient, the same necessity exists. The most liberal county, with every advantage which generous appropriations and the most enlightened effort can secure, must fail to give its insane poor the peculiar treatment their disease requires. This is not merely speculative conclusion, but the experience of many counties in other States, acquired by costly experiments, which it would be worse than idle for us to repeat. Again, in more favored positions, every comfort, luxury and attention which wealth and the tenderest affection can bestow, is of little avail. The restoration of the patient, in almost every case, absolutely required removal from home, and a resort to those means of treatment, medical and moral, which a special institution alone affords. "Although, with great inconvenience, the affluent might provide suitable private accommodations, a large proportion of our best citizens, all in moderate circumstances, no less than those dependent on their daily exertions for support, without some public provision, must be deprived of much that is desirable, almost as completely as the pauper portion of the community. The simple claims of a common humanity, then, should induce each State to make a liberal provision for all its insane, and it will be found that it is no less [in] its interest to do so, as a mere matter of economy."

Eleven years have elapsed since the passage of an act for the establishment of an Asylum for the Insane, in this State. It is not to be supposed that the effort then made was at all premature; and if there really existed a necessity for such provision at that time, how great must be that necessity now! Providence has not arrested the progress of the disease, because the State has neglected to provide for its victims. On the contrary, the causes which produce it have continued in full and constant operation, and the penalty of that neglect has necessarily followed. No institution in our country has cured less than fifty per cent. of all committed to its charge, and in recent cases the proportion of recoveries is far greater. We have no means of ascertaining definitely, but we know that a majority of those upon whom this affliction has fallen during the last ten years, have been allowed to sink into hopeless incurability, and the expense of their life-long maintenance entailed upon the public. The number of insane in the State is now about four hundred and fifty, of whom at least three hundred are, at the present moment, proper subject for Asylum treatment.

The utterly wretched condition of a large proportion of these helpless things, is well known. We do not desire to give greater publicity of the instances of inhuman neglect now disgracing our State. If required, to establish the necessity of at once opening the Institution, the following extract from a late report of the Superintendents of the Poor of one of our counties, upon the condition of its jail, will suffice:

> The whole number of persons confined in said jail, during the six months preceding the first day of November, was one-thousand and sixty four, and they were confined for the following causes, viz: Murder, three; arson, one; burglary, six; grand larceny, eight; drunkenness and disorderly conduct, two hundred and thirty-eight; insane, eighteen. . . . The prison is in a reasonable state of cleanliness. . . . The prisoners say that they have enough to eat; but many are in want of proper clothing. . . . Some are shirtless, and some are without pantaloons. The turnkey of the prison says that those that are destitute have destroyed their clothing. . . .
>
> There are four apartments, four cells in each. Three apartments are for males and one for the females. The prisoners can freely converse with each other in their respective apartments, and it is impossible to prevent it.
>
> The jail is in a dilapidated condition. The cupola is yet

> seriously complained of on account of its leaking every time that it rains, materially damaging the building, and making several of the rooms and halls damp and wet, and the plastering to fall off.

The Superintendents of the Poor, who make the above report, are not so devoid of humanity or so blind to the interests of the county they represent, as to sanction any such course as this. However painful to them, it is their only alternative. The disease fastens itself upon one and another,—eighteen in the short period of six months in that single county—and they must be cast into a prison, because the State has neglected to make the provision she should for their care. It is for no crime committed that they are thus thrust into a jail, and compelled to herd with thieves and murderers. They are suffering under the severest form of disease flesh is heir to, the poor victim may be one whose reason has tottered beneath the cares and responsibilities of some of labor, duty, and affection. A father, perhaps, of broken constitution, who has sunk beneath his anxieties, to provide for a suffering family; a mother, whose night-watches by the sick bed have been exchanged for the sleepless vigils of insanity; or, as was really the fact, a daughter, whose efforts to support a widowed mother and an orphaned family, had been too much for her frail strength. It matters not in what manner God has visited the affliction upon them, they are insane, and the jail is their only refuge and security.

We need not speculate as to the probable condition of these unfortunates thus cruelly incarcerated, nor be surprised if some in their wretchedness should tear the clothing from their bodies and rend themselves. Nor need we ask how many of those eighteen will go forth from that jail "clothed and in their right mind," and be again restored to the domestic circle and to the benefits of society.

Justice, economy, and humanity, therefore, make it the duty as well as the policy of the State, to make suitable provision for all of its insane. This obligation has been already recognized and discharged as far as the establishment and partial erection of the building is concerned.

We have shown the urgent necessity for its immediate completion, and it now remains for us to suggest, and urge upon your honorable body, the adoption of the course best calculated to meet the present exigency. As before stated, a portion of the Asylum is now completed. The Medical Superintendent who was directed in October last to assume his position in order to supervise its internal arrangements, and to assist and advise us in preparing for its opening, is here. We have succeeded, with the limited means at our disposal, in preparing apartments for ninety patients of one sex, and that number can be received as soon as means are provided us for procuring the necessary furniture and fixtures.

When finished, no other institution in our country will be provided with more perfect facilities for the complete classification of its patients, and the entire separation of the sexes. The portion of the house now prepared for use, however, constitutes about two-thirds of the male department, and of course has no provision for such separation. We are fully aware that the relief afforded in receiving only one sex, will be but partial; but we are not to jeopardize the success of our Medical Superintendent or peril the reputation of the institution, by incurring the risks which would attend an attempt to treat both sexes without any means for keeping them apart. The force of this will be readily perceived. Indeed, when Dr. Van Deusen assented to the plan proposed, it was under an assurance we felt no hesitation in giving, that there should be no delay in preparing the entire wing for patients, in order to secure to him and the Asylum advantages for successful treatment, bearing some comparison to those enjoyed by his professional colleagues in sister institutions.

Nevertheless, the reception of ninety patients, even of one sex, will afford great relief throughout the State. But it is quite as necessary, both for the Asylum and the insane, that provision should be immediately made for the other sex. This can be readily accomplished by the reconstruction of the center building, which will render the first longitudinal wing, with accommodations for fifty patients, available, and without which the entire wing will be useless. It will also be necessary to erect the chapel, beneath which are the general kitchen and store rooms, an infirmary, for the purpose of isolation in cases of infectious disease, and the barn and out-buildings.

From estimates carefully prepared in detail, we find that the sum required for this purpose will be $90500, and we respectfully, but very earnestly, urge upon the Legislature the appropriation of that amount. The Asylum can then be opened for the immediate reception of ninety patients, and the following fall, the number will be increased to one hundred and forty four.

In addition to this appropriation, there will also be required the necessary statutory provision for the administration of the affairs of the Asylum, and the control of the officers. This is a matter of the highest importance, as upon the proper organization of the Institution, its success solely depends. It defines the position of the officers, assigns their duties, and creates those close restrictions upon the exercise of power, essential to the perfect discipline of the Asylum, and without which virtue, talent and fidelity, however well directed and combined, would labor under every possible disadvantage. It has been said that "a good organization makes good officers, good officers make good attendants, and good attendants invariably good patients." Poor vessels, properly officered and disciplined, may weather destructive storms, and make successful voyages; but we look for the certain loss of the ship, however good and staunch, which is insufficiently manned and officered, and guided by incompetency and misrule.

Experience, when available, is the surest and safest guide in all these matters; and we are fortunately enabled to secure that of the entire profession devoted to the treatment of insanity in America. As the result of years of observation, they have given us two series of propositions, the one on "Construction" and the other on "Organization," to serve as a guide in the establishment of Institutions for the Insane. By the use of the former, we have secured the building acknowledged to have no superior; and as the more important matter of organization is left with the Legislature, we advise a close adherence to the principles embodied in the latter; and for this purpose present these "PROPOSITIONS" in the appendix of the present report.

A reference to the estimates in detail, as presented on another page, will show that the sum above given, $90500, is the least which can be advantageously used, a less amount will seriously embarrass the operations of the Institution, make it necessary to leave a large portion of the building useless and unoccupied, and materially increase the expense of treating the limited number received.

We urge the claims of the Institution more strenuously, because of a feeling very general throughout the State, that there has been great remissness and an unwarrantable delay in providing for the insane. We have endeavored faithfully and conscientiously to discharge the duty delegated to us, and now leave the matter with the Legislature, trusting that they will feel the great responsibility which is resting upon them, and will hasten to extend that relief which is required by justice and humanity, a sound economy, an enlightened policy, and the gratitude we owe a merciful Providence for our exemption from this terrible affliction.

THE EVIL AMONGST US

Prison Inspectors (1861)

When the state established the Michigan State Prison in 1837, penology was in its infancy. Since the prevailing notion for handling prisoners was retribution for evils done, the regime for inmates was harsh. Prisoners lock-stepped between damp cells and workshops, and were disciplined by the lash, solitary confinement in dark cells, the ball and chain, "iron cap,"[1] bread and water, or shackles. Since Michigan had abolished the death penalty in 1846, persons convicted of first-degree murder were held in solitary confinement at hard labor for life. The solitary confinement cells, however, were damp and poorly ventilated—and injurious to the health of the inmates. By

[1] The "iron cap" was a structure of wire affixed to a iron collar which was placed around a convict's neck for a punishment period. Harold M. Helfman, " 'Good Time' Laws Come to the Michigan State Prison, 1857–1861," *Michigan History* (December 1951) 35:437–46.

the late 1850s, critics charged that brutalizing convicts only made matters worse and succeeded only in their further estrangement from socially useful behavior. In addition, repairs were neglected in an economy wave from 1852 to 1855; the prison had become filthy and the health of the inmates declined. Understandably, the convicts became restive, made weapons in workshops, and between 1855 and 1857 twenty-two convicts escaped.

The prison inspectors' report that follows shows the early idea of retributive justice was at least giving way before a more humane and rehabilitative approach to prison management. The "good time" law of 1861—under which a convict's good behavior might lessen a prison sentence—was successful, and the health and morale of prisoners had improved.

The state took great pride in its penitentiary; it was widely believed that such an institution placed Michigan in the vanguard of reform and enlightened progress. But the inspectors' report shows some of the practical problems of operating a prison in the mid-nineteenth century. The following was submitted as the *Annual Report of the Inspectors of the State Prison of the State of Michigan for the Year 1861* (Lansing: John A. Kerr & Co., 1861).

To the Honorable Secretary of State of the State of Michigan:

Sir: In conformity with the law of the State, the undersigned, Inspectors of the State Prison, beg leave to submit the following report for the year ending the 30th day of November, A.D. 1861:

A majority of them have visited the State Prison, at Jackson monthly, the past year, in accordance with the law under which we are authorized to act, and take pleasure in saying that we have on all occasions found it clean and in most comfortable order, which essentially conduces to the health, comfort, and morals of the convicts, all of which we owe to the incumbency, of W. L. Seaton, Esq., the Agent and his subordinate officers, who have all, in a commendable degree, contributed their united efforts in maintaining this desirable feature in all the departments of the Institution. But especially do we attribute this good order and subordination on the part of the prisoners to the law known as the "Good Time Law" of 1861, increasing it to five days per month to all who comply with the rules and regulations of Prison Discipline.

The health and sanitary condition of the Prison, has been most excellent for the past year, as will be seen by the Physician's Report. . . . This great improvement in the sanitary condition of the prison is attributable in part, to the abundant supply of excellent water produced from the artesian well in the yard, which furnishes a large supply of water for culinary and cleansing purposes about the Prison. But the proportion of credit due Doct. Tuttle, the Physician, for his skill in treating the sick upon the homeopathy system, during two of the last years mentioned . . . which shows much less sickness and cost for hospital stores than is shown in former years, under the treatment of alopathic physicians, we leave the people of Michigan to judge.

We have fortunately escaped all epidemics in the Prison, during the years mentioned above, until on the 31st day of October last, when we were surprised to learn from Doct. Tuttle (who associated with him other eminent physicians of the City of Jackson), that Perry S. Houghton, United States' convict, from the city of Detroit, lay sick with the small pox. The Agent promptly and wisely removed the sick man to an out-of-the-way place in the neighborhood of the Prison, and furnished him with needful attendants, who soon recovered, and is now in his appropriate place within the Prison walls.

As soon as this contagious disease was known to be in the Prison, all the convicts were immediately vaccinated for the kine pox, and by this precautionary measure it was so far checked that only three others had it, and five the varioloid, and these have all fortunately been restored to their good health.

Too much praise cannot be bestowed upon Mr. Seaton and his associates for the prompt and efficient manner with which they acted in stopping the ravages of this loathsome disease.

But we feel that we cannot too strongly censure the sheriff, and officers in charge of the Wayne county jail, for removing the man from that noted pest-house to the State Prison, when they must have known that he had been exposed in the cell which he occupied to the small pox, and thus exposing the lives of all the officers and visitors who daily perambulate the yard, halls and work-shops, as well as the lives of over five hundred prisoners.

In view of such carelessness, if not criminality, on the part of the officers who committed this flagrant act, we would recommend that the Legislature pass a law making it a criminal and penal offense for any sheriff or other officer who may hereafter knowingly or willfully transfer a person from any county jail, or other place of confinement for criminals, in the State, to any other prison, house of correction or asylum, who has been exposed to any virulent epidemic.

Under the law of 1861, which authorizes the inspectors to transfer, during their pleasure, such convicts in solitary confinement as they may deem proper, they have used the power thus conferred by the transfer of eleven such persons to hard labor with other convicts, leaving only nine in solitary confinement.

All of those thus changed are orderly, and conform to the rules and discipline with equal promptitude as do others in prison confined for minor offenses. No one having, for the several months that they have been thus benefited, violated a single rule. Each have been efficient in the respective duties assigned them. The most of those now left in solitary cells, have become insane, in greater or less degree, since their confinement, which fact admonishes us of the necessity of some improvement in the ventilation of those cells.

By reference to page 1504 of compiled laws, section 1, the language used for the penalty for murder in the first degree, is as follows: "Shall be punished by solitary confinement at hard labor in the State prison for life." Our present solitary cells are inadequate to carry out the design of the law, for the want of light and wholesome air, which are necessary for the physical strength and health for a man who labors.

We find the following language used in the report of the Inspectors for the year 1850: In speaking of the construction of suitable cells for life convicts, they say: "Such cells should be so situated that the occupants could have access to the open air in separate yards, leading out from their cell doors. To immure men, without the opportunity of out-of-door exercise, would slowly but surely lead to disease, impotency, lunacy, and premature death." And in the report the Inspectors for the year 1853, they used the following language: "The convicts, sentenced to solitary confinement, from the first day March, 1847, to the second of April, 1849, were kept shut up in the cells of the Prison. It was soon ascertained that such confinement was rapidly wasting away the lives of the occupants. On the representation of the facts, the Legislature by the act of the second of April, authorized the release of the convicts sentenced to solitary confinement, and their employment as other convicts, wherever and for such times as the Inspectors might, by resolution, direct."

The cells which were then used for the confinement of this class of persons, were better ventilated, and consequently much more wholesome than the present solitary ones.

We would therefore call the attention of the Legislature to the propriety of making an appropriation, or authorize the using of the funds already appropriated for building purposes, for the construction of yards, by means of a door-way in rear of each cell, that the inmate may be benefitted by a free circulation of air, which would also afford light to enable those having charge of them, to furnish such as it is thought proper thus to confine, with work, and render it practical for them to do it with benefit to the State.

It is shocking to the sense of humane persons, who are allowed to enter these cells, to come in contact with the unpleasant odor which must necessarily accumulate within these small rooms, when constantly occupied, with only an opening of four and one-half by twenty-four inches, in one end and near the top, for air and light to penetrate.

It is doubted by many whether it would not be more humane to restore the death penalty for the crime of murder, than to cause these unfortunate persons to linger out a few years of existence (such condition cannot be called life) in such illy ventilated rooms as they are known to be.

It is believed that common humanity dictates that so long as it is the pleasure of the Almighty to spare the lives of this unfortunate class of beings, means should be provided for them to spend a portion of their time in the open air, which is furnished by a higher power than man; and should that indispensable element of life and health by man be taken from them?

Great efforts are always made to restore this class of persons to life and health, when attempts are made by them to commit suicide during and after their conviction, which is very humane and proper. Then why not, upon the same principle of humanity, provide means for them, and an opportunity to enjoy all the God-given elements of health, after their confinement for life?

All will agree that to mingle small quantities of poison with their food, and thus shorten their lives by this slow but sure and unnatural process, would be barbarous and cruel in the extreme. How much less so is it to cause them to be so confined in a poisonous atmosphere which is sure to produce the same results?

By section eleven of an act entitled "an act to establish the Detroit House of Correction," &c., approved March 15th 1861, the Inspectors of the State Prison were empowered to enter into contract with the city of Detroit for the confinement and maintenance in their House of Correction, of all the females in the State Prison, and who may be subsequently convicted before any court in this State of any offense punishable by imprisonment in the State Prison, and also for the confinement of such male persons, between the ages of sixteen and twenty-one years, as the Judges of the several courts within the State might sentence to said House of Correction, after the date of such contract.

Conference was had with the authorized agents of the city of Detroit, and the terms on which these prisoners would be received by them were readily agreed upon, viz: that they should receive from the State seven shillings per week each, for the maintenance of females; that such of the younger male prisoners as should be confined in their House of Correction, instead of the State Prison, were to be supported without charge to the State, it being expected that their labor would be sufficient benefit to compensate for the outlay on their account. After careful examination of the law, and consultation with able council, it was found that if any arrangement was made as contemplated by it, the courts would be bound to sentence all who should subsequently be convicted between the ages of sixteen and twenty-one years to the House of Correction. This fact, and the diminution in the number of convicts in the State Prison this year, led us to defer, for the present, the entering into the contemplated contract. We, however, most heartily approve the general features of the law, and should be glad to avail ourselves of the advantages to be derived from some of its provisions, if they could be disconnected.

The females in our State Prison are a burden upon it, and cannot be properly treated in the present arrangements of their apartments. They should be subjected to the routine of salutary discipline, and required to labor regularly at some proper employment.

The small number in confinement would render such an attempt quite expensive as it would require another building in a more suitable place, and does not, in our estimation, promise commensurate results. The larger number of females confined in the Detroit House of Correction, the kinds of employment consequently supplied, and the system of discipline necessarily enforced, seems to make that institution a more suitable place for the confinement of females now sent to the State Prison. Such an arrangement, we think, would be more benefit to this class of females and advantage to the State.

The changes in the management of the younger portion of the prisoners hereafter to be convicted of offenses punishable by imprisonment in the State Prison, contemplated by this law, is eminently worthy of careful consideration.

The number of youths in the State Prisons in the country, mingling freely with the older and more hardened convicts, and for whose reformation no educational or special systematic efforts are being made, is surprisingly large, and is not generally known.

Ohio reports that of the prisoners received into her State Prison, in 1860, forty-nine and thirty-four one hundredths per cent. were between the ages of sixteen and twenty-five years, inclusive.

Indiana, that thirty seven per cent. were between sixteen and twenty-four years. Illinois, that of the whole number in confinement that year, forty seven and forty seven one hundredths per cent. were between sixteen and twenty five. New York, that fifty per cent. were between sixteen and twenty five. And that Massachusetts, fifty-four per cent. were between sixteen and twenty four, inclusive. Of those in our own State Prison in the year 1861, that there were thirty three and one third per cent. between the ages of sixteen and twenty-two years.

Statistics, gathered by both Europe and America, show conclusively that among the varied and complicated causes of crime, ignorance, or the lack of education, together with the surroundings of evil influences in early life, are extremely prominent if not foremost, in the catalogue.

This is almost universally conceded, and has moved the philanthropy of the world to noble endeavors, for the reclamation of the young, from which so much may be hoped in preventing crime.

The wonderful improvement in the public schools of our large cities, and throughout the country, within a few years, the establishing of Houses of Refuge, Reform Schools, and that true Christian benevolence which gathers in and instructs, in varied industrial and benevolent schools, those children who would otherwise remain uninstructed, is full of promise for the future.

But while the vagrant and criminal children, under sixteen years of age, are comparatively well cared for, our young men, too old to be benefitted by such efforts, yet not so old as to be beyond the hope of reformation, are almost entirely neglected. They are "left to themselves," at just that period of life when the character is plastic enough to be moulded easily to the influences with which they are surrounded. The circumstances of their early life, without education, make it almost impossible that they should have any just moral estimates of their duty to themselves and society, which naturally throws them into evil company. Is it a matter of surprise, then, that they are led to violate the law of the land, and incur its penalty?

That these persons should be cast into prison for a term of years, to be educated in crime, by their older and more experienced older prisoners, and be deprived at the same time of all other education, at this rapidly passing and accepted time, the only remaining period of their lives when their minds are capable of expanding and receiving useful knowledge, and thus the seeds of evil implanted in them hereditarily, and by circumstances, often beyond their control, and be allowed to ripen, mature, and solidify, is gross injustice to them and to the highest and best interest of society.

The city of Detroit have provided, at their House of Correction, a convenient school-room which can be approached by convicts, at evening, without hazard of escape; have secured the services of an experienced officer as superintendent, one who has been interested in the school feature of prison for this class of prisoners, and propose to take of those who shall be subsequently convicted of offenses punishable by imprisonment, in the State Prison, between the ages of sixteen and twenty one, such a number as shall enable them to demonstrate by actual experiment, what may be done for the reclamation of this large class of prisoners, by isolation from contaminating associations, by education and a system of short lectures designed to awaken within them desires for a higher and better life, and for pleasures of a more elevated kind.

If the law could be so amended as to give opportunity for this experiment, without detriment to the interests of the State, certainly no injury can result from it, and it is not improbable that the highest welfare of these unfortunate young men and of society at large, might be perceptibly enhanced.

We are sanguine that, between the ages of sixteen and twenty one years, convicts sentenced for a term of years, may be educated in the rudiments at least, of an English education, a taste for reading formed, and the general tone of their feelings so elevated, that on their release from imprisonment by which they are not unduly stigmatized, great hope may be entertained of their permanent reformation.

The reports of prisons throughout the northern States come to us very generally expressing the great need of change and improvement in the class of persons under consideration. In the history of the past, not unfrequently, have important advances been attended with this phenomena. Individuals in different and remote portions of the country, have almost simultaneously given attention to the same subject, and we have the attention being given to prison discipline, particularly as it affects young men in prison, as the harbinger of their improved condition.

It is evident that penal law is not in harmony with the progress of this age, and we trust that the time is not far distant when the judiciary shall not be compelled to administer law at the expense of justice and mercy—when a large discretion shall be vested in them, and they no longer be forced to brand with "State Prison" the youth, who, for the first time, is arraigned in a criminal prosecution, but may instead confine such criminals in institutions which have sprung up since the enactment of the penal code—where the same or greater deterring effects are produced without imparting an indelible mark upon them—when education shall come in to supply the lack of early years, thus removing, for the future, a prominent cause of their degraded and criminal conduct.

In view of trying the experiment of reforming this class of persons, we would recommend that the law referred to be so amended that the courts may sentence such persons as they deem proper to the Detroit House of Correction, instead of the State Prison, between the ages of sixteen and twenty-one years inclusive, after a contract has been made with the proper authorities of said city, as contemplated under the law of 1861.

We cannot forbear again calling the attention of the Legislature to the propriety of their taking measures to carry out the suggestions contained in our last annual report, relative to the appointment of a suitable person as agent to look after the interests of discharged convicts. The reasons assigned, which we think justifies such a policy, will be found in said report, to which we beg leave to call your special attention. . . .

[signed] N. W. Clark A. G. Gates

at Jackson, Dec. 1st, 1861.

THE YOUNG PENITENT

D. B. Nichols

In 1855 the state established a House of Correction for Young Offenders on a thirty-acre site on North Pennsylvania Avenue in Lansing. The institution, one of the first of its kind in the nation and a source of considerable pride, sought to provide a better environment for young offenders than the county jails or the state penitentiary. In 1859 the legislature changed its name to the Michigan Reform School in order to lessen the stigma on its graduates.

For years the institution's nineteenth-century buildings, only recently demolished, served as a visible reminder of mid-nineteenth-century ideas about dealing with juvenile offenders. In the early days, the inmates, dressed in prisoners' garb, worked hard to produce their own food and clothing in shops and farms kept by the school. Their daily regimen consisted of five hours of compulsory work, five and a quarter hours in class, an hour of military drill, and only occasional recreation in a high-fenced three-acre playground. Over time, the institution liberalized this regime.

D. B. Nichols, superintendent of the school and author of this report to the legislature, describes the management of the school and its rationale. He was convinced of the importance of moral instruction in rehabilitating his young charges.

The following is an excerpt from "Fourth Annual Report of the Board of Control of the State Reform School, for the Year Ending November 17, 1860," in *Twenty-Third Annual Report of the Superintendent of Public Instruction of the State of Michigan, with accompanying documents, for the year 1859* (Lansing: Hosmer & Kerr, 1860), pp. 98–106.

Labor Department

It is a fact universally recognized that labor is an indispensable agency in the reformation of wayward youth. Many, if not a majority of the proper subjects of reformatory training, have found their way to these Institutions because [they are] destitute of well formed habits of industry.

This doctrine, that labor is an indispensable agency in the reformation of wayward youth, has long since passed into a proverb. The Roman adage was written of old, "Nehil agendo male agere discimus," (by doing nothing we learn to do mischief,) is a truth as generally believed, as it is widely circulated.

There is but one question as regards labor, upon which reformatories have divided, and that has been as to the manner in which these boys should be employed. What kind of labor pays the best, morally? Is there any kind of labor which does not contribute towards the reformation of the delinquent?

All these questions must be fairly and carefully considered by the friends of Juvenile Reform.

As the fact whether there is any species of labor which does not contribute towards the reformation of the delinquent, we desire to quote the views of a distinguished philanthropist living in Bristol, England, and who has for years been interested in Reformatory education, and has written largely upon the subject of Juvenile Reform, whose views, therefore, are entitled to the greatest respect. In her evidence before the committee appointed by the House of Commons to take evidence upon the subject of Criminal and Destitute Juveniles, page 96, question 819, she speaks as follows: "Now we have heard from Lieutenant Tracy, that he found picking oakum a very useless occupation for the boys; that their minds are not enlisted in it, that they do not take pleasure in it; if they did they have no object in doing it; but when a boy is engaged in labor which calls out his varied powers, in which besides he has an object in view, and where his excitability is worked off, his will is enlisted in the work."

Now the above views are worthy of all deference, not only because they are spoken by one deeply versed in Reformatory education, but because of their agreement with experience upon this subject.

I am aware that different views have been expressed and acted upon by persons who have been reputed wise; yet I cannot but believe that the intelligent and common-sense views expressed in the above abstract, by Miss Carpenter, will be *heartily* acknowledged by every Reformatory Teacher.

As to the question, "What kind of labor pays the best, morally?" I would answer, that it has been my settled conviction for more than three years past, based upon such facts from the experience of others and my own, as I have been enabled to gather, that no species of labor tends more rapidly to develop the whole man, physically, intellectually, and morally, than Agricultural employment. It is congenial to a boy's nature to work on a farm. There is no kind of work which suits equally well the activities of boyhood. But in order to do this kind of work successfully, ample room must be provided, a farm of ample dimensions should be furnished, large enough to furnish every 20 or 40 boys with a building spot for a dwelling house, thus making a neighborhood of Reformatories, where school and church privileges are furnished in common for all. Wherever this plan has prevailed it has been a success.

Successful experiments of this kind of Reformatory labor may be found at the Red Hill School near London, Metray, near Tours, in France, and the Rough House, near Hamburgh, Germany.

But in case the Institution is located in a large city where land cannot be obtained, unless at a vast outlay of expense, or where the facilities for extensive farming are not furnished, of course the managers of Reformatories must look in other directions for employment for the inmates of these schools.

Next preferred to Agricultural is Mechanical labor.

Here again there is a choice as to the best mechanical labor for Reformatories. Some branches of mechanical labor as reformatory agencies are greatly to be preferred to others. For example, take that kind where machinery is used, and where there is no machinery, and the former is greatly to be preferred to the latter, nor is the reason of this preference groundless, it has its foundation in the peculiar constitution of boyhood. Boys are fond of noise and bustle. Life is all astir in the earlier days of childhood. The more stir and noise, the better pleased the child. With this understanding of things, we see why a boy who is placed in a tailor's shop or on a shoemaker's bench, feels all the burdens of labor, while a boy amid spindles and wheels, urged on by a puff of steam, feels that his work is but a pleasant pastime.

The reason for this difference is apparent; the one has an employment congenial to his nature, where his boyish activities have full scope, while the other has not.

In connection with our own shops, more than once I have had occasion to mark this difference. Let our machinery stop to repair a belt, to lessen or increase the friction, and how soon is the magic power of machinery felt—how soon seen in the labor of the boys. Their motions are less rapid, enthusiasm dies, interest in labor flags, and that employment which was but a moment since regarded in the light of an agreeable pastime, now becomes burdensome; but the belt is repaired or friction is increased or lessened, the well known puff of steam is heard, the wheels move, the din of machinery resuscitates the dying zeal and ardor of the boys, enthusiasm is rekindled and the accustomed cheerfulness restored. Our boys love to work in the shops, and I know of no better mechanical labor, as a reformatory agency, than that in which our boys are employed.

We have, at present, five shops where the inmates are employed in the manufacture of chairs, under a contract of Messrs. Woodhouse & Butler. Besides the chair shops, we employ two boys in a shoe shop; these two boys, together with the shoemaker, have furnished shoes for the inmates of the school. In our tailor's shop we have six boys, who, under the direction of a tailor, do all the sewing, making and mending for the school. . . . We have, also, employed about a dozen boys about the establishment in the dining hall, kitchen, dormitories, bake room and laundry. Within the last two months we have also employed a number of boys outside, on the farm and in fitting up the ornamental part of the front yard.

I cannot close this topic without bearing testimony to the general spirit of industry which has prevailed among the inmates of this school since my connection with it.

A willing spirit has pervaded nearly the whole mass, to do according to their ability, and to do what they do with cheerfulness. These boys, even after their days work in the shop is completed, are ever ready and willing to engage in any species of labor which the exigencies of the case may require. The State of Michigan, for all its care and outlay of expense in the education of these boys, has reason to look forward to the time when she will receive an ample reward for all her care, in receiving them into society as industrious members of the same.

Government and Discipline

Our model for imitation in government and discipline is the *family*. The motto of the house, which, displayed in a conspicuous manner is "*We are all one family.*" In accordance with this motto, the

Superintendent and his family, and the resident officers and helpers of the School, eat with the boys in a common dining hall. Our boys are graded into seven classes; each class has its motto, except the fifth, which has a motto in common with the sixth class. The motto of the Most Honorable class is, "*Honor to whom Honor is due.*" That of the first class is, "*Excelsior.*" That of the second class is, "*Onward and Upward.*" "*Perseverance conquers all things,*" is the motto of the third class. The fourth class is the one in which each new comer is graded. The motto of this class is, "*Virtue, Honor and Happiness—Vice, degradation, and Misery: Choose ye.*" This class is called the choosing class. The classes in the downward grades are the fifth and sixth. The motto of these two classes is, "*The way of the transgressor is hard.*"

The grades are read on the first Sabbath of each month, connected with appropriate religious exercises, at which times boys are received into the "most honorable grade," when their names are recorded in the red book, entitled, the "*Book of Honor.*" Boys, on the other hand, who go down to the sixth class, their names go into the "*Black Book.*"

The greatest familiarity exists between the Superintendent of the school and the pupils. My room is at all times accessible to those who desire counsel and sympathy.

Complaints from the work-shop, school-room, and from every other source, are recorded by the principal teacher, in a *Complaint* book kept for this purpose, and at morning prayers on each day of the week, except the Sabbath, these cases come up and are disposed of, according to their respective merits. The disposition of these cases is also a matter of record in the Complaint book.

The punishments used in this Institution are deprivation of privilege, sending the offender to his room, or restricting his diet. Corporal punishment has not been inflicted since my term of service has commenced. We have no dungeons in the Institution. Our dormitories are arranged with separate rooms. In the new dormitories the Most Honorable Class, and [the] first [class], a portion of the second class, have their rooms. These rooms are not locked, nor have they been locked for the last three months past. In the *lower tier* of rooms in the old dormitory all those boys in the second class who are not in the new dormitory, and the members of the third class have recently had their locks taken off, and the same privileges of freedom are granted to these classes which are enjoyed by the new dormitory boys. Our rewards for good conduct are an extension of privilege.

My door-keepers have been chosen from among the inmates of the school from the second day after I entered upon the duties of my office. Since I have been on the ground, no less than 62 boys have worked on the outside with their superintendent at the *same time* with no other guard except inmates. Numbers of boys have visited the town alone and sometimes after dark. The trees which adorn our front yard have been obtained by the boys from 6 to 25 miles distant, with a teamster to drive the team, leaving the 8 or 10 large boys to look after themselves.

This principle of trust has infused itself into the whole school. The officers trust the boys and find that they have *trustworthy* boys to confide in.

At first, for the sake of the *doubting ones*, for they were many, we used great caution in the liberties we gave our boys. Many were the timely remarks which were whispered in my ear, "you don't understand the character of the material with which you deal." "These boys are not like your Chicago boys, they are older and more experienced in crime." One trial after another has removed the doubts of this one, and strengthened the faith of that one, and I cannot but hope that day will come when the inmates of the Michigan State Reform School will enjoy all the privileges that are enjoyed by any well regulated family in our land. God speed the day, when these doubts as to the fact whether words of kindness, and acts of sympathy are better suited to reform these poor unfortunate boys who have been set afloat upon life's rough sea, with no one to give them a friendly hint as to the course they ought to steer, or counsel them how the ship of life is to be manned, than are stern looks, acts of cruelty, whips, reproof without sympathy, dungeons and words of unkindness.

Experience has reiterated the truth of the words of a distinguished American philanthropist, again and again, "that which blows, bars, and dungeons have failed to do, has been easily accomplished by kind words and acts of sympathy."

Moral Instruction

Morning and evening the whole family assemble in the school room for prayers. At these morning and evening gatherings, addresses are often made suited to the condition of the school. A bad habit is pointed out, and the way it is to be rooted up explained; praiseworthy acts commended and their influence upon the future life of the inmate foretold. Besides all this, each day is commenced with a watchword, given at the close of morning prayers, to the school.

This watchword is a sententious saying of the ancients, chosen with reference to its adaptability to the wants and condition of the school. For example, some boy has done a wrong and has not the manliness to come out boldly and confess it. Thus the motto of the day runs thus: "*Daylight will peep through a small hole.*" Is the boy disposed to be wasteful? if so, the watchword of the day would be: "*A small leak will sink a ship*!" A boy runs away and is brought back, and the motto of the next morning would read as follows: "*Haste trips up its own heels.*"

These mottoes are repeated after the Superintendent, in concert, by the school. If by chance the motto should be forgotten, many voices cry out, "The Motto! The Motto!"

Besides all this instruction given out at morning and evening prayers, we have our chapel, school room, dining hall and work shops adorned with appropriate mottoes, so that the eye may all the time come into contact with moral truth. Some of these mottoes read as follows: "*Opportunities are passing.*" "*The diligent hand maketh rich.*" "*God's eye is upon me.*" "*Wisdom is the principal thing—therefore get Wisdom,*" *&c.*

It has been my experience that this class of boys are influenced very much by the eye; thus those Reformatories in this country and in Europe have been most successful in planting truth in the heart where the eye has been appealed to by placards, statues, minerals, cabinets and flower gardens.

Upon the Sabbaths we have preaching in the forenoon and Sabbath School in the afternoon. The Superintendent of the School officiates in the morning, while Mr. Johnson, our principal teacher, conducts the afternoon service. Addresses are often made to the School at the conclusion of the lesson. . . . Our moral instruction is not confined to the Sabbath, to morning and evening prayers, but it is given on play-ground, in the school-room, work-shop, at the table, in the field, by the wayside, here a little, there a little. In fine, this instruction is but a "continual dropping." Bad habits are held up and exposed. The good are encouraged—the weak are strengthened—the timid are emboldened—the smoking flax is not quenched. The faintest aspiration in the direction of right is rewarded. All feel that life is real, that life should be earnest, that each has his part to perform in life's dreams; that each should stand in his appointed lot. Why, then, should not our faith gather strength as we look towards the future? Who has a right to forbid us to hope much for the future, trusting in God's blessing.

D. B. Nichols

Supt. of Mich. State Reform School

THE POLITICAL PROCESS

A. D. P. Van Buren

Van Buren, a copious observer of pioneer life, recorded his impressions of political life in Kalamazoo County in the immediate aftermath of statehood. Party politics were relatively new in the state; the first true Democratic-Whig contest occurred in 1835 over the alien voting issue. Van Buren describes the highly informal manner in which townships were established in newly settled areas; that done, a vital next step was establishing schools: "After our ancestors created the township, that school of self-government," Van Buren wrote, "and provided for a system of voting which would give the freest and most unbiased expression of the popular will, they then established the 'common school,' that sheet anchor of the ship of state." Another important step was the building of roads: "The road is a physical sign or symbol by which you will best understand any age or people. If they have no roads they are savages."

Society, however, got more complicated; the population grew, more complex issues arose, and political parties—organized down to the precinct level—appeared. In this memoir Van Buren recalled the flavor of party politics and the political process in the new state. The fact that Michigan came into being just as the rules of the political game were changing has had a profound effect on its history.

The following excerpt is from A. D. P. Van Buren's "Michigan in Her Pioneer Politics," *Michigan Pioneer and Historical Collections*, vol. XVII (Lansing: Robert Smith & Co., 1892), pp. 238–47.

I have often gone into reflection on the subject of politics; as to what it is, and as to its effect on man, and on the masses. It is not an uninteresting study. The dictionary defines it as the science of government, and politician [as] one versed in that science. But this does not give one a clear idea of the subject. It is the meaning out of the dictionary, where we find politics and politician defined in man's action, that we want. And when we say that as thus defined it is the principle that controls man's political action, although a good general definition, it does not give the meaning of politics in the various party forms that it assumes. In the proper use of politics we see the good citizen, the patriot; in its abuse we see the partisan, or demagogue.

Again, we see in men that political fealty that gives to party what belongs to mankind. And we see, also, that fealty which gives to the party leader what belongs to the party. The first develops the partisan, the second the demagogue. But again, our early politics, like Gaul, was divided into three parts. And each division was different from the other. For instance, as to the question how does politics affect man, the answer would be, that depends on the kind he has. For when applied to a large class of our people it made Democrats of them; when applied to another and smaller class, it made Whigs of them, and when applied to another and [yet] smaller class, it made liberty men or abolitionists of them. Consequently, to get a clear understanding of the politics of the old days we must understand the political principles that then governed the Democrat, the Whig, and the abolitionist. Stated briefly, the first [Democrat] was for free trade, anti-bank, and ignored the slavery question. The second [Whig] was for protection, in favor of banks and neutral on slavery. The third—anti-slavery.

Thus we have given the kind of politics that Michigan started with and that has influenced and shaped her political career; says one of our pioneers, "I remember the time when there were no signs of any politics about the early settlement in Battle Creek, that is, in the partisan sense of that word." The pioneers did not begin their political existence here as voters, till after their homes were established. When there were enough settlers in a certain region, a township was organized, and, when enough townships were created, a county was organized, each township and each county having a distinct civil existence. And the settlers went about the organization of a township, and the election of township officers, as they did in rearing their log cabins, school-houses and churches. It was an important matter, and they gave it their best thought and attention, with an honest endeavor to subserve the public interest. The township being organized, it was divided into school and road districts, and suitable officers were elected in each. Let us for a moment look at the primitive official equipment of a township by its first election. And let us take that of Comstock, Kalamazoo County, at its organization in 1834. It was officered as follows: one supervisor, one township clerk, three assessors, one collector, three highway commissioners, five school inspectors, six overseers of highways and fence viewers, three directors of the poor, three constables, and three pound masters. Here, among other things, we notice the especial attention that was required to be given to schools and highways, by the ample number of officers elected for that purpose. These are two very important factors in our civilization. After our ancestors created the township, that school of self-government, and provided for a system of voting which would give the freest and most unbiased expression of the popular will, they then established "the common school, that sheet anchor of the old ship of State," as Mr. Chauncey Depew calls it. And we cannot give the early settlers too much credit for it. And also in regard to roads, they early gave their attention to them. The road is a physical sign or symbol by which you will best understand any age or people. If they have no roads they are savages. The emigrants who, in the old days, first left Detroit, took a rough road westward, that led to a settlement in the woods. Beyond this they found a mere indistinct wagon track that led to a log cabin among the trees; from the cabin they followed a footpath that led to a log barn, and from that a squirrel track that went up a tree. All beyond was an unreclaimed wilderness, in possession of the red man, with no roads, trackless, save that it was meandered by interminable Indian trails and deer paths. The road then is a creation of man and a type of civilized society.

It was something of an important matter then for a set of men to assume the sworn responsibilities of governing a township, and to faithfully discharge the duties of their offices. As that staunch pioneer, Warren B. Shepard, said: "It may not require us to be deeply versed in State craft in order to govern a township, but I think we should have some township craft in order faithfully to perform our duties; consequently, I move that as we are in a new country, struggling to make a beginning, and as this is new business in which we can all do better when we know better, that instead of taking the formal oath of 'swearing in' to office, . . . we 'swow in' for the first year, and do the best we can at that, and swear in the next year." So, as the story goes, they all "swowed" into office the first year.

Now the environment of the township meeting of those early days was certainly conducive to a free, unbiased vote. The settlers had at heart the interest of the common weal and, for a while at least, no partisan influence was felt at town meetings. But after the township and county organizations were got thoroughly in hand, and the territory became a State, and the whole political machinery of the young commonwealth set going, then we began to see and feel the party man's influence and the partisan's or old demagogue's manipulations. The old Democrat and Whig parties started Michigan in politics. They at least controlled by turns her political interest up to 1852, when the old Whig party after her memorable defeat in that campaign went out of history. At the time Michigan was ushered from her territorial nonage into full statehood, Stevens T. Mason was governor, Isaac E. Crary represented her in the lower house at Washington, and Lucius Lyon in the Senate, and Martin Van Buren was President. The Detroit Free Press was the organ of the Democratic party, the Detroit Advertiser the organ of the Whig party. These newspapers did much in sustaining the cause of their own party. They were ably edited and were about the only political papers that reached the people in various parts of the state. They were weeklies, and in the settlements in the central and western parts of the state, only an occasional copy found its way to the settler's home. A few years later better roads and facilities for conveying news brought the weekly Free Press and Advertiser regularly to people in the interior of the state.

We have spoken of the absence of party spirit at the early elections. To show that this was only of short duration, we give the following instance: At the annual township election in Battle Creek in the spring of 1838, the Democrats on and about Goguac prairie met at Warren B. Shepard's home just south of the village, and there equipped themselves with stout hickory canes or sticks, some four feet long, before going into the village. Here, they were marshaled to a breast, some seventy or eighty in number, and put under command of my brother, Martin Van Buren, as captain. His father being cousin of the president, and he of the same name, made his position as captain of a company of Democrats more appropriate. Being joined by other Democrats, similarly equipped, they presented a formidable array to their political foes as they marched into town.

This election had brought out the Whigs in their full strength. They were on the alert and ready for the onset at the polls; and none was more so than that formidable old Whig, Leonard Starkweather, for short called "old Stark." . . . He, being an incorrigible Whig, could not tolerate the idea of this long file of Democrats, marching to the polls in such a defiant array, and made more especially obnoxious by their carrying hickory canes, that emblem of the [Democratic party] which he detested.

Hence as the column advanced toward the polls, he grew furious, and swore they should not vote in that way, it was an insult to every Whig present. So he made a bold charge in order to throw them into confusion; seizing Henry Eberstine, a young Democrat, he pulled him from the ranks. Upon this Ephraim VanBuren caught "old Stark" by the coat collar and jerked him loose from Eberstine, exclaiming as he did so—"Old Stark, let us alone! We are going to the polls in rank, and vote just as we are. Now keep quiet, and don't molest us again, or you will make us defend ourselves, which may not be as well for you." But the redoubtable old Whig politician was furious with rage, and laid about him left and right with his fists, till some cooler headed Whigs gathered about him, and after awhile, got him out of the excited crowd, and kept him from further interrupting the Democrats voting in the order they had designed. This was the first illustration of party spirit I had ever witnessed. It is said that the sun went down on "old Stark's" wrath that day, and that he awoke the next morning as mad as ever. A few days after this event an old Democrat told him that if he ever wished to succeed in politics he must vote with him. He exclaimed, "what, I join you? Sooner than vote the Democratic ticket, I would crawl on my knees from Battle Creek to Detroit, and be struck by lightning every other mile."

At this time the newspaper and the political speaker constituted a power for each party, and were the means of keeping their adherents informed on all the political issues and topics of the day. The speaker having had the advantage of getting first what the party organs had to say and then personally haranguing the people on the questions at issue in the coming election. They were accustomed to look to him as party leader and counselor, for he was not only the party's orator but oracle as well. And when did the public speaker ever have such listeners?

Listeners who gave him an appreciation that was inspiration itself; and an applause that stimulated him to put forth his best efforts. Webster said that eloquence must exist in the man, in the occasion. Well, here was the occasion in that enthusiastic, appreciative gathering, that put the man at his best, and if there was any eloquence in him it was sure to be brought out. Says an old stump speaker of that day: "When I ascended the platform the upturned faces of the enthusiastic crowd before me fired me for the occasion; there is where I got my inspiration. That was the day for spontaneous eloquence." The notice given out for a political speech at that time was the signal for a rally of Whigs or Democrats.

For every Whig or Democrat had a personal interest in the orator of his own party, and in the discussion of his subject. There was a fealty to party leaders that was true to all the demands made upon it, and he was ever in close sympathy with the masses of the party. He always addressed his adherents in an off-hand speech and manner that seemed born of the occasion, and carried them by a studied, inherent force; and, as this was before the day of stenographic reporting, the speech did not get into print, and the only way for people to get it was at the hustings, where it was delivered. Newspapers gave outlines of these speeches, and ringing editorials on the party issues, and were of great aid to the party's cause, but the party leader or stump-speaker was the director and controlling force in the Democratic and Whig days of fifty years ago.

But today the newspaper has turned the orator into an essayist, and usually a dull one at that. There is such glory in seeing one's speech in print that, as John Borroughs would have it, the thought of the hustings causes the speaker to break out all over with a kind of literary rash that nothing will assuage but some newspaper or journalistic enterprise, which will give the speech with which he is surcharged a chance "to be seen and heard of men."

Now, the essence of a good speech upon ordinary occasions is its adaptation to the tone and spirit of its surroundings—its sympathetic touch with its hearers—the indescribable magnetism born of time, place, and circumstance, and personality, the charm of utterance, the inspiration of the hour. These characterized the speaker and the speaking of the old days. The speaker nowadays cannot address himself to his audience, he must harangue christendom through the next morning's papers, he is encumbered all the time with the thought of how and what he says will be made to read in the papers, and what will be said of it. But, in the old times we refer to, we got the speech fresh, animated from the lips of the speaker, in all the power of argument and impassioned eloquence. We got the speech from the man and not from the manuscript. A great difference that . . . especially where the script hampers the man.

What a change between the now and then of our political meetings! It is difficult for a person of today to conceive of the degree of enthusiasm that pervaded a political gathering in Michigan fifty years ago. Was ever such attention, appreciation and admiration given a political orator? Was ever, we repeat, a public gathering so gifted as listeners?

The day abounded in listeners. And as genuine oratory depends upon the ear and appreciation of the auditors, it was an age of genuine oratory.

Today the reverse of this is largely true. There is a dearth of enthusiastic listeners, hence we have but little genuine political oratory.

For although the present age may be said to abound in public speakers, there is something lacking in the hearers, to fire the speaker's logic, or set his eloquence aflame. The reason for this is obvious, as in any public gathering or convention of our people today, every other man is surcharged with a speech of his own or has a manuscript sticking out of his pocket. Consequently where there are so many people who are impressed with the idea that they have a special mission to publicly deliver to their fellow men, there are very few interested listeners; in such cases you cannot tell people anything.

My earliest recollections of political meetings in Michigan are connected with those held in Battle Creek in the last part of the 'thirties. Edward Bradley, Isaac E. Crary and Thomas B. Church of Marshall, were the political orators at the democratic gatherings I referred to.

Bradley's popularity as a political speaker was unbounded. I can see him now familiarly mingling among the Democrats at their meetings, taking seat with them before the speaking began, and as one of them talking freely on the subjects incident to the occasion. I used to think that here was where Bradley got his power with the masses. That he became so thoroughly identified with his surroundings when he mounted the rostrum, his speech took its thought, it tone and color so much from his environments that it was just what the occasion called for, and the applause that greeted him as he ascended the platform, and the plaudits given him by an animated crowd during his speech, were the natural recognition, the full meed of reward for his oratorical triumph. Nature had endowed Bradley with the rare gift of eloquent speech. Probably no political speaker of his day in the west surpassed him in his power over a public assemblage at the hustings. People went to the meeting because Bradley was to speak. Let it be far or near, time and distance did not hinder them; nor could they hear him too often, nothing staled his infinite variety.

I remember hearing Isaac E. Crary and Thomas B. Church address a crowd of Democrats at Battle Creek sometime in 1838. I was a boy then; and as I recall myself sitting on the rough board seats in

Capt. John Marvin's new store building listening to Hon. Isaac E. Crary's speech, I seem to sit like young Paul getting instruction from a Gamaliel. It was not only fortunate for Michigan that she had an Isaac E. Crary to found (with his co-worker Rev. John D. Pierce) her admirable school system, to represent her in Congress, to fit her for statehood and for her splendid future career, but it was also fortunate for the state that they had so wise and able a statesman to instruct them in their first political duties, on their first party issues, thus making them more useful citizens and more intelligent voters. If he erred in his political course it was an error of judgment, not of intention. That he was a politician is true. But whether discussing party principles at the hustings, or national affairs in legislative council, he was the same candid, able counselor, in the one case as the other. He was foremost among our early statesmen in discovering the wants of the new state, and his master hand is seen not only in its full and thorough organization, but in the establishment of those institutions which have made it a great and prosperous commonwealth. Thomas B. Church was then a young man reading law in the office of Gordon & Woodruff, in Marshall. But he knew then how to make a good political speech. Mr. Church presented his theme in such a manner as to fix the attention of his hearers at the start. He had the power at least to hold their attention, while by forcible argument and illustration, and occasional sallies of wit, discussed the bank question, tariff, and whatever other issue was before the people at the time. Mr. Crary had discussed the same subjects in his speech. There was a local Whig politician by the name of Gillespie, who lived at Verona, two miles north of Battle Creek, and who, being a little deaf, had taken a seat near Mr. Church as he began his speech. The speaker describing that type of politician termed office seeker, exclaimed—"you will find them everywhere, they are the 'hangers-on' in the political camp, the 'fawning Uriah Heeps' at elections, and when elected become the barnacles on the body politic," and at the same time pointing with his fingers here and there at the crowd by way of general expression, he chanced to point towards Gillespie, who, taking it in high dudgeon, exclaimed—"Quite too personal, Mr. Church, quite too personal, sir!" Mr. Church, aware that the wounded bird always flutters, mildly replied, "My reference was to office seekers in general, when I said, 'here is one, and there is one,' but if in thus pointing I have hit a real office seeker, I am not to blame for it. If the coat fits, put it on." The old Whig politician was much nettled by Mr. Church's caustic remark, but kept on taking notes till the speech was finished. And no doubt he answered it the next time he addressed a Whig gathering during that campaign.

What I have said of the Democratic orators in regard to character, to an open and fair discussion of the issues of the day, will apply as well to the Whig orators of that time. It was always a pleasure to listen to Hons. James Wright Gordon and Henry W. Taylor, leading Whig orators of Marshall, as well as to Horace Mower, and Marsh Giddings, prominent Whig orators of Kalamazoo. In these early meetings the Democratic and Whig voters of the state got their first political lessons; their first instruction and training in regard to the duties incumbent on the citizens as electors in a young state.

The hustings were a sort of political school where the politics of the day were discussed for the benefit of the citizen. They were very popular and the two old parties, Whig and Democrat, were noble old foes, and each found in the other a foeman worthy of its steel. The rivalry existing between them was always sufficient to call out the full party strength, and put each one at its bet. They differed in their creeds on the tariff, national bank, and other issues of the time. The general influence arising from party opposition, watchfulness, and scrutiny of each other's movements, resulted in good to the government. Review the political history of this state, from governor down to pathmaster, for the first thirty years of its existence, and you will find a history that not only reads well, but one in which every citizen of the state can take a just and honorable pride. We are in no sense extenuating the sins of the old political parties in Michigan; there was evil enough in politics then, but there was less of it, and both state and national politics were less complicated. And in our young state there was an apparent endeavor on the part of both party leaders, and parties to subserve the best interest of the common weal. I have spoken of the husting as a kind of political training school, that their influence was to inform, instruct, and make more intelligent citizens and voters. The old Judean leaders instructed their followers in this way. The Greek orators enlightened the masses on all public and political affairs, and fitted them for their duties as citizens, at their public gatherings. Our politics, as said, in the past were much simpler, not mixed up with so many political isms, with so many various labor and moral issues, making a political campaign now a much more laborious, intricate, and difficult business, as regards informing and enlightening the people in its issues. For while we have really but two parties today, yet there are half a dozen of what we call party "off shoots," "suckers" to the main party stems, from which they draw their strength and get their growth, thus weakening the main stalks, while they themselves never attain maturity, nor amount to anything but a useless growth, as far as party purpose is concerned. Thus the two old parties stand today, hedged in, assailed and weakened by so many difficulties, while their following is measurably diminished or divided up among these would-be parties, who assume more or less of their principles, thus complicating party issues and discussions, and lessening the old party interest and enthusiasm among the people. And as regards the old "stump speaker," "Othello's occupation is gone"—to the modern editor.

A SEAT OF GOVERNMENT

William W. Upton

The framers of the Michigan Constitution of 1835, unable to agree on where to place the state capital, let it remain temporarily in Detroit, but decreed that a permanent site be chosen in 1847. In the interim, communities all over the lower peninsula—seeking the enormous economic growth certain for the capital site and its hinterland—flooded the legislature with petitions and memorials offering free land and other inducements should the state locate its capital in their midst. As 1847 approached, newspapers in Detroit, Ann Arbor, Jackson, and Marshall—the main contenders—strongly pressed their own claims as capital sites while disparaging the claims of rivals.

Detroit had much to commend it, and it was within the discretion of the legislature to retain the capital there. Of all the communities in the state, Detroit "looked" most like a capital city, with many fine residences, churches, hotels, and public buildings, as well as a history that began in 1701. Keeping the capital there would have saved the cost of relocation, an important consideration for the economy-minded legislators of 1847. And Detroit, despite the marvelous growth of the interior, was a major lake port and terminal for rail and stage lines; it was and would remain the metropolis of the state.

But the temper of the times was against large cities as seats of government. In Europe, a regional or national capital was usually the largest metropolis, a center of culture and finance as well as government. This was not so in America in the 1840s, when the arcadian dream was still alive and many voters shared Thomas Jefferson's mistrust of cities. The American tradition of locating capitals outside large cities was already well established. The District of Columbia was just such a choice, as was Columbus, Ohio, when that state deadlocked between Cincinnati and Cleveland. The neighboring states of Indiana and Illinois had placed their capitals in central, compromise locations. State capitals in Sacramento, Albany, and Atlanta were also compromise choices, and there would be others as new states were formed in the trans-Mississippi west. As 1847 approached, the outcry against the "Detroit influence" and demands for a "healthier political climate" grew more strident.

The selection of Lansing reflects many influences. Hostility towards cities as well as strategic considerations eliminated Detroit as a serious candidate. Even as the legislators met, there were tensions between the United States and Great Britain over the still-unresolved Oregon question. The British, after all, had occupied Detroit during the War of 1812, and that city seemed a likely target in the event of a war. Border incidents had occurred during the Patriot War of 1837–1838; the fact that the United States government was building Fort Wayne on the Detroit River to guard against incursions from the Canadian side shows that strategic considerations played a part in removing the capitol from Detroit. The rivalries and antagonisms of the other important contenders—Ann Arbor, Jackson, and Marshall, as well as the belief that they were too far south—eliminated them as well. The legislators were forced to choose a compromise location, and in doing so had no alternative but to give weight to the arguments in the debate over capital selection. In selecting Lansing, a location they perceived to be in the "north woods," the legislature embraced a vision of the future growth of the state—a vision which they hoped the selection of Lansing would advance.

William W. Upton, a member of the state legislature of 1847, wrote one of the few available first-hand accounts of the legislative maneuvering over the capital site. Upton's account shows how the selection of the capital site was complicated by another and, to some legislators, more important issue—the selection of a United States Senator. Upton's account, "Locating the Capital of the State of Michigan," was written many years after the fact. It is reprinted from *Michigan History*, vol. 23, no. 3 (Summer 1939): pp. 291–97. By permission of *Michigan History* magazine.

I was as a member of the House of Representatives of the State of Michigan that convened, if I recall the date, on the first Monday of January, 1845 [1847].

I had then lived at the village of DeWitt, then the County Seat of Clinton County, two years, and I represented that county. I had been admitted to the bar and had occasionally tried cases more by way of amusement than as a matter of business, for up to that time and for a year afterward I had never supposed I should make the practice of law my business. But being a member of the bar and there not being a very large number of the members of the House who were lawyers and also because I had supported Mr. George W. Peck, who became speaker, I was a member of the judiciary committee of the House, notwithstanding my youth and my want of experience as a lawyer.

This gave me as much prominence as a member, as so young and inexperienced a man was entitled to and I have no doubt a good deal more.

I was greatly aided in avoiding the awkward effects of such inexperience by becoming the roommate and companion of Mr. Charles P. Bush, a man of about forty-five years who was president pro tem of the state senate. He had in his boyhood been a neighbor and friend of my father-in-law, Mr. Joseph Hollister, and although he never saw me until on my way to Detroit to attend the session of the legislature he greeted me cordially because of the acquaintance with my father-in-law and proposed that we should room together during the session. I was wise enough to surmise that his willingness to do me so great a kindness grew out of a design and hope that he would be able to influence my vote on diverse questions and most especially in the election of a United States Senator. But as it seemed to me to be and really was an object to so young and verdant a politician to be on such easy and intimate terms with such a shrewd experienced and influential man I accepted with pleasure. This arrangement enabled me to have in inside view of nearly all that was being done. The business of this first session of the legislature was especially important because in addition to being the session at which a United States Senator was to be elected, it had been provided at the time of adopting the state constitution, that the capital of the state should remain in Detroit until 1845 [1847] and that it should then be permanently located at such a place as the legislature should designate. It had been a topic for several years and as the time approached every town and village in the state became convinced that it was par excellence the place for the capital. It is almost incredible but there was no exception, the people of each embryo city could see abundant reasons why that city ought to be, and for hoping it would be, selected as the capital of the state; some because they were central (and it was wonderful how many were in the center of population, or of the territory or of business, either present or prospective); others because of water power or steam boat or prospective railroad conveniences, or because they were lovely rural situations far from the disturbing and corrupting influences of commerce and trade; others for sanitary reasons, and still others because they were beautifully situated on one of the three Great Lakes.

Detroit was then by far the largest town in the state, yet its adult population was fairly doubled in numbers by the lobbyists who assembled to aid in locating the capital in the respective cities intent on securing its location for themselves. But there were a few individuals who were still more interested in the selection of a United States Senator. The legislature was overwhelmingly Democratic and there were three Democratic aspirants for the position of United States Senator. They were: [Alpheus T.] Felch, who was then governor living in the eastern part of the state; [Epaphroditus] Ransom, a supreme and ex-officio circuit judge living in the west; and [Origen D.] Richardson of Pontiac, in what was then the northern part of the state,—or at least, he had the support of the north, Shiawassee, Clinton, Ionia, then being in the most northern tier of settled or partially settled counties. Ransom had as adherents 28 western members; Richardson, who lived in the north, had 22; and Felch, 22, living in the east. To all appearances the preferences of the members were based entirely on geographic reasons.

A day was appointed for a general Democratic caucus to nominate the senator, and for several preceding evenings the friends of each candidate met in separate rooms in caucus to strengthen each other's ardor, and to devise ways and means of advancing the interests of their respective candidates. From my location in the north and so far as I know for no other reason I was with the supporters of Richardson. President Bush was also with them. Our numbers were equal to the number of Governor Felch's adherents and within six of the supporters of Judge Richardson. Why should we not succeed? I remember we said this to each other when we assembled in our sectional caucus, a great many times and in many different forms of expression, and I don't remember that there was much else that we said or did when we so assembled. While we were repeating these brilliant ideas in various forms I could plainly see that Bush and others of our number were really intending in the end to elect Felch, and that State Senator [Robert P.] Eldridge and another of our number were equally anxious to elect Ransom. It was evident to me that poor Richardson had but 18 bona fide supporters if I counted myself in, and that I could hardly be so counted for I had become satisfied that he could not be elected. When we finally assembled as a caucus composed of the Democratic members of the two houses we took a great number of ballots, 44 I think, prior to any adjournment, each with the same results, namely, Ransom 28, Felch 22, and Richardson 22, and then it was resolved to take a recess for half an hour. Thereupon each of the three factions repaired to separate rooms for deliberation.

When our set of 22 was so assembled it took but a few minutes before Senator Eldridge took the floor and plausibly endeavored to show that it would be better to abandon all hope of electing the man of our choice and to support Judge Ransom who, he claimed, had proved himself the choice of the party. Mr. Bush followed with a speech in favor of electing Felch, then Governor of the State. I followed Mr. Bush and endeavored to show that in as much as we had the same numerical strength with which we entered the contest, and there seemed no probability of coalition between the forces of Ransom and those of Felch, there was now the same reason for adhering to our man that we had at the beginning, and all that was necessary to probable success was persistence and endurance. Of course, the speeches of Bush and Eldridge were as unpleasant and uninspiring to the ten or fifteen earnest and anxious friends who in good faith were supporting Mr. Richardson as could well be imagined, and, of course, those speeches produced an effect too much like a wet blanket to be effective on them. Not one of Richardson's friends was in the least tempted to follow the lead of Eldridge and Bush. By the time I had ended my remarks it was time to repair to the general caucus and as Bush and Eldridge each hoped to draw with him a majority of our set, and neither saw how he was then able to do it, we all again repaired in a body to the general caucus. There a number of additional ballots was taken, each with the same result as before. This continued for an hour or two when at about 2 o'clock another motion for a recess prevailed and each faction again repaired to its special room for further consultation.

Our 22 were no more than fairly seated before Bush and Eldridge renewed their respective propositions. I took a part in this discussion as often as I could obtain the floor with due observance of the modesty that should characterize so young a member of the caucus. No others took part in the debate. The discussion between Bush and Eldridge became heated and acrimonious. The burden of my argument was the importance of cooperation and endurance. I counseled conciliation and harmony and repeated my further assurances based on the truths that we had the same number of voters now as at the outset and that we had as much reason to expect one of the other factions to break from their candidate and disband as they had to hope such a thing would happen to us. As the discussion proceeded I felt convinced by the looks of those who had taken no part in the discussion that I was making the point I was striving for and that neither Bush nor Eldridge was producing the effect each had contemplated. A majority of our set was not only with me in their desire to stand by Richardson but they were becoming doggedly determined not be led away by Bush or Eldridge whom they were beginning to look upon as ingrates and traitors to their set. The most of the silent men were farmers, pioneers, who, though uneducated, had been accustomed to thinking and judging for themselves, men accustomed to have at least an equal voice, if not a controlling influence, in their respective neighborhoods and who would scorn to abandon their colleague in a contest.

As the discussion became more and more acrimonious Eldridge with a flourish, picked up his hat and asking all his friends to go with him to Ransom, left the room followed by only two adherents. Bush declaring this was an unjustifiable act on the part of Eldridge, appealed to all the fair minded men to resent it and go with him and place the matter in its true light by electing our worthy governor, Alpheus Felch, and he left the room also. He left with only three followers. During the excitement of their departure I was earnestly urging them not to be so inconsiderate, begging them not to forsake their friends, and when the last of them disappeared from the door I was conducting my appeal to them and my remaining fellow members in the interests of harmony and good faith and begging them to remain.

The result was that fifteen of us were left in our room and it was evident that if we continued to vote together the nest ballot would stand: Ransom 31, Felch 26, and Richardson 15. At first the talk among the fifteen who remained, favored going into the general caucus and continuing to fight for Richardson regardless of the consequences, and I had no doubt I could have so fostered that sentiment as to have held the fifteen together to the end of the session or until Ransom or Felch had succeeded by depleting the forces of his opponent. But on this point I waited for older men to express their views. There was a good deal of quiet although excited talk and after a time some older members made some observations on the evidence this imbroglio would probably have on the selection of the place for the state capital. This led to a consideration of the question whether the election of Ransom or of Felch would be conducive to the location of the capitol where we desired it to be; that is, in what was then considered the northern part of the state; in other words, at Lansing or that vicinity. The matter of electing Richardson began to be spoken of as almost hopeless, and it began to be queried whether one faction or the other would get consent to locate the capitol in our midst if we should enable them to have their choice for senator. A proposition was made which was agreed to by my fourteen colleagues that before we again entered the general caucus I should go into one or both the other separate caucuses and by sounding the leaders ascertain whether the members of one faction or the other would pledge themselves that we should have the capitol on those conditions. Although a very young man, I was old enough to know that promises made under such circumstances are not very likely to be kept but I did not deem it necessary to mention that point in the hurry of that evening. I felt very great confidence that either faction would make the promise as soon as it was proposed. and with as decent haste as was consistent with modesty, I accepted their commission and repaired to the room of the Felch men.

I informed the door keeper that I desired to see President Bush. It is to be presumed that the message was as welcome to him as any he ever received. He appeared instantly and I communicated my proposition. I told him that if I was called in and given a unanimous promise of the entire twenty-six Felch men that they would aid in locating the capital at Lansing the fifteen votes would be cast for Felch, and he left me for the purpose of presenting the proposition.

It may be thought strange that so many men whose constituents had been and still were so anxious and so hopeful of obtaining the capitol, should be willing to abandon the effort to secure the senator of their choice. But by this time the subject of locating the capitol had been very much canvassed and although the constituents still remained hopeful, most of these twenty-six legislators had become thoroughly convinced that their respective towns had no prospect of being selected as the future capitol of the state.

Bush soon returned, told me my proposition was accepted and invited me into the room to be assured of the pledge of every member.

On entering I found State Senator Jefferson Thurber to be chairman of the local caucus. He welcomed me and asked me if I would be kind enough to state the proposition that had been brought by President Bush, and to state what reason they would have to be assured that the other Richardson men were willing to support Governor Felch. I said, "There are fourteen of those members now in the library awaiting my return who have authorized me to make the proposition brought you by the President of the Senate, and if I receive the assurances I have asked for, they will vote for Governor Felch on the next ballot and until he is nominated. What they expect is the aid of every member present in good faith in locating the capitol at Lansing until it is so located."

Senator Thurber said, "Gentlemen you that join in this pledge will arise." Every man arose and I said, "Governor Felch is elected." I returned to the library room and explained the result to the fourteen. In less than five minutes the roll was being called in the general caucus and at the end of the roll call it was announced, "whole number of votes, 72; necessary to choice 37; of which Judge Ransom has received 31 and Governor Felch 41. Governor Alpheus Felch having received a majority of all the votes cast is declared the nominee of the convention for the office of United States Senator."

How many of these men lived up to the pledge it would be difficult to tell, for independently of any question of that kind the passage of the bill locating the capitol at Lansing resulted in the main from other causes. At this late date without the aid of records of the legislature's proceedings I am unable to recall the exact period in the history of that bill that the senatorial election occurred. The subject had been pretty thoroughly canvassed among the senators at least before any bill was introduced. I think the senate was composed of twenty-two members, and one seat was vacant, so that eleven members constituted a majority, and long before the bill reached the senate and before the senatorial election took place nine senators had secretly pledged to use their utmost endeavors to locate the capitol at Lansing.

James Seymour, a cousin and I think a former partner of Governor [Horatio] Seymour of New York, then resided at Flint, Michigan, and he owned several sections of land in the township of Lansing and had dammed the Grand River and constructed a saw mill at that point. The mill consisted of a rough, upright saw and was probably capable of cutting twelve or fifteen hundred feet of board in a day. There were no buildings in the township of six miles except this mill and four small log houses. The township was pretty heavily timbered and was in every respect a wilderness. Seymour produced to the senators a written proposition that if the majority would locate the capitol on section nine in that township he would construct a capitol building for the state at his own expense as commodious as the one then occupied at Detroit and at his own expense remove the furniture from Detroit to Lansing, and he accompanied this by a good and sufficient bond for its performance.

Probably by the advice of Mr. Bush, and I was selected to introduce the bill and present this proposition to the House. The fact that I lived nearer to this unheard place, Lansing, then any other member (it being seven miles from DeWitt) may have been the reason for selecting me. That I was young, had had no enemies, and there being less reason to suspect a self-interest in me than in more experienced business men, was probably a still stronger reason. I introduced with the bill and proposition a map of all the settled ports of the state. On this map a bright red wafer was placed at the point called Lansing and from this point to each lake town was drawn a broad black line to each port and village on the Three Great Lakes. These lines were so large as to be seen across the hall of the House, and thus ocular demonstration was presented that Lansing was an extremely central point. In fact, on each of these black lines were large figures giving the distance from Lansing to each of the lake ports and towns. In presenting the propositions I read among other things a paper which recapitulated these distances, showing that Lansing was between ninety and one hundred miles from each of these settled points on the lakes.

The first thing that was said after I had finished my remarks and sent the papers to the clerk's desk was by a Mr. [James M.] Edmunds who was then a leading young member and was afterwards Post-Master of Washington, D.C., for many years. Mr. Edmunds said, "Mr. Speaker, will the clerk please read that table of distances again? I did not learn where that place is, although I learned it is a great ways from any other place." The clerk re-read the paper amid some merriment, the proposition being looked upon by most members of the House as an absurdity worthy of but little attention. But before the day was over the scheme of having a capitol building constructed gratuitously began to look like a formidable thing to meet by those who were working for other localities, and that fact together with the favorable comment of a considerable number of senators not supposed committed in favor of Lansing began to make the proposition look at least respectable.

Another feature of the contest grew out of the fact that Lansing, not being a rival town but a mere point in the wilderness, excited no jealousy, and as the representatives of one town after another began to discover that their towns could not succeed, they seemed almost universally to be seized with the determination to prevent any rival from carrying off the prize. Before many days Lansing had acquired many supporters from this cause. Bush was a very zealous and active worker for Lansing, partly from the feeling last mentioned but partly because Howell, his place of residence and his county, generally were to be benefitted, Howell being on the natural line of travel between Lansing and Detroit, and he persuaded members similarly located to vote for Lansing. Wayne County, including Detroit, was so populous as to have a large delegation. I think the number was eleven, and these together with the representatives of two or three counties north of Wayne, including Port Huron, amounting to at least twenty, had placed themselves from motives of policy under the leadership of Mr. [George] Throop, a member of the House from Detroit. He was a brother of Enos T. Throop, ex-governor of New York, a man of some ability who was then looked upon as a very able and experienced manager of affairs, although results proved him not very successful in the matter of the state capitol. Bush managed to send to him a gentleman who was really and decidedly in favor of Lansing. Throop supposed him anxious to secure the capitol at Detroit. This gentleman represented to him that the natural outlet of all the trade of all the counties about Lansing was through Detroit, and that all the representatives of those counties had to pass through Detroit to visit their relatives at the places of their nativity in the eastern and middle states, and if they were not driven away or swerved by unnecessary opposition when they found their project of locating the capitol in that unsettled wilderness an impossibility, they would go for Detroit as a second choice. When Throop had time to ruminate upon this, Bush casually met him and so led the conversation as to induce Throop to point out to Bush that the way of Bush and his constituents to the eastern world led through Detroit and, hence, Bush was standing in his own light in opposing Detroit. Bush says, "My interest would be served in locating it either at Howell or at Detroit but I do not say that we shall secure it at either place. The counties that favor Lansing have the same interest that my county had, and they are about the only counties outside Wayne that have any real interest in locating the capitol at Detroit, but before the fight against Lansing is over I suppose they will be so swerved by you that we can never induce them to see their own interests. I never thought my way to get their support for Howell by fighting them and voting against Lansing." The result of a good deal of management of this kind was to lead Throop to the conclusion that if the bill passed the House in its present form the senate would strike out Lansing, and the great contest in the House would be when the bill came back from the senate and that his true policy was to conciliate the representatives of Enghorne [Ingham], Eaton, Clinton, and adjoining counties by voting for this bill. This accession of Throop and his friends made a very handsome majority for the bill in the lower House and we had long had the pledge of nine senators that if the bill so passed the House there should not be an "i" dotted or a "t" crossed in the senate.

By the time the bill reached the senate a great many towns had offered, like Seymour, to furnish bonds for the erection of a state house if the capitol was given to them. In addition to this, very many town plats were exhibited and the lots offered for sale. Many, if not all of them, cautiously gave out that members of the legislature would be allowed to purchase conditionally and for nominal sums. Soon charges and countercharges of corruption and attempted corruption were heard in every direction. That town lots were offered on such terms to an almost unlimited extent everybody knew. Whether any of them was accepted by any member or senator directly or indirectly I never knew, but the apparent anxiety and timidity of some of them caused suspicion. I knew of only one attempt to make money by any member or senator out of the location. In that instance I was invited to participate but looked upon it as too objectionable and declined. That attempt was made immediately on the passage of the bill by the House. The necessary sum was contributed by senators and members for the purchase price of school section No. 16 in the township of L and an agent was sent to the land office to purchase it but the land office refused to sell. I knew that the money was tendered and refused but I never heard more in regard to it. I also went on the next Saturday from Detroit to DeWitt expecting to purchase from Milo Turner, as agent for the owner, about five sections of valuable timber lands situated near Lansing which Turner had a few months before urged me to buy at $1.25 an acre. These being private lands, I thought the transaction not inconsistent with my official duty and one that I had a right to get into. But when I reached DeWitt, Turner was absent on a business trip to Chicago and I abandoned the attempt to purchase.

The bill to locate the capitol contained in about four short lines, a simple enactment that the capitol is hereby located in the town, designating it, but from the time it reached the senate it was the absorbing topic. After a very little time spent in debate a series of motions and roll calls commenced which were continued with very few and generally brief intervals of debate during about three weeks. This procedure was monotonous and yet nearly all the time very exciting. It was conducted as follows: a motion was made to strike out Lansing and insert, say, Marshall. This was followed by a motion to amend the amendment by striking out Marshall and inserting, say, Saginaw. Upon call of the roll, the motion to amend the amendment would fail and be followed by another motion to amend the amendment. Occasionally the sameness was relieved by an hour or two of debate, occasioned generally by something in the newspaper causing a senator to arise to a question of privilege to repel some accusation or insinuation of corruption or intrigue, and the personal explanation would frequently be followed for a time by a lively debate containing more or less innuendo and insinuations of corruption. With the exception of these interludes of debate filled with personalities and criminations and recriminations, this routine of a motion and roll call continued.

During all of this time it was known to me and a very few others that there were nine senators (within two of a majority) pledged that the bill should never be amended in the senate. Several of the nine senators were compelled by their home interests with their constituents to keep it a profound secret that they favored Lansing as they worked with all ardor and with all appearances of sincerity for their respective towns. As the motions, roll calls, and adverse votes demonstrated to one town after another that it was impossible for it to secure the capitol, the constituents of one after another of these senators came to acquiesce in the inevitable, and began to admit as the senator had long seen, that if the capitol could not be secured, the next best thing was to prevent its being secured by an active and rival town. During all these exciting days and nights but two senatorial votes were lacking to secure the location at Lansing, and they were most diligently sought and worked for especially by the nine committed and pledged senators. One of the two was finally obtained; a grave, honest, but rather stolid senator by the name of Balch, who had finally concluded that his constituents could not secure the prize, and he was casting about in a most anxious and conscientious way to determine what was his duty in making a second choice. Numerous men had interviewed him, especially those who favored Detroit, and he had not been neglected by his nine colleagues who favored Lansing; and for two or three days he had been endeavoring to decide between the two places. Two men who favored Lansing but who pretended to be residents of Detroit and to favor that city took a position in one of the corridors of the state house so that Senator Balch in passing from a committee room on his way to his boarding house must necessarily overhear their conversation which they appeared to be carrying on in a very confidential but excited manner. In the little part of the conversation he heard, he caught something like the following: "Detroit is certain of it. We have the ten votes and the money is raised that will bring the eleventh. The balance of the ten thousand dollars is just paid in and is already." "Are you sure the money is raised?" "Sure, yes, I raised the last myself. It will be located tomorrow before eleven o'clock." Balch passed out.

The next morning Dr. [Samuel] Denton, a senator from Ann Arbor, as soon as the bill was reached arose to a question of privilege and in a most graphic manner stated that he had what he deemed reliable information that the friends of Detroit felt secure of ten votes that were already agreed upon, and the same as counted, and that they were resorting to the most unblushing and nefarious means to carry their point by corruption; that it was an open secret with scarcely an attempt to keep it a secret; that ten thousand dollars was being offered for the eleventh vote and that the rumor pointed to two different senators, either of whose votes it was said could be had for that money. Senator Denton was a fluent and vehement speaker and he indulged in a most withering denunciation of this corrupt proposition, in a speech of about fifteen or twenty minutes, winding up with the declaration that the next roll call would "demonstrate to the world what creature of human form had sunk so low as to cover his name with infamy for the paltry sum of ten thousand dollars."

As the form of Senator Denton sank into his seat, that of Senator [Nathaniel] Balch came up and the latter said, "Mr. President, I will let the citizens of Detroit know they cannot have my vote for ten thousand dollars. Sir, I have heard of this dastardly proposition and I will let the citizens of Detroit know what one senator thinks of their dastardly corruption." Another senator whose name I do not now recollect, but who was not one of the nine, arose and with much heat and indignation made a similar declaration. There was an immediate demand for a roll call, the pending amendment to the amendment being rejected. In the midst of these startling announcements a call for the previous question was sustained which brought the senate to a vote, for the first time, on the original motion, that is, to amend the bill, but striking out "Lansing." The vote stood 10—for and 11—against the motion. The question was then taken on the passage of the bill and it stood "yeas, 11;" "nos 10," and Senator Bush, president pro tem, declared the bill passed.

At this distance of time it seems like a comparatively unimportant incident in the affairs of man, but it did not seem so to the actors at that time. To me and my constituents in Clinton County, it was the opening and building of roads from Pontiac and Ann Arbor and for seventy miles into the wilderness where we lived. It was opening for us a way to markets and bringing us again into connection with the civilization from which we had unwisely but voluntarily exiled ourselves. To the thousands of men who had been drawn from their homes to aid in securing the capitol and who had become partisans in the contest, it had become a matter of the most vital interest on which we were wrought up to the highest pitch of excitement. The hall of the senate was crowded to the utmost capacity and hundreds of men on the outside were crowded together as near to the door as they could get. I well remember that during the brief space while the secretary of the senate counted and noted the votes, there was in that crowded hall the most absolute silence and the most eager watchfulness of every motion of his pen. I remember as if it were yesterday how president pro-tem Charles P. Bush, from his seat of president officer, often leaned forward and craned his neck over the work of the secretary, and how in his unconsciousness of all else but the work at hand he failed to wipe away the perspiration that covered his face and failed to notice the huge drop of sweat that balanced like a glittering jewel from the end of his nose as his eager gaze was riveted on the notes of his secretary.

At a public dinner given a few days afterwards in honor of the results of both senatorial election and the location, good feeling seemed to be in a great measure restored and in general the contending participants were in great degree reconciled and there was much hilarity and good feeling, but occasionally jocular cruelty was indulged in. Among the most flagrant of these was a joke perpetrated by Honorable George W. Peck, then speaker of the House of Representatives (now editor of a Democratic paper in Wisconsin) on Mr. Throop, the leader of the delegation of Wayne County who was roped into voting for Lansing in the expectation that it could not pass the senate. At a late hour when all were hilarious Mr. Peck gave the following toast: "The democracy of Wayne like the Romans of old, they placed a goose to guard the capitol."

THE REFORM AGENDA

Kinsley S. Bingham

In 1833, at the age of twenty-five, Kinsley S. Bingham emigrated from western New York to what would become Livingston County. He bought land and prospered. He had studied law in New York; in Michigan he served as justice of the peace, probate judge, member of the legislature and speaker of the house, and two terms in the U.S. House of Representatives. In 1854 he became the first Republican governor of the state; he served two terms.

Bingham was a fervent reformer and staunch opponent of slavery. During his administration, Michigan passed a Personal Liberty Law, which required prosecutors in the state to use all legal means at their disposal to prevent the return of fugitive slaves.

His message to the legislature, on January 4, 1855, celebrated the achievements of Michigan since statehood, discussed the reform agenda, and summed up the Republican attitude toward the extension of slavery into the territories. It is reprinted from George N. Fuller, ed., *Messages and Papers of the Governors of Michigan*, vol. II (Lansing: Michigan Historical Commission, 1926), pp. 281–301.

In taking the oath prescribed by the Constitution, and in assuming the executive duties to which I have been called by the suffrages of the people of the State, I am impressed with a deep sense of the honor conferred, and of the high obligations and responsibilities imposed by the requirements of that sacred instrument. I enter upon the duties of this important station with an unaffected diffidence of my ability to discharge them, but with a fixed determination to do all in my power to promote the welfare and prosperity of our beloved State, and to meet all the just expectations of our common constituents. I am happy to be able to congratulate you, at your meeting, upon the highly favorable and prosperous condition of the State. During the past year the fields of agriculture have yielded an abundance, and the husbandman is receiving a rich reward for his industry—the mechanic and the laborer have been well requited for their toil—every branch of trade and commerce has met with signal success—the tide of emmigration has brought a large accession to our numbers, of an intelligent and enterprising class of citizens—the unoccupied portions of our state have been rapidly filling up—the interests of education have received unusual attention—our schools and seminaries of learning are in a flourishing condition—and happiness, prosperity and peace prevail throughout our State and country. . . .

By reference to the several reports relating to the subject of education you will have the pleasing assurance that at no period in the history of our State has the attention to learning been so universal and earnest as at the present time. The faculty of the University has been increased and strengthened, and the catalogue exhibits a gratifying addition to the number of those who seek a thorough and finished education.

It is our duty to encourage those having control of that institution, in every well directed effort to make it what its founders designed it should be, one of the first Universities in the land.

Unfortunately, about one hundred thousand dollars of the monies arising from the sale of lands granted by Congress for the University, were invested in buildings from which no income can be derived. The last Legislature authorized the payment of the interest upon that amount out of the Treasury, for the last two years—and to enable them to make such improvements as seem of imperative necessity, I respectfully recommend the payment of the same amount by the State for the two succeeding years.

No estimate can be properly made, of the advantages which the people of this State have already derived from the establishment of the Normal School. Its system of education has been practical and efficient, and from the first, its success has been uninterrupted. Nearly every section of the State can bear witness to the ability of the teachers trained within its walls, and through their influence new life and energy have been infused into our common schools, and the standard of teaching everywhere raised.

The Common School is emphatically the University for the masses. We rely for the permanency of free institutions upon the universal diffusion of knowledge through their instrumentality, and every effort made to improve their character, and make them free, furnishes an additional guaranty against pauperism, and crime, and taxation.

I submit to your judgment, whether any additional legislation is necessary, to give full effect to that provision of the Constitution which requires the Legislature "within five years from the adoption of the Constitution to provide for and establish a system of primary schools, whereby a school shall be kept without charge for tuition at least three months in each year in every school district in the State."

The Constitution also declares that the Legislature shall, as soon as practicable, provide for the establishment of an Agricultural School. I respectfully submit for your consideration whether that "practicable" period has not already arrived. Michigan is eminently an agricultural State, and the great source of our dependence and wealth must ever be in the soil. It has been demonstrated that its productions can be greatly increased by scientific cultivation. Our citizens may indulge a just pride for their efforts in establishing schools for intellectual and scientific improvement, but this most important branch of education has been almost entirely neglected. It seems, therefore, highly proper that provision should be made, for instruction in everything that pertains to the art of husbandry, and practical and scientific agriculture. Our efforts in this direction should never cease, until our young men, engaged in the useful and honorable occupation of farming, shall have received the same high education, as those designed for other professions. . . .

The State Prison has failed to meet the expectations of former Legislators and the people, in making the labor of convicts meet its current expenses. Every year we find a large deficiency. Great complaints are made of a want of discipline and efficiency in the management of the prisoners, and of that cleanliness and other which is characteristic of a well managed penitentiary.

I recommend an increase of the salaries of the officers and keepers of the prison, in order that a higher grade of talent may be employed in the management of its affairs.

It is believed that great improvement can be made in the condition of the prison, financially and otherwise, and that if men of the highest character for integrity and capacity are entrusted with its concerns, not only can the Treasury of the State be relieved from a grievous burden, but that by a more perfect system of discipline, and greater attention to the moral culture and training of the convicts, they will be less likely to again violate the laws of society, when the terms of their sentence have expired, and they are restored to freedom.

The presence of several boys and youth, among the more hardened criminals in the State prison, induces me to urge upon your attention the propriety of establishing a House of Refuge or Correction, where a milder course of treatment more especially adapted to their reformation can be employed. The State has not discharged its duty to these unfortunate victims of ignorance and temptation, until it has made provision by a proper system of discipline, for their instruction, in useful knowledge, morals, and piety—taught them some mechanical trade or other proper employment, and prepared them upon their release from confinement, to become good citizens and useful members of society, as they return to its duties and privileges. . . .

The common schools and the University have each been very amply endowed by a grant of lands from the General Government. So far as the expense is concerned there is nothing to hinder every child in the State from receiving a good common school education, and the fullest provision is made for free instruction in all the higher grades of education at the University; but the Union schools and intermediate classes of Academic education have been obliged to rely mainly upon private support, rather than upon any public educational fund.

A want is also seriously felt for seminaries of the highest grade for the education of young ladies. Their education is an object as intimately connected with our social well being, and as important in every moral and religious point of view, as that of the stronger sex; and if you should deem it expedient to set apart a portion of the income of this fund to the endowment of high schools for females, there can be little doubt that the measure will prove highly acceptable to the fathers and mothers of the State, and be welcomed by all, as an auxiliary for the cultivation and refinement of the daughters of the land. . . .

The subject of slavery in the U.S. is one, which for generations past has attracted the anxious attention of our statesmen and philanthropists; and the deep concern produced in the minds of thinking men by the existence of this anomalous element in our condition, has not been confined to the period which has elapsed since our revolutionary struggle. . . .

[The Missouri Compromise of 1820] furnished to the country a pledge—ever from that time and until within a few months considered inviolable—that for the future, slavery should not exist in all that part of Louisiana [Territory] lying in latitude 36 degrees 30 minutes, which is the Southern limit of Missouri. This compromise the present Congress, by an act for the organization of the territories of Kansas and Nebraska, have repealed, and thus opened to the ingress of slavery a region hitherto sealed against it, and embracing a geographical area quite equal to the thirteen original States, limited on the west by the territories of Utah, New Mexico, Oregon and Washington, on the north by the line of the British Possessions, and on the east by the States of Missouri and Iowa and the territory of Minnesota—lying in the heart of the North American continent, possessing, as we have good ground to believe, a highly fertile soil and salubrious climate, capable of containing a vast population, and fitted in every respect to exert at no distant day a powerful influence upon the destinies of the nation. . . .

Perhaps no measure could have been passed more repugnant to the feelings of the North-Western States, whose political and social life has been shielded from the blighting touch of slavery by the same prohibition which has been repealed, and in no part of the country have the evidences of popular dislike been more marked and decisive.

The sentiments of the people of Michigan are known and unequivocal; and at the commencement of this recent struggle to extend slavery, their views were expressed by the Legislatures of 1847, '48, and '49. In the last named year a joint resolution was passed affirming the power of Congress to impose the anti-slavery restriction upon the territories, and instructing our Senators, and requesting our Representatives, to use all honorable means to incorporate it into any territorial bill upon which they might be called to act. . . .

The Fugitive Slave Act and the mode of its enforcement, awakened the deep sensibilities of the people of the free States. They have been aroused to a still higher pitch by the repeal of the Missouri prohibition.

Originally, the American policy excluded slavery from all the National Territory—next to the Missouri Compromise tolerated the increase of Slave States, carved out of Slave Territory, on the condition of excluding the evil from all north of 36 deg. 30 min. by positive prohibition. Then, by the Utah and New Mexico acts, Free Territory made such by foreign law, was converted into Slave Territory, and now faith is broken and solemn pledges violated in order that soil from which the curse was excluded by a law which for thirty-four years, was well understood and regarded as a *compact*, shall be converted into Slave soil. The people of the free States are now satisfied that the question is of an importance paramount to that of every other, and that the effort of patriots can be devoted to no higher object, than a real and permanent settlement of it.

That such a permanent settlement is practicable, I believe. That it can be effected without dishonor to either, and with incalculable advantage to both sections of the country, I am thoroughly convinced. The great principle of such a settlement, should be the divorce of the General Government from slavery. Neither Congress or the President should take any part in upholding or extending such an evil. Without any interference whatever, with the internal concerns of States, not committed by the Constitution to the supervision of Congress or the Executive, the power and influence of both departments, should be exerted for the benefit of freedom, rather than for the benefit of slavery. There should be no slavery in the District of Columbia—none in National Territories—no slave catching under national law—no slave trade in American vessels, allowed or regulated by acts of Congress—no slave auction under process, out of the Federal Courts. These things done, the example and influence of the National Government would be on the side of freedom, and the power of reason and the force of sympathy, might be safely relied upon, to bring about universal emancipation.

I respectfully recommend the consideration of these subjects to the Legislature, in order that the position of the State may be clearly expressed. The people of Michigan are represented in the Senate of the United States, by two eminent men, both of whom voted for the repeal of the Missouri Prohibition. I submit to the Legislature the expediency of instructing them to vote for, and to urge the passage of such measures as are intended to restrict and denationalize slavery. Their repeated declaration of readiness, to abide the will of the State, will suggest to them the duty of either obeying the instructions, or allowing the wishes of the people to be represented by others.

Permit me to say, in taking leave of this subject, that the rapid strides which slavery has made of late—its bold encroachment upon free soil and the still bolder schemes which it nourishes—has seemed to require this notice at my hands. Like other free states, Michigan has a deep and abiding interest in the question. In reference to it the heart of the people is sound—their purposes are steadfast; and believing it to be their will, it is our duty as their representatives, to resort to all the Constitutional means in our power, to counteract this dangerous policy—a policy hostile to the interests of the State—disturbing the internal tranquility of the country—unfriendly to the Constitution and the Union.

For several years past the subject of a "Homestead Law," has been fully discussed by the American people, and but little doubt is entertained that the correctness of its policy has been settled and affirmed by the public judgment. The Congress of the United States has hitherto failed to give effect to the popular will. Your predecessors passed a joint resolution indicative of the course of the people of Michigan upon that subject, and I recommend a renewed expression on your part, in favor of the passage of a bill granting to every head of a family who is a citizen of the United States, one hundred and sixty acres of land of the public domain, upon condition of settlement and cultivation for a number of years. The public lands are rapidly passing away from the government of the United States into the hands of wealthy capitalists and gigantic corporations. Let us urge upon our Senators and Representatives the necessity of speedy action, to secure the benefits which this great measure is destined to confer.

The Sault Ste. Marie Ship Canal had progressed so far towards completion, that by the opening of navigation the approaching season, it will be prepared for the passage of vessels. This noble work of internal improvement, rivaling in its magnitude and the fitness and excellence of its structure, the most celebrated works of a similar character in the Old World, has been prosecuted with an energy highly creditable to the able direction under which it has been constructed. A less diligent and energetic management would have been intimidated by the serious obstacles which have interposed to impede the progress of the work; as it is, it will undoubtedly be completed within the time specified by the contract for its construction.

Our State will have just cause for congratulation, when this last connecting link in the chain of our ample lakes shall have been completed.

It is an improvement which our own increasing prosperity, and the prosperity of the country at large, imperatively demand. It will peculiarly redound to our advantage as a State, by affording a facile and uninterrupted communication with the northern portion of our Peninsula, whose vast resources, mineral and otherwise, will secure a more rapid development and readier transportation, thus at once increasing our commerce and wealth, and promoting the general prosperity.

It will also become a great national highway, connecting our richly endowed State, more intimately than at first thought would be obvious, with the ports and cities of the Eastern Hemisphere.

The Capital was removed from Detroit to this place in 1848. Its site was established in the heart of a dense forest, and all the improvements which we witness have been made since that time. Its fortunate location upon the center of a school section has added more than one hundred thousand dollars to the Common School Fund by the sale of the adjoining lots. It is now permanently fixed by the Constitution. The State should therefore regard its increase in population and wealth with favor, and cherish its growth and improvement. With such fostering care as the Legislature can give, it will soon become a Capital worthy of a flourishing and populous State. . . .

INDEX

Printed in the USA
CPSIA information can be obtained
at www.ICGtesting.com
JSHW010715130124
55309JS00007B/11